ID0961323

AUGUSTA LEIGH

Other books by Michael Bakewell

Lewis Carroll

AUGUSTA LEIGH

Byron's half-sister: a biography

MICHAEL & MELISSA BAKEWELL

Chatto & Windus
LONDON

Published by Chatto & Windus 2000

2 4 6 8 10 9 7 5 3 1

Copyright © Michael and Melissa Bakewell 2000

Michael and Melissa Bakewell have asserted their right under the Copyright, Designs and
Patents Act 1988 to be identified as the authors of this work.

First published in Great Britain in 2000 by
Chatto & Windus
Random House, 20 Vauxhall Bridge Road,
London SW1V 2SA

Random House Australia (Pty) Limited
20 Alfred Street, Milsons Point, Sydney,
New South Wales 2061, Australia

Random House New Zealand Limited
18 Poland Road, Glenfield,
Auckland 10, New Zealand

Random House South Africa (Pty) Limited
Endulini, 5A Jubilee Road, Parktown 2193, South Africa

Random House Group Limited Reg. No. 954009

A CIP catalogue record for this book
is available from the British Library

ISBN 018 561 9754

Papers used by Random House are natural,
recyclable products made from wood grown in sustainable forests.
The manufacturing processes conform to the environmental
regulations of the country of origin.

Typeset by Deltatype Ltd, Birkenhead, Merseyside
Printed and bound in Great Britain by
Mackays of Chatham PLC

Contents

Illustrations

Queen Charlotte. By John Downman (The *Connoisseur*, Extra Number No. 2, 1907, property of authors)

Portrait of George IV when the Prince of Wales. By H.P. Bone after Marie Elisabeth Vigée Lebrun (By courtesy of the Ashmolean Museum, Oxford)

Robert D'Arcy, 4th Earl of Holdernesse and Mary D'Arcy (née Doublet van Groenveldt), Countess of Holdernesse. By Jean-Etienne Liotard (Bildarchiv Preussischer Kulturbesitz)

Lady Amelia D'Arcy (9th Baroness Conyers). By François Hubert Drouais. (By kind permission of the Richard Green Gallery, London)

Francis Osborne, Marquess of Carmarthen (later 5th Duke of Leeds) by Benjamin West. (By courtesy of National Portrait Gallery, London)

Captain John Byron ('Mad Jack'). Artist unknown. By courtesy of the City of Nottingham Museums and Galleries: (Newstead Abbey)

George Osborne (later 6th Duke of Leeds). Miniature by Richard Cosway. (By courtesy of the National Portrait Gallery and with acknowledgements to Christie's Images Ltd.)

Lord Francis Osborne (later 1st Baron Godolphin). By Sir William Beechey (By kind permission of Christie's Images Ltd.)

Lady Mary Osborne (later the Countess of Chichester). Miniature by Mrs Anne Mee, after Cosway. (By kind permission of Sotheby's Picture Library)

The Reverend Christopher Alderson by Joseph Wright of Derby (The Witt Library)

Eckington Rectory (photographed by the authors)

Thomas Pelham, 2nd Earl of Chichester, by Sir Joshua Reynolds, after Hoppner. (By courtesy of the National Portrait Gallery, London)

The Hon. Mrs Harcourt by John Downman (The *Connoisseur*, Extra Number No. 2, 1907, property of the authors)

Frederick Howard, 5th Earl of Carlisle by Sir Thomas Lawrence. (By courtesy of the National Portrait Gallery, London)

Castle Howard, from an engraving by W.M. Dome. (Authors' collection)

vii

Augusta Leigh: drawing by Sir George Hayter. (By courtesy of National Portrait Gallery, London)

Lieutenant Colonel George Leigh in the uniform of an officer of the 10th Hussars: engraving after Dighton. (Courtesy of the Director, the National Army Museum)

Six Mile Bottom. A drawing by J.S. Clarke, 1891 (Cambridgeshire County Libraries)

Newmarket Heath in 1787 from the print after James Pollard reproduced in *Newmarket: Its Sport and Personalities* by Frank Siltzer (Cassell & Company Ltd., London, 1923)

William Harry Vane, 3rd Earl of Darlington, by Ben Marshall. (Reproduced by kind permission of Lord Barnard, Raby Castle)

Sir Harry Fetherstonhaugh at Uppark by Pompeo Batoni. (By kind permission of National Trust Photographic Library)

George Gordon, 6th Lord Byron. Miniature by James Holmes, 1816, engraved by Meyer. By courtesy of the City of Nottingham Museums and Galleries: (Newstead Abbey)

Augusta Leigh. Miniature by James Holmes. (By kind permission of the Earl of Lytton)

Lady Byron. Drawing by Mary Anne Knight, 1820. By courtesy of the City of Nottingham Museums and Galleries: (Newstead Abbey)

Newstead Abbey. Engraving. (The authors' collection)

The Reverend Francis Hodgson. Mezzotint by William Walker. (The authors' collection)

John Cam Hobhouse. From a drawing by A. Wivell, engraved by J. Hopwood. (The authors' collection)

Theresa Villiers, née Parker. By Henry Eldridge, 1798 (By courtesy of National Portrait Gallery, London)

George Anson, 7th Lord Byron. (Photograph courtesy of Jacqueline Viognier-Marshall)

Georgiana Trevanion. By James Holmes, 1828 (By courtesy of the National Portrait Gallery, London)

Elizabeth Medora Leigh. Drawing by Thomas Wageman. By courtesy of the City of Nottingham Museums and Galleries: (Newstead Abbey)

St. James's Palace. Engraving. (The authors' collection)

The Reverend Frederick Robertson: daguerrotype from *Life and Letters of Frederick W. Robertson M.A.* (Smith, Elder & Co., 1865)

For
Megan Boyes

The Byron Descent

Names marked * appear in the table twice

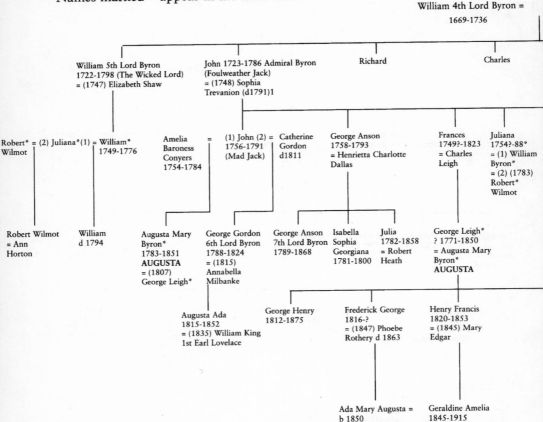

[1] Sophia Trevanion's mother-in-law, Frances Berkeley, was also her aunt.

(1720) (3) Frances Berkeley

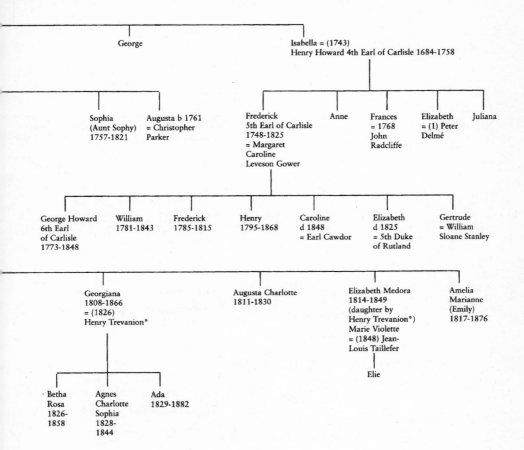

George

Isabella = (1743)
Henry Howard 4th Earl of Carlisle 1684-1758

Sophia
(Aunt Sophy)
1757-1821

Augusta b 1761
= Christopher
Parker

Frederick
5th Earl of Carlisle
1748-1825
= Margaret
Caroline
Leveson Gower

Anne

Frances
= 1768
John
Radcliffe

Elizabeth
= (1) Peter
Delmé

Juliana

George Howard
6th Earl
of Carlisle
1773-1848

William
1781-1843

Frederick
1785-1815

Henry
1795-1868

Caroline
d 1848
= Earl Cawdor

Elizabeth
d 1825
= 5th Duke
of Rutland

Gertrude
= William
Sloane Stanley

Georgiana
1808-1866
= (1826)
Henry Trevanion*

Augusta Charlotte
1811-1830

Elizabeth Medora
1814-1849
(daughter by
Henry Trevanion*)
Marie Violette
= (1848) Jean-
Louis Taillefer

Amelia
Marianne
(Emily)
1817-1876

Elie

· Betha
Rosa
1826-
1858

Agnes
Charlotte
Sophia
1828-
1844

Ada
1829-1882

The Holdernesse Descent

Names marked * appear in the table twice

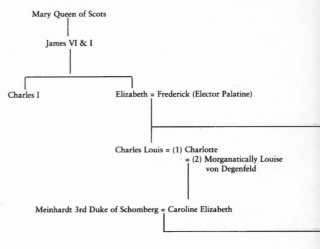

Mary Queen of Scots

James VI & I

Charles I   Elizabeth = Frederick (Elector Palatine)

Charles Louis = (1) Charlotte
= (2) Morganatically Louise
von Degenfeld

Meinhardt 3rd Duke of Schomberg = Caroline Elizabeth

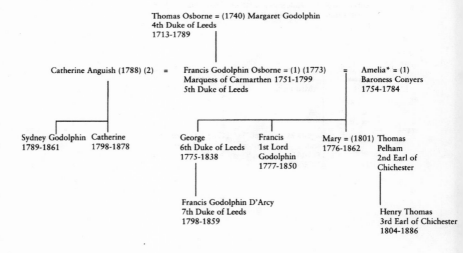

Thomas Osborne = (1740) Margaret Godolphin
4th Duke of Leeds
1713-1789

Catherine Anguish (1788) (2)   =   Francis Godolphin Osborne = (1) (1773)   =   Amelia* = (1)
Marquess of Carmarthen 1751-1799   Baroness Conyers
5th Duke of Leeds   1754-1784

Sydney Godolphin   Catherine   George   Francis   Mary = (1801) Thomas
1789-1861   1798-1878   6th Duke of Leeds   1st Lord   1776-1862   Pelham
     1775-1838   Godolphin   2nd Earl of
     1777-1850   Chichester

Francis Godolphin D'Arcy
7th Duke of Leeds
1798-1859   Henry Thomas
     3rd Earl of Chichester
     1804-1886

Sophia
Electress of Hanover

George I

Frederica = Robert 3rd Earl of Holdernesse
        | & 7th Baron Conyers

Robert 4th Earl of Holdernesse = (1743) Mary Doublet (d 1801)
& 8th Baron Conyers 1718-1778   van Groenveldt

Amelia* = (2) (1779)   = John Byron = (2) (1785) = Catherine Gordon
Baroness Conyers   1756-1791   (d 1811)
1754-1784   (Mad Jack)

Augusta Mary = (1807) George Gordon
Byron   George 6th Lord Byron
1783-1851   Leigh   1788-1824
AUGUSTA

The Trevanion/Byron Connection

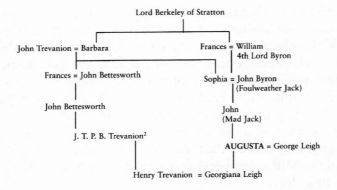

Lord Berkeley of Stratton

John Trevanion = Barbara   Frances = William
                                      4th Lord Byron

Frances = John Bettesworth   Sophia = John Byron
                                        (Foulweather Jack)

John Bettesworth   John
                     (Mad Jack)

J. T. P. B. Trevanion[2]   AUGUSTA = George Leigh

Henry Trevanion = Georgiana Leigh

[2] John Trevanion Purnell Bettesworth adopted the surname and arms of Trevanion.

A Note about Names

The fact that the same Christian names were generally passed on from father to son makes for great confusion in following many of the families in this story. We have tried to distinguish some of the major characters by using their nicknames – 'The Wicked Lord', 'Foulweather Jack', 'Mad Jack'. As for George Gordon, the 6th Lord Byron, we have referred to him throughout as Byron, the style used by his friends and by which he is universally known.

Many men at that time, from the King and Prince of Wales downwards, were called George. Two of Augusta's half-brothers, two of her cousins, her husband and one of her children were all Georges. Mad Jack's brother George was christened Anson and so was his son. The latter, who became the 7th Lord Byron, we have referred to throughout as George Anson, although he would not have been addressed in this way. Similarly, Augusta's eldest son George becomes, for the purposes of this book, George Henry.

Where members of a family inherit a title or a change of name – the Marquess of Carmarthen for example becomes the Duke of Leeds and the Milbankes become the Noels – we have done our best to make this clear.

As for Augusta's third daughter, Elizabeth Medora, although in the family she was called Libby or Elizabeth, we have referred to her throughout as Medora since that is the name by which she is generally known.

A Note about Spelling

Where possible we have tried to retain the original spelling and usage in the quotations from letters, without wearying the reader with innumerable 'sics'. We have left Queen Charlotte's highly idiosyncratic French as she wrote it. To correct it would have been *lèse-majestée*.

Preface

Although no one has ever drawn attention to the fact, and she herself may not have known it, Augusta Leigh, through her Holdernesse grandfather, was a direct descendant of Mary, Queen of Scots. In her impulsiveness, her lack of judgement, her stubborness, her genius for doing the wrong thing at the wrong time, her fatally romantic imagination, her generosity, her gaiety, her loyalty, Augusta resembles, admittedly on a less dramatic scale, her tragic ancestress. And like the Scottish queen, she had the misfortune to incur the unremitting enmity of a woman more intelligent and more resourceful than herself.

Peter Gunn published his pioneering biography *My Dearest Augusta* over thirty years ago, and there has been little since then in the biographies of Byron, his wife or his daughter that has shed much light on Augusta's character. She has been variously portrayed as 'docile and devoted' as 'the mother he [Byron] wished had been his', as 'intensely mischievous' and duplicitous, as simpleminded with a revealing fondness for baby-talk. What most of these books do have in common is that they unquestioningly repeat the same old errors about Augusta's life – even including her date and country of birth – without offering anything that is new.

In this book we have drawn on new material to present as fully rounded a picture of Augusta as possible and to explore the circumstances that shaped her life – the scandalous love affair which led to her birth and to her mother's downfall, her childhood in a remote Derbyshire vicarage, her years at Holdernesse House where George III and Queen Charlotte were frequent visitors, her circuit round the great houses of her family, from Gogmagog to Castle Howard, and the events which led to her ill-considered and disastrous marriage. We have tried to show Augusta not simply as part of the Byron legend but in the context of her own private world, her friends, her relatives, her children and, above all, of her husband, George Leigh.

Inevitably much of her life was dominated by the relentless war of attrition against her carried out by her sister-in-law, Annabella (Lady Byron). We have done our best to be fair to Annabella but to present her sympathetically has proved an impossible task.

Prologue 1853–6

In the spring of 1853, Harriet Beecher Stowe paid her first visit to England. A vast, cheering crowd assembled at Liverpool Docks to welcome the writer of *Uncle Tom's Cabin*. The book had created a sensation when it was published the previous year and British sales had far eclipsed those in America. England was swept by Uncle Tom mania and Harriet was fêted wherever she went. 'She cannot ride or show her face without crowds and hurrahs,' said her brother, Charles Beecher. She was received by the Lord Mayor of London, who gave a banquet in her honour, and was presented to Lord and Lady Palmerston and to Mr Gladstone. The Duchess of Sutherland gave her a bracelet fashioned like a slave's shackle. At a lunch party she was introduced to the Dowager Lady Byron, widow of the poet. Their conversation, inevitably, centred on the abolition of slavery, a subject on which Harriet found Lady Byron singularly well informed. They were just settling down to an earnest assessment of the impact of the Oxford Movement, on which Lady Byron also had decided views, when the famous authoress was whisked away to be presented to 'other persons'.

Lady Byron had made a profound impression on Harriet. 'I had found one more pearl of great price upon the shore of life,' she wrote. On a subsequent visit to England in 1856, she sought Lady Byron's advice on how best to answer the *Edinburgh Review*, which had savaged her most recent novel, *Dred*. 'Oh, do not be susceptible to these "darts", my dear friend,' came the reply.

Byron had been dead for more than thirty years. Now his widow was having urgent thoughts about her own mortality. Her health had always been her chief preoccupation and she was beginning to fear that she was in a more precarious state than ever. There was to be a new edition of her husband's works. Was this, perhaps, the time to put before the public her own account of Byron's life? She decided to approach Harriet, as an 'unprejudiced person', and ask her advice. After a lunch to which Harriet's sister was also invited,

Lady Byron arranged a confidential tête-à-tête and began to tell her story, a story to which Harriet listened with mounting horror.

> ... there was something awful to me in the intensity of repressed emotion which she showed as she proceeded. The great fact upon which all turned was stated in words that were unmistakable: 'He was guilty of incest with his sister!'

CHAPTER I

'An Imprudent Conduct'

Augusta Leigh was at the heart of what the Victorians chose to call the 'Byron Mystery'. Without her there might have been no separation, no exile, no tragic death in the fever-ridden swamps of Missolonghi. Augusta, Byron's dear 'Goose', as he called her – muddle-headed, warm-hearted, remarkable neither for her intelligence nor for her beauty, trusting blindly in a providence that never came to her rescue – was doomed to be her half-brother's Achilles' heel and the instrument of his fall.

Certainly there were no fairy godmothers at her christening. She was the child of one of the most scandalous escapades of an age not noted for its propriety, the notorious liaison of Amelia, Baroness Conyers, wife of the Marquess of Carmarthen, and Captain 'Mad Jack' Byron.

Amelia was one of the brightest ornaments at the court of George III, the darling of the royal family, a leader of fashion, pretty, talented and distinctly wilful. Born on 12 October 1754, she was the only surviving child of Robert D'Arcy, Earl of Holdernesse, and his Dutch-born wife, Mary Doublet van Groenveldt.

The Holdernesses were directly descended from the Stuart kings, while Amelia's mother, Mary, came from one of the most distinguished families of the States of Holland. By the time the Earl of Holdernesse brought 'the lovely Dutch girl' to England, he was firmly entrenched at court. Already Lord Lieutenant of the North Riding of Yorkshire, and a Gentleman of the Bedchamber to George II, he had attended the King on the battlefield of Dettingen and was to go on to become Ambassador to Venice at the court of the only doge to be elected a member of the Royal Society. After nearly five years there he was appointed Minister Plenipotentiary at The Hague, where he remained until 1751 when he was recalled to London to join the government as a Secretary of State.

'That formal piece of dullness', as Horace Walpole described the

3

Earl of Holdernesse, seems to have had an endearingly lighter side to his nature. His great passion was for the opera and for a time he shared with Lord Middlesex the management of the King's Theatre, putting on a series of second-rate Italian opera in the vain hope of rivalling Handel and finding leading roles for Middlesex's mistress, La Muscovita. Walpole, whose native waspishness seems to have been readily provoked by Holdernesse, noted with delight a temporary fall from royal favour: '... the calamity of Lord Holdernesse was singular; he was for some days in disgrace for having played Blind Man's Buff at Tunbridge in the summer...'

The accession of George III in 1760 effectively put an end to Holdernesse's career in government. After some devious political shuffling, he was abruptly relieved of his office, which was required for the Earl of Bute, the young King's friend and mentor. Holdernesse was appeased with the promise of the Wardenship of the Cinque Ports and a golden handshake worth £4,000 a year. The money enabled him to buy a sizeable piece of ground on the corner of Hertford Street and Park Lane. There he built the great mansion known then as Holdernesse House,* which became the family's London home.

Removed as he now was from the political arena, the Earl still maintained his position in court circles, which Walpole had always attributed, rather snidely, to the fact that 'his mother was distantly related to the Royal Family'. While that was true, it had rather more to do with Mary Holdernesse's close friendship with Queen Charlotte and her position in the Queen's household as Lady of the Bedchamber. 'Vous savez que je vous aime personellement,' her royal mistress had told her.

In 1771 the Earl of Holdernesse was made governor to the nine-year-old Prince of Wales and his brother the Duke of York (who, thanks to an arrangement enshrined in the Treaty of Westphalia, also found himself, at the age of six, with the title of Bishop of Osnabrück). To judge from a letter sent by the Queen, the royal children seem to have felt a genuine affection for the Holdernesses: 'Mes enfants, ma chère Mylady vous font tous leurs compliments. Ernest demande souvent après Lady Holy. Vous voyez ils sont tous de mon goût...'

---

* Holdernesse House was rebuilt in the 1820s by Lord Castlereagh's brother the 3rd Marquess of Londonderry and renamed Londonderry House.

Ernest was the Queen's fifth son, the Duke of Cumberland and future King of Hanover. 'Lady Holy' was a not inappropriate name for Lady Holdernesse, who was renowned for her exemplary piety and was in the habit of exchanging sermons and religious treatises with her royal mistress. Her daughter Amelia was seven years older than the Prince of Wales, who adored her, but then at no time in his life could he resist a pretty face or a witty woman. The Queen, too, had a great affection for 'Ma chère Lady Amelia'. 'I not only love you,' she told her, 'but shall always be happy to number you among my friends.'

As heiress to a considerable fortune, it was imperative that Amelia should make a suitable marriage, but with the world at her feet she was in no hurry to commit herself. It was not until 1773 when the young Marquess of Carmarthen appeared on the scene that she decided to give the matter serious thought. When he proposed, Amelia accepted him.

'The prettiest man in his person; the most polite and pleasing in his manners', and, more importantly, the only son and sole heir of the 4th Duke of Leeds, Francis Osborne, Marquess of Carmarthen, was all the Holdernesses could have wished for their daughter, who would herself be a decidedly valuable acquisition to the Leeds family. A marriage settlement was drawn up providing Amelia with a handsome dowry of £20,000, and the Duke of Leeds engaged to provide £1,600 a year, with an extra £400 per annum for Amelia's pin money. However, when the two sides reviewed the deal in practical terms, it was felt that the income fell far short of what was necessary for two young people required to reflect their rank and position in society. The Earl of Holdernesse came to the rescue and agreed to allow the couple a further £1,500 a year, while the Duke of Leeds managed to find another £500 for them, thus increasing their annual allowance to a very acceptable £4,000.

The first indication that all did not bode well made itself evident even before the marriage. It is possible that Amelia was simply playing up, or that Carmarthen had not managed to extricate himself from a previous entanglement; whatever the cause, their intended union was suddenly in jeopardy. But too much was at stake for the families: pressure was brought to bear and Carmarthen was soon writing to his aunt that 'Lady A.D. . . . has consented to make me happy . . .'

The marriage was now set to go ahead, but was further delayed when Lady Holdernesse fell and gashed her head at Syon Hill, the Earl's riverside house near Isleworth. William Mason, the poet, former chaplain to the Holdernesse family and a crony of Horace Walpole, took a ribald view of the incident in one of his regular bulletins to his old friend, who liked to be kept up to date with Holdernesse gossip:

> I had heard that Lady Holdernesse had broken her head, but am yet to hear when Lord Carmarthen is to break her daughter's head. I wish it was fairly broke, though my poor living and this goodly estate are to pay for it . . .

William Mason had entered the Holdernesse family as chaplain about the time of Amelia's birth, when he was also presented by the Earl with the living of Aston, near Rotherham. The Aston estates, which included Mason's parish, had been broken up and sold piecemeal to provide the cash for Amelia's marriage settlement, but his living was retained, as was the handsome new rectory he had built for himself opposite the church. His duties to his patron required Mason to spend rather more time than he would have liked in London and at Syon Hill. Lady Holdernesse had never cared for the Yorkshire weather, and visits to her husband's family seat, Hornby Castle, were limited to the summer months. Mason, not a man to take kindly to being at anyone's beck and call, had become terminally bored with his chaplaincy and resigned, pleading unconvincingly that the journey to London was too taxing. When nineteen-year-old Amelia and Carmarthen were joined in matrimony at Holdernesse House on 29 November 1773, it was not William Mason who married them, but his successor, the Reverend Christopher Alderson.

The following spring Lord Holdernesse, whose health was never very robust, was taken ill. Walpole duly passed on the news to William Mason: 'Your old friend passes by here very often looking ghastly and going . . .' he reported. The Earl was probably suffering from consumption. In the hope that he might benefit from a change of climate, he set off for Switzerland with his wife. When his condition showed no sign of improvement he decided to move on to Montpellier for the winter. There, painful operations for piles debilitated him even further and it was several months before any real improvement was noticed.

In London the young Carmarthens took possession of their new house in fashionable Grosvenor Square. When Amelia found she was pregnant, the Queen (who for once in her life was not) took upon herself the role of surrogate mother, claiming the right, as she put it, *'de mettre comme un bonne example'*.* Queen Charlotte had produced ten children in twelve years. The Carmarthens' first child, George William Frederick, Earl of Danby, was born on 21 July 1775.

The Earl of Holdernesse had recovered sufficiently to return to England in 1775, where he found that his long absence abroad had seriously undermined his authority in the royal schoolroom. The Prince of Wales had grown into a rude, obstreperous teenager, and his behaviour was completely out of hand. It was more than Holdernesse was prepared to put up with and he resigned as governor.

There had also been a brief disagreement with the Carmarthens – Walpole, with his gift for hyperbole, referred to it as 'a great breach' – when they took the part of an eloping couple, causing eyebrows to be raised and bringing down on Amelia's head the full force of her mother's disapproval. But the storm soon blew over and the arrival of Juliana Henrietta Mary (always known as Mary), the Holdernesses' first granddaughter, had restored the peace. A second son, Francis Godolphin Osborne, was born to the Carmarthens on 18 October 1777.

On 16 May 1778, a month short of his sixtieth birthday, the Earl of Holdernesse died suddenly at Syon Hill. It was an event that passed virtually unnoticed by the public, overshadowed as it was by the Earl of Chatham's spectacular collapse in the House of Lords and Voltaire's death from overexcitement at being allowed to return to Paris to direct a performance of his tragedy *Irène*.

On her father's death, not only did Amelia inherit a great deal of money, but she also succeeded to the title of Baroness Conyers. She was now a peeress in her own right and it looks very much as if she felt that this gave her *carte blanche* to behave precisely as she pleased. Within a few months of William Mason conducting her father's funeral at Hornby, Amelia had met Jack Byron.

Jack, known to his friends as 'Johnny' or, more fittingly, 'Mad Jack', was twenty-two – sixteen months younger than Amelia. He

---

* Queen Charlotte's French was considerably more fluent than it was correct.

7

was the eldest son of Admiral John Byron and was destined to be the father of both Augusta and Byron.*

Mad Jack had been educated at Westminster and at a small military academy run by a Frenchman† in Little Chelsea. In 1772, when he was sixteen, he took up a commission in the Coldstream Guards. During the War of American Independence Jack was sent with his regiment to America. He served with the army that defeated Washington at Brandywine in September 1777 and went on to take Philadelphia, but, when that town proved to be of no strategic importance, was holed up there for the winter. True to form, Jack gambled, drank and made merry and got himself seriously into debt. By March 1778 he was back in London, leaving behind him a string of unpaid bills which, to avoid his arrest, his father's business agent, James Sykes, was forced to settle on his behalf.

That June, Jack was appointed adjutant to the regiment. England was in the grip of invasion fever. The French had entered the war on the side of the American colonists in March and everywhere volunteer militias were springing into action. The nobility and local gentry were decking themselves out in military attire and energetically raising recruits. Camps were set up at Salisbury, Winchester, Bury St Edmunds and, most spectacularly, at Coxheath near Maidstone. It was here that Amelia reputedly had her first meeting with Jack Byron.

Coxheath had rapidly become a public attraction, 'one of the most striking military spectacles ever exhibited in this country', according to the *Morning Chronicle*, and 'no coaches are to be had for love or money'. 'Camps are the new things,' wrote an officer stationed there, 'everybody of course must see them ... it is impossible to help laughing at the prodigious number of women.' It was not long before the camp acquired a notorious reputation. At first the practice of sneaking in ladies to spend the night under canvas was restricted to the officers, but 'the plan was suddenly extended; and every *fille de joie* who was happy enough to light on a gallant was stole within the lines to the tent of her paramour'.

---

* Nobody had a good word to say about Mad Jack, except his children, both of whom would feel the need to defend his memory. 'He was,' wrote Byron, 'according to the testimony of all those who knew him, of an extraordinary and amiable and joyous character, but careless and dissipated.'
† Monsieur Locheé.

Although the Coldstream Guards were not quartered at Cox-heath, Jack Byron would undoubtedly have seen to it that he had regimental business there. The prospect of a good time, where ladies of the town might be found mingling freely with ladies of the *ton*, was more than he could have resisted. Certainly when Amelia was asked to make up a foursome by friends planning a visit to the camp, it was a prospect she could not resist either. Nor could she resist Jack Byron, whom she had been invited to partner. 'It is true', Byron was to write of his father, 'that he was a very handsome man, which goes a long way.' It certainly went a considerable distance with Amelia.

Amelia was spoilt, independent, headstrong and capricious, the prisoner of her own desires. 'Passion', her husband warned her, 'has hitherto proved to both our miseries the bane of mutual happiness', which suggests that Amelia was already given to living dangerously close to the edge. She had been a dutiful and ornamental wife to Carmarthen, had brought considerable wealth to his family and had presented him with three children, including the all-important son and heir. No one would have been greatly shocked or unduly surprised if she had discreetly accepted the advances of a lover: unfortunately, however, discretion seems to have been the last thing that either Amelia or Jack had in mind. From the very beginning, their love affair was driven by a recklessness that defied caution or concealment. Danger seemed only to spur them on. No risk was too great.

In November, the Duke of Leeds became ill on a visit to Bath, and Carmarthen went down there to be with his father for a few days. Amelia remained in London and, since the children had conveniently been sent to stay with their grandmother at Syon Hill, the lovers therefore had the house in Grosvenor Square to themselves. The fact that the place was in the throes of alteration and redecoration can only have added a useful element of confusion, and Jack frequently stayed the whole night. At first he made token attempts to avoid being seen by the servants, sneaking up the back stairs, but soon he was brazenly coming in by the front door, and using Carmarthen's powdering room, where he was spotted sitting in the window reading by the light of a candle. Next morning it was he who ordered the footman to bring the breakfast and 'her ladyship's chocolate'. He then followed the footman down the stairs, 'whistling and singing at the same time'. On another occasion one of the servants 'plainly heard the voice of a man in bed with her Ladyship . . . they laughed a good deal and it appeared that they were very merry'.

All this may have been deliberately calculated on Jack Byron's part. It was characteristic of his ruthless bravado to make his cuckolding of Carmarthen as obvious as possible. The temptation to broadcast the fact that he had captured the beautiful Marchioness, known to be possessed of her own fortune, was irresistible.

Amelia was in a very different position. Her maid wanted to give notice and the servants were in open revolt. Confronted with the situation, she promised that it would never happen again. The housekeeper was given money to distribute among the maids in the vain hope of buying their silence. But her great terror was that her mother would get to hear of the affair.

For all her protestations, Amelia was entirely at the mercy of her infatuation and, while she was still insisting that there would be no repetition of her folly, she was sending footmen to Pall Mall with messages for Mad Jack. Even after Carmarthen's return from Bath, the lovers continued to meet in the house. On one occasion Amelia contrived to leave a dinner party early and to return home, where she was immediately joined by Jack. When Carmarthen got back, he found that she had gone to her room. He went out again and Jack took the opportunity to make good his escape. A little later Carmarthen returned with a clergyman friend, Amelia came downstairs and the three of them had supper together. It was a situation that would have been excessive in *opera buffa*.

Early in December Carmarthen, who had recently been appointed Lord Lieutenant of the East Riding, left London for a ten-day visit to Yorkshire on official business. In his absence the lovers grew more reckless than ever and Jack 'scarce missed a day without coming in some part of the day or evening'. By this time the servants could no longer keep silent and soon letters from Carmarthen's friends were flying up to Yorkshire.

An account in the St James's *Chronicle* stated that when his wife's adultery was confirmed, Carmarthen 'fainted away three times successively'. He returned and went directly to Hampstead where a house had been taken for him.

The reports in the popular press varied considerably. According to one account, the Marquess descended on Grosvenor Square and began questioning the servants, at which Amelia exclaimed, 'Then I cannot think of staying here!' and ordered the servants to carry her, in her sedan chair, to Admiral Byron's house, round the corner in Green Street. A rival version had the lovers eloping to Dover, where they were 'taken' and brought back to town. However, to judge from a letter written to Amelia by Carmarthen on 15 December, she had, in fact, confronted her husband with a full confession:

> At the moment I write this letter, my heart is so sorely afflicted, that God knows if I write sense or not. I am thunderstruck! Confounded! I never suspected the heavy blow that has fallen upon me, but I thank heaven that notwithstanding all I have suffered I bore the trying scene this day with fortitude, had my life only been concerned my affection would have been predominant, my honour being so deeply wounded, to my joy and pride it sustained itself against any other contending passion and I went through the most dreadful scene with, I hope, a becoming not a savage firmness . . . we never must meet again under those sacred ties which once connected us; as to the leaving of Grosvenor Square, it is an inevitable consequence of the fatal business.

However, Carmarthen begged her to remain in the house until she had 'thought of some proper decent place of residence'. Perhaps it was his own devout religious belief that prompted him to suggest that she might find it helpful to spend a few months in a convent in Antwerp, 'if only to give time for reflection', and urged her 'for God's sake . . . put reason in the scale against passion'. Passion was, unfortunately, in the ascendant, and a convent in Antwerp certainly did not figure in Amelia's plans. For her, life without Jack Byron was simply not an option.

Carmarthen's next task was to break the news to the King:

> Your Majesty will I am sure be shocked when you learn that Lady Carmarthen has by an imprudent conduct forever forfeited ye protection of your Majesty and ye Queen so graciously afforded her, ye favour of her own family and ye affection of mine.

Even so, Carmarthen was prepared to help Amelia. She was to keep her carriage and her favourite horse, and even her own footman, provided the livery was changed, and he would do all that he could to further the progress of their divorce. Evidence was being collected from the servants of 'marks and stains on the sheets' giving every appearance 'of a man and woman having lain together and been connected with one another that night in the same bed'. It was also arranged that the guilty pair should be discovered together in bed in a private house 'at Rotten Dean', near Brighton.

Amelia obediently went along with all this, relying on her husband for guidance at every step – 'for God's sake tell me what method I can follow without appearing to coincide too much with you' – but there was one problem. She was pregnant and she felt obliged to tell Carmarthen that the child she was carrying was not his. Again, with almost superhuman understanding, he assured her that he would make no claim on it and promised to pay all the expenses of her confinement. It was, however, impossible for him to avoid bringing a case against Jack for stealing Amelia from him. In the eyes of the world it was a matter of personal honour that he should do so, but he promised Amelia that he would not take a penny of the damages that he was certain to be awarded. He assured her that he was bringing the case only for the sake of form and to enable the divorce action to proceed. In the event, the Court of King's Bench ruled that Jack Byron should pay £600 for injury to Carmarthen, which he did not claim.

Carmarthen had behaved with generosity, even to the extent of allowing Amelia to see the children. 'I cannot think of depriving you of ever seeing your sweet children again,' he told her, his only condition being that on such occasions Jack Byron must not accompany her. But Amelia was far from happy. Jack was clearly not giving her the emotional support and understanding she badly needed. Desperately vulnerable, she was at the mercy of her mother's unpredictable temper and the barely concealed disapproval of her friends. After one unusually distressing confrontation with Lady Holdernesse, she was driven to write to Carmarthen:

> . . . you are the only friend I have left and think what must be my dreadful situation to apply to you whom I have so much injured for the only comfort I can receive. I really wish not to see my mother anymore for the present as from such another scene I should have everything to dread for my health . . . Crime should be punished and could you know what I have suffered for these six weeks you would be sufficiently revenged.

When the divorce finally came before the House of Lords in April 1779 their Lordships were exercised by the possibility of collusion and worried about the little charade that had been acted out at 'Rotten Dean'. Did this not seem to 'insinuate that her L-yship concurred in this design and also wished to afford the most ample Demonstration of Criminality on her side?' However, what evidence there was for collusion was not considered sufficient foundation for rejecting the bill, which was passed on 4 May, receiving the Royal Assent on the last day of the month. A week later the following announcement appeared in the *Morning Post*:

> London. A few days since, Lady Amelia D'Arcy (Marchioness of Carmarthen) was privately betrothed to Mr Byron with the full consent of her Ladyship's mother the Countess of Holdernesse.

Since Amelia was by now heavily pregnant, her mother could scarcely object, and the lovers were married shortly afterwards at St George's, Hanover Square, by the Reverend Christopher Alderson, who was once again required to provide a nuptial blessing for Amelia. Six weeks later, on 19 July, Amelia gave birth to a daughter. The baby was christened Sophia Georgiana on 11 August, but survived for only a few more weeks.

As a result of the divorce, Amelia forfeited her right to all money settled on her at the time of her first marriage. She was now dependent on £600 a year maintenance awarded her by Parliament after the divorce, and on a further £1,500 a year allowed her by Carmarthen from the money she had inherited from her father and which, thanks to the divorce and property laws, he now controlled. It was not an unreasonable income, had Jack Byron not been part of the equation.

In the autumn Jack was ordered to Sheffield and Rotherham with a recruiting party and Lady Holdernesse prevailed upon William Mason to lend the newly married couple his rectory at Aston. Mason was at York, where he was a canon at the Minster. 'This was by no means a pleasant sacrifice on my part,' he informed Horace Walpole, but 'as Lady Holdernesse asked it, I could not decently refuse'.

On 7 December he wrote again to his old crony that he had received a letter from Alderson, who was looking after his parish for him:

> . . . telling that the West Wind which blew violently on Thursday night had torn off a great deal of my fine Westmoreland slate, that the slate in falling has broken all the panes in the very window of that best bedchamber where my lady Conyers and Mr Byron so conjugally reposed. That not only my lady but even her military

spouse were greatly alarmed and obliged to quit their apartment – to this sad detail I hear you cry very composedly, 'a just judgement!' However, I find they are not so frightened but they will still keep their headquarters at Aston . . .'

By the time spring arrived, Mason's unwelcome guests had moved on and his rectory was once more his own.

Jack was weary of his military duties and, with a wife happy to support him, he decided it was time to get rid of his commission. By the middle of September 1780 he had resigned from his regiment and become a gentleman of leisure. He soon discovered that in London, where Amelia was shunned by her friends and they were both ostracised by society, it was impossible to lead the life he had visualised. They took the only course open to them and went abroad, where they set up house in Paris.

Marriage had not changed Jack, and in Paris he was in his element, lording it among the French aristocracy and behaving more wildly than ever. Amelia, still infatuated, could deny him nothing. Another child was born to her. This time it was a boy, who lived for only an hour.

Now and again she managed to slip quietly back to England to see her children by Carmarthen, who spent much of their time with Lady Holdernesse. William Mason reports that in September 1781 he was visited at York by 'Holdernesses and Conyers', which suggests that Amelia had been at Hornby Castle with her mother and the children.

In the early summer of 1782, she knew that once again she was pregnant. She had been finding it increasingly difficult to keep pace with Jack's hectic way of life and the demands it made on her constitution; now, anxious for her health and for her unborn child, she decided to return to London for her confinement. There were other reasons too for her decision. Jack Byron's extravagances were forcing her to face up to some unwelcome realities. Never in her life had Amelia known what it was to be short of money, but now the rigours of the divorce settlement and Jack's fecklessness were causing her severe financial embarrassment.

On their arrival in London, they moved into a house in Audley Square where Amelia awaited the birth of her child. She was in low spirits and a bleak little note that she wrote to Carmarthen's lawyer provides a clear indication that all was not going well:

Jan 25th, 1783

I am very much surprised to hear from my mother that you have not yet paid her the quarterly sum which has now been due one month, nor even appointed a time for it, as I am in want of the money I must desire you will send me a written answer . . . mentioning what day you will fix for the payment.

Within hours of dispatching the note, Amelia went into labour and the following day, 26 January 1783, a daughter, Augusta Mary Byron, was born.* The infant was put in the care of a wet-nurse, to be suckled until she was of an age to wean. To everyone's relief, she was a healthy child – but Amelia herself was far from well and her recovery from her confinement seemed to be a slow process.

An ailing wife was not in Jack's scheme of things and it was only a matter of time before he lapsed into the habits of his bachelor days, no doubt bragging of his conquests to Amelia. In what may well have been a desperate bid to regain her husband's interest, she dragged herself from her sick-bed and, in Byron's words, 'imprudently insisted on accompanying my father to a hunt'. She became acutely ill as a result, and her health continued to deteriorate, as did the marriage.

In May, Jack was living in his parents' house in Green Street, where, according to his father, he was behaving 'as usual but where the money was coming from except from one quarter I cannot imagine . . .'

Reports of Amelia's health and rumours about her marriage reached Queen Charlotte's ears:

> Lady Conyers passera son hyver à Londres. Elle est toujours malade à ce qu'on dit et devienne plus maigre de jour en jour, il y a un bruit en ville . . . qu'une séparation doit se faire entre elle et son mari, j'en doute, au moins je crois que Lady Holdernesse s'y opposera.

Whatever Lady Holdernesse may have felt, it was too late for opposition. Amelia was dying. In a first-hand account of her death there is no mention of Jack Byron and it was 'a deeply afflicted' Lady Holdernesse who kept vigil at her daughter's bedside and watched over her during the final, harrowing days. At last, on the evening of 26 January 1784, Amelia relinquished her hold on life. It was her little daughter Augusta's first birthday.

---

* It is a sad irony that probably Amelia's last action before Augusta's birth was to write a letter asking for money.

The *Morning Herald* took the opportunity to make her death the occasion of a sermon:

> Ye who give encouragement to the fops and profligates of the age, and prefer their company to that of the worthy and sedate, learn from the unhappy Lady C— that all your boasted resolution will not protect you in an hour of levity. She died literally of a broken heart. The tender remembrance of what she had been . . . remorse for what she had done, soon laid her low in the dust. Remember this ill-fated penitent! And place her unhappy story before your eyes!

There was a rumour that Carmarthen had visited Amelia on her deathbed, but no one gave a thought to Jack Byron; it was as if he had ceased to exist. The *Annual Register* even managed to get his name wrong: '26th January. In Upper Brook Street, of a lingering disorder, aged 29, the Rt Hon. Amelia, Baroness Conyers, Lady of George Byron esq.' The *Morning Chronicle* ignored Jack's very existence, referring to Amelia as the 'Lady of the Right Honourable, the Marquis of Carmarthen'.

Amelia's 'lingering disorder' was, in all probability, consumption, the disease that had caused her father's death and would, in due course, kill Jack Byron.

Two days after Amelia's death the Queen wrote to Lady Holdernesse:

> Your present melancholy situation . . . is of such a kind that it requires time to gather strength and comfort after so long and so severe a tryal you are gone through I very sincerely partake of your grief which I hope you do me justice to believe, I shall not now attempt to say much more upon the subject, but beseech you to take care of yourself for the sake of those dear infants who are the remains of your now I daresay Happy Daughter . . .

The 'dear infants' were George, Mary and Francis, the children of Lord Carmarthen, and 'poor Miss Byron' – Augusta Mary – the daughter of Mad Jack.

CHAPTER 2

'A Passion for My Ancestors'

Although Augusta looked upon the children of her mother's first marriage as her siblings, she always thought of herself as a Byron. Her mother's grand ancestors never had, for her, the allure and fascination of her father's turbulent family, in whose history she was always passionately interested.

The Byrons had first come over from France in the eleventh century, part of the land-hungry band of knights who had thrown in their lot with William the Conqueror. Their descendants were reputed to have fought in the Crusades, falling valiantly before the walls of Ascalon, but one of the few solid facts known about the early history of the family is that Godfrey de Buron (the Byron name appears spelled in many ways) was recorded in 1191 as owing money to Aaron the Jew, thus establishing a family tradition almost unbroken until the mid-nineteenth century. 'That disease', wrote Byron, 'is epidemic in our family.'

Romantic Augusta's ancestors may have been, but they were hardly distinguished role-models. They robbed and poached, pillaged and burned, respecting neither God nor man, although over the centuries they steadily established themselves in royal favour. During the Wars of the Roses, Sir John Byron (a bewildering number of the Byrons were called John) declared for Henry Tudor and is said to have fought at the Battle of Bosworth Field in 1485.

Sir John's loyalty to the House of Tudor was rewarded when he was appointed Constable of Nottingham Castle and, at the Dissolution of the monasteries, the Byrons acquired, for the knock-down price of £810, 'The Priory of Newstead within the Forest of Sherwood ... and all our messuages, houses, buildings, barns, stables, dovecotes, pools, fishponds, kitchen gardens, lands and soil ...' The Priory had been built in the twelfth century for the Augustinians by Henry II, reputedly out of contrition for ordering the murder of Thomas à Becket. 'Religion's shrine! Repentant

Henry's pride', as Byron put it. Sir John somewhat magnified the place by calling it Newstead Abbey and considerably diminished it by pulling down the church, leaving only the thirteenth-century façade as the picturesque ruin familiar from dozens of romantic engravings.

At the outbreak of the Civil War in 1642, no fewer than seven Byron brothers and their uncle declared for Charles I, and the Sir John of the time, 'Bloody Braggadochio John', fought ferociously for his royal master, being rewarded with a 'noble scar on the face' – which he defiantly displayed on William Dobson's portrait of him – and with a peerage. He took the title of Baron Byron of Rochdale.

So fanatically did Sir John fight on, when all hope of a royalist victory had been abandoned, that when the war ended he was refused a pardon by Parliament and died in exile in Paris. His widow, Eleanor ('that whore my Lady Byron who had been the King's seventeenth whore abroad', as Samuel Pepys, with his habitual regard for statistical accuracy, put it), died trying to extract £4,000 worth of plate from the clutches of her royal lover. The Civil War left the Byron fortunes in a sorry state. The Abbey had been pillaged and the estates sequestrated; the Chaworths, the Byrons' rivals and enemies for many years, now had control of them. That situation was happily resolved by the marriage of Elizabeth Chaworth to the 3rd Lord Byron, but this was by no means to be the end of the conflict between the two families.

At the Glorious Revolution in 1688, the Byrons prudently transferred their allegiance to William of Orange, and the 4th Lord became Gentleman of the Bedchamber to Queen Anne's husband, the charmingly indolent Prince George of Denmark. Unlike his belligerent forebears, the 4th Lord seems to have been a quietly civilised man and an amateur painter of some capability. He married three times, on each occasion making a valuable strategic alliance, but only the children of his third wife, Frances Berkeley, survived beyond childhood. There was Isabella, who married the 4th Earl of Carlisle; William, known to posterity as the 'Wicked Lord'; Admiral John Byron, nicknamed 'Foulweather Jack', the father of Mad Jack; Richard, who became a clergyman and, like his father, had a talent for painting; and George, a rather weak-willed character, who had the good sense to marry a girl with respectable connections, Frances Levett, the daughter of a Nottingham surgeon.

So many wild and improbable stories have clustered round the life of William, the 5th Lord, that it is difficult to extricate fact from fantasy. By the time Thomas Moore came to write his life of Byron in 1830, the legend had reached its fullest flowering: the Wicked Lord had thrown his wife into a pond, had shot his coachman and bundled his corpse into the coach where his wife was sitting; and had become a total recluse, living in an Abbey that he had deliberately let go to rack and ruin, attended only by a horde of crickets and by his servants, Joe Murray and Elizabeth Hardstaff, who was reputed to be his mistress and whom the locals derided as 'Lady Betty'.

The sober facts are only a little less fantastic. The Wicked Lord was still at school at Westminster when in 1736, at the age of thirteen, he succeeded to the title but, already showing signs of an aversion to any form of discipline, he was packed off into the Navy. In time he became a Second Lieutenant on the *Victory*, but had either the good fortune or the good sense to leave the ship before it was wrecked on the rocks off Alderney in 1744. The following year, after subscribing £2,000 to the Duke of Kingston's Light Horse, he rode off with the regiment to check Bonnie Prince Charlie's advance into Lancashire. However, by the time the Highlanders were being slaughtered at Culloden, the Wicked Lord was back in London and making a reputation for himself as a man of fashion.

In 1746 they were laying bets at White's as to when the Wicked Lord would marry Elizabeth Shaw of Besthorpe Hall in Norfolk, an heiress with a fortune of £70,000, but by the time the marriage took place the following year William had become totally obsessed with a young actress, the 'enchanting' George Ann Bellamy. He somehow persuaded a close friend to abduct the girl on his behalf, but Miss Bellamy was rescued by her brother and was widely lampooned for failing to put up more than a token show of resistance.

At Newstead, following the Gothic fashion of the time, the Wicked Lord erected a folly castle where he entertained his friends with concerts and parties, but such was his reputation that these were soon transformed by the imagination of local families into wild orgies. The folly, long since demolished, was reputed to be haunted, but by then there can have been few parts of the Abbey that were not.*

* The ghosts of Newstead were always to exercise an irresistible fascination for Augusta and Byron.

Two miniature forts were built on the lake, where the Wicked Lord, assisted by Joe Murray, played at battle games with a miniature fleet. Horace Walpole, who visited the Abbey, was not impressed:

> the present lord has lost large sums and paid part in old oaks, five thousand pounds of which have been cut near the house. In recompense he has built two baby forts to pay his country in castles for the damage done to the navy.

It was not just the Newstead oaks that were being sold off to finance William's follies. He was now making considerable inroads on the fortune brought to him by his wife. Apart from the vast sums he was squandering on his compulsive gambling, cock-fighting and horse racing, he was regularly searching the auction rooms for jewels or paintings, not to mention less likely acquisitions such as a pair of statues of libidinous satyrs, and a live wolf that played contentedly with the Newstead cows.

In January 1765 occurred the event that was to mark William Byron for posterity with the name of the 'Wicked Lord'. It was his custom to join the association of Nottinghamshire gentry at their regular gatherings at the Star and Garter Inn in Pall Mall. There, on the evening of the 26th, he became involved in an argument over dinner, on the subject of the management of game, with his neighbour William Chaworth, a member of the family whose Nottinghamshire estates adjoined those of the Byrons and to whom they were now related by marriage.

William Chaworth was no less hot-tempered than William Byron and, as the argument grew more heated, he blurted out what sounded like a challenge. However, the moment passed and the row seemed to simmer down. Some time later, when both protagonists had been drinking deeply, they encountered one another on the staircase and tempers flared again. A waiter was sent for and showed them into an empty room, lit only by a 'poor little tallow candle and a dull fire'. William Byron drew his sword, as did Chaworth, making a thrust at his opponent's waistcoat. Blundering about in the dark, William drove his sword six inches into Chaworth's stomach. 'Good God, that I should be such a fool as to fight in the dark,' the Wicked Lord is said to have told the other members of the club when they rushed in to part them.

William Chaworth died the following day, leaving his fortune to his mistress and gallantly forgiving his murderer who, he said, had conducted himself like a gentleman. William Byron was arrested and imprisoned in the Tower of London and on 16 April stood trial before his peers in Westminster Hall charged with unlawfully killing Chaworth 'with a certain sword made of iron and steel of the value of five shillings . . . not having the fear of God before his eyes but being moved and seduced by the intrigues of the Devil'. The Lords found him not guilty of murder but guilty of manslaughter. After invoking a convenient statute of Edward VI, granting immunity to the peerage, William was set at liberty.

He seemed none the worse for his experience and travelled abroad, continued to haunt the sale rooms and to play with his toy warships. In October 1770 he celebrated the coming of age of his son and heir (another William) with a cannonade of twenty-one guns, 'the report being heard all over Nottingham and some of the adjoining counties'. He was looking forward to marrying the boy off to Miss Danvers, a wealthy heiress on whom William was counting to restore the family's now seriously depleted fortunes. Unfortunately his son had other ideas and the following year he brought all his father's carefully laid plans crashing down by eloping to Scotland with his cousin Juliana Elizabeth, the second daughter of the Wicked Lord's younger brother, Admiral Byron, a girl possessed of no fortune and no prospect of one.

Admiral (John) Byron, Augusta and Byron's grandfather, was a man of very different calibre indeed from the Wicked Lord, and the two brothers cordially detested each other. Nicknamed 'Foul-weather Jack', the Admiral was renowned for his nautical misfortunes. The story of his first major voyage reads as if it had been concocted by Jonathan Swift or Daniel Defoe. Setting out in 1741, his ship was wrecked while attempting to round Cape Horn. He was befriended by a tribe of natives, the daughter of the richest priest on a neighbouring island fell in love with him, he was hauled off to Valparaiso and thrown into a flea-ridden cell, imprisoned in France on his way back to England and, after countless storms and shipwrecks, returned to London in 1746.

Two years later, by then a Captain, he married his first cousin Sophia Trevanion. The Trevanions were an old Cornish family whose history curiously paralleled that of the Byrons. They too had done their fair share of plundering and poaching and house breaking. They too had declared for Henry Tudor and fought at

Bosworth. They too had fought for the King in the Civil War and a Trevanion had died at the siege of Bristol. Like the Byrons, with the coming of the eighteenth century they had begun to send their sons into the Navy.

According to her good friend Mrs Thrale-Piozzi, Sophia Trevanion was a woman for whom 'men would willingly have run through fire'. She was certainly very pretty, if her portrait by Rosalba Carriera can be believed, but she cannot have been easy to live with. There was an air of fragility about her and she was the victim of excessive sensibility, prone to outbursts of hysteria and self-pity. She had, at the same time, a high opinion of herself, 'an odd way of coveting the servants of neighbours' and was a friend of the diarist and novelist Fanny Burney and, through Mrs Thrale-Piozzi, part of the circle that revolved round the great Dr Johnson.

Her husband's frequent infidelities were a constant trial of her patience. Known in the scandal sheets as the 'nautical lover', Admiral (John) Byron had a girl in every port and Sophia, like so many naval wives, saw very little of her husband. He was always on the high seas, fighting the French in Canada and the West Indies, discovering the tribe of giants in Tierra del Fuego, formally taking possession of the Falkland Islands in the name of George III, but managing to return home with sufficient frequency to keep Sophia in a state of almost permanent pregnancy.

The Admiral and his wife were not entirely fortunate in their children. Their elder son, 'Mad Jack', was a constant drain on their finances and, although Sophia may have derived some brief excitement at her son's elopement with so celebrated a society figure as the Marchioness of Carmarthen, she was deeply embarrassed by the popular press reporting the exploits of the 'Boisterous lover and the Capricious Marchioness' and by the knowledge that the name of Byron had been reviled in the House of Lords. She had barely recovered from her 'mortification and humiliation' when she heard that her second son, George Anson, was returning from Barbados with a bride, Henrietta Charlotte Dallas, whom he had known for barely ten days before he married her on board his ship, HMS *Proserpine*. 'A pleasant situation for this proud family' was Fanny Burney's comment.

Nor did Sophia fare much better with her daughters. Frances, her eldest surviving child, was a woman of determinedly independent spirit who, after the failure of her early marriage, went on to lead a distinctly rackety life, had at least one illegitimate child and was shunned by the majority of her family.

Sophia's second daughter, Juliana,* who was always known as Julia, seemed destined for a highly desirable marriage when, barely sixteen, she was courted by John Delap Halliday, a young Ensign in the Coldstream Guards and heir to a sizeable fortune. But Sophia soon began to make excessive demands on her daughter's behalf – 'House, servants, equippage etc.' – and young Halliday seems to have had second thoughts about what he was letting himself in for. At this point he had the good fortune to meet another sixteen-year-old, the Earl of Dysart's daughter, Lady Jane Tollemache, who was herself a considerable heiress. The two promptly fell in love and eloped. Sophia's wrath at this jilting of her daughter knew no bounds and letters flew across the Atlantic to her husband (who had been appointed Governor of Newfoundland in 1769), insisting that he bring an action against Halliday for breach of promise.†

Under the circumstances it is not surprising that Julia decided to elope with her cousin William Byron the following year, confounding the Wicked Lord's marriage plans for his heir. The old man was said to have made himself ill with rage, but by the time Julia had presented him with a grandson – yet another William – a year later, he had become reconciled.

Julia's first husband William Byron died four years later at the age of just twenty-six, cheating her of the chance of inheriting Newstead and the title, but seven years later she married again. Her new husband was the extremely wealthy Sir Robert Wilmot of Osmaston in Derbyshire, who showered his bride with gifts, including three of the finest coach horses in town, a phaeton, an elegant sedan chair and 'a large quantity of plate, curious birds, with the prettiest terrier she ever saw with her name on the collar'. Sadly, Julia did not live long to enjoy all this grandeur, but died at the age of thirty-four in 1788, though not before producing a son and heir for her sorrowing second husband. The child was named, like his father, Robert Wilmot.

No different from the rest of the family, Admiral Byron was invariably short of money. 'I have on coming home so many things

---

* Not her elder sister, Frances Byron, as stated by A. L. Rowse in 'The Byrons and the Trevanions'.
† The action was in the end settled out of court by Halliday's father.

– alas – to pay,' lamented his wife Sophia, 'it distresses me – nay near drives me mad – if I can't save it out of next quarter – what will become of me – I know not.' The convenient death of a Berkeley uncle in 1772 eased their situation slightly. The Admiral was left £20,000 and a further £22,000 was put in trust for the children, who would inherit it on coming of age. The Admiral spent much of his money on rebuilding a country house at Pirbright in Surrey, which he renamed 'Byron Lodge', where he planted a mile-long avenue of pine trees still known today as the 'Admiral's Walk'.

As far as his children were concerned, the Berkeley inheritance served only to accelerate the break-up of the family and the third daughter, Sophia Maria (known as Sophy), was determined to leave home as soon as she came of age. Devoted as she was to her father, and much as she loved the house at Pirbright, she seized the first opportunity created by her independent fortune to get away from her mother and to travel abroad with her widowed sister Julia and little William Byron.

The last of the daughters of Admiral Byron, Augusta Barbara Charlotte, 'my romantically partial young friend', as Fanny Burney called her, could not wait to get away from home either. 'She flatters herself with the pleasing prospect at such an event being not very far distant & counts the hours,' the Admiral told her sisters. In the spring of 1783 she travelled with Sophy to France. Within the year she had married Christopher Parker,* who was later to become, like his father-in-law, an Admiral.

As for Mad Jack Byron, he spent his share of the Berkeley inheritance the moment he could get his hands on it, and by the time he was twenty-two there was nothing left.

Six weeks after Amelia Byron's death in London on 26 January 1784, Mad Jack turned up in Frankfurt, out of funds as usual. On 14 March 1784, he wrote to James Sykes at his office in Crutched Friars:

> I have taken the liberty to draw upon you for forty four pounds. I intended to have sent the Bill to my Mother but they would not give me money on a Bill drawn on my Mother. Therefore I was obliged to draw on you. I have wrote to Grosvenor Square about it. I desir'd

---

* Rear Admiral Christopher Parker (1761–1804) was the son of Nelson's patron, Admiral Sir Peter Parker (1721–1811).

my Mother to repay my Father, whom I hope will be so good as to advance the sum for me till my affairs are settled.

James Sykes had long been familiar with Mad Jack's ways and with his little tricks to get hold of money. Sykes was a valued friend of the Byrons, and his daughter Sarah was to marry the son of the Admiral's younger brother, Richard. As Navy agent to the Admiral and his general man of business, Sykes knew all too well that Mad Jack's affairs would never be 'settled' until he found himself another source of income. As far as Jack was concerned this could only be another susceptible woman possessed of her own fortune. It was with that end in view that the following year he set up his headquarters in Bath and proceeded to open his campaign in the Assembly Rooms.

Although Bath was no longer the elegant and glittering city it had been in the heyday of Beau Nash, it was still a highly fashionable spa, much frequented by society and an important marriage market to which young women resorted in quest of eligible husbands. Jack Byron may not have been in any material sense eligible, but he was handsome and elegant, could be irresistibly charming when he put his mind to it and had a formidable reputation as an accomplished lover, which his liaison with Amelia had widely publicised.

It was not long before he found what he was looking for in the plump, plain and eminently available Catherine Gordon, the 13th Laird of Gight, descended from a family that could trace its ancestry back to James I of Scotland and the Earls of Huntly. Catherine was twenty-one and in search of a husband. Her fortune was comparatively modest, amounting to some £22,500, but the gossips of Bath, always on the look-out for a new heiress, had blown this up into a huge sum. Jack must have considered this boisterous, impressionable little dumpling of a girl easy prey. Music and dancing were her passion, and dancing was something at which Jack excelled. Catherine was won in a mere matter of days, and on 13 May 1785 Jack Byron married his second heiress in Saint Michael's Church, assuming the name of Gordon to secure her fortune.

Jack did not even trouble himself to inform his parents of his marriage, nor did he linger long with his bride in Bath, where too many creditors, having heard that he had married money, were clamouring to be paid. Instead he made directly for Scotland and Catherine's ancestral home at Gight.

Stories of the Gordon Byrons' wild life, with music and dancing, feasting and shouting and shooting, suggest that they were living at a very extravagant rate, and Jack was capable of running up the most alarming bills on his wardrobe alone. It came as no surprise to anyone when Gight was put on the market, and Jack was soon writing to his father asking him to advance money on the sale so that the estate could be freed from the debts that already encumbered it.

The Admiral, who had come to his son's rescue once too often, was in no position to advance money on anything. He was ill and weighed down by financial burdens of his own. In April 1786 he died, and Mad Jack hurried down from Scotland to find out what had been left to him in his father's will. To his disbelief all that awaited him was £500. He had already pledged far more than that many times over to a host of creditors. The proceeds of the sale of the Admiral's estates were to be divided between his children, but from this Jack was specifically excluded. There was a further complication: the Admiral had made a provision for an annuity to be paid to his widow but, when it became clear that there would not be sufficient funds to cover this, Sophia was reduced to the rather desperate expedient of suing her own children for payment. 'I believe there never was a will like it,' George Anson Byron wrote to his sister Frances, 'and I always thought my Father did not owe a farthing.'

Refusing to accept the terms of the will, Jack exasperated his brother George by lodging a claim, as the elder son, to their father's property at Pirbright and to a farm at Crondall in Hampshire and by lying to him 'that lawyers had given in his favour'. The reverse, of course, was the case. Since he had promised his 'legacy' in so many directions, Jack was now in serious trouble. His letter to Sykes, written on 4 May 1786, trying to raise £20, is breathtaking in its naïvety: 'if you chuse to have the other part of the Legacy, you shall have four hundred and fifty pounds – & I give you my word of honour that I will not mention a syllable of it . . .'

Two days later Jack's creditors pounced. He was arrested for debt by an officer with the name of Goodflesh and thrown into the King's Bench prison. His tailor, James Milne, to whom he was considerably in debt, took it upon himself to bail him out in exchange for a promise of the increasingly elastic £500, thereby stealing a march on the other creditors. Perrigaux, a Parisian banker known to the Byron family and who had funded Jack in the past on the strength of his expectations, wrote rather forlornly to James Sykes:

> Some time after the Admiral's decease Mr Byron had proposed making an assignment of his legacy for £500 to you partly for the purpose of discharging another debt of about the same amount as mine, and that you had expressed much pleasure at the proposal hoping that it would enable you to secure mine; but he soon after changed his mind and assigned it to a Mr Milne, a Taylor, to whom I conclude he owed the whole and to whom probably it has since been paid. Thus I fear I am cut off from every prospect of recovering my debt . . .*

Clearly, with so many creditors on his tail, Jack could not remain in London and out of gaol. In the summer of 1786, he rented a house in South Warnborough in Hampshire, conveniently close to the farm at Crondall to which he had laid claim. A dash to Cornwall to scrounge money from his Trevanion relatives failed and he was forced to lie low until the following year, when Gight was at last sold. Unfortunately, virtually all the proceeds of the sale were swallowed up instantly by his creditors and Jack was still in debt. The only solution was to do what so many improvident Englishmen did at that time: to take refuge on the continent where living could be cheaper and it was out of reach of the duns. As a preliminary step, in the early summer of 1787, he leased a house in Cowes on the Isle of Wight, where he was joined by Catherine and his four-year-old daughter, the Honourable Augusta Mary.

After Amelia's death, Lady Holdernesse had taken on the responsibility for her little granddaughter and, as far as is known, Jack had never shown the slightest interest in her. Perhaps it was Catherine's idea to take over the care of Augusta; perhaps Jack had hopes of material benefit or of getting back at his former mother-in-law, who would have been legally powerless to prevent him from having custody of his child if he chose to do so. Lady Holdernesse loathed Jack Byron, whom she regarded as the instrument of Amelia's disgrace and death. Now, confronted with his uncouth new wife, she made no attempt to conceal her disdain, for which Catherine never forgave her.

---

* Much about the same time, the ever-gullible Perrigaux had been persuaded by the Duchess of Devonshire to assist her in sorting out her enormous gambling debts.

Early in July, Jack hired a boat and slipped across the Channel into France, leaving Catherine in Cowes with Augusta. It was September before she plucked up enough courage to follow him – by which time she was nearly five months pregnant, or as a family friend described: 'She is big with bairn for certain, he is off to France for debt, where the poor unhappy woman must soon follow.' Follow him Catherine did, for, despite everything, she was still infatuated. Taking Augusta with her, she made her way to Chantilly, where George Anson Byron and his wife, Henrietta Charlotte, had moved earlier in the year from St-Germain-en-Laye. 'Our house is completely furnished,' George Anson told his sister Frances Leigh, 'with old furniture – not very elegant to be sure – but we have a large garden and likewise stabling for three horses . . . everything dear as at Paris . . .'

At Chantilly there would have been company for Augusta, for the Anson Byrons had two daughters, six-year-old Isabella Georgiana and Julia Maria Charlotte, who was five, but the Gordon Byrons did not remain there long. Jack was still on uneasy terms with his brother after his attempt to cheat over their father's will and he soon found out that George Anson was in no position to subsidise him. So Jack took off for Paris with Catherine and Augusta, where the unfortunate Perrigaux, who had been mollified by partial payment after the sale of Gight, was coaxed into advancing him a further £200. There is no reason to suppose that Jack did other than live it up, while Catherine remained miserably in their lodgings with Augusta. It was during this time that Augusta, for whom all the moving about had proved far too much, became seriously ill and was nursed back to health by Catherine, a fact that she was determined never to allow her stepdaughter to forget:

> I still recollect with a degree of horror the many *sleepless* nights, and days of *agony* I have passed by your bedside drowned in tears, while you lay insensible at the gates of death. Your recovery certainly was wonderful, and thank God I did my duty . . .

Realising that her spendthrift husband was drinking and gambling what little money they had left, Catherine resolved to return to England to await the birth of her child. When Augusta was well enough to travel, she returned with her to London and took rooms at 16 Holles Street,* off Cavendish Square. There she was

---

* A site now occupied by the department store John Lewis.

introduced to the wife of a young solicitor, John Hanson, who helped her to arrange for her approaching confinement.

As for Augusta, she had become a luxury Catherine could no longer afford – and, with the arrival of her own child, there would be neither money nor space to spare for Jack's daughter by his first wife. The solution was to return the little girl to her grandmother, Lady Holdernesse. What happened then can only be conjectured, but it seems likely that Lady Holdernesse, convinced that Augusta had not been properly cared for, refused point-blank to have any personal dealings with Catherine and instead sent her maid, Deborah Bradshaw, to remove the child from Holles Street and bring her back to the security of Holdernesse House, thereby incurring Catherine's enduring enmity and resentment.

Catherine was expecting the return of her husband 'everyday', and Jack did in fact land in England early in January 1788, since we know that he incurred debts in Dover. Wisely he did not risk showing his face in London and was not present when his son, the future Lord Byron, was born on Tuesday 22 January. Jack, who was never strong on dates, places or names, reported to Catherine's agent in Edinburgh that Mrs Byron was 'brought to bed of a son on Monday last, and is far from well'.

Four days after the birth of his son, Augusta celebrated her fifth birthday with her grandmother in the comfort of the house in which her mother, Amelia, had grown up.

Catherine slowly recovered and Jack probably took advantage of a curious legal anomaly, by which debtors could not be arrested on the Sabbath, to pay a quick visit to Holles Street, impelled not so much by a desire to see his son as by the need to persuade Catherine to give him the means to travel to Scotland. She was all too well aware that if he asked her for money she would be unable to refuse him, but now, as far as she was concerned, her little boy took priority over everything else. She wrote to James Watson in Edinburgh:

> I shall make Mr Beckett give you an account of all Mr Byron's debts that we know of as soon as possible, but I hope the money won't be given to him but to have somebody to pay them, for he will only pay what he is obliged to pay and there will be more debts coming in and more demands for money. I am sorry he is getting a new carriage . . . I hope by the time my little boy is able to travel Mr Byron will have

got a house in some cheap country whether Wales or the North of England. I want money to be sent me while in Town and I must have it as if Mr Byron gets it it will be thrown away in some foolish way or other and I shall be obliged to apply for more . . . I will live as cheap as I can but it was impossible till now as there was a great many expenses that could not be avoided – direct for me No. 2 Baker Street Portman's Square – my little boy is to be named George.

She added, 'Don't show Mr Byron this.'

CHAPTER 3

'Poor Miss Byron'

On 10 June 1789 William Mason wrote to Earl Harcourt* from his rectory at Aston:

> I expect the honour of a visit from Lady Holdernesse very soon, she is coming to Alderson in my neighbourhood, and I believe she brings poor Miss Byron to live for some time in his family with a gouvernante, but whether this be a secret or no I know not, and therefore would not have it mentioned.

Christopher Alderson was now the Vicar of Tickhill in South Yorkshire and had succeeded William Mason as the Holdernesse family chaplain in 1773. Since the Earl's death he had become a close and trusted friend of Lady Holdernesse, acting as her adviser in legal and financial matters, and she had him in mind, almost from the first, as the most suitable person to whom to entrust Augusta. To all intents and purposes Alderson was to become her granddaughter's guardian.

However, Tickhill, situated as it was on the Great North Road, was not considered a sufficiently secluded setting for Augusta's childhood and when the living of Eckington fell vacant Lady Holdernesse persuaded the Queen to prevail upon William Pitt to confer it upon Alderson. Eckington, where Augusta was to pass the next seven years of her life, was on the edge of the Derbyshire coal fields, some seven miles outside Sheffield. As far as Lady Holdernesse was concerned, the great virtue of the place was its remoteness. Mason's caution about whether or not the child's presence there was to be treated as a 'secret' referred to the fact that Jack Byron, as ever in hiding from his creditors, was known to be 'skulking in Town under a feigned name' and Lady Holdernesse was anxious to put her granddaughter in a place where there would be little chance of her father attempting to carry her off again.

* George Simon, 2nd Earl Harcourt, d. 1809.

Not that this was the only reason for exiling Augusta to a remote corner of Derbyshire. It was time, too, for her to be removed from a place and a situation still overshadowed by her mother's tragic and scandalous history. In the household of a country clergyman, far removed from the perils of fashionable London, Augusta could be assured of a stable and God-fearing upbringing.

On an evening in early July, Lady Holdernesse arrived in Eckington with six-year-old Augusta and her governess and deposited them at the Rectory. Tired and bewildered by the long journey from London, the little girl, with her great woebegone eyes, was warmly welcomed into her new home by the Rector's wife, Elizabeth Alderson, whom all her life Augusta would remember with devotion and gratitude. In 1817, hearing of Elizabeth's death at a time when she was at her lowest ebb, Augusta wrote: 'Poor Mrs Alderson – she was in my younger days as a mother to me – and loved me so well that I feel grateful for every unhappiness she has been spared on my acct.' Growing up as a child of the Rectory gave Augusta a glimpse of domesticity and a sense of family that she would never have found in the stiff formality of life in Holdernesse House. Of the Aldersons' three children, it was their eight-year-old daughter, Mary, who became her particular companion, sharing with her the schoolroom as well as their games and secrets, and Augusta would always look upon her as 'my earliest friend'.

The Reverend Christopher himself was a wise and kindly man, but generally much preoccupied with his passion for garden design. In 1791, two years after Augusta's arrival at Eckington, Lady Holdernesse recommended Alderson to Queen Charlotte as the best man to advise her on the construction of her 'little paradise', the garden at Amelia Lodge (named after the Queen's daughter) at Frogmore. Queen Charlotte found him 'a man of great natural taste but not of the World' and was delighted by the 'pleasing diversity of mounts, glades, serpentine walks and canals, with bridges and other erections' that he created for her. He also laid out a fine garden at Eckington, though this was not completed during Augusta's time there.

Lady Holdernesse's decision to hide her precious granddaughter where the Byrons could not discover her proved both successful and expedient. Jack was continually trying to ferret out his child's whereabouts, but it was kept a close secret: 'Do you ever hear anything of little Augusta and how she is?' Catherine Byron enquired of Mad Jack's sister, Frances Leigh. 'Is she in the country or with Lady Holdernesse?'

When Catherine wrote this letter in 1791 she had lost touch not only with her stepdaughter Augusta but with her erring husband Jack as well.

Sometime after the birth of their son, Catherine had returned to Scotland to live in Aberdeen, where Jack had eventually joined her, but they had soon fallen into raucous quarrelling. Jack had moved to the other end of the street, but Catherine continued to scream at him at the top of her voice, calling him a scoundrel and a spendthrift. He managed to extract £100 from her and beat a hasty retreat.

Catherine never saw him again. 'She is very amiable from a distance,' he told his sister Frances Leigh, 'but I defy you and all the Apostles to live with her for two months, for if anybody could live with her it was me. *Mais jeu des Mains, jeu des Vilains* [rough play oftens ends in tears].'

Frances Leigh was Jack's senior by several years. She had married in July 1770 a young Guards Captain, Charles Leigh. It seems to have been rather a perfunctory ceremony, for apart from the bride and groom the only persons present appear to have been the parish clerk of the Church of Saint Marylebone and one Grace Barnett, whose names figure so frequently in the parish records that they must have enjoyed quite a business as token witnesses.* The Leighs' only child, George, was born within a year of the marriage.

Charles Leigh came of a plantation-owning family from St Kitts in the Leeward Islands and was the son of a George Leigh whose name appears as an executor to a will of 1738 in the parish records of Saint Anne. Leigh's service record gives no date or place of birth, but he cannot have been born much earlier than 1748, which would have made him very little older than Frances Byron. He had been in England at least since 1764, when he enlisted in the 3rd Regiment of Footguards as an Ensign. The Byrons evidently regarded Charles Leigh as a responsible character and a man of probity, for he was invited to replace one of the trustees of the Byron/Trevanion marriage settlement (another trustee being the 'Wicked Lord' himself).

---

* No mention is made in the register of Frances having her father's consent, which suggests that she was not a minor.

Leigh also seems to have tried his hand as a financial adviser. Writing to her brother in Mecklenburg Strelitz, Queen Charlotte commented on the difficulty of finding officers to fight in the American war, 'as owing to their continued sojourn in the city, a great many of them had taken profitable professions'. Profitable or not, Charles Leigh certainly entered into a rather dubious financial arrangement with his sister-in-law Sophy, persuading her to allow him to invest her Berkeley legacy and agreeing to pay her a high rate of interest every six months to give her a regular income from it. It would be twelve years before she realised that getting the money back at all, not to mention the arrears of interest, would be a very difficult business indeed.

If Sophy came to detest and distrust her brother-in-law, Frances could hardly bear the sight of him. By the time Charles Leigh had embarked for the war in America, their marriage was as good as over. Exactly what triggered their split is a mystery but, from what is known about her later life, it is fairly safe to assume that a lover was involved. There was never a divorce, but there was nothing amicable about their separation and, having taken custody of their son, George, Charles Leigh seems to have severed all connection with her. Nor did Frances fare much better with her mother and her two youngest and highly respectable sisters, to whom her scandalous way of life was a profound embarrassment. The men of the family were a different matter and she managed to remain in contact with her father and both her brothers, as well as the Wicked Lord and the Nottingham relations. By 1787, however, although they continued to correspond, her brother George Anson had not seen Frances for twelve years and she was living in Raismes, a small village near Valenciennes in northern France. Along the way she acquired numerous lovers and a couple of children.

Valenciennes was an ancient frontier town, known somewhat optimistically as the 'Athens of the North' – a city that had suffered many wars and was to suffer more. Mad Jack, needing somewhere he could lie low out of reach of his creditors, now decided to make it his bolt-hole. When he turned up there in September 1790 he seems to have had no trouble in persuading Frances, who was by then living in the town itself, to let him stay with her.

Frances was doing her best to live in style. She had acquired the use of a carriage, bought a harpsichord and had her own box at the theatre, provided by one of her admirers. She was, though, like all the other members of the Byron family, seriously short of money and seriously in debt. With their similarly cavalier approach to sex, brother and sister wasted little time in falling into bed together. Evidence for this is provided by a series of letters written to Frances by Jack after she had gone back to England:

> I declare I can find no woman so handsome as you. I have tried several, but when I do anything extraordinary I always think of you. The Marigny slept with me two nights running, but she is the worst piece I have ever slept with.

Their incestuous liaison was cut short when news reached them that their mother, Sophia Byron, had died in Bath on 5 November. She had been ill with various neurotic ailments for years and, with the exception of her younger son, 'the best of men and my Heart's most dear George', was estranged from her remaining children. Of Jack she had heard not a word since the trouble over the Admiral's will and she 'knew no more of him than if he were not so . . .' Both Sophy and the youngest daughter, Augusta Parker, had long ago lost patience with Sophia's endless complaints and never went near her if they could avoid it – and they generally could – while Frances no longer really counted. It was perhaps the realisation that she had been virtually deserted by her children that led Sophia to cancel the bequest of a little gold and ivory prayer book she had intended for Augusta Mary, the granddaughter she had so seldom seen. Instead she decided to leave it to her friend Mrs Piozzi's daughter, Cecilia Thrale.

Jack and Frances did not spend long mourning the demise of their unfortunate mother. Their only concern on hearing the news was the will and what they had been left in it. Since it was out of the question for Jack to show his face in England, where he would have been instantly clapped into gaol, Frances went to London, leaving Jack in charge of the house in Valenciennes, with special instructions to look after her harpsichord and her pet bird.

At first all went well. Jack slept in Frances's room, trained her little bird to fly out of the window and return to him and, in anticipation of his expectations from his mother's will, drew three drafts on his London banker for £100 each. He gave parties for the neighbours – 'we had 3 bottles of wine and punch – all drunk and *le petit mari* farted to such a degree by eating too much sallad that he was beastly . . .' – and every night he appeared in Frances's box at the theatre. 'The woman who opens your Loge said she should never see any person so good to her as you was. I immediately gave her 3 Livres and told her the Byrons were always so.'

He continued to send Frances detailed accounts of his escapades with the ladies of the town, leaving out nothing that he thought might appeal to her fancy:

> As for La Marigny she is as wide as a church door and I really was resolved [not?] to do it with her, because Renaud said that one must give her money, and quoted the P.[rince] de Ligne. Although not so young nor so handsome as him, still the Birons are irresistible. You know that Fanny ... as for La Henry she told me that I did it so well, that she always spent twice every time. I know this will make you laugh but she is the best piece I ever ...

At the same time Jack asked his sister to send someone to Hertford Street to make enquiries about his daughter's health from Lady Holdernesse's maid Deborah Bradshaw and to find out where Augusta was living. Much as one would like to believe that this was a rare instance of paternal concern, it is more likely that, as Lady Holdernesse had anticipated, he was calculating that, once he had discovered his daughter's hiding place, someone might pay him to keep away from her.

In Valenciennes Jack was living his life as he had always done, womanising indiscriminately and running up massive bills, but gradually he began to grow uneasy. Letters from Frances became increasingly rare and money from her to meet the escalating bills still rarer. To make matters worse, he was showing unmistakable symptoms of tuberculosis, the disease that had carried off both Amelia and her father: 'I have been very ill, and have been spitting blood for these three days ... it is owing to a cold I have had for some time.'

The Revolution was strengthening its hold upon society in Valenciennes and Jack was not making himself popular by shouting out '*Vive le Roi*' from his loge at the theatre, 'and now they say *Cet Anglais est Aristocrat au diable*'.

Frances began to lose patience with her brother's incessant demands for money and his continual complaints that he did not have a shirt to his back or a pair of stockings. Someone in Valenciennes, probably her former lover Talusbrus, was keeping her fully informed of the way Jack was living. He wrote to her in what sounds like genuine misery:

> You do not know how much I have suffered in this d—ed town – and much more so since you have wrote to Talusbrus – who mentions that you are angry with me, for what reason I do not know. God knows, I love only you, and if we part we must be miserable, therefore dear sister do not always listen to what they say.

In February 1791 came the final blow. Frances told her brother that there would be nothing coming to him from his mother's will. In April their creditors in Valenciennes lost patience. The bailiffs seized her clothes and her harpsichord, and somehow in the confusion her bird was killed: 'Your bird was not trod to death,' Jack wailed, 'but died a natural death. I have got another as good.'

Jack was now constantly drinking brandy 'in order to drown care'. The bailiffs were coming to take away the furniture and soon he would not even have a bed to sleep on. 'A prison will be my lodging.' Jack had cried wolf before and had continued to live in his old extravagant style. Now no one, least of all his sister, would believe him. He had dreams of joining the Army and finding his way back to England, 'or go to India to my brother – he must do something for me'. By now he realised that Frances was not coming back to rescue him. She was more concerned with the other men in her life.

Against all reason he still clung to the futile hope that something might still be salvaged from his mother's will, by paying a fee to the executors, the 5th Lord Byron and Charles Leigh. Jack had been prepared to pay £20 to the Wicked Lord 'with the little I have', but now 'I would give sooner the £20 for Colonel Leigh than to remain in the situation I am in.' Since Frances could not bear even to hear her husband's name mentioned, this was not likely to be well received, and like all Jack's desperate remedies it came to nothing.

The gates of the town were shut against him by order of the magistrate, he told her. 'I would rather be a Galley Slave than what I am at present, and suffer the indignity I do now – for I have neither help nor comfort.' And yet, in the midst of all his misery, the old Mad Jack Byron flared up one last time: 'Here is an English woman who plays on the Stage & is the first actress. She is married to an Actor who is the second, Bastalle. I do not know how but she has wrote to me.'

This proved to be the final spark. Years of dissolute living and the consumption of formidable quantities of brandy had steadily undermined his health, which now failed completely. Six weeks later, on 2 August 1791, Jack was dead. He bequeathed Frances the by now mythical £500 that, in a final access of self-delusion, he believed was due to him.

Whether she was with him at the end is impossible to say. Augusta was always convinced that she was, and Frances was at pains to reassure Catherine that she had been present at his deathbed. 'You wrong me very much when you suppose I do not lament Mr Byron's death,' Catherine wrote to her. 'It had made me very miserable and the more so since I had not the melancholy satisfaction of seeing him before his death, if I had known of his illness I would have come to him . . . you say he was sensible to the last, did he ever mention me?'

Frances was certainly not above telling a lie to cover up her callousness. Catherine's cries of distress when she learned of her husband's death could be heard, it was said, all the way down the street. It is doubtful whether Frances mourned the death of the man who had been her lover and was also her brother. Nor is it known whether she ever returned to Valenciennes, where so many creditors awaited her. A letter from Catherine the following November declining an offer to go abroad with her suggests that Frances may have been planning to do so, but it is more likely that she remained in Sandgate, where George Anson wrote to her on 19 June 1792, after apologising for the cardinal sin of having consulted her husband about her dire finances.

> I am afraid my dear sister that the many years we have been deprived of each other's company has likewise deprived us of understanding each other . . . I spoke to Mr Leigh not with an intention of giving you offence nor could he in return think of setting me against you.

In February of the following year France declared war on England.

> The continent is in a pretty state of uproar – and the *sans culottes* ran well without breeches [wrote George Anson]. They never had a shirt and Desmouriez* says they are in want of shoes – they must

---

* Charles François Dumouriez (1739–1823), French general and statesman. He commanded the revolutionary forces in the campaign in northern France 1792–3 but after their defeat by the Austrians at Neerwinden he went over to the Allies. He died in England.

be an indecent corps without they carry a large latoush Box in Front.

By a magnificent irony, when the British attacked and captured Valenciennes in July 1793, it was Charles Leigh who led the storming party.

CHAPTER 4

'A Very Nice Child'

Augusta was eight and a half when her father died in Valenciennes. She had barely known him and could only have preserved a few memories of his devil-may-care exuberance, his temper and his irresistibly handsome appearance, for it is unlikely that she saw very much of him. Mad Jack Byron was neither a domestic being nor much exercised by fatherhood. Nevertheless, enough remained in her memory to sow the seeds of a legend. The very fact that on the rare occasions when she did hear her father's name mentioned, he was spoken of with bitterness and contempt served only to intensify her loyalty. Many years later she recalled:

> the adoration almost I felt for my poor father from hearing him constantly abused and cried down – the romantic schemes I formed and which I never mentioned to anybody, because there was no one to whom I could open my heart.

Did her romantic schemes include running away to find him? If they did, she took care to keep them to herself. She learned at Eckington how to conceal her true feelings, to become the person Christopher Alderson and his wife wanted her to be, and she soon fell into the habit of telling people only what she believed they wanted to hear. Her devotion to her father's memory was the most closely guarded of her many secrets.

In June 1793, almost two years after Mad Jack's death, his brother, George Anson, died. Severely injured while on service in India, he had barely survived the long voyage home and the death of his wife in childbirth proved to be the final blow. He never recovered his health or his spirits and died of consumption, leaving his three children, Isabella Georgiana, Julia Mary Charlotte and his namesake, four-year-old George Anson, wholly destitute, 'for there is no provision', wrote James Sykes, 'but the hopes of Assistance from Friends which may God grant them'. Guardians had been appointed by George Anson before his death, but it was their aunt

Sophy Byron who unhesitatingly stepped into the breach. By far the most sympathetic and practical of the Byron sisters, she was endowed, unlike some of her family, with a sense of responsibility and, with the help of the Sykes family, set about making a life for the children. Isabella Georgiana and Julia were old enough to go to boarding school, while little George Anson remained with Sophy, doted on and probably a little spoiled, until he too was of an age to go to Dr William Burney's Academy at Gosport,* returning to her for the holidays.

Sophy's difficulty was that she had little money of her own, for she was still locked in an increasingly acrimonious struggle with her brother-in-law Charles Leigh to reclaim the money he owed her. She had reached a point where she could take no more of his lies and his evasions:

> I shall expect with some impatience an account of what new subterfuge Mr Leigh will avail himself of not to pay when he learns I am not really the dupe he imagines and wishes to make me, indeed the patience I have hitherto submitted to his delays may have given him reason to suppose I shall not continue it, but in this he must be undeceived.

Eventually a naval pension of £50 each was secured for the children and was matched by a similar amount from the East India Company, in whose service George Anson had been injured. It was paid to Sophy Byron in trust for the three children, but £300 a year was still a pathetically small sum on which to bring up two girls and the boy who would eventually become the seventh Lord Byron.

Barely more than twenty miles, as the crow flies, from where Augusta was living at Eckington, her great-uncle the 5th and 'wicked' Lord Byron had withdrawn from the world and was living a hermit-like existence among the ghosts of Newstead. His sudden descents on London to indulge in gaming and cock-fighting under an assumed name were now things of the past. He lived frugally on bread, cheese, butter and ale, still attended by his two devoted servants, Joe Murray and Betty Hardstaff. His only remaining diversion was the horde of crickets (or so Byron called them – they were probably cockroaches) that swarmed over the kitchen floor.

One of his few visitors at the Abbey was Frances Leigh. As the

---

* This was the school to which Trelawney, Byron's 'Corsair', was sent in 1806.

black sheep of her generation, ostracised by polite society and alienated from her sisters, she saw the old man as a kindred spirit, sharing a contempt for the world whose rules and values they had both defied. Frances was also undoubtedly hoping that he might leave her something in his will. On one of her visits to Newstead, according to Augusta:

> she slept in what was termed the Haunted Room and she was obliged to be removed from it to another! Because a sort of *Black Mass* regularly appeared and flung itself across the foot of her bed and vanished!!!!! Mrs Hardstaff was accordingly summoned to complain of this, who replied that she was not surprised for everyone who slept in that room saw the same!!!

In 1794, William Byron, the Wicked Lord's grandson and heir, was killed at the siege of Calvi in Corsica. Augusta would have been told of her cousin's heroic death and the fact that the little half-brother she had never seen was now heir to the Barony of Rochdale, but no one thought it worth their trouble to inform Catherine Byron. Frances Leigh had long since given up replying to Catherine's letters, since they were invariably pathetic requests for money, but when Catherine did eventually get news of William Byron's death she wrote to Frances:

> You know Lord Byron. Do you think he will do anything for George, or be at any expense to give him a proper education, or, if he wish to do it, is his present fortune such a one that he could spare anything out of it?

The Wicked Lord could spare nothing and would do nothing. He was not even remotely curious about his successor, to whom he referred as the 'brat from Aberdeen'. There were more important matters on hand. He had discovered that if he called the crickets they would come rushing out to greet him.

In March 1796, Augusta, now thirteen years old, left Eckington – which had been her home for nearly seven years – and the woman who had been 'as a mother' to her, to journey to London where she was to be prepared for her entrance into society. John Milbanke, with whom Lady Holdernesse discussed everything and upon whom she relied for advice, wrote to another friend, Thomas Pelham: 'Miss Byron is come up to Lady Holdernesse – with ye consent of all ye Leeds family, she is going to place her with a French Protestant Marquise who takes 12 pupils at Barnes . . .'

The Marquise was one of a colony of French émigrés who had been lucky enough to get out of France before the Terror and settle in Barnes. Her establishment would have been something like the equivalent of a finishing school, where Augusta would perfect her French and be taught the elegant accomplishments – deportment, dancing, music and drawing – that were indispensable for a young lady about to be launched into the fashionable world. Even taking into account the possibility that Augusta made occasional visits to Lady Holdernesse during her years at Eckington, the sudden transition from a remote Derbyshire village set among coalfields must have been overwhelming. Small wonder that Augusta soon developed a reputation for excessive shyness.

Augusta's half-sister, Lady Mary Osborne, had been just fifteen when in 1791 Lady Holdernesse presented her to Queen Charlotte and she had made her début in society, becoming a great favourite with the royal family. The year before Augusta's return from Eckington, Mary had been one of the maids of honour at the wedding of the Prince of Wales to Princess Caroline at which her father, now Duke of Leeds,* had been deeply shocked by the spectacle of the Prince, suitably fortified with brandy, swearing that he would never love any woman but Mrs Fitzherbert and being led to the altar looking, according to Lord Melbourne, 'like Macheath going to execution'.

In 1797, when Augusta was fourteen, Lady Holdernesse, now in her late seventies, was found to be suffering from breast cancer, which, in her doctors' opinion, 'rendered amputation necessary'. With stoical determination she kept her condition 'a secret from everybody and preserved her cheerfulness and courage in an astonishing degree', but in April, fearing that she might not survive the operation, she added a codicil to her will, making special provision for Augusta, who would otherwise have had nothing to support her. After directing payment of her debts, specific legacies and an annuity of £80 to her maid, the faithful Deborah Bradshaw, Lady Holdernesse:

gave and bequeathed all her leasehold messuage or house wherein she then resided . . . and all the rest and residue of her household

* The Marquess of Carmarthen had succeeded to the title on the death of his father, the 4th Duke of Leeds, on 23 March 1789.

goods and chattels and all her personal estate to be placed in the hands of her executors and trustees in Trust to be sold ... to invest for the education and maintenace of her granddaughter, Augusta Mary Byron.

As it happened, Lady Holdernesse survived the brutally primitive mastectomy that she was forced to undergo, and by the end of the year was sufficiently recovered to concentrate on her plans to bring out her younger granddaughter the following season. Augusta, having completed her time at the Marquise's school in Barnes, had now returned to Holdernesse House. As Mary Osborne, all of seven years older than Augusta, wrote:

> This child of mine is a great dear and the greatest comfort to me from her cheerfulness and goodness which together make her society very agreeable to me, with whom she is perfectly at ease. With every other creature in the world she is (more or less) shy to a degree beyond all shyness I ever saw before, and yet shy as she is at this minute, she is *impudent* comparatively speaking to what she was when I first knew her. Her manner is very genteel and gentle, and with her very pretty face and expressive countenance, makes her *tout ensemble* very striking and interesting at first sight. She grows handsomer every day as she grows less thin.

Augusta, she said, was taller than Catherine, Mary's step-mother,* but not as tall as herself. Her head was small, with a long train of dark brown hair:

> which with her long neck and falling shoulders becomes her much and gives her whole bust an air *dégagé*. The upper part of her face is very handsome, her eyes being beautiful and her nose pretty and retroussé. Her mouth is very large – her worst feature – but a very fine set of teeth make up for this disadvantage. She has a fine complexion and fine colour, but is rather freckled. She is 'as light as a feather'.

Her sister's 'favourite amusement', she continued, was 'the play'. Did Lady Holdernesse, one wonders, permit her granddaughters to see Mrs Jordan, the mistress of the Duke of Clarence, in 'Monk' Lewis's sensational melodrama, *The Castle Spectre*? Augusta's

---

* Catherine Anguish was the second wife of the former Marquess of Carmarthen and 5th Duke of Leeds. There were two children of the marriage – Lord Sydney Osborne (b. 1789) and Lady Catherine Osborne (b. 1798). In 1813, by that time the Dowager Duchess of Leeds, she was appointed governess to Princess Charlotte.

cousin Lady Gertrude Howard said that it had been 'received most miraculously to the great astonishment of most people. I hear there is a gunpowder plot which has a sublime effect.'

According to Mary Osborne:

[Augusta's] taste is remarkably good and *nice* in everything, and memory astonishing when she *wishes* to fix anything on it. She has been very happy lately, having had so much of Carmarthen company and of Lady Carmarthen in the house.* Next to me Lady Carmarthen is the person she is most at ease with. She has been excessively kind to her and is very fond of her, as are likewise both my Brothers and she worships them quite . . . All this makes a very nice child, does it not? Pray tell this all to Miss Byron, as it must please her to know her niece is so amiable and so happy.

'Miss Byron' was Aunt Sophy, the acceptable face of the family. Its unacceptable face, the Wicked Lord, died on 21 May 1798 and was added to the roll of Newstead's ghosts. His faithful friends, the crickets, promptly left the house *en masse*. Augusta's ten-year-old half-brother George Gordon, whom she had never met and about whom she was endlessly curious, was now the 6th Lord Byron. The old Lord lay unburied while his solicitor, John Hanson, and the other executors tried to find out whether there was enough left in his estate to pay for the funeral: 'I am apprehensive we shall have to bury the poor lord ourselves after all.' Eventually, three weeks after his death, he was laid to rest in the family vault at Hucknall.

In August 1798, Catherine Byron with her son and her maid arrived at the gates of Newstead after a seemingly interminable journey from Aberdeen. John Hanson was there to greet them and looked with some curiosity at the 6th Baron Byron of Rochdale. 'The young Lord is a fine sharp boy, not a little spoiled by indulgence but that is scarcely to be wondered at.'

The Abbey was in a dreadful state of dereliction. There was no roof over the east wing, the refectory was full of the tenants' hay and the monks' parlour was being used as a cowshed. Hanson advised Catherine and her son to stay with their relations in Nottingham, the Honourable Mrs Frances Byron, widow of the Wicked Lord's youngest brother, George, and a noted eccentric.

---

* On 17 August 1797 Lady Charlotte Townshend married Augusta's half-brother George Osborne, Marquess of Carmarthen. The Marquess of Camarthen was the courtesy title that automatically went to the eldest son of the Duke of Leeds.

However, the Young Lord would stay nowhere but in the hall of his fathers, so he and his mother camped out amid the decaying splendours of the Abbey, while the 'hollow winds' whistled about them.

On 31 January 1799 the Duke of Leeds, whose children Mad Jack Byron had robbed of their mother, died two days after his forty-eighth birthday. Mary Osborne was so distracted with grief at the loss of her father that the Queen felt it necessary to write to Lady Holdernesse with a little advice:

> I hope you will soon be enabled by your religious precepts to restore the amiable girl to some degree of serenity and resignation which I am advised she stands greatly in need of . . .

Augusta had been treated kindly by her mother's first husband and his second wife since her arrival in London and she would have been expected to join in a period of family mourning following the Duke's death. There would have been no question of attending public entertainments or going out into society for several months. This did not, however, prevent the royal family paying private visits to Lady Holdernesse, and the King, Queen Charlotte and their family were now beginning to become familiar figures to Augusta, who was slowly learning to control her shyness and timidity. In June that year the Queen and the royal Princesses came to Hertford Street to watch from the windows of Lady Holdernesse's drawing room the 'sublime spectacle' of the King's birthday review in Hyde Park, which began with a royal salute from the Honourable Artillery Company at 9 a.m. and continued doggedly, through the pouring rain for the rest of the morning.

Lady Holdernesse was now almost eighty and could not be expected to live much longer. She had done everything in her power to make sure that both her granddaughters grew up with a proper sense of moral rectitude and an appropriate fear of the Almighty. Amelia, the child she had loved and indulged, had fallen a victim to 'passion'; Lady Holdernesse was determined that Amelia's daughters should be protected from following her example. There was never any question of Mary kicking over the traces and she never deviated from the straight and narrow, becoming a devoted wife and mother and, with the years, increasingly pious. In Augusta's case, Lady Holdernesse's influence was not so marked. While the girl was unquestionably (and unquestioningly) devout, her faith expressed itself in a stubborn belief in the benign workings of providence rather than in a strict conformity to traditional morality. She was a creature of impulse, with a streak of her mother's recklessness. She had become expert in hiding her real emotions behind a blushing incoherence, leaving trailing in the air sentences that could mean everything or nothing. In what may represent one of her own attempts at poetry, expression is given to the conflict between conformity and rebelliousness which she may have perceived in herself:

> The home of thy youth may be lonely,
> The friends of thy youth may be cold;
> The morals they teach may seem only
> Fit chains for the feeble and old:
> Yet though they may fetter a spirit
> That soars in the pride of its prime
> The friends of thy infancy inherit
> All thy love – in the dark winter time.

In 1800 the cancer that Lady Holdernesse had believed cured returned to attack her mouth and spread to her jaw and tongue. Thomas Pelham, Mary Osborne's would-be suitor and twenty years older than his prospective bride, was desperate to get the old lady's permission, before her illness grew any worse, to pay court to her granddaughter. But he was continually frustrated by her 'extreme weakness' brought about by her physicians regularly bleeding her, or, on the occasions when she did receive him, by her conversing 'only upon general subjects'. He was also sworn to secrecy about his visits to her, since she had been unable to see the Prince of Wales. Eventually, after weeks of waiting 'for a fair opportunity of saying something specific', he did manage to secure her concentration for long enough for her to consent to the marriage.

The King and Queen were delighted, and Queen Charlotte wrote to Lady Holdernesse telling her that her husband had expressed the hope that Augusta would soon follow her sister's example and make an equally good marriage; adding, for good measure, in a postscript: 'I shall be glad to hear the King's wish fulfilled about Miss Byron.' Princess Elizabeth too echoed her parents' sentiments: '. . . tell Miss Byron that I have not forgot her and sincerely hope that she may follow your example in every respect . . .'

With that charming informality that was one of their most endearing qualities, the King and Queen had taken to dropping into the house in Hertford Street to do what they could to comfort their old friend. Princess Augusta wrote:

> My dearest Lady Mary, Lady Holdernesse not being well enough for the Queen to venture to ask her to the Queen's House of an evening – the King and Queen propose themselves the pleasure of *spending this evening with her*. They particularly desire and command that Lady Holdernesse will remain *above stairs* and that you and Miss Byron will receive them *below* which will prevent Lady Holdernesse having any alarm from the staircase.

Augusta Byron had certainly come a considerable way from the little waif who had arrived at her Derbyshire refuge that summer evening in 1789.

In 1801, since provision for Augusta's education was no longer necessary, Lady Holdernesse revoked the codicil to her will of four years before. In a new codicil Augusta was to receive, on her grandmother's death, a sum of £7,000 to provide her with a modest income for life.

Mary and Thomas Pelham were married in July and left for their honeymoon with Augusta tagging on behind like Mary's little lamb. Three weeks later Pelham's father was created 1st Earl of Chichester and in August the trio were at Stanmer Park, the Chichester family seat under the South Downs not far from Lewes. Anne, Pelham's mother, was the daughter of Sir Thomas Frankland and a descendant of Cromwell and there were many relics of the Protector displayed in the house, including his four-volume Bible, with his own annotations, which would have provided a sombre diversion on rainy days.

When Augusta returned to Hertford Street she found her grandmother terribly changed. 'The accounts of Lady Holdernesse are very indifferent,' Princess Amelia reported to the Prince of Wales. 'I hear her face grows larger every day.' The Queen asked Princess Elizabeth to send pork from her model farm at Frognal to tempt her old friend's appetite. 'She flatters herself that dear Lady Holdernesse will like them,' the Princess told Lady Mary, but the old lady's mouth and tongue were so badly affected by the disease that she could barely manage to eat at all. Pelham ordered game to be sent her from Stanmer, since he had heard that 'game soup does her good', but Lady Holdernesse was beyond all help and died on 13 October 1801.

It was the end of the only period of real security that Augusta would ever know. Now the house in Hertford Street, with its gardens and wide views across Hyde Park, which had been home to her since her return from Derbyshire, was to be sold. The proceeds were to provide Lady Holdernesse's legacy of £7,000 to Augusta, which the old lady had hoped would assure her granddaughter a degree of independence and even a modest fortune. But the matter of most immediate concern following her grandmother's death was the question of where Augusta was going to live: 'A point I have very much at heart,' wrote Thomas Pelham, 'for I perceive that her intention is if possible to fix with us, and Mary has too much love for her to resist . . .'

Pelham, perhaps a little jealous of Augusta, was determined not to share his marriage with his eighteen-year-old sister-in-law, and he resorted to rearguard action. Since no decisions affecting Augusta's future could be taken without the sanction of the trustees and of Lady Holdernesse's executor, Christopher Alderson, Pelham decided to corner Alderson. 'I took the first opportunity of explaining my sentiments . . . he perfectly agreed with me on the subject . . .' Having won Alderson over, there was no difficulty in persuading old John Milbanke that it was high time that Augusta's Byron relatives did something for her. Four weeks later, on 24 November, Pelham was able to announce triumphantly that her aunt Sophy Byron had been approached and had accepted an invitation to Stratton Street. 'Miss Byron has come from Brighton,' he crowed, 'and I am in the hopes that everything will be arranged for her niece's return with her and their future permanent establishment . . .'

But Pelham's plan misfired. He had not reckoned on the fact that Aunt Sophy did not possess an establishment in Brighton or anywhere else. After parting a few years earlier with young George Anson, whom she had been forced to hand over to the care of his guardians prior to his entering the Navy, Sophy had slipped back into her old semi-nomadic existence, which she shared for much of the time with George's surviving sister, Julia. When they were not on extended visits to friends with large country houses, she and Julia lived in a state of penny-pinching and spartan simplicity. 'I do not indulge myself in anything I can do without,' Aunt Sophy explained. 'I never even dine in a room with a fire, the one I live in being too small for two persons to eat in . . . everything is so dear here and with the most rigid economy, money will go . . .'

However sympathetic Augusta may have found her aunt's company, it was not a life in which she would have wanted to participate for long, nor could anyone have expected her to do so.

Pelham had no option but to resign himself to sharing his wife with her half-sister on a fairly regular basis, while ensuring that Augusta was kept in a state of more or less perpetual motion round the houses of her other grand relatives and friends. Her half-brother George, now 6th Duke of Leeds, had inherited Hornby Castle, but Augusta seems to have found herself staying more frequently at Kiveton, another Leeds estate in Yorkshire, for which she did not greatly care. Far more to her liking was Gogmagog House near Cambridge, where her other half-brother, Lord Francis Osborne, and his family lived. It had been built at the centre of an ancient hill fort and had its own ghost, which would have appealed to her Gothic fancy.

The place where she was undoubtedly happiest was Castle Howard near York, the home of Frederick Howard, 5th Earl of Carlisle. Lord Carlisle was Augusta's cousin. The son of the Wicked Lord's famously eccentric sister, Isabella, he had, since the old man's death, come to regard himself as the elder statesman of the Byron family.

As a young man, Carlisle had been something of a rake, 'fond of dress and gaming by which he greatly hurt his future', or so Horace Walpole said. In 1770 he had rashly agreed to stand guarantor for the gambling debts of his close friend Charles James Fox and had forfeited one-fifth of his fortune in consequence. In his more sober middle years he had served in government as Lord Lieutenant of Ireland and was one of the few English statesmen ever to have understood the Irish problem:

> It is beyond doubt that the practicability of governing Ireland by English laws is become utterly visionary. It is with me equally beyond a doubt that Ireland may be well and happily governed by its own laws.

A man of culture and a discriminating collector of art (he was said to have bought a Titian for one guinea), Carlisle had written a tragedy entitled *The Father's Revenge* of which Dr Johnson had grudgingly approved, an ode on the death of William Mason's friend Thomas Gray, and a great deal of satirical verse.

Carlisle's marriage to Margaret Caroline Leveson Gower was a particularly happy one, and he was a devoted father to his four sons and three daughters. He was, however, something of a despot. Firmly of the opinion that as 'head of his house' he should be deferred to on all matters concerning his family, he insisted on being informed before his sons of any appointments they were in line for, and demanded reports of the progress of his heir, Lord Morpeth, as a Parliamentary speaker. He could be formidable and remote, but Augusta was devoted to him. He became her father figure, the man to whom she could turn for advice and guidance.

Castle Howard was one of the junction points where some of the greatest families in England, all of them linked by a network of marriages, came together, and the house was always filled with Howards, Leveson Gowers and Cavendishes. Augusta took her place there with a natural ease, in spite of her shyness. Lady Harriet Cavendish, who was nicknamed 'Hary-O', noted with some amusement the close attachment that had developed between Augusta and her new friends:

> Lady Charlotte,* Lady Gertrude† and a tall, reserved, alarmed lady, called Miss Byron, are inseparable, which leaves me more time to be with G. [her sister Georgiana], but it is a formidable coterie, as the intrusion of a fourth person, even for a minute, causes such pains and tremors that one suffers more from their shyness and gravity than they do themselves.

The following year she recorded an instance of Augusta's tantalising (and infuriating) manner of hinting at everything and saying nothing:

> Miss Byron used to abuse Duncannon's‡ looks to me rather, at least said she was rather surprised at his appearance as she had heard he was handsome. She used in her tiresome way to joke me to the last and say 'it would certainly be – but what can make you ask – pray let me know'.

* Lady Charlotte Leveson Gower.
† Lady Gertrude Howard.
‡ John William Ponsonby, Viscount Duncannon (1781–1847), eldest son of the 3rd Earl of Bessborough and brother of Caroline Lamb.

Lord Carlisle's sons were as devoted to Augusta as were his daughters, and his grandson (Lord Morpeth's little boy) George adored her and, unable to get his tongue round her name, always called her 'Miss Bear'. One of the reasons why she was so readily welcomed by the Howards may have been that she was instantly recognisable as one of the family. Isabella Byron, traces of whose features were to be found in most of her children and grandchildren, was Lord Carlisle's mother and Augusta's great-aunt.

> Somebody who saw Augusta for the first time lately was struck by her likeness to Elizabeth Garnier [Carlisle's sister]. She is like all the Carlisles but most to Lady Elizabeth Howard,* not so regularly handsome but with much expression and a better figure.

Augusta always spoke affectionately of 'poor dear Castle Howard where indeed I have spent many a happy hour'. Some of her most precious memories were of the Ray Wood – once a maze winding between statues, summerhouses and fountains, but in her day a secluded wilderness where she could read to herself, or sketch, or simply indulge in romantic dreaming.

Much of Augusta's year was, of course, passed in London where there were a number of places she could call home. The Duke of Leeds had a house in Grosvenor Place, as did the Earl of Carlisle (it overlooked the grounds of Buckingham House, to the great annoyance of George III). In Portland Place, close to where Charles Leigh had lived with his son George, were old family friends, General and Mrs Harcourt,† who had known Augusta since she first came to live with Lady Holdernesse. The Harcourts had no children of their own and enjoyed having young people about them. Augusta was made welcome at their house, as was her young half-brother, Byron, who was making his first uncertain venture into London society.

---

* Lady Elizabeth Howard, second daughter of Frederick, 5th Earl of Carlisle. She married John, 5th Duke of Rutland, on 22 April 1799.
† William Harcourt (1743–1830) was a distinguished soldier, courtier and close friend of the family of George III. His wife Mary was chosen to escort Princess Caroline of Brunswick to England for her wedding to the Prince of Wales. In 1809 Harcourt succeeded his brother as 3rd Earl Harcourt.

CHAPTER 5

'Ties of Blood and Affection'

On 18 October 1801, six days after the death of Lady Holdernesse, Catherine Byron wrote from Brighton to her stepdaughter:

Dear Augusta

As I wish to bury what is past *in oblivion* I shall avoid all reflections on a Person now no more, my opinion of yourself I have suspended for some years the time is now arrived when I shall form a very *decided* one.

I take up my pen now however to console you on the melancholy event that has happened, to offer you every consolation in my power, to assure you of the unalterable regard and friendship of myself and son, we will be extremely happy if ever we can be of service to you, now or at any future period. I take it upon me to answer for him, although he knows so little of you, he often mentions you to me in the most affectionate manner, indeed, the goodness of his heart and amiable disposition is such that your being his sister had he never seen you would be a sufficient claim upon him and ensure you every attention in his power to bestow.

Ah Augusta, need I assure that you will ever be dear to me as the daughter of the man I tenderly loved, as the sister of my beloved darling boy, and I take God to witness you *once* was dear to me on your own account, and may be so *again* . . .

I don't intend being in Town for some time, I shall be anxious till I hear from you, I am the more easy on your account as I hear a very amiable character of Lady Pelham.

Your Brother is at Harrow school and if you wish to see him I have no desire to keep you asunder . . .

She added a postscript giving a brisk round-up of the Byron family:

Your Aunt Miss Byron [Aunt Sophy] is here, and Julia Byron is with Mrs Gregor in Cornwall, her brother George [Anson] is at Sea, Captain Byron is married to Miss Sykes, the army agent's daughter.

This must rank as one of the clumsiest letters of condolence ever written. Not even death could diminish Catherine's resentment of

Lady Holdernesse, but she was, in her rough-and-ready way, extending the hand of friendship. She was also curious to discover what, if anything, had been left to Augusta in Lady Holdernesse's will. 'I wish you could find out for me,' she beseeched Hanson, 'I shall be quite anxious till I hear. I had a letter from her recently but it is impossible for me to ask herself.'

Nothing now stood in the way of a meeting between Augusta and her thirteen-year-old half-brother. From a very early age, Byron had been fascinated by the idea of having a sister at all. Years later he recalled a time when, as a young boy, he was reading a history of Rome and found out that one of the Emperors had married his sister. Did this mean, he asked his mother, that he could marry Augusta?

Augusta would soon be confronted with her brother's precocity where girls were concerned. In 1800, when he was only twelve, he had conceived a 'passion' for his thirteen-year-old cousin, Margaret Parker,* who had died of consumption two years later. Years afterwards Byron remembered:

> My sister told me that when she went to see her shortly before her death – upon accidentally mentioning my name – Margaret coloured through the paleness of her mortality to the eyes – to the great astonishment of my sister who . . . knew nothing of our attachment – nor could conceive why my name should affect her so at such a time . . .

Augusta had also heard a great deal about Byron and his mother – none of it very much to their credit – from Lord Carlisle and his family. In 1799 Hanson, now firmly established as the family lawyer, had approached the Earl to ask if he would become the boy's guardian. Carlisle had very reluctantly agreed, stipulating that it should only be in a strictly limited capacity.

From the start, Byron took against the Earl of Carlisle, resenting what he termed his 'magisterial presence'. At their first encounter he had become bored and had asked Hanson to take him away, although this may have been the result of Byron's inveterate shyness, which could be considerably more disabling than his sister's. As for Catherine, she clearly came as a terrible shock to the Earl's sensibilities. Very unwillingly he had been drawn into a

---

* The daughter of Admiral Byron's youngest daughter, Augusta Barbara Charlotte, and her husband, Rear Admiral Christopher Parker.

dispute between her and Dr Glennie, the headmaster of Byron's school at Dulwich. Catherine had developed an infatuation for a French dancing master from Brompton – she was, it must be remembered, still only thirty-five – and Glennie somehow got hold of a rumour that they intended to run away to France, taking the boy with them. He wrote in some alarm to Hanson, who passed the matter on to Carlisle. The Earl told Glennie that he must under no circumstances let the boy go and insisted that Mrs Byron be prevented from having access to her son at weekends. Then, in a gesture that Pontius Pilate might have envied, he added: 'I can have nothing more to do with Mrs Byron – you must manage her as best you can.'

Word of this would certainly have got back to Augusta who was becoming irritated by Catherine's attempts to interfere in her affairs. Catherine had written to her, fulminating against Aunt Sophy, and had received a very sharp rebuff.

> It was by the desire of my Guardian as well as my own, that I have spent and mean to spend some of the year with my Aunt. I have felt perfectly happy with her, and have discovered none of those failings which you seem to suppose in her, and you must excuse me Dear Madam, if I do my cousin, Julia, the justice to say that she had ever appeared to have the Love and regard for our Aunt* which she so justly deserves from all her nephews and nieces.

Augusta had become a determined and relatively self-assured young woman and under no circumstances was she going to bow to her stepmother's opinion; nor did she have any intention of letting Catherine dictate the terms under which she and her brother could meet. Since their early letters to one another have not survived, we do not know exactly when or where Augusta and Byron saw one another for the first time, but it was not in Catherine's presence. Both urged Hanson to find some way in which they could meet and it seems probable (although it is possible that they met earlier) that brother and sister were first brought together at the Harcourts' house in Portland Place in the spring of 1803.

Byron was just fifteen and about to enter his third year at Harrow. Augusta would have looked at this fat, rather bashful, self-conscious boy who walked with a slight limp curious to find any signs of resemblance. Byron saw a tall, graceful, twenty-year-old

* Sophy Byron and not, as has generally been supposed, Frances Leigh.

whose social ease and manner masked a shyness as acute as his own. They were meeting as total strangers, but strangers who knew they had more in common with one another than with anyone else in the world. 'Recollect, My Dearest Sister,' Byron wrote in the first of his letters to survive, 'that you are the *nearest relation* I have *in the world by the ties of blood and Affection.*'

One of the first things that they discovered was their mutual gift of laughter, a way of putting the world and its inhabitants into their own absurd perspective. Augusta had an unexpected comic talent and was a brilliant mimic. In her brother she had a perfect audience and she found that she could very easily laugh him out of his sulks and 'grumps'. In turn she became the butt of his affectionate jokes, his 'Goose'. Very soon they were exchanging confidences and secrets and finding a strong bond between them in their shared devotion to the memory of their dead father – a fierce idolatry in which they were determined to defend Jack Byron against the world. 'Augusta and I have always loved the memory of our father as much as we have loved each other,' wrote Byron.

For all their excitement in their discovery of one another, they managed to meet very rarely. They were far too preoccupied with their separate concerns. In September 1803, probably at Carlisle's town house in Grosvenor Place, his son Frederick Howard introduced Augusta to the Colonel of his regiment, her first cousin George Leigh (the son of General Charles Leigh and his estranged wife, Mad Jack's sister Frances). George Leigh was twelve years older than Augusta, tall, and striking, with a high opinion of himself and something of that brand of audacious charm and easy self-assurance with which his uncle Jack Byron had so effortlessly won over Augusta's mother, Amelia. Unfortunately for Augusta, she had inherited her mother's susceptibility and fell in love with him.

At the time of their first meeting, George was riding high in the favour of the Prince of Wales. He was Colonel of the 10th Hussars, the Prince's own highly fashionable regiment, and his Equerry. He was a first-class horseman, a good judge of horse flesh, a compulsive gambler, a daredevil, the life and soul of any party, and money ran through his hands like water – hardly the kind of husband that the Duke of Leeds or the Earl of Carlisle had in mind for Augusta. Although she was virtually penniless, her pedigree entitled her to a much more advantageous match. However, she was determined to marry George Leigh, or, as her brother later put it, 'she would have him'. To mark their engagement George gave her a pearl ring inscribed 'to Augusta M. Byron from George'. Byron must have been one of the first to be drawn into the secret, for even in the earliest of his surviving letters to his sister he was writing:

> When you see my cousin and future brother, George Leigh, tell him that I already consider him as my friend, for whoever is beloved by you, my amiable sister, will always be equally dear to me ...

What did George Leigh see in Augusta? She was attractive, she had an endearing personality, some very grand relatives and she worshipped him, but all this would have been counterbalanced by her lack of a fortune. The General had calculated on his son making a wealthy marriage and the idea of George saddling himself with Mad Jack's impecunious daughter was intolerable. His own experience of being married to a Byron had been disastrous and the bitter legal dispute with his sister-in-law Sophy had only served to make him detest the family on principle. He refused to give George his assent.

This only made Augusta more stubbornly determined than ever. She was not prepared to give George up, but George was not prepared to defy his father. George was not, one suspects, greatly agitated over the matter. There was no shortage of pretty women in his life and he was in no hurry to be tied down. Byron was careful to warn Augusta that his mother, too, was fiercely opposed to the match: George was exactly the kind of spendthrift rake to arouse her disapproval. Furthermore, he was the son of Mad Jack's sister Frances, whom Catherine had never forgiven for ignoring her and her letters. Nor would Sophy have been any happier at the prospect, for she would hardly have given her blessing to a marriage between Augusta and the son of the man who had tried to cheat her of her inheritance.

Meanwhile Byron, too, was in love and, with a fatalism that might have been borrowed from a Gothic novel, the girl on whom he had set his heart was a descendant of the man who had been dispatched by the Wicked Lord in the ill-lit room in the Star and Garter Inn. Her name was Mary Chaworth. In April 1803, Catherine Byron had moved into Burgage Manor, a handsome house on the green in Southwell, twelve miles from Newstead.

Southwell had not the slightest appeal for Byron – 'no society but old parsons and old Maids' – and he longed to be back at Newstead. The Abbey had been leased to Lord Grey de Ruthyn until Byron came of age, since Catherine could neither afford to live there nor to cope with its upkeep. However, Byron found its closeness to Southwell too great a temptation and decided that, if he could not live in the Abbey, he would at least put up at the Lodge. This was not at all to the liking of the steward and Byron was told that he was free to visit the Abbey whenever he wished, but since there was no accommodation for him there he must put up at Annesley Hall, the home of Mary Chaworth. He took to staying there frequently and it was only a matter of time before he had fallen desperately in love with Mary.

She was little more than two years older than Byron, but she was besotted with a neighbour, the dashing Jack Musters, and was not in the least interested in a callow adolescent. She was prepared only to offer him sisterly affection and to play the piano for him, which was not entirely what he had in mind. Mary did not respond to the 'rough boy', as she called him, and he rather confirmed her judgement by firing off his pistols into the terrace door.

When the time came for Byron to return to Harrow he refused to go and persisted in sitting it out at Annesley. This was not the first time that Byron had absented himself from Harrow, and Catherine wrote frantically to Hanson:

> . . . the truth is I cannot get him to return to school, though I have done all in my power for six weeks past. He has no indisposition that I know of, but love, desperate love, the worst of maladies in my opinion.

Relief presented itself in the form of Lord Grey de Ruthyn, who was now all too happy for Byron to come and stay at Newstead. At first everything went swimmingly; Byron agreed to return to Harrow in the new year and stayed on at Newstead, shooting pheasants by moonlight with Grey. Then, without warning, Byron insisted on breaking off their friendship but stubbornly refused to give any explanation. It seems highly probable that Grey had made advances to the boy or, as Byron's friend Hobhouse noted rather laconically many years later: 'a circumstance occurred during intimacy which certainly had much effect on his future morals'.

Even Augusta was not taken into Byron's confidence over his

reason for breaking with Lord Grey, although he could not resist dropping tantalising hints:

> He was once my *Greatest Friend*, my reasons for ceasing that Friendship are such as I cannot explain, not even to you my Dear Sister (although were they to be made known to anybody, you would be the first), but they will ever remain hidden in my own breast . . . My mother disapproves of my quarrelling with him, but if she knew the cause (which she will never know) she would reproach me no more . . .

Byron could never entirely keep a secret, even one of his own.

Once he was back at Harrow, a series of skirmishes with Mark Drury, the headmaster's brother, whom Byron had been told had called him a blackguard, drove all thoughts of his sister from his mind, and he was soon imploring his mother to remove him 'from a place where I am goaded with insults from those from whom I little deserved it'. Augusta's letters went unanswered; she was doing her best to fulfil her brother's request and find employment for the Wicked Lord's servant, Joe Murray, almost the last relic of the old Newstead. 'While I live he shall never be abandoned in his old age,' Byron had promised her. She had managed to find Murray a place with the Duchess of Leeds, but it was not a success: the old man was set in his eccentric ways. Fearing that she had failed in what she saw as her family duty, she wrote to Hanson about it:

> I saw poor Joe Murray the other night who wishes me particularly to apply to Colonel Leigh to get him into some City Charity which the Prince of Wales is at the head of I cannot understand what he means, nor can anybody else, and therefore as he said he was advised by you I think it better to apply to you on the subject. I am sure Col Leigh would be happy to oblige him; but in general he dislikes asking favour of the Prince, and this present moment is a bad one to chuse for the purpose, as H.R.H. is so taken up with public affairs. I am very anxious about poor Joseph, and would do almost anything to serve him. I fear he is too old and infirm to go to service again.

Byron and Augusta's correspondence was now beginning to fall into a set pattern. When he was bored or in low spirits, he would beg her to write letters 'as long as may fill twenty sheets of paper' and would even take pains to write to her. When he had better things to do, as he invariably did at Harrow, Augusta never entered his thoughts and she was reduced to writing plaintive letters to Hanson:

> I don't know whether to direct to Mrs Byron as the last I heard of her and indeed my brother too was that they were in Town. I conclude that he is gone back to Harrow but I cannot get him to write which makes me uncomfortable as at one time he seemed to like doing so.

Augusta was at Castle Howard in the autumn of 1804 and needed someone with whom she could share her frustration at the continuing stalemate of her proposed marriage to George Leigh, which his father was still blocking. George's inability to take any kind of initiative should have served as a warning. For all his braggadocio and self-importance he was, as Byron later put it, 'helpless' and always needed others to carry him through anything that went much beyond the management of horses.

Byron's reply, when Hanson eventually managed to goad him into writing at the end of October, was far from what Augusta had hoped for, since his good intentions were limited by his desire to keep up a pose as a jaded and cynical man of the world:

> Can't you drive this Cousin of ours out of your pretty little head . . . or if you are so far gone, why don't you give old L'Harpagon (I mean the General) the slip, and take a trip to Scotland, you are now pretty near the Borders. Be sure to Remember me to my formal Guardy Lord Carlisle, whose magisterial presence I have not been into for several years, nor have I any ambition to attain so great an honour . . .

Up to this point Byron had managed to keep his running battle with his mother out of his letters, but now, knowing that he had at last found a sympathetic audience, he began to let himself go. Catherine was, he told his sister, 'in a monstrous pet with you for not writing, I am sorry to say the old lady and myself don't agree like lambs in a meadow, but I believe it is all my own fault, I am rather too fidgety, which my precise mama objects to . . .' This tone of gentle self-mockery was not to last. Only a week later he was writing in a very different vein:

> Now, Augusta, I am going to tell you a secret, perhaps I shall appear undutiful to you, but, believe me, my affection for you is founded on a more firm basis. My mother had lately behaved to me in such an eccentric manner, that so far from feeling the affection of a Son, it is

with difficulty I can restrain my dislike. Not that I can complain of
want of liberality, no, She always supplies me with as much money
as I can spend, and more than most boys hope for or desire. But with
all this she is so hasty, so impatient, that I dread the approach of the
holidays, more than most boys do their return from them . . .

Catherine and her son had fought and screamed at one another
since the boy could walk, but what particularly infuriated him now
was his mother's embarrassing infatuation with Lord Grey. She was
constantly upbraiding her son for refusing to be reconciled with
Grey and demanding to know his reason for breaking off the
friendship – '. . . once she let slip so odd an expression,' he told
Augusta, 'that I was half inclined to believe the dowager was in love
with him'. Augusta was all too willing to believe ill of Catherine
Byron.

'I thought, my dear Augusta, that your opinion of my *meek
mamma* would coincide with mine,' Byron began his next letter.
'Her temper is so variable, and when inflamed, so furious, that I
dread our meeting . . .' It was a long letter – longer than any he had
yet written to her – and it was calculated to engage his sister's
sympathy on a point on which he knew she was most sensitive and
most vulnerable:

> . . . she flies into a fit of phrenzy, upbraids me as if I was the most
> undutiful wretch in existence, rakes up the ashes of my *father*,
> abuses him, says I shall be a true Byrrone, which is the worst epithet
> she can invent.

He was beginning to learn how to manipulate his sister by telling
her exactly what he knew would please her most: 'You, Augusta,
are the only relation I have who treats me as a friend.' She was
mistaken, he insisted, in supposing that he disliked Carlisle; he
respected him and might come to like him if he knew him better. It
was his mother who had an 'antipathy' towards his guardian, not
him: 'I am afraid he could be of little use to me in separating me
from her, which she would oppose with all her might but I dare say
he would assist me if he could . . .'

Byron hoped that, at the very least, he might be allowed to spend
the Christmas holidays with John Hanson and his family.

An impartial observer would have reckoned that the boy was
simply letting off steam, but not Augusta. She became obsessed with
the notion that the life Byron was living with his mother was wholly

unsuitable for a young man of his rank and that he was being denied every opportunity to take his place in polite society. Catherine cannot have been a prepossessing character, but she had very real qualities that Augusta, blinkered by her innate snobbishness, could not perceive. She spoke to Carlisle, who was easily persuaded to authorise Byron to spend Christmas with the Hansons, saying that it would 'put it in his power to see more of him or shew him more attention than he has hitherto, being withheld from doing so from the dread of having any concern whatever with Mrs Byron'.

Of course, Augusta told Hanson, her own involvement must in no way be mentioned to Catherine:

> as she would only accuse me of wishing to estrange her son from her, which would be very far from the case further than his happiness and comfort are concerned. My opinion is that *as* they cannot agree, they had better be separated, for such Eternal scenes of wrangling are enough to spoil the very best temper and Disposition in the universe . . .

Byron's strategy had proved rather more successful than he had anticipated or even desired, and he now began to have second thoughts. His turbulent existence with his mother, however much he complained about it, was essential to him:

> I thank you my dear Augusta for your readiness to assist me, and will in some manner avail myself of it. I do not however wish to be separated from *her* entirely, but not to be so much with her as I hitherto have been . . .

With a little adroit manoeuvring Catherine was persuaded to agree to her son spending his holidays away from the 'edifying conversation of Old Maids' at Southwell. There were several visits to Drury Lane to see the theatrical sensation of the season, thirteen-year-old William Henry Betty, 'Young Roscius', whom Byron found 'tolerable in some characters'. On Saturday 26 January 1805, to Augusta's great satisfaction, even though she was not present herself, her brother dined with the Carlisles and the evening turned out to be surprisingly successful. She told Hanson:

> I hear from Lady Gertrude Howard that Lord Carlisle was *very much* pleased with my brother, and I am sure, from what he said to me at Castle Howard, is disposed to show him all the kindness and

attention in his power . . . You will easily perceive that [my brother] is a *great favourite of mine,* and I add the more I see and hear of him, the more I *must* love and esteem him.

Byron had, for once, managed to overcome his intense reserve and, for that evening at least, enjoyed being in the company of Carlisle and his family, where he was greatly entertained by anecdotes of his sister's equestrian exploits at Castle Howard:

> . . . on further acquaintance I like them very much. Amongst other circumstances, I heard of your *boldness* as a *Rider,* especially one anecdote about your horse carrying you into the stable *perforce.* I should have admired amazingly to have seen your progress, provided you met with no accident . . .

Augusta's particular friend, Lady Gertrude, he judged to be 'a sweet girl' and he commented, with his habitual condescension: 'If your taste in love is as good as it is in friendship, I shall think you a *very discerning little Gentlewoman.* His Lordship improves too upon further acquaintance.'

The Easter holidays of 1805 found Byron in 'very bad spirits', he told Augusta, 'out of humour with myself and all the world except *you*'. His days at Harrow were coming to an end and he was reluctantly trying to make up his mind between Cambridge and Oxford universities. Throughout his life, once he had settled anywhere, he would stubbornly resist change. There was, however, the chance that they might be able to meet while she was staying at Carlisle's house in London, 'a pleasure, which as I have been long debarred of it, will be doubly felt after so long a separation'.

Much of his gloom was caused by the knowledge that a visit to the 'Dowager' could no longer be put off. At first he managed to avoid any open argument with his mother, but a casual remark about Southwell not being 'peculiarly' to his taste opened the floodgates of Catherine's wrath:

> Within one little hour, I have not only [heard] myself, but have heard my *whole family,* by the father's side, *stigmatised* in terms that the *blackest malevolence* would perhaps shrink from and that too in words you would be shocked to hear. Such, Augusta, such is my mother; my mother!

Swept along on the torrent of her rage, Catherine informed her son that Carlisle had 'behaved very ill to her' and forbade Byron to have any further contact with him. When she discovered that her son and Augusta had met clandestinely in London, where he had gone to attend a debate at the House of Lords, she hurled at her stepdaughter one of her 'epistles in the *furioso* style', as Byron described them, and banned any further communication:

> Believe me, dearest Augusta, not ten thousand *such* mothers, could induce me to give you up ... and nothing now can influence your *pretty sort of a brother* (bad as he is) to forget that he is your *Brother*.

Augusta had been ill; the protracted inactivity over her marriage to George was beginning to wear her down. Byron gently teased her over 'throwing herself into the fidgets about a trifling delay of 9 or 10 years ...' He was hoping that she would put in an appearance at his last Speech Day at Harrow so that he could show her off to his fine friends:

> I *beg, Madam*, you may make your appearance in one of his Lordship's most *dashing* carriages, as our Harrow *etiquette*, admits of nothing but the most *superb* vehicles, on our Grand *Festivals*.

But Augusta was in no mood to be shown off, even by her brother, and did not attend, although they did manage to meet briefly in London that summer before Byron returned to Southwell to prepare to go up to Cambridge. He was in no hurry and put off his arrival at Trinity until the end of October, that last day permitted by the regulations. He told Augusta:

> As might be supposed I like a College Life extremely, especially as I have escaped the Trammels or rather *Fetters* of my domestic Tyrant Mrs Byron ... I am allowed 500 a year, a Servant and Horse, so Feel as independent as a German Prince who coins his own Cash, or a Cherokee Chief who coins no Cash at all, but enjoys what is more precious, Liberty.

He added, rather ominously, that he was still suffering from the after-effects of 'last night's claret'.

By the end of his first term at Trinity his extravagances had landed him in deep financial trouble. He did his best to blame Hanson, whom he now treated with lofty contempt, for deceiving him about the extent of his allowance. He had severed all contact with his mother and swore that if she ever came up to Cambridge he would quit it instantly, 'though Rustication or Expulsion be the consequence'.

Byron was rapidly drifting into the kind of situation that had brought about his father's ruin. He had committed himself to a manner of living far beyond his means, which he would not and could not amend. At the centre of the problem lay his need to outdo the other men of his year at Trinity, particularly those whom he considered his inferiors. His rank still sat rather self-consciously upon him; nothing in his upbringing had prepared him for it and he tried too hard to act in the way he believed a young man of his station should behave. Where his companions had one servant, he would have two; where they had one horse, he would have three.

When the term came to an end he would not even consider returning to that '*execrable* Kennel' in Southwell, but took rooms with a Mrs Massingberd in Piccadilly where his mother had stayed some years before. It was from here that he wrote to Augusta on 26 December 1805 hoping that they might meet when she came to London from Castle Howard in January:

> I hope your everlasting negociation with the Father of your *Intended* is near a conclusion in *some* manner; if you do not hurry a little, you will be verging into the '*Vale of Years*', and though you may be blest with sons and daughters, you will never live to see your *Grandchildren*.

He was deliberately keeping in the dark the real reason for wishing to meet her – 'I have some subjects to discuss with you, which I do not wish to communicate in my Epistle.'

Events were moving rather too quickly for him, however, for he wrote more urgently to Augusta the following day. First he found it necessary to issue a warning: '. . . before I disclose it, I must require the most inviolable secrecy, for if ever I find that it has transpired, all confidence and all friendship between us has concluded'. This exordium was not, he assured her, a 'threat' to ensure her compliance with what he was about to ask, but a request to keep it a secret:

> The Affair is briefly thus; like all other young men just let loose, and especially one as I am, freed from the worse than bondage of my maternal home, I have been extravagant, and consequently am in want of money.

The last thing he had in mind, he assured her, was to borrow from her:

> All I expect or wish is, that you will be joint Security with me for a few Hundreds a person (one of the money lending tribe) has offered to advance in case I can bring forward any collateral guarantee that he will not be a loser, the reason of this requisition is my being a Minor, and might refuse to discharge a debt contracted in my non-age.

She was, he told her, the only person he could approach. Most of his friends were in the same predicament as himself 'and to those who are not I am too proud to apply'. He ended on a mildly threatening note:

> I know you will think me foolish, if not criminal; but tell me so yourself, and do not rehearse my failings to others, no, not even to that proud Grandee the Earl, who, whatever his qualities may be, is certainly not amiable, and that Chattering puppy Hanson would make still less allowance for the foibles of a Boy. I am now trying the experiment, whether a woman can retain a secret; let me not be deceived.

Augusta was horrified. Nothing in her very sheltered life had brought her into contact with a situation of this kind. She had no acquaintance with debt and money lenders did not enter into her world. Signing a contract with one would have been unthinkable.

She was thrown into a hopeless muddle of indecision. Her first instinct was to do what Byron had told her he would not accept, which was to offer him money of her own. This he refused. He alone would be injured by his own extravagance. Then she tried to suggest to him that the situation was not as serious as he had made out – was he unwell, or suffering from some kind of melancholia? He assured her that it had nothing to do with his health.

Since Augusta could not bring herself to tell him outright that she would not do what he had asked, he was left with the impression that she was prepared to sign the bond:

> I fear the business will not be concluded before your arrival in Town, when we will settle it together, as by the 20th these *sordid Bloodsuckers* who have agreed to furnish the Sum, will have drawn up the Bond.

Augusta had no intention of signing a bond which, as she saw it, would be the first step on the road to her brother's ruin. The only person to whom she might have turned for advice was the husband of her half-sister Mary, Thomas Pelham, who had succeeded his father as Earl of Chichester in 1805, but, isolated as she was at Castle Howard, this was out of the question and she was running out of time. In her growing panic she did what her brother had expressly forbidden her to do, and told Carlisle. He decided to return to London and instructed Hanson to arrange a meeting with Byron at Grosvenor Place.

Byron was in no mood to put up with any interference from Hanson or Carlisle. He went ahead, persuading Mrs Massingberd, who probably brokered the initial contact with the money lenders, to stand security for the bond in his sister's place.

As for Augusta, he behaved as if she had ceased to exist. He had chosen her to be his ally in a private conspiracy and she had betrayed him. He cut himself off from her completely, refusing to speak to her or to answer her letters. In February 1806, she wrote desolately to John Hanson:

> I am afraid from your not having written to me that you have nothing of a favourable nature to communicate. I own I perfectly despair of my Brother's ever altering his Tone towards me, for when one has put oneself very much in the wrong, it is difficult to get right again. The only excuse I can make for troubling you again on this sad subject is the wretchedness it has inflicted on me, *time* seems rather to increase than to remove it, and to have lost his affection and esteem appears to me as a still more severe affliction than his Death would have been.

CHAPTER 6

'The Amusement of George Leigh'

In the winter of 1806, when Napoleon was knocking down his opponents like ninepins and while Byron was inscribing copies of his first book of verses, *Fugitive Pieces*, to the belles of Southwell, at Castle Howard Augusta discovered that her matrimonial predicament was beginning to turn her into a figure of fun. Lady Morpeth* received regular bulletins from her sister Lady Harriet Cavendish at Devonshire House – 'Your joke about Colonel Leigh is the drollest I have heard for some time, but not to poor Miss Byron I fear . . .' – while Lady Harriet wondered whether 'poor Miss Byron' might do better with one of Carlisle's nephews: 'Is there any prospect of Miss B. and him joking into a mutual attachment?'

Augusta was miserable, but as determined as she had ever been to marry no one but George Leigh. Accounts of his scandalous carryings-on only increased her resolution. Her misery was made worse by the fact that Byron was still remorselessly refusing to acknowledge her existence. In London she caught sight of him at the theatre, she heard stories about his escapades, but she was still having to rely on Hanson for any real information about him: 'I cannot forget that I have a brother or cease to feel anxiety about him and I know no other means of obtaining an intelligence.' In February 1807, when Byron published his *Poems on Various Occasions*, it was Catherine – doubtless relieved that Augusta was no longer playing any significant role in her son's life – who sent her two copies of the book.

By now it was being openly stated that Augusta's marriage to George had been called off and, had the Prince of Wales not decided to intervene at that point, she would have had no alternative but to break her engagement. The insurmountable obstacle was that the

---

* Georgiana, elder daughter of the 5th Duke of Devonshire and his Duchess, Georgiana. She married George Howard, Viscount Morpeth, eldest son of Frederick, 5th Earl of Carlisle, on 21 March 1801.

couple had no prospect of a home. Now, and perhaps with a little prompting, the Prince recalled a modest property that he owned at Six Mile Bottom, six miles south-west of Newmarket. It was neither splendid nor particularly large, but it was his to bestow. At the same time, he prevailed upon his old friend General Leigh to withdraw his opposition to the match, even if he still stubbornly refused to give it his blessing.

On the eve of setting out for what was to be her last visit to Castle Howard before her wedding, Augusta made one final attempt to make contact with her brother through Hanson, although she did not mention her forthcoming marriage:

> If you are in Town and have heard of my Brother, will you tell me if you think there is the slightest hope of his forgiving me – or the least possibility of my doing *any* thing in the world to obtain his forgiveness. I would not torment you, but that I am sure you wish for a reconciliation between us and that I am *perfectly wretched* at his continuing angry, and you know there is not anything I would not do to regain his good opinion and affection, which I trust I don't *quite deserve* to have lost – for that idea would greatly augment my distress . . .

Hanson's appeal went unheeded. Byron still refused to speak or write to her.

On 17 August 1807 Lieutenant Colonel George Leigh, who gave Carlton House as his address in the register, and the Honourable Augusta Mary Byron were married at St George's, Hanover Square. The witnesses were Augusta's half-sister Mary and her husband, the 2nd Earl of Chichester. Their marriage united the son of Frances Leigh with the daughter of her one-time lover and brother, Mad Jack Byron. Augusta's marriage to George Leigh proved to be the most serious mistake of her life.

When Frances Leigh decided to walk out of her ill-starred marriage, George was still a very young child. Fortunately his paternal grandmother, by then a widow and living in London, was able to take charge of him, for Charles Leigh, more concerned with making his way up the military ladder, can have had little time to give him. George was about nine years old when his father was chosen to be one of the military aides attached to the Prince of Wales.

In 1787, after the uproar over his secret marriage to Mrs Fitzherbert had died down and he was enjoying a temporary reconciliation with his parents, the Prince of Wales appointed Charles Leigh to his household as Equerry. By then, young George was already beginning to acquire something of a reputation on his own account:

> The Prince of Wales understands from young Mr Leigh yt [that] Sir John Lade has five white or grey ponies yt he was inclined to dispose of and yt 12 guineas apiece was their price, if yt price is agreeable to Sir John ye Prince would be very glad to take them on those terms.

Horses were to be George's whole existence: choosing them, breeding them, training them, riding them and, above all, betting on them. Sir John Lade was one of the most celebrated and notorious figures in the world of the turf, a gentleman jockey and brilliant whip who was one of the Prince's more disreputable companions. If, by the age of sixteen, George was already acting for him, then he must have been well in with the Newmarket coterie.

The late 1780s were the years of the Prince's most successful seasons at Newmarket. Charles Leigh, as his Equerry, would have been in frequent attendance there, with George at his heels, joining his father at the Equerries' table after dinner. It was a time when the heady excitement of gambling would have been irresistible to any young man. The Prince won no fewer than 185 races, bringing him in over 32,000 guineas, a prodigious sum, and it is little wonder that George became instantly and incurably addicted to the turf.

Gambling had become a national mania. Fortunes were won and lost overnight, sometimes in a matter of minutes, and betting was by no means confined to the turf. Wagers would be made, quite literally, on anything: when a man might marry or a Duchess die, when the King of France would lose his head. Lord Barrymore, who managed to run through £300,000 in four years, once bet the Duke of Bedford that he could produce a man who could eat a cat alive – and won!

In this life of riding, betting and gaming, interspersed with a good deal of whoring, George, still in his teens, was in his element, and his father began to grow alarmed at the great chasm that was appearing between his son's increasingly extravagant way of life and his lack of means to support it. He decided that George should make the Army his profession. For the sum of £650 he purchased him a commission in the Prince of Wales's Own 10th Light Dragoons, and on 27 October 1790 George was officially gazetted as Cornet, though it was the following year before he got round to the idea of turning up for regimental duty.

That was to be the last year that the Prince ran his horses at Newmarket. On 20 October 1791, his horse, Escape, ridden by his favourite jockey, Sam Chifney, came last in a field of four. The following day, Escape was an easy first in a field involving two of the same horses at much longer odds. Chifney was accused of deliberately losing the first race and the Prince was informed that if he ever permitted Chifney to ride one of his horses at Newmarket again, 'no gentleman would start against him'. Outraged, the Prince stood by Chifney. A Jockey Club inquiry proved nothing either way, but the Prince removed his horses from Newmarket and swore that he would never race there again.

George Leigh's role in the affair is unclear, but he was given leave of absence from the regiment at the time of the Jockey Club inquiry, at which he may have given evidence. His military career was more remarkable for the time he spent away from his regiment than for the time he spent with it, invariably on the Prince's business and generally in connection with the turf.

The 10th Light Dragoons had been granted the privilege of calling themselves The Prince of Wales's Own Regiment in 1783 but, because the King was violently opposed to the heir to the throne taking up any military appointment that might involve him in active service, the Prince's initial connection with 'his' regiment was entirely unofficial and he was forced to content himself with what was virtually playing at soldiers. When the King finally relented in 1793 and appointed his son Colonel of the 10th, the Prince was at last in a position to put into force the schemes he had devised over the years for the dragoons, gradually transforming the regiment into what amounted to a highly exclusive club and appointing its officers from among his friends. In 1794, at a time when Britain was at war with the Revolutionary Government in France, the Prince brought into the 10th his protégé, the sixteen-year-old George Bryan Brummell, who managed to get away with even less serious soldiering than George Leigh. That summer the 10th pitched camp at Hove outside Brighton, where the Prince celebrated his thirty-first birthday. Marquees of astonishing splendour were erected and all the town turned out to see the Prince and his regiment in their splendid uniforms.

While George and his companions were dancing attendance on

the Prince and enjoying the favours of the ladies of Brighton, his father had been putting in a little real soldiering in the war against France. He had covered himself in glory at the assault on Valenciennes and had won the special approbation of the Duke of York. In the wake of his success, Charles Leigh was given leave to return to England to raise a volunteer regiment, '. . . which I hope for his sake will answer to him, though I think the terms are very hard,' the Duke of York told the Prince of Wales. Four days later, on 27 September 1793, Charles Leigh took command, as its Colonel, of the 82nd Regiment of Foot, known as the Prince of Wales's Volunteers. A fortnight after that his promotion to the rank of Major General was announced. It was a step that involved him in great personal expense and would cost his family dear.

George, too, was rapidly making his way, purchasing a Captaincy in 1794, gazetted Major in 1796. Army regulations stipulated that no officer should be promoted to the rank of Field Officer until he had been seven years in the service and had held a Captaincy for two, but the Prince was not a man to trouble himself about regulations when he was transforming his regiment into the finest in the country, 'of which the Corps of Officers is entirely composed of men of fashion'.

In 1799, one of the regiment's two lieutenant colonelcies was about to fall vacant. George had had his eye on this, but the grossly inflated purchase price of a colonelcy in the 10th was far beyond his or his father's means. In any case he was not next in line for it. First refusal went to the senior Major, Josiah Cottin. It came to George's ears, however, that while Cottin was proposing to purchase, he was also planning to sell on the colonelcy immediately and transfer to a less glamorous regiment, making a tidy profit in the process. Feigning indignation, George easily persuaded the Prince of Wales to confront Cottin and force him to sell to George at the basic regulation price, which his father was prevailed upon to put up for him. The Prince contrived to present the whole affair as if George had reluctantly purchased the colonelcy in strict conformity with the regulations and to restore 'good humour and unanimity in the Corps'.

But George was becoming greedy. As he climbed ever higher in the Prince's favour and ingratiated himself with the Duke of York, he was always on the look-out for more perquisites to be put in his direction. The Treasurer of the Prince's household complained:

Colonel Leigh came here on Thursday to dinner with a commission to give a large sum of money for a horse Sir F Pool would not part with. He also told me he was to farm the hounds at either 12 or 1500 pounds a year. Surely these sums could be dispos'd of to the credit of H.R.H. and not for the amusement of George Leigh?

There were more signs of ill feeling from another quarter. Sam Chifney, the Prince's jockey, had for some time been dropping dark hints about George mixing with some of the murkier members of the racing fraternity, whom he considered:

> . . . improper people for him to employ training the Prince's horses. This gang that impose upon a field of noblemen and gentlemen who run horses for sport for themselves and the nation upon the most noble and honourable motives.

George had further incensed Chifney by employing his two sons as stable lads for eight guineas a year while using them to race the Prince's horses for no extra pay. If that were not enough, George had arranged for Chifney's daughter to work at Carlton House, the Prince's famously extravagant establishment in Pall Mall, and she was being paid nothing at all. It was in fact not uncommon for the servants at Carlton House to receive no wages, but what really maddened Chifney was that when he confronted George he denied all knowledge of the girl.

The discord between George and the Chifneys soared to a dizzy climax in October 1803 when George, who had been complaining to the Prince that his jockey was 'the worst fellow living', caught sight of Chifney on the exercise ground at Newmarket and called out to one of the stewards of the Jockey Club to join him in giving Chifney a good hiding. '. . . and he knew that I had been ill for 2 years,' Chifney wrote. 'My son William knowing of this and other insulting injurious usage of George Leigh to me, himself and his brother licked Colonel Leigh.'

George was not the kind of man to pass over what must have been a public humiliation, and brought an indictment against William Chifney 'for an assault and misdemeanour'. Young Chifney was eventually persuaded to plead guilty and was gaoled for six months. As for his father:

> I received a letter dated November 7th 1803 for me to be discharged from the Prince's service and for my pension to cease from this date

for my ingratitude to the Prince and my son's atrocious behaviour to
Colonel Leigh.

By the middle of 1804, relations between the Prince of Wales and
his father had once again taken a turn for the worse. It was the
same old story: the Prince was fretting at not being given an active
military command and the King, whose mental state was again
giving much cause for anxiety, was determined to do what he could
to distance the Prince from his glamorous regiment. The 10th were
ordered to leave Brighton and set up their headquarters in the
distinctly less fashionable area of Guildford.

Left to its own devices in a town where there were few or no
diversions, morale and concord in the 10th began rapidly to go to
pieces. The resentment caused by the way in which George had
procured his colonelcy with the Prince's connivance suddenly boiled
over. George was abusing his own authority by his continual
absences from duty and, when he was with the regiment, his
overbearing and bullying attitude towards anyone who crossed him
was making him more unpopular than ever. On 20 September
1804, when George was once again away from his regiment, the
acting commanding officer wrote to the Prince of Wales to
complain, claiming that George had humiliated him in front of his
fellow officers and accused him of organising a faction against his
Colonel. 'You will not Sir,' he ended, 'I am confident, suffer me to
be subject to treatment so degrading and so unlike that which every
officer has a right to expect . . .'

The regiment was now split between George's supporters and his
opponents, and the Duke of York, as Commander-in-Chief, was
called in to arbitrate. But the Duke, too, was a friend of George
Leigh and depended on his advice on the buying, selling and racing
of horses and also on betting on them. He concluded that all parties
were equally to blame, but it was George's enemies who were
moved out of the regiment and his own position was, if anything,
strengthened. George was encouraged to believe he was above the
law and that there was nothing he could not get away with.

By the time of his marriage to Augusta, only the Prince of Wales
was senior to George Leigh in regimental command. George
continued to fly high in royal favour and was regularly in the
Prince's company. On the Prince's birthday in August 1806, 'the
Prince entertained five of his Royal brothers . . . Of the splendid
party were also, the Duke of Orleans . . . Mr Sheridan, Colonels

Turner and Leigh . . .' Colonel Leigh was also among the 'distinguished personages' at a dinner and ball hosted by the Prince the following evening. Three weeks earlier, he had accompanied his royal master to Lewes Races, when the *Morning Post* reported:

> . . . his Royal Highness, seated on the dickey box of his barouche, with six beautiful spirited blood horses, has just moved from the Pavilion. To the right of his Royal Highness on the box is Sir John Lade . . . In the interior of the carriage is Lord Darlington* and Lieutenant Colonel Leigh.

* Harry William Vane, 3rd Earl of Darlington and 1st Duke of Cleveland (1766–1842). Patron of the turf and celebrated sportsman who kept a famous pack of hounds at his home Raby Castle in Co. Durham.

CHAPTER 7

'Le Moins Marié Que Possible'

The house at Six Mile Bottom – it was known as 'the Lodge' – lay off the old road from London to Newmarket, south-east of Cambridge. It was an ideal base for George, and the place was steeped in the apocryphal history of the turf. In 1750 it had been the scene of a wager between Lord March and Theobald Taafe over whether a four-wheeled vehicle could cover nineteen miles in an hour (a phenomenal speed at that time). The fact that March's vehicle consisted of not much more than a seat slung in a light frame between the wheels and that each of the four horses had its own postillion was not considered to depart from the terms of the wager and he won his bet easily. Across the road from the house stood (and still stands) the Green Man, an inn much frequented by the racing fraternity, where in the reign of Charles II the celebrated poet-rake Lord Rochester had once carried off the young wife of a miser by disguising himself as a woman and drugging the sister-in-law who was acting as the girl's chaperone.

Although the place was well suited to George's needs – with its large stable-block and extensive paddocks and location so conveniently close to Newmarket – its attractions for Augusta were less obvious. Compared with the great houses to which she was accustomed, Six Mile Bottom was uncomfortably small. Yet it possessed one great virtue: for the first time in her life she had a home that was exclusively her own. It was, as she put it, 'the house I have so long wished for and in which I am so completely happy'.

George and Augusta spent the three weeks after the wedding settling into the house, organising the domestic arrangements and unpacking wedding presents. While George occupied himself with the business of the stables, Augusta wrote letters of thanks for the gifts they had received. One of these has survived, a note to Colonel John McMahon, the Prince's private secretary, acknowledging the safe arrival of 'the most beautiful clock which is most highly valued not only for its beauty but for the sake of its giver whose friendship and kindness will ever be remembered . . .'

Augusta herself had not met 'its giver', but McMahon, who had instant access to the ear of the Prince, had many a time extricated George from 'moments of distress and perplexity'.

Augusta's talent for home-making and her readiness to roll up her sleeves and 'scrub and scour' must have owed more to her life at the Rectory at Eckington than at Holdernesse House or Castle Howard, and she seems to have been blissfully content. For George, with so many demands on him from the Prince, the regiment, the turf and his friends, there was little opportunity to relax into a life of quiet domesticity, even if he had been inclined to change his deeply ingrained way of life now that he was a married man. By 9 September 1807 he was back in London with the Prince.

Fortunately for Augusta, she was by nature undemanding, unambitious and unselfish. She consoled herself for George's frequent absences by writing long letters, sketching and reading; she also began to compile a commonplace book. Nor was she deprived of society. Her half-brother Francis Osborne and his wife lived only seven miles away at Gogmagog outside Cambridge, while her cousins the Duke and Duchess of Rutland had a house nearby at Cheveley where they stayed on their very regular visits to Newmarket and where the Duke had his racing stables.

Towards the end of September the Duke and Duchess of Rutland, as a curtain-raiser to the Autumn Meeting at Newmarket, had a large house party at Cheveley Park for the shooting. It was an annual event at which at least one royal duke could be expected to be present, as were George Brummell and most of London's fashionable sportsmen and gamblers. For Augusta it was a chance to catch up with her Howard cousins while George, with the Duke of Cambridge and other guests, 'enjoyed three days of excellent sport' and drank and gambled into the small hours.

In October George was recalled to Carlton House on equerry duty and, among other things, was given the task of finding a suitable pony for Princess Charlotte, as a present from her father. Augusta remained at Six Mile Bottom, settling into what would be the pattern of her life, an existence punctuated by George's absences. Lady Harriet Cavendish, whose notice little escaped, could hardly wait to tell her sister, Lady Morpeth:

Colonel Leigh is said to be always in Town and it is another subject on which people are tempted to be very ill-natured, but to be sure with some reason for he certainly is *'le moins marié que possible'* and everybody, excepting his wife, meets him at every place in England save Six Mile Bottom.

When in the spring of 1808 Augusta knew that she was pregnant, with the prospect of George being away so much, the family decided to arrange for her confinement to take place in London at the Chichesters' house in Stratton Street. There, if George was on Carlton House duty, it would be easier for him to be with her and she would also have the comforting presence of her sister, Mary.

Byron at last broke his long silence, but only to ask a favour of her. He wanted Augusta to persuade George to use his influence with the Prince of Wales and put in a word on behalf of a friend, who was trying to avoid having to rejoin his regiment in the East Indies: 'I shall feel particularly obliged by Col Leigh's interference, as I think from his influence the Prince's consent might be obtained . . .'

Byron had still not met George Leigh, but he had seen him, parading with the regiment on the Steyne in Brighton.

The 10th had by now been transformed into the 10th Hussars and looked more spectacular than ever in their Hungarian trappings, with mirlitons and sabretaches; when the Prince reviewed them on their arrival in Brighton in August, the papers reported a 'very fine sight'. The traditional junketings for their Colonel's birthday on 12 August were, however, overshadowed by the news from the Peninsula.

In March 1808, as part of his overall plan to seize control of western Europe, Napoleon had taken advantage of a struggle for power within the Spanish royal family to install his brother Joseph Buonaparte on the throne. There were uprisings against the French all over Spain and Sir Arthur Wellesley was sent out to the Peninsula with an army of 13,000 men. A further British force was to follow under Sir John Moore. The 10th, along with the other Hussar regiments, began training for war.

'I don't know if my Hussars would fight well,' wrote Lord Paget, 'but they certainly look well which is all we are likely to want of them.' As it happened, considerably more was wanted of them and they were ordered to embark as soon as possible for active service in the Peninsula. Paget was given overall command of the cavalry regiments, while George Leigh was to command the 10th in the field.

Augusta was by this time more than seven months pregnant. 'Mrs Leigh is very dismal and unhappy,' reported the Duchess of Rutland, who had rushed over from Cheveley, 'the Colonel was obliged to leave her and go to Town yesterday and perhaps may be obliged to join his regiment without being able to come back to her, I want her to come here, and not stay there by herself . . .'

The regiments began to assemble in Portsmouth and on 14 October the Prince, wearing the uniform of the 10th Hussars, addressed his troops, telling them that they would win honour for themselves and do him credit. In pouring rain, buffeted by heavy gales, the men and their horses began to embark, but it was two weeks before the fleet actually managed to set sail. By the time the ships reached Corunna in northern Spain at the end of the first week of November, the Hussars were thoroughly debilitated by sea-sickness and the discomforts of their cramped and insanitary quarters.

On Friday 4 November, at her sister's house in Stratton Street, Augusta gave birth to a daughter, who was named Georgiana Augusta. Aunt Sophy travelled up to London to see this new addition to the family and was delighted to report that 'both my nieces are well'. Since she was aunt to George as well as Augusta, she was in fact great-aunt twice over to Georgiana Augusta. At the end of the month Byron, for whom his sister was once again 'my dearest Augusta', wrote to her: 'I return you my best thanks for making me an uncle and forgive the sex this time, but the next must be a nephew.' Motherhood suited Augusta and, but for George's absence, she would have been completely happy. She was desperately anxious for news of him.

Predictably George was proving a poor correspondent and Augusta had to rely for news on the letters that Frederick Howard was sending back to his father: 'Leigh begs his compliments to you – perhaps you will have the goodness to send to Mrs Leigh to say he is quite well . . .' He also noted with some surprise: 'Leigh has weathered all the fatigues amazingly well.' The 10th were slowly making their way across Galicia, battling through winter storms and watched balefully by an inhospitable and indifferent local population.

On 23 December news reached Sir John Moore that the entire

French army in Spain, with Napoleon at its head, was marching against him. There was nothing for it but to retreat. During the long trek back through steadily increasing snow and ice, George Leigh had his one moment of military glory.

On 26 December 1808, the 10th Hussars were about to enter Mayorga, fifty miles north of Valladolid, when they were warned by the locals that a troop of French cavalry had taken up position on the other side of the town. Paget ordered Brigadier Slade, whom he heartily despised, to advance and attack. The regiment set off at a trot, but Slade halted, apparently to readjust his stirrups. Once again the 10th moved forward, and again Slade stopped to fiddle with his stirrups. Paget, seething with impatience, dispatched an aide-de-camp to urge him to move on, but Slade was still preoccupied. Now beside himself with rage, Paget ordered George Leigh to lead the attack.

With George at their head, urging them forward, the Hussars made their way up the hill to Mayorga through the snow and slush and, when they came to the gates on the other side of the town, halted so that the horses could recover their breath, while shot from the French rained down upon them. The charge was sounded and in no time at all the 10th had carried the day, with three French dead and forty or fifty taken prisoner. The only casualty among the English officers was Frederick Howard, who received a cut on the arm.

On 11 January 1809 the British army, by now utterly demoralised and exhausted by the long retreat across the Galician mountains, constantly harried by French chasseurs, reached Corunna. The Hussars were 'almost horseless, shoeless, gagged, dirty and something worse' and there was no sign of the fleet that had been summoned to carry them home. Twelve thousand barrels of powder were blown up to prevent them being seized by the enemy, greatly alarming the town's inhabitants and breaking all the windows. Hundreds of the horses were shot on the beach or driven over the cliffs. At last the ships struggled into the harbour and the army began to embark, while Moore did his best to hold the French at bay. Two days after the 10th had sailed for home, the French mounted an attack on the town. Moore was severely wounded and died that evening.

It was 23 January before the battered transport ship carrying George Leigh and Frederick Howard finally reached Plymouth.

'Many of the Officers who landed today have not changed their linen for 20 days . . .' the *Morning Herald* informed its readers. Augusta had heard no news of her husband's return and two days later Georgiana Augusta's christening went ahead at Stratton Street without him. Her godfather was the Prince of Wales.

The day before George landed, Byron had celebrated his twenty-first birthday. He had moved into Newstead in September but on this occasion he dined quietly by himself at Reddish's hotel in St James's, leaving Hanson to feast the tenantry at the Abbey and to drink his health in ale and punch. Now that he had come of age, it was time for him to take his seat in the Lords, and he wrote to the Earl of Carlisle asking him if he would introduce him.

The second edition of his verses, *Hours of Idleness*, had been dedicated to the Earl 'by his obliged and affectionate kinsman' and Carlisle had responded with a 'tolerably handsome letter' in which he had given his ward some words of cautious advice:

> Be not disconcerted if the reception of your work should not be that you have the right to look for from the public. Persevere, whatever the reception may be, and though the Public may be found very fastidious . . . you will stand better with the world than others who only pursue their studies in Bond Street or Tattershall's . . .

When it came to introducing Byron into the House of Lords, Carlisle was not so obliging. He was reluctant to put himself out for his ward at the best of times but now, suffering from a neurological disease and seriously unwell, he ignored Byron's request, confining himself to informing him of the correct procedure for entering the House and leaving Byron to go through the business of proving his pedigree.

Byron chose to take offence. His guardian's refusal to sponsor him meant that he had to go through what he saw as the humiliating business of proving not only his own legitimacy but that of his father and grandfather. He was still in the surliest of moods when he took his seat on 13 March and determined to take his revenge. The means lay ready to hand. *Hours of Idleness* had – as Carlisle had warned him it might be – been roasted by the *Edinburgh Review* and Byron was preparing a riposte, tentatively entitled *The British Bards*, in which he savaged not only his critics but any contemporary poet whom he considered worth his scorn.

Originally he had intended to make a brief complementary reference to his guardian's verses, but now they were dismissed as 'the paralytic puling of CARLISLE' and he attacked the old man with vitriolic ferocity:

> Lord, rhymester, petit-maitre, pamphleteer.
> So dull in youth, so drivelling in his age,
> His scenes alone half damned our sinking stage;

Carlisle was hurt and angry, but the person who was most distressed was Augusta, who loved Carlisle and respected him. Byron knew this very well, but nothing could be allowed to come between him and his revenge.

In July 1809, Byron set off, with his Cambridge friend John Cam Hobhouse as his travelling companion, for a Grand Tour of those parts of Europe and the Levant that Napoleon had not overrun. He did his best to put the whole matter out of his mind, although his conscience was still troubling him a little.

> Though I was happy to obtain my seat without Ld C.'s assistance, I had no measure to keep with a man who declined interfering as my relation on that occasion, and I have done with him, though I regret distressing Mrs Leigh, poor thing! I hope she is happy.

Augusta was far from happy for, by the time her brother left England, her husband's career was on the brink of collapse.

George had returned home feeling something of a hero, convinced that he had acquitted himself well in the campaign in Spain, but any satisfaction was rapidly dampened by the realisation that, as far as the country at large was concerned, the retreat to Corunna had been an inglorious fiasco for which Moore, despite his heroic death, was allotted most of the blame.

By a curious twist, the 'shameful disaster' of the failure of the military expedition became inextricably entangled in the mind of the public with a scandal that had broken just as the battered army was returning to England. It had been revealed in the House of Commons, by a member of the Opposition, that the Duke of York's former mistress, Mary Ann Clarke, had taken money from officers who had hoped that she would use her influence with the Duke, as Commander-in-Chief of the Army, to secure their promotion. The nation was predictably outraged at this revelation of corruption in high places and, although the Duke was cleared by Parliament of any direct involvement, the majority vote in his favour was so narrow that he was forced to resign.

It was against this unsavoury background that George Leigh's own shabby fall from grace was played out. Some time before the regiment embarked for Spain, he had been involved in the sale of a horse belonging to the Prince of Wales – the kind of deal he had frequently negotiated over the years. Unfortunately, in his absence it had come to light that he had omitted to hand over all the proceeds of the sale to the Prince.

George suffered from an unfortunate combination of optimism, stubbornness and stupidity. He may have hoped that by adjusting the books a little the discrepancy might never be discovered; he may even have intended to pay the money back, having probably borrowed it to back a horse that he mistakenly reckoned would be a certain winner and, in the confusion of the regiment's sudden departure, the whole matter may have slipped his mind. But by the time of George's return from Spain, the Prince had been informed and was greatly shocked. He had gone out of his way to further the career of his protégé and that George should betray his trust in such a squalidly petty fashion both distressed and angered him. Even so, he was not disposed finally to turn his back on a man who had been his close associate, and the Prince seems to have done all that he could to keep George in the royal household, while giving him an opportunity to make public amends by opening up the possibility of a transfer to another regiment.

George was never capable of subtle thinking and, in his anger and embarrassment at being caught red-handed, he chose to behave as if he were the injured party and abruptly resigned his position as Equerry. Even now, the Prince was prepared to be generous and understanding, perhaps out of concern for Augusta and the baby who was his godchild; certainly out of consideration for General Leigh, as becomes clear from his letter to his private secretary McMahon:

> Whatever may have been the ungrateful return I have met with from this man, for now two and thirty years unremitting protection and kindness, still in consideration for his family, and the sincere regard I ever shall feel for my old friend, his father, who is the most honourable of men, you will acquaint General Hulse that though in the option that was propos'd to Lt Col Leigh at my desire through

Lord Paget, he has chosen to dismiss himself from my Family, yet, that I mean not to withdraw his salary from him but to continue it as a pension . . .

At the same time the Prince arranged for the deeds of Six Mile Bottom to be transferred to George.

The news of George's fall was soon the talk of the clubs and messes. His overbearing behaviour had made him many enemies both inside and outside the regiment who had long hoped to see him toppled. By May his disgrace had become public knowledge, and Catherine Byron gleefully passed on the news to her son: 'I hear the cause of Col Leigh's quarrel with the Prince is that he cheated him in selling a horse for him, that he retained for himself part of the purchase money.'

Shocked though Augusta was, she did not allow her faith in her husband to be shaken. Her concern was for George and to find some way to help him out of his troubles. Carlisle was approached for his advice. Was it really necessary for George to resign from the regiment and should he, as the Prince had stipulated, quit Newmarket and the turf for good? Carlisle's memorandum* suggested the line that George might take:

> for not leaving Newmarket he is heartily repentant and will for every reason lose no time to disengage himself from a pursuit no way consistent with his fortunes, and with the consideration he owes to his family or to his friends . . .

But George had not the slightest intention of giving up the turf, since it was the very centre of his existence. His marriage, the regiment, the Prince, were all secondary.

As for leaving the Prince's regiment, this would effectively finish off his career in the Army. Could a little more be squeezed out of the Prince's devotion to George's father?

> Colonel Leigh will consider whether he ought to have any repugnance to say to the P.O.W. either in a personal interview or by writing that his reason for not leaving the regiment, which seemed to meet the P.'s wishes, was that he'd have acted in direct opposition to his father's wishes.

George, unfortunately, did not realise that in a very short time there

---

* The memorandum is a draft and unsigned but the handwriting is remarkably like that of the 5th Earl of Carlisle. We also know George visited Castle Howard at that time.

would be no question at all of his remaining in the regiment. In May 1809, possibly as a result of the heavy losses of horses and equipment during the Corunna campaign, a detailed inspection of the accounts and resources of the 10th was set in motion. This may have begun as a purely routine affair, but it soon brought to light a series of discrepancies and irregularities, most of which led directly back to George Leigh. Rumours of his peculations and high-handedness were now common talk:

> from fear of his tyranny, for which he was universally disliked, the men forbore from making public clamour, but at last his conduct was reported and it became necessary to notice it.

George chose to ignore the storm that was gathering about him. He was becoming increasingly obsessed with his quarrel with the Prince and his conviction that it was everyone else who was in the wrong. At Augusta's insistence he consulted the Earl of Chichester, whose advice was eminently sensible: George must make a personal apology to the Prince and offer to resign:

> ... write to the Prince expressing your obligations and gratitude to him for past favours and your concern at having incurred his displeasure but that as long as you remain in that predicament it is impossible for you to continue in his Regiment with any satisfaction to yourself or advantage to the service and that accordingly you beg leave to lay your commission at H.R.H.'s feet to be disposed of in the manner most agreeable to his wishes ...

Still George did nothing. He was wearing himself out protesting about the injustice that had been done him, but he seemed incapable of taking any step to save himself.

> Col Leigh arrived 8–9 last night in a most miserable condition [Augusta told Lady Carlisle]; tired to death as you may imagine and *wet to the skin*. I really was afraid he would be seriously ill he seemed so chilly but I prescribed with success and he is quite well this morning ...

The inquiry had unearthed a whole series of malpractices and frauds, which went back as far as 1806 – some of them petty, others of great consequence. George had connived at and shared in 'exorbitant profits' made by the Paymaster in supplying the regiment with clothing, and in 'neglecting to credit the regiment with the amount of the half yearly allowances from Government for

Postage, Stationery, carriage of ammunition and coals . . .' He had compelled men who were allowed to be discharged on finding substitutes 'to pay large sums of money for that purpose – instead of permitting the said men to find their own substitutes'.

George Leigh was by no means the only culprit, but it was clear that he was going to be made the regimental scapegoat. Injustice always moved Augusta to anger. She wrote an indignant letter to Colonel McMahon protesting that her husband had been singled out for blame, while others guilty of far worse got off scot-free – she may even, one suspects, have brought the Duke of York's case into the argument.

McMahon, for once, had 'nothing consolatory to offer' George and there was nothing he could do to 'avert the Blow . . . the Deed is already done and no palliatives will soften the King's Determination . . .' He could only advise George to request an audience with the Prince as soon as the business was over:

> I am confident that it will still be your own fault if his Feelings are not kind and good towards you . . . I return Mrs Leigh's note in preference to burning it for no one ought to see it . . .

Knowing as they did the extent to which Augusta idolised George, the Carlisle family was afraid that his situation was placing her under intolerable strain. When, resisting all advice, George decided to put in an appearance with the 10th in Brighton that August, as if nothing had happened, Lady Gertrude took the opportunity to persuade Augusta and her nine-month-old daughter to stay with her at Paultons, the Sloane Stanleys' house in Hampshire.* Time among friends in which to collect her spirits was exactly what she needed and those August days must have been tinged with nostalgia for the old life at Castle Howard – even Hary-O, caustic as ever, was there, observing the presence of 'Mrs Leigh but not the Colonel'. For the Colonel in Brighton things looked very black.

Just before the findings of the inquiry were due to be made known, George received an anonymous letter warning him that a court martial was inevitable unless he immediately resigned from

---

* Lady Gertrude Sloane Stanley (1783–1870). The youngest daughter of the 5th Earl of Carlisle, in 1806 she married William Sloane, who assumed the name Stanley when he inherited Paultons. William Sloane was a grand-nephew of Sir Hans Sloane – whose elder daughter had married George Stanley of Paultons near Ramsey. A failure to produce a continuity of Stanley heirs brought the estate to the Sloanes.

the 10th. Even now, on the brink of total ruin, he could not bring himself to admit what was happening. When the 10th moved to Romford in October 1809, he was clinging to the wreckage of his career, still signing the Regimental Returns as Colonel and hoping that some miracle might save him. He had put himself beyond the possibility of intervention – divine or otherwise – but although his friends could not save him, they at least managed to cushion his fall from grace. He was not dismissed or court-martialled, but was allowed to phase himself out. At the beginning of 1810, he was given leave of absence and in February this was extended until May. On 25 April he signed the Regimental Returns for the last time and resigned his commission.

George was thirty-nine. He had no occupation and no prospects, he had forfeited the personal friendship of the Prince of Wales and had been lucky to escape a court martial. Years of being cocooned in the royal circle had not equipped him to fend for himself. Now he was faced with the bleak prospect of making his own way for the first time in his life and without the protection of patronage.

For a time he retired to Six Mile Bottom to lick his wounds and be comforted by Augusta. Adversity would always bring out the best in her and, with her unshakeable trust in providence, she could convince herself that all that had happened would eventually turn out to be for the best. At least she no longer had to compete with the Prince of Wales or the regiment for her husband's attention. And she was expecting another child.

CHAPTER 8

'Materially Altered for ye Worse'

On 14 July 1811, the frigate *Volage*, which had carried Byron back from the Mediterranean, docked at Sheerness. He had been out of England for two years and twelve days, had journeyed to Greece and the Levant, eating oranges in Portugal, watching the moon rise over Actium and swimming the Hellespont. He had admired the beauty of the ladies of Cadiz, been involved in an affair with a married woman in Malta, made love to Greek boys and to Greek girls. But, most importantly, he had discovered himself. He had affirmed his destiny as a poet watching eagles soaring over Mount Parnassus, he had embraced the cause of philhellenism on the Plain of Macedon and he had written an account of his 'Pilgrimage' in 'a long poem' in the Spenserian stanza.

Yet in all that time, although he had dashed off long and entertaining letters to his mother and to his friends from Harrow and Cambridge, he had written not a single line to Augusta, his reason apparently being that he had heard she had been 'annoyed' by his attack on the Earl of Carlisle:

> Had I been aware she would have taken it to heart, I would have cast my pen and poem both into the flames . . . But the mischief is done, Lord forgive me! that it is to have tender hearted she-relations.

Nor did he show any inclination to write to her on his return. There were more pressing affairs. The financial problems he had left behind him had not disappeared in his absence and he was trying to rescue Mrs Massingberd, who had signed the agreement with the money lenders after Augusta had refused to do so and was now threatened with prison.

At the end of July, Catherine Byron was suddenly taken ill. She had been intermittently unwell for the past three years and was probably suffering from cancer. Borrowing forty pounds from Mrs Hanson, Byron set out for Newstead, but his mother died before he could reach her. She was buried in the church at Hucknall. Byron took care that the plate on her coffin recorded, as she would have wished, her descent from the royal house of Scotland.

Augusta wrote to him immediately she heard the news and he sent her a mourning ring set with a moonstone. It was not until the third week of August that he was able to bring himself to reply to her, and then in a curiously guarded manner, addressing her as 'My dear Sister':

> I ought to have answered your letter before, but when did I ever do anything I ought – I am losing my relatives & you are adding to the number of yours, but which is best God knows . . .

Augusta's second child, Augusta Charlotte, had been born at Six Mile Bottom on 20 February. Byron continued to dwell, rather edgily, on the subject of Augusta's fecundity:

> I hear you have been increasing his Majesty's Subjects, which in these times of War & tribulation is really patriotic, notwithstanding Malthus tells us that were it not for Battle, Murder & Sudden death, we should be overstocked, I think we have latterly had a redundance of these national benefits, & therefore give you all credit for your matronly behaviour.

Byron was still uneasy about the way he had treated Augusta, first causing her pain and embarrassment, then neglecting to write to her because he felt guilty about her. But his apprehensions were groundless. Had he known her better, he would have been aware that it was not in her nature to harbour resentment, least of all where he was concerned. All Augusta wanted was a reconciliation.

Hoping to involve her brother more in her world, she wrote to him enthusiastically about her young family, having got the impression, from a chance meeting in London with Scrope Berdmore Davies, one of his closest friends, that Byron was fond of children. Augusta had been charmed by 'his quaint dry way of speaking' and quite won over when with his 'irresistible stammer' he pronounced that her three-year-old Georgiana was 'exactly the kind of child that Byron would delight in' – but she was oblivious to the fact that Scrope Davies was not being entirely serious:

> I am determined not to say another word in her praise for fear you should accuse me of partiality and expect too much. The youngest (*little* Augusta) is just 6 months old and has no particular merit at

present but a very sweet placid temper. Oh! That I could immediately set out to Newstead and shew them to you. I can't tell you *half*
the happiness it would give me to see it and *you*; but, my dearest B.,
it is a long journey and serious undertaking all things considered . . .

Byron replied by return:

I don't know what Scrope Davies meant by telling you I liked
Children, I abominate the sight of them so much that I have always
had the greatest respect for the character of Herod. But, as my house
here is large enough for us all, we should go on very well, and I need
not tell you that I long to see *you*. I really do not perceive any thing
so formidable in a Journey hither of two days, but all this comes of
Matrimony, you have a Nurse and all the etceteras of a family. Well,
I must marry to repair the ravages of myself and prodigal ancestry,
but if I am ever so unfortunate as to be presented with an Heir,
instead of a *Rattle* he shall be provided with a *Gag*.

In the past it had been Byron who had needed a confidante and an
ally – now their positions were reversed and Augusta needed
somebody to whom she could unburden herself without feeling
disloyal.

I have indeed much to tell you [she told her brother], but it is more
easily said than written. Probably you have heard of the many
changes in our situation since you left England; in a *pecuniary* point
of view it is materially altered for ye worse; perhaps in other respects
better.

It was over a year since George had resigned his commission and
during that time he had made no effort to reinstate himself in the
Prince's favour or to show the least sign of remorse. Now it was
becoming a matter of urgency to resolve this, for soon the Prince
would be beyond George's reach. George III was no longer capable
of fulfilling the role of monarch and a cautious Parliament had
allowed the Prince a limited Regency – but, with no hope of the
King's recovery, it was only a matter of time before George's former
friend would be King in all but name.

George continued to be unrepentant. As his spirits revived, he
was finding extremely pleasurable ways to occupy his time,
spinning out the days on a range of commissions, finding for a
friend a 'clever' horse or a suitable 'lad', selling a pony for another
and generally receiving payment in kind – 'a valuable mare to breed
from Lord Egremont for thanks', 'handkerchiefs', or perhaps a gift

of game. A series of letters written in 1811 to Sir Arthur Paget,* the brother of the man who had commanded the cavalry in the Corunna campaign, opens this window into George's world. The letters are full of gossip about 'Sir Harry F.',† who 'was in great form when he was with us and shot every day'; about Chester, who 'was capital the other day having met with some very good brandy to which he did justice'; about Lord Rivers, whose greyhounds had died; and Brummell and Lord Alvanley, who 'sat up till 4 o'clock playing at whist and were the losers'. He arranged for Paget to send venison from Dorset to his in-laws at Gogmagog – 'which I am sorry to say was spoilt in the intense heat of the weather' – and even found a man to make a cot for the Pagets' baby son: 'Mrs Leigh made him measure our own and hopes it will answer.'

George's fall from grace did not affect his standing with his old friends and whenever they gathered together at Sir Harry Fetherstonhaugh's at Uppark, with Delmé Radcliffe‡ at Hitchin Priory or at the Pagets' house near Blandford, he was always a welcome guest. His life began to fall into a yearly routine, dictated by the principal race meetings and the shooting and hunting seasons. All this only served to take him away from Augusta for weeks on end. In between times he was absorbed with his horses and at the end of 1811 actually refused the present of a brown horse, on the grounds that 'I have so many horses in my possession, at this time and I shall not want a hack again soon, as the mare Lord Paget gave me is perfect.'

One of the fixed points on George's itinerary was Castle Howard, where he could meet up with his former comrade-in-arms, Frederick, and attend the race meetings at York and Doncaster. Augusta had not been there since her marriage and Lady Carlisle was complaining that she never heard from her. 'Col L. said that you accused me of idleness in that respect,' Augusta told her. 'I hope however you received a long letter from me some time ago, after I received the Frocks you was so good as to send my little girls, you must otherwise think me more *mad* than all the Byrons.'

* Sir Arthur Paget (1771–1840), second son of the 1st Earl of Uxbridge. An eminent diplomat, he scandalised the nation by running off with the wife of Lord Boringdon, the former Lady Augusta Fane, whom he married two days after a highly publicised divorce was granted.
† Sir Harry Fetherstonhaugh (1754–1846). Celebrated rake, racing man and art collector. He installed Emy Hart (Nelson's Lady Hamilton) at his house Uppark.
‡ Emilius Henry Delmé Radcliffe was a nephew of the 5th Earl of Carlisle and son of the Earl's sister Lady Elizabeth (Betty) Garnier by her first husband, Peter Delmé.

The Carlisles urged her to visit them that September and it suddenly occurred to Augusta that she might be able to break the long journey to Yorkshire at Newstead and meet the brother she had not seen since well before her marriage:

> Now, if I could contrive to pay you a visit *en passant*, it would be delightful, and give me the greatest pleasure. But I fear you would be obliged to make up your mind to receive my *Brats* too. As for my husband, he prefers the *outside of the mail* to the *Inside of a Post-Chaise*, particularly when partly occupied by Nurse and Children, so that we always travel *independent* of each other.

By now she was sufficiently confident of the renewal of their friendship to indulge in a little banter about his 'determination' to get married:

> . . . I really hope you are serious, being convinced that such an event would contribute greatly to your happiness, PROVIDED *her Ladyship* was the sort of person that would suit you; and you won't be angry with me for saying that it is not EVERY *one* who would . . .

She concluded: 'Are you going to amuse us with any more *Satires*? Oh, *English Bards*! I shall make you laugh (when we meet) about it!' This was telling Byron as clearly as she could (without being positively disloyal to Carlisle) that he was forgiven. He replied immediately and gratefully:

> My 'Satire!' – I am glad it made you laugh for Somebody told me in Greece that you was angry, and I was sorry, as you were perhaps the only person who I did *not* want to *make angry*. – – – But how you will make *me* laugh I don't know, for it is a vastly *serious* subject to me I assure you; therefore take care, or I shall hitch *you* into the next edition to make up our family party.

But almost as soon as she had suggested the idea, Augusta began to have second thoughts. The prospect of a long journey to Yorkshire with a child of not quite three who was always in indifferent health and an eleven-month-old baby began to look 'a very serious undertaking', particularly since Georgey was becoming rather a handful. Little Augusta was also giving her mother cause for anxiety. 'I feel very uncertain about her,' she told Lady Carlisle. 'She is certainly by no means well and I cannot exactly make out what ails her. I have till only lately thought it must be entirely owing to her teeth, but as I think she must have cut them all I begin to fidgit very much on the subject.'

Byron then proposed coming to Cambridge that October. If Augusta were not prepared to make the journey up to Castle Howard, he could collect her from her home and drive her up to Newstead: '. . . we will travel in my *Vis* & can have a cage for the children & a cart for the Nurse. Or perhaps we can forward them by the Canal . . .'

In the end, as had happened so many times in the past, Byron's and Augusta's plans to meet came to nothing. This did not, of course, prevent George from going to the Doncaster races, where he met up with Brummell, whose compulsive gambling was beginning to land him in serious financial trouble.

The Leighs too were having money difficulties, and Christmas at Six Mile Bottom that year cannot have been a very joyful affair. George wrote miserably to Arthur Paget on the last day of the year, heading his letter 'Poverty Bottom' and lamenting the fact that he hardly ever went away from home (although he was in fact planning an excursion to Uppark the following month). At Newstead, Byron was getting joyously drunk with his old friends from Cambridge and becoming 'totally enamoured' of 'a Welsh Girl whom I lately added to the bevy . . .'

That winter at Hucknall and in Nottingham the stocking-makers and lace-makers, who saw their existence threatened by the introduction of mechanical means of production, made a last-ditch attempt to ward off the inevitable by destroying the machines that would make them redundant. In February 1812, a bill was put before Parliament making the 'destroying or injuring' of stocking- and lace-frames a capital offence and Byron seized the chance to make this the occasion of a passionate maiden speech to the House of Lords:

> How will you carry the Bill into effect? Can you commit a whole country to their own prisons? Will you erect a gibbet in every field and hang up men like scarecrows?

Augusta read reports of his speech in the papers, and, though she may have been pleased with her brother's moment of glory, she would hardly have shared his opinions. Like most of her friends, she was deeply reactionary in her political views and shared the general fear that the frame-breakers were the forerunners of an English reign of terror.

Early in March 1812 she received a copy of the poem in which Byron had commemorated his journey through 'Spain, Portugal, Epirus, Acarnania and Greece', *Childe Harold's Pilgrimage*, suitably inscribed:

> To Augusta, my dearest sister, and my best friend, who has ever loved me better than I deserved, this volume is presented by her *father's* son, and most affectionate brother, B.

In the poem itself she received only the most oblique of mentions, reflecting how small a part her brother's 'best friend' had played in his life for the past four years:

> Childe Harold had a mother – not forgot,
> Though parting from that mother he did shun;
> A sister whom he loved, but saw her not
> Before his weary pilgrimage begun:

John Murray, a practised publicist as well as a discerning publisher, had privately circulated the sheets of the poem so that it was being enthusiastically discussed even before it was offered to the public. When it did go on sale, priced at thirty shillings a copy, the whole edition was snapped up in three days. It was the sensation of the season and, if no letters came to Augusta from her brother, she would at least read about him in the gossip columns.

> 'Nobody reads, talks, or thinks of anything else' [wrote a young American visitor to his mother]. 'He has become the idol of fashionable society. His admirers are never tired of telling how he was the guest of honour at a certain duchess's ball, and how another duchess was quite ill with chagrin because she could not secure him for her dinner party.'

And the Duchess of Devonshire* told her son:

> The ladies, I hear, spoil him, and the gentlemen are jealous of him. He is going back to Naxos, and then the husbands may sleep in peace. I should not be surprised if Caro William were to go with him, she is so wild and imprudent.

'Caro William' was Lady Caroline Lamb. Capricious, wilful,

---

* Second wife of the 5th Duke of Devonshire, the former Elizabeth Foster.

eccentric, the licensed tomboy of Whig society, she had been bowled over first by the poem and then by its author. Lady Caroline and Byron were soon involved in a reckless love affair in which they were intent on breaking every taboo and which they made little attempt to conceal, even from her husband, William Lamb. The progress of the affair was observed with ironic detachment, even amusement, by Caroline's mother-in-law, Lady Melbourne. Now past sixty, she had been one of the great beauties of her day and had numbered among her lovers the Prince of Wales. She had grown rather stout, but was still capable of exercising a certain fascination, particularly on Byron: 'If she had been a few years younger, what a fool she would have made of me, had she thought it worth the while.'

On 25 March, at a morning party of Lady Caroline's, her cousin (and Lady Melbourne's niece) Anne Isabella Milbanke saw Byron for the first time and, as was her custom, subjected him to a cool critical analysis:

> His mouth continually betrays the acrimony of his spirit. I should judge him sincere and independent – *Sincere* at least in society as far as he can be, whilst dissimulating the violence of his scorn . . .

Anne Isabella Milbanke, always called Annabella, was nineteen, a cousin of Caroline Lamb and the only child of Lady Melbourne's elder brother, Sir Ralph, and the former Judith Noel, daughter of the first Viscount Wentworth. Born fifteen years after their marriage, when they had given up hope of having a child, Annabella had been spoiled and indulged. She had been led to believe that in everything that she did, whether riding or dancing, taking her medicine or dutifully saying her prayers, she was perfect, 'a little Angel', as everyone called her. Worse still, she had been encouraged to think that she could never be wrong.

Annabella had a brilliant, if limited, mind, shone in mathematics and astronomy and had written verses that had been highly praised by a coterie of admiring friends. Although no one could have called her a beauty, she was small and neat and attractive and very self-confident. She had many suitors, none of whom came up to her exacting standards – one of them had been dismissed because he had shown no sympathy for her 'high aspirations'. She lived far away in Seaham in County Durham, and this was her third season in town.

It was not until 13 April that she actually managed to speak to Byron, but the following evening she succeeded in luring him into a discussion on the merits of her family's protégé, the shoemaker poet Joseph Blackett. By 15 April, Annabella had come to the conclusion that Byron was more agreeable in conversation than anyone she knew and, in a letter that ought to have sent shivers of apprehension running down her mother's spine, she announced:

> He really is an object of compassion . . . I consider it as an act of humanity and a Christian duty not to deny him any temporary satisfaction he can derive from my acquaintance – though I shall not seek to increase it. He is not a dangerous person to me.

Byron, who had no great opinion of clever women, as he had more than once made clear to Augusta, now began to be intrigued by Annabella's unfashionably natural personality. He even had generous words for the specimens of her verses that Caroline Lamb had sent him: 'She certainly is a very extraordinary girl; who would imagine such strength and variety of thought under that placid countenance.' Lady Caroline, scenting competition from this very unexpected quarter, went out of her way to warn her cousin off: '. . . shun friendships with those whose practice ill accords with your principles'. To make doubly certain she told Byron that Annabella was engaged to George Eden, the son of Lord Auckland.*

Byron was under the impression that Annabella was an heiress and this undoubtedly added to his interest. He may have been the most sought-after man in England, but he was desperately short of money and had reluctantly decided to put Newstead on the market.

No one could have been more astounded than Lady Melbourne when, on 13 September, Byron declared his interest in Annabella Milbanke – 'one whom I wished to marry, had this affair not intervened'. She asked him whether he knew what he was doing. 'I admire [her] because she is a clever woman,' Byron told her, 'an amiable woman & of high blood, for I have still a few Norman & Scotch inherited prejudices on the last score, were I to marry – As to *Love*, that is done in a week . . .'

Lady Melbourne acquainted Annabella with Byron's proposal. Annabella, incapable of action without first drawing up a balance sheet, sat down and wrote a character assessment of her suitor:

* In fact he had proposed to her the previous year and had been turned down.

When indignation takes possession of his mind – and it is easily excited – his disposition becomes malevolent. He hates with the bitterest contempt. But as soon as he has indulged those feelings, he regains the humanity which he had lost – from the immediate impulse of provocation – and repents deeply. So that his mind is continually making the most sudden transitions – from good to evil, from evil to good.

Annabella could hardly have been unaware of the Caroline Lamb imbroglio and Byron had spoken to her openly about his admiration for other women, but she would not admit to herself that this was a stumbling block. It was his '*theoretical* idea of my perfection' and 'the Irreligious nature of his principles' that were her real objections. In a letter positively overflowing with exalted sentiment, she told Lady Melbourne that she rejected Byron's proposal. It must have given her great satisfaction to turn down a man who undoubtedly represented the catch of the season.

Byron was considerably piqued by her rejection: in fact he was more wounded by it than he cared to admit. However, he was determined to put on as brave a face as possible where Lady Melbourne was concerned:

> I thank you again for your efforts with my Princess of Parallelograms, who has puzzled you more than the Hypothenuse; in her character she has not forgotten '*Mathematics*' wherein I used to praise her cunning. Her proceedings are quite rectangular, or rather we are two parallel lines prolonged to infinity side by side but never to meet. *Say* what you please for or of me, & I will mean it.

A few days later, he was all affability: 'Tell A. that I am more proud of her *rejection* than I can ever be of another's acceptance.'

CHAPTER 9

'A New Sensation to Both'

Byron had written in the summer of 1811, '... at all events and in all situations, you have a brother in me', and early in 1813 Augusta took him at his word and wrote asking for financial help.

In the year since George had written his 'Poverty Bottom' letter to Sir Arthur Paget, their situation had changed greatly for the worse. Another child, their first son, had been born the previous June and christened George Henry John by a friend and neighbour, Charles Wedge, the vicar not of their parish of Bottisham, but of nearby Burrough Green. The new baby had his uncle the Duke of Leeds and his father's old friend from Uppark in Sussex, Sir Harry Fetherstonhaugh, as godparents, but the Leighs' circumstances were in sorry contrast to the splendour of their connections. Now, with another mouth to feed, two sickly daughters (the younger one in particular giving her every reason for anxiety), barely enough money to pay the servants and remorselessly mounting debts, Augusta was at the end of her tether.

Their only income was George's irregularly paid pension and Augusta's own £350 a year allowed her under the terms of her grandmother's will. She always aimed to be frugal in her housekeeping but she had never known how to make a little money go a long way, and it was pointless looking to her husband to extricate them from their plight. George had still made not the slightest effort to apologise to the Prince Regent and even a plan to set up his own stud had failed to materialise. He may not have grasped fully the gravity of their position, since Augusta had always devoted herself to protecting him from the harsher realities of their life. She handled all his business correspondence and did her best to fend off their creditors, taking charge of anything liable to cause him the least disquiet. She saw it as her duty to ensure that his life was as trouble-free as she could make it and, when he was at home, the household was run according to his wishes and, therefore, far beyond their means. This was done partly out of genuine concern for him, but partly also in an attempt to head off the fits of depression that invariably followed his being forced to confront any unpleasant truth.

By the middle of March, Augusta had received no reply to her plea for help from her brother and she wrote again, this time a more urgent appeal that he could not ignore. He replied on 26 March:

> I did not answer your letter, because I could not answer as I wished, but expected that every week would bring me some tidings that might enable me to reply better than by apologies . . .

The problem was that the prospective purchaser of Newstead, a Lancashire lawyer named Claughton, was doing everything he could to avoid handing over the deposit of £25,000, and Byron's own debts were racing out of control. He was clearly discountenanced by Augusta's appeal and by his failure to respond to it; embarrassed by her embarrassment at having to ask again – and ask at all. He was guilty, too, of having failed to contact her for a year and a half, and tried to laugh off a little shamefacedly the various amours that had put her completely out of his mind:

> . . . You have perhaps heard that I have been fooling my time with different 'regnantes' but what better can be expected of me? I have but one *relative* and her I never see.

Everyone had heard of Byron's romantic entanglements and Augusta was no exception. What she did not pick up from the scandal sheets, her relatives were eager to tell her, and in particular Aunt Sophy, who took great delight in keeping up with her nephew's exploits. The 'regnante' with whom Byron was currently entangled was Lady Oxford, sixteen years older, but still a beauty and one of the leading political hostesses of the day. Byron confessed rather sheepishly that he was off to spend a fortnight with Lady Oxford and her husband at Eywood, their house near Presteigne, on the edge of Radnor Forest:

> I see you put on a demure look at the name, which is very becoming and matronly in you; but you won't be sorry to hear that I am quite out of a more serious scrape with another singular personage which threatened me last year . . .

That 'singular personage' was, of course, Lady Caroline Lamb, and Byron was greatly deceiving himself if he thought that she was going to bow out of his life quietly. He went on to give Augusta a

brief summary of his inclinations – both matrimonial and parliamentary – and expressed his wish to see her before he went abroad
again, as was his plan, while bewailing the fact that she 'was always
buried in that bleak common near Newmarket'.

What he does not seem to have realised was the effort it cost
Augusta to approach him like that, particularly in the light of her
own failure to come to his rescue over the money lenders' bond all
those years ago. There were other matters pressing him more
closely. Lady Caroline began to bombard him with demands for a
meeting and Lady Oxford suspected she was pregnant – 'A slight
perplexity', as Byron put it, which led to a distinct cooling off on
the part of her normally complaisant husband.

Marooned on 'that bleak common near Newmarket', Augusta
was left to weigh up her unsuccessful appeal to Byron and
concluded that she had not made sufficiently clear how desperate
their situation really was. She also brooded over the implied
accusation of his having 'but one *relative* and her I never see', and
realised how little she knew her brother; how little either of them
knew of the other. Over the years they had made so many plans to
meet, which had always miscarried, and for this he clearly blamed
her.

In June a new crisis in George Leigh's affairs drove him to ask
Augusta to make a fresh appeal to Byron. Rather than write yet
another begging letter to her brother, she now decided to descend
immediately on London.

Byron's immediate reaction on hearing of his sister's imminent
visit was one of mild annoyance. Lady Oxford had discovered that
she was not, in fact, pregnant and she and her husband were leaving
for Sicily, where he was intending to join them later that summer,
but he had planned a visit to Portsmouth to take a sentimental
farewell of his inamorata. He did, however, do his best to cover up
his irritation at having to alter his arrangements. On 26 June, he
sent off a note from his rooms at 4 Bennet Street:

> My dearest Augusta – Let me know when you arrive – & when &
> where & how you would like to see me – any where in short – but at
> *dinner* – I have put off going into ye country on purpose to *waylay*
> you –

Augusta had arranged to spend the first day or two of her stay with the Hansons at their house in Bloomsbury Square.* They were not particularly close friends, but she had known them almost as long as she could remember – ever since, as a bewildered four-year-old, she had arrived in London with a very pregnant Catherine Byron and Mrs Hanson had been kind to her. Hanson himself had often acted for her as go-between with her brother and, when Byron was still a schoolboy, had done all he reasonably could to make it possible for them to meet. It shows an unexpected shrewdness in Augusta that she should now turn to the Hansons to be assured of making contact with her brother. Furthermore, no one was in a better position to put her in the picture about Byron's affairs and give her an accurate update on the sale of Newstead.

She arrived in Bloomsbury Square on the evening of Saturday 26 June and immediately sent a note round to Byron. His reply came back at once, leaving her in little doubt as to the sacrifice he was making in order to see her:

> If you knew *whom* I had put off besides my journey – you would think me grown strangely fraternal – However I won't overwhelm you with my *own praises* – Between one & two be it. – I shall in course prefer seeing you all to myself without the encumbrance of third persons . . . P.S. Your writing is grown like my Attorney's – & you gave me a qualm – till I found the remedy in your signature.†

Byron and Augusta had last set eyes on one another when he was still a schoolboy at Harrow. Now he was considered the most dangerously attractive man in London. Of their first meeting 'between one & two' on 27 June, we know nothing, other than that Byron evidently felt sufficiently confident afterwards to ask her to accompany him to a party, in the evening, at Lady Davy's:‡

> There you will see the *Stael* – some people whom you know – & me whom you don't know & you can talk to which you please – & I will watch over you as if you were unmarried & in danger of always being so – Now do as you like – but if you chuse to array yourself before or after half past ten I will call for you – I think our being together before 3rd people will be a new *sensation* to *both*.

* In a letter to Lady Melbourne, Byron says that Augusta stayed at first with 'My old friends the Hs in B-l-y Square . . .' which has been interpreted as alluding to the Harrowbys in B[erke]l[e]y Square. However, the Harrowbys' house was in Grosvenor Square.
† It is probable that Augusta left Hanson to address the envelope.
‡ Wife of Sir Humphrey Davy (1778–1829), inventor of a safety lamp for miners known as the Davy Lamp.

The evening at Lady Davy's must have been a severe challenge to Augusta's reputed shyness. The guest of honour, Germaine de Staël, was considered one of the most brilliant women in Europe. A formidable personality, she dominated any gathering at which she appeared, pontificating on art and literature, politics and morals, even love. Augusta must have been amused and delighted by Byron's refusal to take Madame Staël in the least seriously. He rallied her unmercifully and, never giving her a chance to protest, insisted that her celebrated novels were far too dangerous to be put into the hands of innocent young women.

As for 'watching over' his sister, Byron was as good as his word: always at her side when they were in company, assiduous in his attentions to her, behaving more like her suitor than her brother. None of this escaped the sharp eyes of Annabella Milbanke, who spotted them together at the Glenbervies' one evening:

> His playful and affectionate manner towards her, as they sat together on the sofa, was favourable to both in my opinion: it seemed to prove that *he* had gentler qualities & she had the power of educing them.

On 2 July they went together to an assembly at Almacks, the 'Seventh Heaven of the Fashionable World'.* Admission to these most sought-after and highly exclusive gatherings was by ticket only and was strictly regulated by a committee of seven ladies, all of them leading society figures. On requesting a '*she* voucher' for the occasion from Lady Melbourne, Byron commented wryly and rather ominously on the role Lady Melbourne had played in facilitating Augusta's marriage:

> I wish she were not married for – (now I have no house to keep) she would have been so good a housekeeper. Poor soul – she likes her husband – I think her thanking you for the abetment of her abominable marriage (7 *years* after the event!!) is the only instance of similar gratitude upon record. – However now she is married I trust she will remain so. –

After spending a few days with the Hansons, Augusta moved to the

---

* The chief entertainments at Almacks were the weekly balls which were held throughout the season. Until 1814 the dancing was limited to reels and country dances and refreshments restricted to the mildest of wines and cordials. The strictest etiquette was observed at all times. On one occasion the Duke of Wellington was refused admittance for being incorrectly dressed.

house of her friend Theresa Villiers, in North Audley Street, to be more central. Although most of her time in London was given over to renewing old acquaintances, to visiting relatives and friends, Byron contrived to meet her nearly every day. Part of her uncomplicated appeal for him was that – unlike Caroline Lamb with her passions and tantrums, or Lady Oxford, who was forever trying to manoeuvre him into a more active role in Whig politics – his sister was neither a threat nor a challenge to him. It was an easy and unexacting relationship, in which Byron did not need to adopt a pose or take refuge in brooding melancholy (his so-called 'Wertherism'), as he had with Lady Oxford. Had he attempted to do so, Augusta would have simply laughed him out of it.

'He told me,' Annabella later recalled, 'he only wanted a woman to laugh, *and did not care what she was besides.* The peculiar charm of A.'s society is a refined species of comic talent . . .' One of Augusta's more unexpected talents was her gift for mimicry, and Byron delighted in her irreverent and accurate impersonations, egging her on to do his valet William Fletcher, Lady Melbourne, Madame de Staël, Lord Carlisle and, best of all, the heavily accented English of her grandmother, Lady Holdernesse. On such occasions they were like a pair of naughty children convulsed with giggles at the hilarity of their jokes. 'I can make Augusta laugh at *anything*,' boasted Byron. More to the point, no one could make *him* laugh with greater ease than Augusta could.

But laughter sometimes conceals more than it reveals. What they were actually doing was exploring one another, finding what was common between them and what was different, comparing their likes and dislikes, echoing thoughts, testing opinions, increasingly aware that they were being drawn irresistibly closer by a physical attraction that became more electric as each day carried their discovery of one another a little further. There was a terrible inevitability that such a voyage of discovery would end in their becoming lovers. Exactly how or when that happened, we do not know – only that it did. Nor do we know which one of them was the driving force, although Lady Melbourne most emphatically laid the blame on Augusta, which Byron was quick to deny. 'You are quite mistaken . . . and it must be from some misrepresentation of mine that you throw the blame on the side least deserving. – Pray do not speak so harshly of her to me – the cause of all . . .'

Byron never deviated from his insistence that it was his fault and his alone. Caroline Lamb said that he told her the seduction had not cost him much trouble, but this comment can hardly be relied on. It seems more likely that it was not a matter of seduction but rather a spontaneous happening. 'We fought first and explained afterwards' was a phrase that Byron rather obliquely applied to it. Augusta may have succumbed without a struggle, but she was no helpless victim. She was not, as has been suggested, amoral; nor is there evidence that she had had other lovers before Byron. She was, however, a creature of wholly natural impulse, who approached life with a kind of muddled pragmatism, never paying very much thought to the consequences.

It is unlikely that she gave much thought to her infidelity to George. Adultery was, after all, the name of most people's game then; incest, however, was quite a different matter and one that society did not view with the same leniency. The reality of their situation did not immediately dawn on Augusta, or she chose not to allow it to do so. But the truth was that the two of them had not simply become lovers; they were in love – a love that neither would ever be able entirely to escape, a love that was to change their lives irrevocably and bring Augusta, at least, untold misery and suffering.

The problem was that Byron could not leave it at that; he could not simply accept his love for his sister for what it was. His relentless need to dramatise his life, allied with the Calvinistic outlook that he had inherited from the Gordons, led him to remind himself continually that in making love to Augusta he was committing a deadly sin. For him this added a sense of danger and excitement, a *frisson* of evil, to their passion and gave a new dimension to his role as the Byronic hero, hurling defiance at his creator. 'Great is their love who love in sin and fear,' he wrote in *Heaven and Earth*. He was not content for them both to be merely themselves. In his imagination they became Paolo and Francesca, carried eternally on the warring winds of the inferno, or John Ford's Giovanni and Annabella, showing 'a matchless beauty to the world'.

Incest was one of the major themes of epic and saga, of classic and Jacobean drama, and had become one of the trappings of Romanticism. Chateaubriand had rather gingerly touched on it in *René* and, in *Laon and Cythna*, Shelley's first version of *The Revolt of Islam*, the lovers are brother and sister. For all the undoubted depth of feeling in his love for Augusta, the creative spirit in Byron was stockpiling material for the future.

> ... we were not made
> To torture thus each other, though it were
> The deadliest sin to love as we have loved.

Deadly sin though incest may have been, it was not technically a crime, as both bigamy and homosexuality were, but it comprised, in the eyes of the law, incontestable grounds for divorce and even the most remotely incestuous marriages – affinity was judged equal to consanguinity – were invalid. But in spite of the fact that it meant social ruin, it was far from unknown in Georgian society. The brother of Fanny Burney had run off with his half-sister, and in 1789 there had been a scandal so shocking that even Walpole hardly dared hint at it, though Annabella Milbanke's great-uncle Lord Wentworth had no such qualms in reporting to his sister that 'Lord Bolingbroke is going off with his Sister, Miss Beauclerck, who is in the way to make him at once an Uncle and a father.' (Lord Bolingbroke's abandoned wife was, as it happened, a close friend of Byron's and Augusta's Aunt Sophy.) Napoleon was popularly supposed to have slept with his sisters, and even the children of George III were not above suspicion. In 1829 Thomas Creevey recorded the efforts of Captain Garth to prove that he was the illegitimate son of Princess Sophia by her brother, the Duke of Cumberland. The claim was proved to be false, but the Princess was driven to admit that her brother's conduct towards her had been 'imprudent'.

Byron, who had once taunted Augusta as to whether a woman could keep a secret, was burning to tell someone. He had made no attempt to hide his affair with Caroline Lamb and he had kept Lady Melbourne informed of the progress of his relations with Lady Oxford. So accustomed was she to receiving regular updates on his amours that she grew suspicious at his sudden silence and, although he did not at first rise to her bait, he could not resist the temptation to mention Augusta's name:

> 'I don't tell you anything!' – very good – every body rates me about my confidences with you – Augusta for example writes & the last thing she says – is 'this must not go to Ly M.' – & to punish you it *shant*.

By the third week of July, it was time for Augusta to return home and she could at least justify her long absence to George, for she had achieved what she set out to do. Byron had agreed to help George out of his immediate financial impasse. A month later, on 16 August, Byron gave him £1,000.

Prepared to go to any lengths to delay the moment of parting, Byron escorted Augusta back to Six Mile Bottom, where George was on the verge of leaving for Sussex now that the July Meeting at Newmarket was over. Byron returned to London but, as soon as he could be certain that the coast was clear, made his way back. The house at Six Mile Bottom – unlike London, where prying eyes were inescapable – was ideal for the orchestration of a love affair. The 'bleak common' that Byron had once complained about had after all certain advantages, for there they could be together undisturbed and relatively unobserved.

Byron had long been planning a journey abroad and both destination and travelling companions were subject to frequent alteration. Now a new possibility occurred to him – to leave England taking Augusta with him. It is some measure of Augusta's despair at the state of her marriage, and of her love for Byron, that she seriously considered going along with the idea. She was weary of having to fight all George's battles as well as her own. The weeks she had spent with her brother had brought home to her most forcefully that she craved someone who would look after her. Byron blithely informed Lady Melbourne on 5 August:

> My sister who is going abroad with me is now in town where she returned with me from Newmarket – under the existing circumstances of her lord's embarrassments – she could not well do otherwise – & she appears to have still less reluctance at leaving this country than myself.

Lady Melbourne, frantic to know exactly what was going on, urged Byron to visit her:

> If you have any Secret you wish to confide to me, you may do it Safely, but I shall not plague you to tell me – do what is most pleasant to yourself – I am not given to make professions but so far I will say that you will never find me either deceive or betray you – come and see me if you can . . .

For once Byron did not succumb to the temptation to call on her, but he could not resist a chance to wind her up, tantalising her with hints:

> I should have been glad of your advice how to untie two or three 'Gordion knots' tied round me – I shall cut them without consulting anyone – though some are rather closely twisted round my *heart* (if you will allow me to wear one).

Byron was still looking around for possible additions to his travelling party and, on 12 August, he invited James Wedderburn Webster to join them:

> I am going very soon – & if you would do the same thing – as far as Sicily – I am sure you would not be sorry – my Sister, Mrs L. goes with me – her spouse is obliged to retrench for a few years (but *he* stays at home . . .).

Six days later plans were still not resolved and were complicated by the news that plague was rife in the Mediterranean. Both Byron and his friend Lord Sligo, who had each laid out a great deal of money in preparation for the trip, were anxious to get on their way, but Augusta was now having second thoughts. Reality began to reassert itself. She had been discussing the proposed plan with some of her relatives, who were understandably shocked that she would even contemplate such a step. Gertrude Sloane Stanley, with whom she had talked over the reasons for her flight, was not at all happy: 'It would be a terrible bad plan & it is a sad thing indeed that poverty and distress should make her think of it,' she told her sister-in-law Lady Morpeth, who doubtless passed the alarming news on to Lady Carlisle, who would certainly have made sure that the Duchess of Rutland was in the picture.

By the time all her family had argued the sheer folly of running off to Sicily with her brother, deserting her husband and children, Augusta was visibly wavering. Perhaps it was Mary Chichester who finally convinced her. No one was better placed to point out to Augusta what it was like to be an abandoned child, for Mary had been only two and a half (the same age as Augusta's little ailing Guss) when their mother ran away with Jack Byron.

Now very unsure, Augusta talked it all through again with Byron, telling him that it would be impossible to go away with him without taking at least one of the children with her, a prospect that did not in the least appeal to him, although it seemed to have slipped his mind that he had already agreed to it. On 21 August he wrote rather tetchily to Lady Melbourne:

> She wants to go with me to Sicily or elsewhere – & I wish it also – but the intelligence of the progress of the plague is really too serious – & she would take one of the children – now Lady O[xford] sickened me of, *every body's* children – besides it is so superfluous to carry such things with people – if they want them why can't they get them on the spot? After all I shall probably go alone.

Three days later, the crisis seems to have passed and Lady Gertrude felt able to reassure her mother and sisters:

> I am in great hopes Augusta has changed her mind about going abroad with Lord Byron – in her last letter she says she thinks it will end in her staying at home, which I hope with all my heart will be the case . . .

It is tempting to wonder whether Byron and Augusta would have been worse off had she decided to brave the world's opinion and go away with him.

While Augusta was doing her best to forget what might have been and to resign herself to a life of 'poverty and distress' with her feckless husband, Byron was demonstrating his inability to keep a secret. On 22 August, in a postscript to the Irish poet Thomas Moore, he observed:

> the fact is, I am, at this moment, in a far more serious, and entirely new, scrape than any of the last twelve months, – and that is saying a good deal. *** It is unlucky we can neither live with, nor without these women.

Although, when he published this letter in his life of Byron, Moore denied that there was anything concealed by the asterisks, it seems certain that Byron told him about Augusta and that Moore cut out the offending passage.

Six days later, Byron wrote again to Thomas Moore, and again there is a provocative line of asterisks:

> After all, we must end in marriage; and I can conceive nothing more delightful than such a state in the country, reading the county newspaper, &c, and kissing one's wife's maid. Seriously I would incorporate with any woman of decent demeanour to-morrow – that is, I would a month ago, but, at present, *****

By the time he wrote that letter there had been two significant new developments: Annabella Milbanke had reopened negotiations and he had confessed all to Lady Melbourne.

Flattered though she may have been at having finally extracted this horrifying information from him, Lady Melbourne left him in no doubt as to her opinion: 'If you do not retreat, you are lost for ever – it is a crime for which there is no salvation in this world, whatever there may be in the next . . .' And she spoke of the 'cruelty of depriving of all peace and happiness a woman who has hitherto, whether deservedly or not, maintained a good reputation'. It was an unusually subdued and seemingly contrite Byron who wrote to her on 31 August:

> Your kind letter is unanswerable – no one but yourself would have taken the trouble – no one but me would have been in a situation to require it. – I am still in town so that it has as yet had, all the effect you wish . . .

In other words, he had resisted the temptation to return to Six Mile Bottom.

On the same day that Byron composed this humble and repentant letter he sent off another, in a very different style, to Lady Melbourne's niece, Annabella Milbanke:

> I am too proud of the portion of regard you have bestowed upon me to hazard the loss of it by vain attempts to engage your Affection – I am willing to obey you – and if you will mark out the limits of our future correspondence & intercourse, they shall not be infringed . . .

If this reads rather like an exceptionally prim epistolary novel, it was nothing compared with the enormous letter – a positive three-decker – written to him by Annabella a week earlier, offering to renew their friendship. Although she continued with the pretence that her affections were engaged elsewhere, Annabella uncompromisingly proceeded to stake her claim:

> I have the right of a constant and considerate zeal for your happiness, and the right which you have given and will not reasonably withdraw. I entreat you then to observe more consistently the principles of unwearied benevolence. No longer trust yourself to be the slave of the moment, nor trust your noble impulses to the chances of life. Have an object that will permanently occupy your feelings and exercise your reason. Do good . . .

It is safe to say that Byron had never received anything like this before and he set about replying in the same manner. It was a game that diverted him from dwelling on Augusta, but he was in no doubt as to the kind of person he was dealing with. As he told Lady Melbourne:

> She seems to have been spoiled – not as children usually are – but systematically Clarissa Harlowed* into a narrow kind of correctness – with a dependence upon her own infallibility which will or may lead her into some egregious blunder . . .

Lady Melbourne was still striving to keep him away from Augusta, but by 8 September his resistance had been worn down and he wrote rather shamefacedly: 'I leave town tomorrow for a few days – come what may – and as I am sure you would get the better of my resolution – I shall not venture to encounter you . . .' He lingered in town for another two days, perhaps waiting for George Leigh to depart on his travels again, but the possibility of taking some irrevocable step with Augusta was still greatly in the front of his mind. He wrote again to Lady Melbourne: 'You say "write to me at all events" depend upon it I will – till the moment arrives (if it does arrive) when I feel you ought not to acknowledge me as a correspondent . . .'

On 11 September Byron returned to Six Mile Bottom and seems to have been more determined than ever to persuade Augusta to give up the idea of taking even one of the children away with her, but to make a clean break and commit herself absolutely to him. It was, after all, only what her mother had done with his father. By then, however, Augusta had realised that what he was asking was impossible.

Byron was in no mood to be thwarted. There was a bitter quarrel and he left abruptly for Cambridge and Scrope Davies's rooms at King's, where they 'swallowed six bottles of his burgundy & Claret' in less than three hours. This, not surprisingly, left Scrope Davies unwell and Byron 'rather feverish'.

The letter that he wrote to Augusta on his return to London was humourless and uncompromising. He was about to leave either for Newstead or Aston:

* A reference to the intransigent virtue of the eponymous heroine of Samuel Richardson's novel *Clarissa*.

I have not yet determined – nor does it much matter – as you perhaps care more on the subject than I do – I will tell you when I know myself. – When my departure is arranged – & I can get this long-evaded passage – you will be able to tell me whether I am to expect a visit or not – I can come for or meet you as you think best . . .

The letter was both an ultimatum and a threat. The threat came in the mention of Aston, for this was the home of James Wedderburn Webster and his wife Lady Frances, and Augusta would have been well aware that her brother had already noted the 'conjugal contempt' that the lady had shown for her husband. She knew too that Byron had Lady Frances in his sights as a possible conquest. It was an attempt to make Augusta jealous.

By the time Augusta received his letter she had other concerns: she was pregnant. The widely held belief that Byron was unquestionably the father of her fourth child is based on the chivalrous assumption that Augusta, out of romantic consideration for Byron, would not have let George make love to her; but this was not the case. Augusta did not, as Annabella later put it, suffer from 'moral idiocy from birth', but took life as it came and was generally inclined to settle for the easy way out. She had slept with both Byron and George. She would, in any case, have regarded it as her conjugal duty not to deny herself to George, and to do so would only have provoked an unnecessary scene.

CHAPTER 10

'One Step Will Lead to Another'

Aston Hall in South Yorkshire had once been the property of Augusta's grandfather, Lord Holdernesse, and was only six miles from Eckington, where she had passed her childhood. Byron was not yet aware of her pregnancy and it was possibly in a spirit of petty vengeance that he set out for Aston, taking care to inform Lady Melbourne that one of his purposes was 'to vanquish my demon . . . *transferring* my regards to another'. But his advances towards Frances Webster were, at this stage at least, decidedly lukewarm.

It was impossible for him to banish Augusta from his thoughts: 'I wanted to go elsewhere,' he informed Lady Melbourne. He managed to engineer an invitation for his sister from the Websters to join them in Yorkshire, but to his great annoyance Augusta declined. She had no wish to be with her brother in the company of strangers and face to face with a woman whom she had good reason to believe was a rival, particularly at a time when she was carrying a child that might well be Byron's. She pleaded ill health, which, in view of the way her pregnancies usually went, was probably true.

Byron was piqued. Mistakenly, he was also under the impression that Aston Hall was, as he told Thomas Moore, 'the same house which came to my sire as a residence with Lady Carmarthen (with whom he had adulterated before his majority – by the bye, remember *she* was *not* my mamma) . . .' Perhaps he had hoped that he and Augusta might commemorate the occasion by emulating the example of Amelia and Mad Jack but it was not in fact the same house.*

Augusta's refusal acted as a spur to Byron's hitherto rather half-

* It was the Rectory, and not the Hall, that Lady Holdernesse had persuaded her poetical chaplain William Mason to lend to the couple (and Jack Byron was by then already three years past his majority).

hearted pursuit of Lady Frances and he now proceeded to step up his offensive, recounting his progress in a series of blow-by-blow commentaries* to Lady Melbourne. Lady Frances began to respond beyond Byron's expectations, asking him, during the course of a game of billiards, 'how a woman who liked a man could inform him of it – when he did not perceive it'. In the midst of all this excitement came a forlorn letter from Augusta, who had been made miserable by his failure to write to her and asked if he were angry. He replied:

> I have only time to say that I am not in the least angry – & that my silence has merely arisen from several circumstances which I cannot now detail – I trust you are better – & will continue *best* . . .

Poor pregnant Augusta could no longer treat her brother's amours as lightly as she had once done and would have been in no doubt as to what the 'several circumstances' were. Byron pressed ahead with his campaign and was soon receiving billets-doux from Lady Frances – passed to him under the eyes of the 'Marito', which must have given added spice to the proceedings – the details of which were passed back in bulletins to Lady Melbourne: 'the topography of the house is not the most favourable – I wonder how my father† managed.' Thinking that a change of scene might facilitate matters, Byron invited the whole party over to Newstead. That night Webster drank deeply and at two o'clock in the morning Byron's intended victim mildly informed him that she was entirely at his mercy. Byron, rather to his surprise, 'spared her' – or so he said.

On his return to London on 20 October, still trailing clouds of regret for having been the dupe of his good feelings towards Lady Frances, yet longing to be with Augusta, Byron threw himself into a new Turkish tale, to be called *Zuleika*. It was a tale of incestuous passion and his first attempt to capitalise on his dark but not very well-kept secret. It took him a little over a week to complete it. 'I believe the composition of it kept me alive,' he noted in the journal

---

* Lady Melbourne was only too happy to take on the role of Madame de Merteuil, in the manner of Laclos' *Les Liaisons Dangereuses*.

† Not only had Byron got the wrong house, he had failed to realise that by the time of their sojourn at Aston, Jack and Amelia were married and there would hardly have been any need for them to creep down corridors.

that he had begun to keep, 'for it was written to drive my thoughts from the recollection of – "Dear sacred name, rest ever unreveal'd ..."'* By then, however, he had had second thoughts and his hero and heroine had become cousins:

> ... Oh! never wed another –
> Zuleika! I am not thy brother!

and he had changed the title to *The Bride of Abydos*.

He still had not banished Annabella Milbanke entirely from his mind, nor had she any desire that he should do so. He sent off to her a copy of his new poem and indulged himself in a few complacent reflections about her:

> What an odd situation and friendship is ours! – without one spark of love on either side, and produced by circumstances which in general lead to coldness on one side and aversion on the other. She is a very superior woman, and very little spoiled, which is strange in an heiress ...

Had he only known what thoughts were shaping themselves in Annabella's mind, he would have been less sanguine and far less generous, for she was beginning to fix her sights on nothing less than his salvation: 'It is not the poet – it is the immortal Soul lost or saved.'

Augusta, for all her piety, had no such pretensions to glory, although undoubtedly she would have preferred to see Byron a better Christian. Her thoughts at this time were not of his or her own salvation, but of her overwhelming love for him and the bitter frustration of not being able to be with him. On 29 November she sent him a curl of her hair, tied with white silk and wrapped in a piece of paper on which she had written:

> *Partager tous vos sentiments*
> *ne voir que par vos yeux*
> *n'agir que par vos conseils, ne*
> *vivre que pour vous, voilà mes*
> *voeux, mes projets, & le seul*
> *destin que me peut rendre*
> *heureuse.*†

---

* *Eloisa to Abelard* by Alexander Pope. Byron is misquoting. Pope wrote: 'Dear *fatal* name ...' (our italics).
† To share all your feelings
  to see only through your eyes

Byron kept the lock of hair with its message for the rest of his life, writing on the outside of Augusta's folded paper: 'La Chevelure of the *one* whom I most *loved*', and adding one of their crosses.

He was drifting listlessly, constantly on the point of setting out for Six Mile Bottom, but never managing to bring himself to do it. He could settle at nothing, taking up books and throwing them down again, smoking cigars and writing 'puling, petrifying, stupidly platonic compositions' to Frances Webster. In the middle of December, Augusta, feeling miserable, neglected and exasperated by her brother's inactivity, suddenly arrived in London and told him what she had not been able to put down in her letters: that she was five months pregnant with a child that might well be his.*

Byron immediately cancelled all his engagements to be with Augusta. Excusing himself from a visit to Leigh Hunt,† who had been imprisoned in the Surrey Gaol for libelling the Prince Regent, he told Hunt that she was 'almost ye only friend I possess'.

When she returned to Six Mile Bottom, he went with her and stayed there throughout Christmas.

Frances Shelley and her husband, Sir John,‡ had driven over from Gipping for the Boxing Day shoot and her diary gives one of the very few eye-witness accounts of life at Six Mile Bottom, and of Byron and Augusta together.

> The house is far too small even for the company it contained. Lord Byron was there. Mrs Leigh told me that he spent most of the night writing a poem which is to be called The Corsair. As he did not leave his room until mid-day our intercourse was restricted ... He is decidedly handsome and can be very agreeable. He seems to be easily put out by trifles, and, at times, looks terribly savage. He was very patient with Mrs Leigh's children who are not in the least in awe of him. He bore their distracting incursions into his room with imperturbable good humour. Mrs Leigh has evidently great moral

to act only by your advice, to
live only for you,
these are my
desires,
my schemes, and the only
destiny which can make me
happy.

* Byron noted despondently in his journal: 'December 14, 15, 16. Much done but nothing to record. It is quite enough to set down my thoughts – my actions will rarely bear retrospection.'

† Leigh Hunt (1784–1808), poet, essayist and editor of *The Examiner*.

‡ Sir John Shelley (1772–1852), racehorse owner, sportsman, gambler and friend of the Prince of Wales, distantly related to the poet.

influence over her brother, who listens to her occasional admonitions with a sort of playful acquiescence. But I doubt the permanence of their effect upon his wayward nature. Her manner towards him is decidedly maternal; it is as though she were reproving a thoughtless child. She looks very much older than her brother and does not make the most of herself. She is dowdy in dress, and seems to be quite indifferent to personal appearances.

The fact that Augusta was pregnant seems to have escaped her notice.

Byron did not stay long, for he was back in London on 27 December and working at a great pace to finish his poem. Believing that the sale of Newstead would soon be completed, he had persuaded Augusta (without, one imagines, very much difficulty) to spend a few days with him at the Abbey, while it was still his own. The sale would enable him, he told her, 'to do something further for *yours & you*'. First, however, he needed some indication of how much George owed.

> I shall be able to make some arrangement – for *him* – but at all events you & the children shall be properly taken care of – what I did for *him* might be *seized* &c. anything done for yourself would be safer & more advantageous to both.

And with the prospect of his brother-in-law stepping in to clear his debts George could hardly raise any objection to the Newstead trip.

Awaiting Byron in London was a reminder of the most painful episode of his youth, a letter from the 'Starlight of his Boyhood', Mary Chaworth, now Mary Musters:

> My dearest Lord,
>   If you are coming into Notts, call at Edwalton nr Nottingham where you will find a very old and sincere friend anxious to see you.

Mary's marriage to Jack Musters, for whose sake she had spurned the schoolboy Byron's passionate declarations of love, had gone badly wrong. She had been steadily broken down by her husband's persistent infidelities and the revelation that he had fathered an illegitimate child had finally driven her to leave him.

Byron was flattered and intrigued, and not in the least concerned about admitting yet another complication into his life, but Augusta had other ideas. She knew Byron all too well and, with the chance of passing a few days alone with him at Newstead, had no intention of sharing him with Mary Musters. 'For,' she said, 'if you go, you will fall in love again, and then there will be a scene; one step will lead to another, *et cela fera un éclat.*'

Mary Musters remained unconsoled, but she did at least provide Byron with a smoke-screen. 'A very old & early connection or rather friend of mine has desired to see me,' he informed Webster, 'as now we never can be more than friends I have no objection.'

The person whom he really hoped to deceive was Lady Melbourne, who, despite all Byron's protestations to the contrary, continued to hold Augusta responsible for what had happened and what, she suspected, was continuing to happen. Byron did his best to defend his sister but failed to make a very convincing job of it:

> . . . it must be from some misrepresentation of mine that you throw the blame so completely on the side least deserving and least able to bear it – I dare say I made the best of my own story as one always does from natural selfishness without intending it – but it was not her fault – but my own *folly* (give it whatever name may suit it better) and her weakness . . .

Augusta came up to London in the middle of January 1814, with leave of her 'lord and president', and stayed with Mrs Villiers. The weather was so bad that it was several days before the lovers could set out for the North. The snow held off long enough for them to reach Newstead, but once they were installed it fell so heavily and so continually that they were soon cut off from the outside world. On 22 January, his birthday, Byron wrote contentedly to John Murray:

> The roads are impassable – and return impossible – for ye present – which I do not regret as I am much at my ease and *six* and *twenty* complete this day – a very pretty age if it would always last. – Our coals are excellent – our fire places large – my cellar full – and my head empty – and I have not yet recovered my joy at leaving London – if any unexpected turn occurred with my publisher – I believe I should hardly quit the place – but shut my doors & let my beard grow.

For Byron and Augusta – alone, apart from the servants, in the 'Huge Halls, long galleries, spacious chambers' of their forebears – the whole adventure became a chance to create for themselves a kind of fantasy childhood: the childhood that had never been theirs to share, endlessly exploring, telling stories, summoning up ghosts out of the dark shadows. At the same time it became a honeymoon.

Byron even felt sufficiently defiant to inform Lady Melbourne that his sister was with him in:

> this Lapland ... which renders it much more pleasant – as we neither yawn nor disagree – and laugh much more than is suitable to so solid a mansion – and the family shyness makes us much more amusing companions to each other – than we could be to anyone else.

For Augusta, the first sight of Newstead had been a revelation and her arrival there a homecoming. The great houses in which she had spent her childhood were known and familiar, but the west front of the ruined Abbey, with its vast, empty, ivy-clad window and the pitted, ruinous walls of the house itself, awoke feelings that she had never experienced at Kiveton or Castle Howard. For all her cautious Georgian upbringing, Augusta was instinctively a romantic and Newstead was for her the embodiment of her colourful and lawless Byron ancestors. From the moment she entered its walls she felt herself 'a child of the place', and she always referred to it afterwards as 'our dear old Abbey'. 'Mrs Leigh is with me,' Byron told Murray, 'much pleased with the place – & less so with me for parting with it – to which not even the price can reconcile her.' Augusta would always remain fiercely opposed to the sale of Newstead and once said that, rather than have let it go, she would have wished that she and her brother had been buried beneath its ruins.

By the end of January the roads were still blocked with snow and the Trent was frozen so hard that fires were lit on it. 'From this place there is no stirring till the weather is better,' Byron told Hanson. 'Mrs Leigh is with me & being in ye family way – renders it doubly necessary to remain till the roads are quite safe.' Poor Mary Musters, the ostensible reason for his journey to Newstead, remained unvisited. In a letter to Lady Melbourne designed to conceal Augusta's opposition to his meeting Mary, he wrote:

> You will very probably say that I ought to have gone over at all events – & Augusta has also been trying her rhetoric to the same purpose & urging me repeatedly to call before I left the County – but I have been one day too busy – & another too lazy ...

But the snowstorms died down and the roads became passable enough for Claughton, still attempting to negotiate the sale of

Newstead, to reach the Abbey. There were now no excuses for not returning to the outside world.

By the time Byron and Augusta were ready to set out, the unfortunate Mary Musters had been struck down with erysipelas, which provided them with yet another excuse for not seeing her. On 6 February, braving the river Trent, swollen by the thaw, they arrived at Newark. The following night, intent on prolonging their idyll until the last moment they stayed at the Haycock Inn, near Wansford, one of Byron's favourite staging posts. From there they reluctantly went their separate ways, Byron to London and Augusta back to Six Mile Bottom.

She tried to resign herself to taking up life at home where she had left it, but George had never seemed more inadequate nor the house more confined. Newstead she now felt to be her spiritual home and she was horrified by the thought that, in a few weeks' time, it would be lost to the Byrons for ever. The sale of Newstead would mean that her brother would be in a position to ease their more immediate money problems and relieve George of a few of his debts, but this seemed a very inadequate compensation for the sacrifice of what was not only the home of her ancestors, but had also become her emotional centre.

From Byron she heard very little, although she heard a great deal about him. *The Corsair* had caused a sensation and 10,000 copies were sold in the first day. The poem that he had instructed Murray to bind in with it, 'Lines to a Lady Weeping', had resulted in a sensation of a very different kind. It was an overt political attack on the Prince Regent, and the press were in uproar.* To add fuel to the flames, one paper had reprinted his attack on Carlisle from *English Bards and Scotch Reviewers* and the Earl was said to be very angry indeed. As the 'clash of paragraphs and conflict of Newspapers' raged on, Byron told Lady Melbourne that he was astonished that at a time when peace and war in Europe were trembling in the balance, the pro-government press should devote half its columns, day after day, to '8 lines written two years ago'.

Lady Melbourne was more interested in keeping up the attack on Augusta. Since his return from Newstead, Byron seemed to have

---

* *The Corsair* went to seven editions in a little over a month. Hobhouse said that 'the abuse showered upon Byron for "Lines to a Lady Weeping" helped it along'.

been deliberately avoiding Melbourne House. Had his sister forbidden him to call on her? Byron replied that this was very far from the case, but he admitted, for the first and the only time, the power that Augusta now had over him:

> She seemed more assured (and not very pleased) of your influence than of any other – but – I suppose being pretty certain of her own power – always said 'do as you please – & go where you like . . .'

Away from Augusta, Byron had fallen back into restless melancholy. He wrote letters and tore them up, tried to keep her out of his mind by reading Hobhouse's anecdotes about Napoleon's curious sexual predilections, went to see Edmund Kean playing Richard III, but he ground his teeth in his sleep – and sleep did not come very often. He sat down to commit his feelings about Augusta to paper, but the following morning destroyed what he had written.

In the first week of April, when her confinement was barely two weeks away, Augusta summoned him to Six Mile Bottom. George had gone off to Yorkshire and this would be their last chance to be together before the baby was born. Byron stayed for almost a week but the only memorable thing that he recorded about his stay was that he:

> . . . swallowed the D—l in ye shape of a collar of brawn one evening for supper (after an enormous dinner too) and it required all kinds of brandies and I don't know what besides to put me again in health and good humour.

At King's College, Cambridge, Hobhouse and Scrope Davies had been looking forward to a merry evening with him, but Byron had overstayed his time and returned to London 'alone and not over pleased at being so'.

Augusta too was alone, awaiting the arrival of her fourth child without either of the men who might have been the father to support her.

CHAPTER 11

Elizabeth Medora

On 15 April 1814, Augusta gave birth to a baby girl. The child was christened by the Reverend Charles Wedge at Six Mile Bottom on 20 May and given the names Elizabeth Medora. Her sponsors were the Duchess of Rutland, Mrs Robert Wilmot* and Byron himself.

Elizabeth was the name of the Duchess of Rutland, but Medora, as everyone was quick to point out, was one of the two heroines of *The Corsair*, a fact that would seem to link her very positively with Byron. But it was not as simple as that, for Medora was also the name of one of the Duke of Rutland's most successful racehorses, and the reference would certainly have appealed to George Leigh and to the Duke. It looks very much as if Augusta (and perhaps Byron) was indulging a private joke.

However much Byron may have wished to believe that the child was his, he must have known that this was no foregone conclusion. His first reaction seems to have been to make yet another attempt to persuade Augusta to go away with him, an impulse that Lady Melbourne, writing to him on 25 April, was determined to do her best to forestall:

> I wish I could flatter myself I had the least influence . . . for I could talk and reason with you for two hours, so many objections have I to urge, and after all, for what ~~for the sake of Augusta~~ [crossed out] is it worth while! And to involve – – indeed, indeed, if I had powers of persuasion on this Subject, and could use them with effect you should fall down and adore me.

Byron replied on the same day:

> Oh! but it is 'worth while' – I can't tell you why – and it is *not* an 'Ape' and if it is – that must be my fault – however I will positively reform – you must however allow – that it is utterly impossible I can

---

* The wife of Byron's and Augusta's first cousin and the inspiration for his poem 'She walks in beauty like the night'.

ever be half as well liked elsewhere – and I have been all my life trying to make some one love me – & never got the sort that I preferred before – But positively she & I will grow good – & all that – & so we are *now* and shall be these next three weeks & more too . . .

Apart from being one of his open professions of his love for Augusta, this letter raises more questions than it solves. The 'Ape' is a reference to the superstition that the child of an incestuous love would be born a monster, but is Byron saying that the child is his or not? Or is he simply confirming that it is impossible to tell? Perhaps the clue to the whole conundrum lies in his subsequent behaviour towards Medora, for, despite comments by Hobhouse and others that she was Byron's favourite niece, he always showed far more interest in Augusta's eldest daughter, Georgiana, of whom he was particularly fond. Compared with the concern that he showed for the girls who certainly were his daughters (Ada Byron and Claire Clairmont's child Allegra), he showed very little interest in Medora, who was just two when he left England. He never wrote to her and never even possessed a portrait.

Medora's birth had confronted the lovers with the very real danger of their situation. Since Augusta continued to hold out against the idea of defying the world and going off abroad to live together, they could not reasonably hope to keep their affair going indefinitely, but they were neither of them as yet ready to face up to the implications of this.

'I believe that to marry would be my wisest step,' he had told Lady Melbourne at the beginning of the year, 'but whom?'

The only woman who continued to intrigue him was Annabella Milbanke, partly because she was the niece of Lady Melbourne:

> One of my great inducements to that brilliant negociation with the Princess of Parallelograms was the vision of our *family party* – & the quantity of domestic lectures I should faithfully detail with our mutual comments thereupon.

The previous year, Annabella, bored with life in Seaham and increasingly troubled with misgivings over her rejection of Byron's proposal, had made an attempt to throw her cap back into the ring. Her great difficulty was that she did not know how to account to Byron for the fact that she had lied to him, in leading him to believe that her affections were given elsewhere and that she was still involved with George Eden.* Annabella always made a great virtue out of her truthfulness. She was not prepared to admit that she had misled him, but she realised that some sort of explanation was needed before she could announce her availability, and she took refuge behind a fog of words:

> You have understood *me* at least as well as I understood myself. Both may have been partly deceived, though unwittingly by me; but I have found that Wisdom (often the most difficult Wisdom, Self-Knowledge) is not less necessary than Will, for an absolute adherence to Veracity. How I may in a degree have forsaken *that* – and under an ardent zeal for Sincerity – is an explanation that cannot benefit either of us . . .

Not surprisingly, Byron had been baffled by this and had asked her what she meant. Annabella was still not willing to admit that there had been no rival for her affections, and that Byron had been the only man in her thoughts for some time, but she ventured a little further into the open.

By now aware of exactly what she was up to, Byron entered into the game and provocatively increased the stakes: 'I was told yesterday that you had refused me "a second time" so that you see I am supposed to be the most permanent of your plagues – & persevering of Suitors . . .'

To this Annabella had replied at length. She discoursed on Man and the Supreme Being, and on the Woman of Samaria and self-despair, and eventually came round to the point:

> As for the report, it is absurd enough to excite a smile – false in *name* as well as *number*. In avoiding the possibility of being in a situation to refuse, I *cannot consider myself as having refused.*

This was every bit as provocative as Byron's letter to her and, for Annabella, surprisingly pert. Byron noted in his journal on 15 March: 'A letter from *Bella* which I answered. I shall be in love with her again, if I don't take care.'

But after that there had been no further progress. Annabella had been advised by her doctors that she should not travel to London. Byron's thoughts were beginning to drift in the direction of Lady Charlotte Leveson Gower, whom he had glimpsed at a party at Lansdowne House: '. . . there is that shyness of the antelope (which

---

* George Eden (1784–1849), 2nd Baron Auckland, Governor-General of India 1836–1841. Having been rejected by Annabella in 1811, he never married.

I delight in) in her manner . . . She is a friend of Augusta's and what she loves I can't help liking.'

There was one great difficulty standing in the way of approaching Lady Charlotte: her aunt was the wife of Lord Carlisle and Byron's relationship with his former guardian was at an all-time low. Augusta, reluctantly following in the wake of her brother's matrimonial quest, suggested that he should make an effort to patch things up with Carlisle, preferably through a disinterested intermediary. The person chosen for this ticklish task was their first cousin Julia Byron's son, Robert Wilmot, an aspiring politician with a positive passion for interfering in the affairs of others. Early in April, Wilmot sent off a letter to Carlisle, attempting to prepare the way for reconciliation:

> Had I no other motive perhaps I might have been induced by the satisfaction which its accomplishment would afford Mrs Leigh who feels, and has just cause to feel, every sentiment of regard & gratitude to yourself and your family.

The Earl refused to be drawn.

Two days before Augusta gave birth to Medora, Annabella had decided that it was time to renew the pressure on Byron. She wrote to him that her parents, Sir Ralph and Lady Milbanke, would have 'the most sincere pleasure' in seeing him as their guest. She was, however, not at all happy about news of this reaching the ears of her aunt, Lady Melbourne.

Byron, too, was apprehensive about Lady Melbourne's reaction, but for very different reasons. Knowing what she did about his affair with Augusta, would Lady Melbourne forbid him to visit her niece? He need not have worried. She may have considered Annabella and Byron to be singularly ill-matched, but she was not going to stand in the way of anything that might undermine Augusta's corrupting influence. Byron had been passing on to her his sister's letters and she was more certain than ever that it was Augusta who was the guilty party: '. . . is not the tempter most to be blamed? And have I not seen in black and white – "I was so provoked because I could not make you love me" or something like that . . .'

Byron was well aware that by passing on Augusta's love letters he was guilty of an act of betrayal, yet his need to confide in Lady Melbourne was almost pathological: 'you must always know everything concerning me,' he told her. At the same time, having exposed his sister to attack, he did his best to mount a rather half-hearted defence of her, which did her an even worse disservice:

> *she* was not to blame – one thousandth part in comparison – she was not aware of her own peril – till it was too late – and I can only account for her subsequent 'abandon' by an observation which I think is not unjust – that women are much more *attached* than men – if they are treated with anything like fairness or tenderness.

He was, at the same time, beginning to show unmistakable signs of jealousy and resentment of George Leigh: 'it is true she married a fool – but she *would* have him – they agreed – and agree very well – and I never heard a complaint but many vindications of him'.

The deposit on the sale of Newstead had at last been paid, but George was now showing unexpected scruples in his apparent reluctance to accept a loan of £3,000 from his brother-in-law. An exasperated Byron wrote to Augusta:

> . . . for Godsake let me have the satisfaction of at least relieving you from the most worrying and pressing of petty vexations – if the Prince should *come* forward at last or the General *go* – he can then repay me or not as he likes – I am sure I don't care . . . if any accident happened to G. – you know my dearest A. – that as your *father's* son – I am more deeply interested than your *Mamma*['s] brothers can be.

It was not, of course, a matter of the Regent coming forward but of George approaching him, which he was still obstinately refusing to do. As for General Leigh, there was no sign of him 'going' and whether he had anything to leave his only son was something of a mystery.

Byron's half-hearted matrimonial designs were doing nothing to take his mind off Augusta. When Thomas Moore asked him to write some lines that could be set to music, Byron sent him a poem on 4 May, 'which has cost me something more than trouble', and which was clearly inspired by the joys and frustrations of their love affair:

> 'Too brief for our passion, too long for our peace,
> Were those hours – can their joy or their bitterness cease?
> We repent, we abjure, we will break from our chain, –

We will part, we will fly to – unite it again!'*

When he began *Lara*, intended as a sequel to *The Corsair*, which he wrote 'while undressing after coming home from balls and masquerades', it was Augusta who dominated his thoughts, and not the feudal chieftain of his poem:

'When thou art gone – the loved, the lost – the one
Whose smile hath gladdened though perchance undone –
Whose name too dearly cherished to impart
Dies on the lip but trembles on the heart . . .'†

That June saw the beginning of what came to be known as the 'Summer of the Sovereigns', weeks of frenzied celebration following the downfall of Napoleon and his exile to Elba. Byron still had hopes that 'my little Pagod [i.e. Napoleon] will play them some tricks still', but London was determined to enjoy itself and roaring crowds dragged Marshal Blücher's carriage through Horse Guards Parade and greeted the Tsar and his sister with hysterical huzzahs.

Every night there were balls and masquerades. At Lord Grey's, Byron was at last introduced to the woman whom Augusta would have preferred him to marry, Lady Charlotte Leveson Gower. They found themselves together in the middle of a large, empty room. Byron was overtaken by a severe attack of the family shyness and blushed and stammered, while the equally bashful Lady Charlotte did her best to begin a conversation on the only possible topic of conversation between them – Augusta – which Byron nervously took up: 'I uttered your respectable name and prattled I know not what syllables and so on for about 3 minutes – and then how we parted I know not.' Their meeting could hardly be judged a success, but Byron was now of the opinion that Lady Charlotte was pretty.

Annabella Milbanke was still languishing in Seaham. Byron had made no attempt to take up her parents' invitation and her long letters to him had gone unanswered. She was, she told him, made uneasy by his silence.

Meanwhile Caroline Lamb had taken to appearing in his rooms at Albany, defying the regulations – it was an exclusively male preserve – and outwitting the doorman‡ who was there to enforce them. He protested, rather feebly, to Lady Melbourne:

* Stanzas for Music – 'I speak not, I trace not, I breathe not thy name'.
† These lines were removed from the published edition.
‡ She generally disguised herself as a page.

You talked to me – about keeping her out – it is impossible, she comes in at all times – at any time – and the moment the door is open in she walks – I can't throw her out of the window . . .

In fact, since Byron's rooms were on the ground floor, he could perfectly well have done so. Instead, since he could never resist telling a secret, he was soon dropping dark hints to Caroline, and rather more than hints about the truth of his relationship with his sister, 'he showed me letters, and told me things I cannot repeat and all my attachment went . . .' Although nothing that Caroline Lamb said or wrote can generally be relied upon, in this instance she was speaking no less than the truth.

Towards the end of June, Augusta sent Byron word that George would be away from home and on 3 July Byron set out for Six Mile Bottom. This was his first sight of Medora. He remained for only four days, but during that time they made plans to spend a seaside holiday together. Byron then went on to Cambridge for a drunken evening with Hobhouse and their old friend Douglas Kinnaird in Scrope Davies's rooms at King's, which left them 'a little head-achy with free living as it is called'. Outside, Cambridge was noisily celebrating the Treaty of Paris. The town was illuminated with 'transparencies and devices', there was a ball at the Town Hall attended by 'nearly all the fashionable in the university and town' and a dinner of cold roast beef and plum pudding at Parker's Piece for 'all the inhabitants who chose to partake of it', concluding with sports on Midsummer Green, which included a 'Royal Pig Hunt with a soaped tail'.

Byron decided on Hastings as the place where he and Augusta would spend their holiday and the arrangements were handed over to his old Cambridge friend Francis Hodgson. Seven years older than Byron, Hodgson was a poet and translator and, like Scrope Davies, a fellow of King's College. In his youth he had enjoyed rather a rakish reputation, but he had put all that behind him and in 1812 had taken Holy Orders. He had even once made a quixotic and wholly unsuccessful attempt to convert Byron to orthodox Christianity. Now he was staying in Hastings so that he could be near his fiancée, whom he hoped (with the help of a financial rescue package from Byron) soon to marry.

Augusta was proposing to bring with her all four children accompanied by three maids, so the house, Byron told Hodgson, had to be 'tolerably large': 'let my bedroom be some way from the

127

Nursery or children's apartments – and let the women be near together – and as far from me as possible . . .'

Augusta came up to London in the middle of July and stayed at the London Hotel in Albemarle Street, close to John Murray's premises. However, Byron was forced to delay their departure, since Claughton was once again dragging his feet over the purchase of Newstead. Then he heard that Mary Chaworth Musters had arrived in London determined to see him, which was enough to send him off immediately down the road to Hastings with Augusta, the children and Captain George Anson Byron, his cousin and heir presumptive, who had now joined the family party. Poor Mary, hearing that Byron had fled from London leaving no word for her, broke down completely and burned all his letters.

Hastings House, which Hodgson had leased for them, was on East Hill, looking down over the old town. Its gardens led on to the Rock-a-Nore cliffs, where Byron and Augusta went for walks and where he 'hobbled' up and 'tumbled' down the hills with five-year-old Georgiana, running races and making light of his lameness.

Byron had promised Hodgson that he would 'like Augusta much – she is as shy as an antelope – but the best hearted gentle inoffensive being in the world'. Augusta took to Hodgson immediately (which was not often the case with her brother's friends); she was won over by his directness and sincerity and by his religious faith. It was the beginning of a warm friendship, which was to last for the rest of their lives.

Byron had chosen Hastings because of the sea-bathing. There was the added advantage that he knew no one there and the town was not much frequented by society. He described their three-week holiday as 'dolce niente', although on one occasion he 'got into a passion with an ink bottle' and flung it out of his window, where, to his dismay, it broke over a statue of Euterpe, the muse of lyric poetry. There were more serious matters than besmattered muses to trouble them. The marriage question would not leave them in peace. Just before he left London, Byron received letters from Annabella and her father renewing the invitation to visit Seaham, although Annabella made a point of telling him not to come unless he were in earnest.

The decision could not be postponed indefinitely. It was imperative for Byron to find an heiress and Augusta's conscience was beginning to trouble her. For over a year her love for Byron had dominated her thoughts and emotions. As she had promised, she had been guided only by him and lived only for him. But she could not keep her religious scruples at bay forever.

Augusta's was an infinitely compassionate God; both incest and adultery would be forgiven, she was sure, perhaps because, like Mary Magdalen, she had 'loved much'. But she also knew that the time was coming when, in the words of the New Testament with which she was so familiar, it would be required of her to 'go and sin no more.'

'She wished me much to marry,' Byron told Lady Melbourne, 'because it was the only chance of redemption for *two* persons . . .' There were endless discussions in Hastings about whether Byron ought to renew his proposal to Annabella. Augusta was not at all in favour. In her view, it was essential that her brother's wife should be someone whom she knew and liked. With that thought, she wrote to Charlotte Leveson Gower to suggest a meeting take place as soon as possible.

On 9 August the holiday came to an end and Byron and Augusta returned to London, deftly avoiding the arrival in Hastings of the distraught Mary Chaworth Musters, who had come there in pursuit and, finding them gone, moved into the house they had just vacated. She wrote to Byron, not without a touch of acidity: 'I very much fear we hastened your and Mrs Leigh's departure . . .'

Awaiting Byron's return was a letter from Annabella that seemed designed to raise the temperature of their correspondence: 'My doubt then is – and I ask a solution: Whether you are in *any* danger of that attachment to me which might interfere with your peace of mind?'

Despite the fact that Augusta's negotiations with Charlotte Leveson Gower were still proceeding, Byron chose to see what would happen if he increased the temperature still further:

> I did – do – and always shall love you – and as this feeling is not exactly an act of will – I know of no remedy and at all events should never find one in the sacrifice of your comfort.

He was testing her, still playing a game of words to discover how she would respond, but he was not prepared for her frigid reply. She informed him that she considered that their characters were ill adapted to each other: 'you do not appear to be the person whom *I* ought to select as my guide, my support, my example on earth, with a view still to Immortality . . .'

Annabella was, of course, correct. His wild romantic spirit and her rigid piety and intellectual pretension were completely at odds. If only they had left it at that, Annabella and Byron and, even more so, Augusta would have been spared years of misery.

By the third week of August it had become clear that there was little hope of Claughton ever completing his purchase of Newstead, and Augusta persuaded her brother to take her and the children to the Abbey, for what she suspected might be their last stay there. At Newstead the lovers soon fell back into their accustomed lazy, laughing way of life. Augusta roamed through the halls of her ancestors or walked in the woods and played with the children, while Byron whiled away the time 'fishing, shooting, bathing and boating', reading books he had devoured many times over and exploding soda-water bottles with his pistol.

He had informed Annabella that there was no longer any chance that he would be able to take up Sir Ralph's invitation to Seaham that year. Her parents were considerably put out by this and Annabella, who had regretted her crushing letter to Byron almost as soon as she had posted it, was miserable and contrite. If only they could have met, 'all my apparent inconsistencies would have been dispelled' and she begged him to write to her. He sent her a cool and formal letter of reply, but Annabella had done exactly what he had hoped and put herself back into the running.

Her rival was soon to be decisively out of it. Augusta had shown more enthusiasm than common sense in her pursuit of Charlotte Leveson Gower, ignoring the fact that the sticking point in any negotiation was the Earl of Carlisle. Wilmot, with his fussy, opinionated manner, had failed to bring about a reconciliation between the Earl and his cousin, and what was needed was for Augusta herself to try her powers of persuasion on the old man. Instead, she arranged a meeting in London with Charlotte and flustered the bewildered girl into allowing Byron to make an approach to her. But no sooner was she out of Augusta's orbit than Charlotte began to have second thoughts. She was terrified of incurring her uncle's displeasure and, seized with a wild panic, pleaded a 'contract elsewhere'. Convinced that Augusta had thoroughly mismanaged the whole business, Byron decided, as he told Lady Melbourne, 'to try the next myself' and to make another, more positive approach to Annabella. It is difficult to understand why he did not stand back and give himself a chance to consider alternative candidates. He needed a rich wife but there were ladies in the field other than Charlotte Leveson Gower and Annabella Milbanke who were much better suited to him and possessed of far larger fortunes. What blinded him to all else, and sharpened his determination to make Annabella accept him, was the fact that she had at first refused him and then chosen to pour icy water over his professions of love.

Augusta was well aware that Annabella had become something of an obsession and did everything that she could to dissuade Byron. She argued that Annabella had no immediate fortune and that, in the present state of his affairs, it would be folly to marry a woman who would bring him no money. She also reminded him how much he detested 'learned women'. Byron had shown some of Annabella's letters to her and Augusta could not make hear or tail of them. Admittedly, her attitude was not entirely disinterested. Recent events had shown all too clearly how dependent she and George had become on her brother. It would hardly benefit them if Byron were to marry a tiresome blue-stocking with virtually no money of her own, whatever her future expectations might be.

What finally seems to have swung the balance in Annabella's favour was the arrival of Aunt Sophy, who, like her niece and nephew, wanted to spend a few days at Newstead while it was still in the hands of the family. Once more the necessity of Byron's marriage was talked through and Sophy, to whom Sir Ralph Milbanke had been 'an early and old requaintance', came out strongly in favour of Annabella. She had heard very good reports of her and thought that she would make Byron an excellent wife. Byron needed no further encouragement and on 9 September drafted a cleverly contrived letter, which would enable Annabella to extricate herself gracefully from all her lies and evasions:

A few weeks ago you asked me a question – which I answered – I have now one to propose – to which if improper – I need not add that your declining to reply to it will be sufficient reproof. – It is this – Are the 'objections' – to which you alluded – insuperable? – or is there any line or change of conduct which could possibly remove them? – . . . When I believed you attached – I had nothing to urge – indeed I have little now – except that having heard from yourself

that your affections are not engaged – my importunities may appear
not quite so selfish however unsuccessful.

It was hardly a letter to sweep a girl off her feet, but it was a well-
judged climax to the game of words they had been playing since
February.

Augusta read the draft and for the final time tried to persuade
him that Annabella was not the right wife for him. Byron put the
letter away in his desk. But when the time for the post arrived, he
took it out again. Once more Augusta looked it through. She said,
'It is a very well written letter,' and on that Byron rang the bell,
sealed the letter in haste and sent it off 'as if anxious to deprive
himself of the power of retracting'.

From the tone of Byron's letter it would not have been easy to
judge whether it was an offer of marriage or merely a cautious
exploration leading up to one, but there was no doubt in
Annabella's mind that it was a proposal and she wrote back to him
a few hours after she had received it:

> It would be absurd to suppress anything – I am and have long been
> pledged to myself to make your happiness my first object in life. *If I
> can* make you happy, I have no other consideration. I will *trust* to
> you for all I should live up to – all I can love . . .

The arrival of her letter at Newstead was preceded by all manner of
alarms and portents that might have come out of a tale of terror by
Mrs Radcliffe. The previous night in his dressing room Byron had
seen the ghost of the Black Monk, the traditional warning that ill
fortune was about to fall upon a member of the family. That
afternoon a gardener at Newstead had come across Catherine
Byron's wedding ring, which had been lost since her death. When
Annabella's reply was brought in, Byron, who was sitting at dinner
with Augusta and the local doctor, said, 'If it contains a consent, I
will be married with that ring.' He read Annabella's letter and
handed it over the table to Augusta, 'looking so pale that she
thought he was going to faint away', and remarked, 'It never rains
but it pours.'

Byron and Augusta lingered at Newstead until 20 September,
knowing that it was unlikely that they would ever be there together
again, and certainly never as lovers. In the Devil's Wood, where the
Wicked Lord had set up his statues of a malignant male and female
satyr, there were two elm trees that had grown into one another and

which Byron had named after himself and his sister. On one of them he carved their names: 'Byron and Augusta'.

CHAPTER 12

'One Whom I Hope Soon to Call My Sister'

Augusta had been away from Six Mile Bottom for the best part of two months and for most of that time she had been continually in Byron's company. Now, in the last week of September 1814, she was having to come to terms with the prospect of a future without him, or at least one in which she would no longer play the central part.

Fortunately for Augusta, she was not much given to gloomy introspection. Resolutely she determined to turn her back on the past. She brushed aside all her doubts about Annabella and threw herself behind the marriage. She had always trusted in providence and now she strove to convince herself that what had happened would turn out to be for the best.

Annabella and her parents had fully expected that her betrothed would set off immediately for Seaham, to be welcomed into the Milbanke family and to receive their blessing, but as the days passed and Byron showed no sign of leaving London they began to grow increasingly uneasy. The arrival of Lord Wentworth,* the senior member of the family, to give his approval to the match served only to increase the tension and embarrassment.

Lady Melbourne was convinced that it was Augusta who was holding Byron back. '[Augusta] never threw any obstacles in the way,' he protested, 'on the contrary she has been more urgent than even you that I should go to S[eaham].' The real reason for the delay was that Byron was attempting to put his financial affairs in order before discussing details of the marriage settlement with Sir Ralph Milbanke. Byron had rather grandly committed himself to putting up £60,000, which would involve finally selling Newstead or the Rochdale estates, or both, but nothing could be set in motion without the services of John Hanson. Dilatory at the best of times,

---

* Thomas Noel, 2nd Viscount Wentworth (1745–1845), Judith Milbanke's brother.

Hanson was now entirely immersed in the troubles he had brought down upon himself by marrying his daughter off to the feeble-minded Earl of Portsmouth, whose relatives were demanding that the union should be annulled and were accusing Hanson and his daughter of foul play.

Byron had begun by writing every day to his intended bride but, as his vexations over Hanson's inactivity increased, he was beginning to go off the boil. He turned to Augusta as the one person whom he could trust to make his excuses and explain the difficulty in which he found himself. Augusta, who had been uncertain what role, if any, she was to play in her brother's new life, made the most of the opportunity and wrote to Annabella on 1 October:

> I am afraid I have no better excuse to offer for this *self introduction* than that of feeling unable any longer to reconcile myself to the idea of being *quite* a *stranger* to one whom I hope *soon* to call my *Sister*, and one – may I be allowed to add – whom I already love as such. If I could possibly express how deservedly dear my brother is to me, you might in some degree imagine the joy I have felt in the anticipation of an event which promises to secure his happiness . . . I have been most anxious to write to you for the last fortnight, but delayed it from day to day in the hope that my Brother would be at Seaham to *chaperone* the arrival of my letter and make excuses for the writer who is but too sensible of her inability to express her feelings on this occasion. But on finding he is still provokingly detained in Town by business, and unable to fix a day for his departure, I have resolved not to wait any longer, and trust entirely to your indulgence for forgiveness.

Annabella appears to have been rather nonplussed by Augusta's nervous charm. She asked Byron whether his sister were not shy. She is 'like a frightened hare with new acquaintances', he told her; 'she is the least selfish and gentlest creature in being – and more attached to me than anyone in existence can be' – which was certainly true. 'She was particularly desirous that I should marry,' he continued and only regretted, '– what I must regret a little too – that she had not earlier the pleasure of your acquaintance'.*

At Newmarket, George Leigh and his confederates had set up a book and were taking bets on whether the marriage would ever

---

* Neither Augusta nor Annabella ever seems to have realised that there already existed a tie between their two families, since Lady Holdernesse's friend and financial and legal adviser, the late John Milbanke (who had been one of the trustees of her will with its particular provisions for Augusta), was, in fact, Annabella's great-uncle.

happen. George, with his vested interest in Byron's attachment to his wife, was far from enthusiastic at the prospect of the coming marriage. When he happened to run across his brother-in-law in London, he strongly urged Byron 'to be in no hurry'.

> He knows that I have made + [Augusta] my heiress [Byron told Lady Melbourne] & though it is not a stupendous inheritance – yet as he supposes the life a bad one &c, I can see that he don't like any chance of my wife's being in his way.

By 15 October Byron was still dragging his feet and once again Augusta was pressed into service to account for the continuing delay. Her second letter was considerably less poised than her first and contained more of her habitual hurry and flurry. She did her best to calm Annabella's 'doubts and fears' about being able to make 'my dear Brother' happy:

> He writes me word that he hopes *very* soon to see you. It is most provoking that his departure to Seaham should have hitherto met with so many impediments. I am writing in such haste for the post (having been so fortunate as to obtain a frank) that I hope you will forgive ye numerous imperfections of this letter and allow me to write again. Whenever you have a moment to bestow on me and *think it not irksome to you to write* pray indulge me with a few lines. I feel that I have a thousand things *at least* to say to you and that the *subject* of them *all* would perhaps ensure them a kind reception . . .

Lord Wentworth, who had better things to do than sit in Seaham waiting for the arrival of his niece's dilatory fiancé, took his leave. The Milbankes began to wonder whether the reluctant bridegroom might be speeded on his way if the 'charming Mrs Leigh' were to accompany him. Augusta was all too willing to exchange pleasantries with Annabella from afar, but she knew that she was not yet in sufficient command of her emotions to meet her brother's bride-to-be face to face:

> You cannot imagine how very sensible I am of yours and Sir Ralph's and Lady Milbanke's kind wish of seeing me at Seaham, and how much, how *very much* I should like to go there . . . I fear it is more than difficult for me to leave home at present. I am a *Nurse* to my Baby – Governess to my eldest Girl and something between both to my two intermediate Babes.

What Augusta found difficult to suppress even in her letters was her love for her brother, which she trusted she could disguise as sisterly affection:

> You would not be surprised at my attachment surpassing that of Sisters in *general* if you knew all his kindness to *me & mine*. It is indeed beyond all praise. I hope you will soon see him my dear Miss Milbanke. It seems as if I were as impatient as he is for his joining you, but I am so anxious for you to know him better, being convinced he will gain by it in your estimation – and I am anxious *too* for his sake & that of the *family shyness* that his first arrival at Seaham should be over.

Hanson had still not put in an appearance and was now pleading illness as an additional excuse for not coming to London. Byron was becoming incoherent with rage and embarrassment, and Augusta was constantly lamenting that she could not be with him, 'to afford him at least the consolation of *talking over* all this *worry* . . .'

This was not how she put it to Annabella, to whom she was writing nearly every day without any prompting from Byron; her letters were becoming quite shameless in her eagerness to please and to paper over the cracks:

> I feel already *so much* as if we *were Sisters*, that I am divided (or *should* be if I had the power to choose) between the wish of going to *Seaham* or to *Albany*. Do you know I think I should decide upon the former . . .

By 27 October Byron felt that he could no longer wait for Hanson to show up and set off for the north. In her next letter, Augusta, who had been hoping that Byron might break his journey at Six Mile Bottom, told Annabella regretfully that she would not have her 'promised glimpse which I had anticipated with so much pleasure' as her brother would go directly by the Great North Road, but Byron had no intention of missing an opportunity to be with his sister for even a few hours and rather undermined Augusta's exercise in self-denial by telling Annabella that he would make his 'inn' at Six Mile Bottom.

Byron reached there on the evening of 29 October. For the past weeks he had struggled to keep his thoughts in order, and away from Augusta, by concentrating on the problems of the marriage settlement. But now they were briefly face to face and had, as Augusta told Hodgson (with whom she was now in regular correspondence), 'but a short time to hear and say a thousand things'. Byron left the house late on the Sunday night in a state of blackest gloom. He passed the night at the Haycock Inn at Wansford, where he and Augusta had stayed on their way back from snow-bound Newstead. There he learned that another incestuous pair, the notorious roué Sir Henry Mildmay and his sister-in-law, Lady Rosebery,* had dined at the inn during the course of their recent elopement and flight from England, Sir Henry having previously been caught, disguised as a bearded sailor *in flagrante* with Her Ladyship. They had been, or so Byron confided to Lady Melbourne:

> in very good spirits & quite at their ease . . . Don't you think they are not much better than some people you may have heard of who had half a mind to *anticipate* their example – & don't yet know whether to be glad or sorry they have not . . .'

Byron had not committed himself to a date for his arrival at Seaham, but the Milbankes could not have expected him to take five days over the journey. When eventually he got there he raised Annabella's proffered hand and kissed it, muttering that it had been a long time since they had met, but then the family shyness took over and he was at a loss for words. Annabella likewise was tongue-tied. They were, after all, virtual strangers who had barely exchanged more than an hour of polite and very formal conversation. It was one thing to be animated and even mildly flirtatious in their letters, but when brought face to face there seemed to be nothing for them to say to each other. Annabella rose early the following morning in the hope of having a few moments alone in the library with her uncommunicative suitor, but, to her chagrin, he did not emerge from his room until well after noon.

As the days passed, conversation continued to prove an almost insurmountable obstacle and Byron informed Lady Melbourne that her niece was 'the most silent woman I ever encountered'. Annabella was, however, very curious to find out more about Augusta. Was it true tht he had broken with her completely for three years 'on account of some trivial offence'. He replied that it was true, adding darkly, 'You might have heard worse than *that*.' Already Byron could not resist the temptation to play with fire, and

* Sir Henry Mildmay's late wife, Charlotte, was sister to the Countess of Rosebery.

he added mysteriously, 'Had you married me two years ago, you would have saved me *that* for which I can never forgive myself.'*

While Byron was at Seaham, he wrote only one letter to Augusta, who confided to Hodgson that she was beginning to grow uneasy, 'but it is very selfish to be so, for I know he is happy, and what more can I wish'.

Byron was in fact far from happy and he was keeping his old confidante Lady Melbourne fully informed about what was happening. The terms of the marriage settlement had been agreed and he was getting on 'to admiration' with Sir Ralph, cheerfully putting up with his interminable and frequently repeated anecdotes. Judith Milbanke he did not care for at all – 'She seems to be everything here' – and she was keeping a very wary eye on him. The real difficulty, however, continued to be Annabella herself: 'Do you know I have great doubts – if this will be a marriage now – her disposition is the very reverse of *our* imaginings – she is overrun with fine feelings.'

Byron's response to his fiancée's fine feelings was to resort to what he called 'the eloquence of action' – in other words, to make love to her. She began to respond to his kisses and embraces rather more wholeheartedly than he had expected: 'In fact entre nous it is really quite amusing – she is like a child in that respect – and quite *caressable* into kindness and good humour.' Annabella soon began to fear that her feelings, and Byron's, might very rapidly get the better of her. Urging on him the necessity of making her preparations for the wedding, she asked him to leave and on 16 November he swept out and off down the Great North Road in a foul temper.

By the time he reached Six Mile Bottom on 19 November, he was determined to call the whole thing off and wrote a letter to Annabella breaking their engagement. Augusta was horrified. During the course of their rather artificial correspondence she had begun to feel protectively disposed towards her future sister-in-law. She understood, as Byron did not, that pulling out of the marriage at so late a stage would not only cause Annabella limitless psychological damage but would severely undermine her standing

---

* It is well to remember that for much of what happened at Seaham, and during the course of the honeymoon, we have only Annabella's subsequent statements and memoirs to go on, compiled when she was concerned only to build up a case against her husband and Augusta.

in society. Jealous of her brother's future wife she may have been, but she had no desire to see her hurt. She persuaded him to tear the letter up.

However, Augusta had no intention of exposing herself to the emotional ordeal of the wedding. Her family, as always, provided her with an easy way out:

> The fact is that *Medora* would require my *head* Nurse, and taking her I should leave my other with only the *subaltern* whom I cannot trust with such a charge – particularly my little boy who is too young to be reasoned with on such an occasion . . .

Byron had returned to London to find that Hanson was still hopelessly embroiled in his daughter's affairs – 'the brother of Ld P[ortsmouth]. wants to lunatise him – or stultify him' – and was likely to be of very little assistance to him over the marriage settlement; nor was Augusta's growing opposition to the sale of Newstead making his task any easier. However, he was in no great hurry to return to Seaham. Edmund Kean was playing Macbeth, and an artless young poetess, Eliza Francis, wanted to hold his hands and look deep into his eyes.

Annabella's letters were now as warm and affectionate as she could make them and she was doing her best to keep up what sense of humour she possessed. 'There is a wedding cake in preparation that makes Ossa* like a wart', she told him, and Sir Ralph was penning an epithalamium. Byron wanted the ceremony to be as simple as possible – just two cushions to kneel on in the drawing room at Seaham – and was going to obtain a special licence from the Archbishop of Canterbury so that 'we can be married at any hour in any place without fuss or publicity'. However, he was still no nearer to setting a date and, as day after day passed, Annabella grew increasingly impatient:

> I begin to think that after the great cake is baked and the epithalamium composed, with all other prologues to the perform-ance, the part of the Spouse, like that of Hamlet, will be omitted 'by particular desire'.

Augusta did what she could to keep up the momentum, and

---

* Ossa was a mountain in Thessaly. When the giants Otuz and Ephialtes attempted to make a stairway to Heaven, they planned to pile Mount Pelion on top of Ossa (Odyssey XI, 315).

Queen Charlotte.
'If I can always have the pleasure of counting you among the small number of My Friends, I shall be happy,' she told Augusta's grandmother, Lady Holdernesse, whom she appointed to her household as a Lady of the Bedchamber.

The Prince of Wales was the patron and friend of Augusta's husband, George Leigh, with whom he shared a passion for horses and the turf, as well as a remarkable capacity for getting into debt.

The Earl of Holdernesse, Augusta's grandfather, diplomat, statesman and polished courtier. George III gave him the unenviable task of overseeing the education of the young Prince of Wales.

The Countess of Holdernesse took charge of her granddaughter, in tragic circumstances when Augusta was only a year old. An exceedingly pious woman, she was
nicknamed 'Lady Holiness' by the royal princes.

Lady Amelia D'Arcy, Augusta's mother. The pampered only child of the Earl and Countess of Holdernesse, she took as her first husband Francis Osborne, Marquess of Carmarthen, 'the prettiest man in his person' (*below left*) but, five years and three children later, she ran off with 'Mad Jack' Byron, 'a giddy young man whose finances were in a very ruined state'. Mad Jack (*below right*) was the father of both Augusta and Byron.

The children of Amelia's first marriage: George, Mary and Francis. Byron referred to Augusta's half-brothers as her 'Mamma Brothers'. The devoted if strait-laced Mary never wavered in her loyalty and affection for her half-sister Augusta.

The Reverend Christopher Alderson, Rector of Eckington in Derbyshire. Chaplain to both the Holdernesses and Queen Charlotte, he was also a celebrated landscape gardener. Lady Holdernesse sent Augusta to live with his family.

The Rectory at Eckington was home to Augusta from the ages of six to thirteen.

Thomas Pelham
(2nd Earl of
Chichester) married
Augusta's half-sister,
Mary. He was the
person to whom
Augusta most often
turned for advice.

The Hon Mrs William
Harcourt, a family
friend of long standing.
Augusta sometimes
stayed with her after
the death of her
grandmother, Lady
Holdernesse. It was
at the Harcourts'
house in Portland Place
that Augusta had her
earliest recorded
meeting with Byron.

The Earl of Carlisle (*right*) took Augusta under his wing after the death of Lady Holdernesse had deprived her of a home. Augusta spent part of each year with his family, generally in Yorkshire at Castle Howard (*below*). While some people complained about 'the family's prejudice against stoves', Augusta always enjoyed her visits. 'I need not tell you what pleasure it wd give me to go to Castle Howard,' she wrote.

supplied Annabella with a steady stream of letters, both reassuring and flattering her. Annabella wrote to her on 9 December:

> I am not 'wiser than yourself' as you are pleased to suppose me. However I will keep up this character of an *owl* as long as my *quill* does not betray the *goose*. After post yesterday – 'I am sure you have a letter from Mrs Leigh, you look so pleased,' said my mother, and she was right.

For weeks there had been no progress over the sale of Newstead, and Byron began to explore the possibility of using this as a reason for postponing the wedding: Annabella would have none of it:

> Byron, my own, there shall not be any delay to our marriage on account of these circumstances if you are sure you can reconcile yourself to the privations necessarily attendant on so limited an income.

He was left with no alternative but to press ahead, and on 23 December he at last obtained the licence from the Archbishop of Canterbury and announced his intention of setting out 'tomorrow but stop one day at Newmarket'. He was still, however, hinting at a 'postponement' and his letter to her was hardly reassuring: 'Hobhouse I believe accompanies me – which I rejoice at – for if we don't marry I should not like a 2nd journey back quite alone.' It was intended as a joke, but it did not relieve the tensions that were growing at Seaham.

Byron's letters to Augusta at this time have not survived, but one of hers to him has, and it perfectly conveys the charm of her personality, her manner of speaking, her infectious laughter, her impulsive gooseishness and her way of using crosses as if they were a succession of light kisses. It also shows that she was far from sanguine at the prospect of the wedding:

> Mr Dearest B.+
>
> As usual I have but a short allowance of time to reply to your tendresses + but a few lines I know will be better than none – at least I find them so + It was very + very + good of you to think of me amidst all the visitors &c. &c. I have scarcely recovered *mine* [sic] of yesterday. La Dame did talk so, oh my stars, but at last it saved me a world of trouble. Oh, but she found out a likeness in your picture to Mignonne* who is of course very good humoured in consequence

---

* The 'likeness in your picture to Mignonne' was later claimed by Annabella and the

+ I want to know Dearest B. – your plans – when you come + when you go – umph! When the writings travel, when ye cake is to be cut, when the Bells are to ring, &c. &c. &c. By the bye, my visitors are acquainted with A. & did praise her to the skies. They say her health has been hurt by studying &c. &c, &c.

I have not a moment more my dearest + except to say ever thine.

It was not until noon on 24 December that Byron and Hobhouse, who was to be Byron's best man, finally managed to set out from London. When they reached Great Chesterford they went their separate ways: Hobhouse to Cambridge, where he was to have Christmas dinner at Trinity, and Byron to Six Mile Bottom.

Hobhouse had the best of it, for Christmas at Six Mile Bottom was bleak and comfortless. It was bitterly cold, so that everyone was forced to remain indoors; Byron was in a state of deepest gloom at the prospect of finally parting from Augusta; and George Leigh, swathed in blankets, was suffering from a cold:

> Col L. is opposite to me, making so many complaints of illness and calls for medicine that my attention is called off and the rest of my letter will be like a prescription if I don't leave off. – A. is looking very well – and just as usual – in every respect – so that better can't be in my estimation . . .

He told Annabella that he was 'as warm as love can make one with the thermometer below God knows what', sent his love to her parents and ended, 'I wish you much merriment and minced pie – it is Xmas day . . .'

But he did everything he could to delay the moment of leaving Augusta and it was not until three o'clock on Boxing Day that he arrived at Trinity to collect Hobhouse. 'Never was lover less in haste,' Hobhouse noted in his diary. That night they got no further than the by now very familiar Haycock Inn at Wansford, 'the bridegroom more and more *less* impatient . . . Indifference, almost aversion . . .'

The Milbankes had gone ahead with the wedding preparations on the assumption that Byron would be at Seaham at least by

Lovelace faction to be proof positive that Medora was Byron's child, since Augusta's friend Theresa Villiers had claimed that 'Mignonne' was Byron's pet name for Medora. However, it is obvious that Augusta was referring to Georgiana. An eight-month-old baby would hardly have been put in a good humour by being told that she resembled her uncle.

Christmas and their plans had been thrown into considerable disarray. Christmas must have been a nerve-racking time for Annabella, doing her best to keep up her spirits in the face of her parents' mounting impatience and anger, never knowing when Byron would arrive, or if he would arrive at all. 'I have little to tell you except my happiness at his nearer approach,' she wrote bravely to Augusta. 'Perhaps he is with you at this moment . . .'

It took Byron and Hobhouse four days, travelling slowly through heavy snow, to cover the 220 miles between Wansford and Seaham. They arrived late on the evening of 30 December and, not surprisingly, their reception was even bleaker than the weather. Only the servants were there to greet them. Lady Milbanke had gone to her room and Sir Ralph, when he eventually put in an appearance, was, Hobhouse observed, 'somewhat cool . . . Our delay the cause. Indeed I looked foolish in trying to find an excuse for it.'

Annabella ran into the room, threw her arms around her bridegroom's neck and burst into tears. Hobhouse was not greatly impressed with her looks: 'Rather dowdy looking, and wears a long and high dress, though her feet and ankles are excellent.' That night she wrote to Augusta. Augusta's reply for once made no attempt at cheerfulness, merely reflecting the bleakness of her own unhappiness:

> I am relieved to think ye first moments of it [Byron's arrival] are passed. I sincerely hope they will be the *last* of *pain* to you . . . I had written so far when I was interrupted by visitors (a *rare* occurrence in this place) . . .

The wedding ceremony, simple as Byron had stipulated, with kneelers on the floor of the drawing room, took place on 2 January 1815. Annabella wore a plain muslin gown and was attended by her mother's former maid, Mrs Clermont. The Reverend Thomas Noel,* who had been waiting for the best part of two weeks for the privilege, conducted the service, assisted by the Rector of Seaham. According to Hobhouse:

> Miss M. was firm as a rock, and during the whole ceremony looked steadily at Byron. She repeated the words audibly and well. Byron hitched at first when he said, 'I George Byron,' and when he came to

* The illegitimate son of Judith's brother, the 2nd Viscount Wentworth.

143

the words, 'With all my worldly goods I thee endow', looked at me with a half smile.

The bells of Seaham church rang out – Byron had a particular aversion to church bells – muskets were fired outside and the formidable Lady Milbanke kissed her son-in-law. After the register had been signed and Annabella had 'completed her conquest, her innocent conquest', Hobhouse noted bleakly, 'I felt as if I had buried a friend.' If Sir Ralph delivered his epithalamium, no one thought it worthy of notice.

As Hobhouse handed Annabella into the carriage, in which he had placed as a gift to her (rather superfluously, one might have thought) a complete edition of her husband's poems, he wished her many years of happiness. 'If I am not happy,' she replied, 'it will be my own fault.' Byron clung desperately to his friend's hand as the carriage moved off. As they made their way towards Halnaby Hall, the Milbanke family seat, where they were to spend their honeymoon, the newly married couple sat for a long time in silence. Then suddenly Byron broke into a 'wild sort of singing', snatches of the Arnaout songs he had heard at Tepelene on his Grand Tour.

CHAPTER 13

'The Art of Making B. Happy'

For the whole of what Byron chose to refer to as the 'Treaclemoon' – in fact for all of January and February 1815 – he wrote not one word to Augusta. This was partly his way of dealing, or of failing to deal, with the pain of their separation, but to a great degree he found it convenient to make her the scapegoat for his marriage. He had forgotten that it was against his sister's advice that he had insisted on renewing the proposal to Annabella; he could only remember that when he had wanted to break off the engagement after his first visit to Seaham, it had been Augusta who had talked him out of it. As a result she found herself yet again frozen out of his life, and for news of him she had to rely entirely on letters from Annabella.

Byron wrote plenty of letters to other people – to Lady Melbourne, Thomas Moore, Hobhouse and Hanson. He was at pains to point out that he and Annabella were 'getting on extremely well'; 'we agree admirably'; 'we may win the Dunmow flitch of bacon for anything I know'. But Annabella had a very different story to tell. On their first night in the old Milbanke house at Halnaby where they were entirely alone together for the first time, Byron told her that he hated sleeping in the same bed as a woman and that 'one animal was as good to him as another'. He gave her the impression that some kind of remorse was preying on his mind: 'I have done that for which I never can forgive myself'; 'I was a villain to marry you'; 'I am more accursed in this than any act of my life'.

Annabella had been confident of her ability to handle Byron. Now she realised that she did not know him at all, nor had she the least notion how to cope with his violent swings of mood, his bursts of anger, his self-dramatisations and what Lady Oxford would have called his 'Wertherism'. Unfortunately he had in Annabella the perfect victim. 'When Byron did not get a reaction from his audience,' observed his old Harrow friend William Harness, 'he very soon came to the end of his performance. But Lady Byron was too conscientious, too severe to allow the fire to thus die out. She took seriously every word he uttered.'

Since Byron refused to write to her, Augusta had to rely on Annabella, whose letters to her at first painted a rosy picture. Augusta had always doubted whether Annabella would be able to cope with Byron, whose temperament she knew all too well. She may even have hoped that Annabella would fail. Augusta would have had to be superhuman not to be jealous and, for all the buoyant cheerfulness of her replies, there is a slightly patronising tone and an underlying hint of envy in her letters, a need to emphasise the fact that she knew Byron better than Annabella could ever hope to. When eventually Annabella began to reveal that all was not entirely well, Augusta made light of this, praising her sister-in-law for her ability to handle her brother's whims, while at the same time suggesting that she was making a great fuss about nothing.

If Augusta had had the least idea of some of the games that Byron was beginning to play at Halnaby, she would have taken the situation more seriously. He could never resist the temptation to dangle before Annabella tantalising hints that he and Augusta were rather more than mere brother and sister. He made a point of reading aloud extracts from Augusta's first letter to him after the marriage, which began, 'Dearest, first and best of human beings,'* and went on to speak of her sympathy for his feelings of agitation during the marriage ceremony, 'as the sea trembles when the earth quakes'. Annabella also recounted (though this needs to be viewed with some caution) that she chanced upon some lines in Dryden's *Don Sebastian*:

> Alas, I know not what to call thee!
> Sister and wife are the two dearest names;
> And I would call thee both! And both are sin.

When she happened to mention to Byron this story of an accidental incestuous union:

> His terror and rage were excessive. He said, 'Where did you ever hear of that?' with an air of distraction. I quietly explained. He took up his dagger, which with his pistols, lay on the table and left the room.

* At least, so Annabella said.

Byron was so continually lamenting his sister's absence, and telling his wife how no one loved him or knew how to make him happy as Augusta did, that Annabella decided that she had little option but to ask her sister-in-law to join them at Halnaby Hall. (Or so she said; it is more likely that she was finding Byron too difficult to handle on her own.) Augusta had not the least wish to join the happy pair, and her usual excuses lay ready to hand:

> *Would* that I COULD go to you! But I'm sure you will understand ye difficulties attending such a removal, and that ye power not the *will* or *wish* is wanting. I feel not a little grateful for all the kindness you express on the subject and hope that we shall meet and *soon, somehow, and somewhere* . . . Colonel Leigh would be too happy *to be able* to remove the difficulties in ye way of moving from hence . . . B will tell you what a helpless person I am, which you will think somewhat excusable considering MY YOUNG FAMILY.

Over the next few days Annabella continued to send 'Gussie' dispatches from the front line at Halnaby, where Byron was becoming increasingly fractious. She did her best to put a cheerful face on things, referring to the 'comical proceedings' and receiving encouraging notes from Augusta making light of Byron's blackest moods: 'It is so like him to *try and persuade* people that *he is disagreeable and all that.* Oh dear!' As far as Annabella was concerned, it was considerably more than 'Oh dear!' Byron had taken to stalking up and down the long gallery in the middle of the night with his pistol and dagger, threatening to kill himself. He spoke so constantly of some terrible dark secret that Annabella was beginning to believe that, like the Wicked Lord, he had actually committed a murder. Unfortunately, Annabella aroused and unconsciously encouraged the undeniable streak of sadism in Byron's make-up.

Not that the 'Treaclemoon' was the constant nightmare that Annabella later made it out to be. They read together and talked about poetry and Annabella dutifully copied out Byron's compositions. They gave one another pet names – he became 'Duck' and she became 'Pippin' – and she enthusiastically allowed herself to be initiated into the pleasures of lovemaking.

By the end of the second week Annabella was telling her sister-in-law that all was going smoothly, and Augusta was permitting herself to be somewhat reluctantly convinced:

I think and with joy that you are a most sagacious person and have in one fortnight made yourself as completely Mistress of the 'art of making B. happy' as some others would in 20 years – to be sure, when that is understood the task is not difficult . . . I will own to you my dear Sis *all my folly*, as it now is proved to have been – which was that you might not understand all his 'comical ways' – 'facons de parler' and 'grumps' and that such *misunderstanding* would have made *you* unhappy – which he would soon have discovered and his own candid representation of his qualifications for domestic life would have had *beau jeu* – but I now give my fears to the Wind – and I am sure you do right 'to laugh away' all anxieties for not even *I* can know him better . . .

Some of Byron's 'comical ways' were evidently no laughing matter, despite Augusta's attempt to make them seem so:

I think I see the Waistcoat consuming! I hope it was not one with *gold Buttons* – and then the decanter full of Wine – oh yes! I know his malicious insinuations on these occasions . . .

It was not only burning waistcoats that Annabella had to contend with, but Byron's continual attempts to rouse her jealousy of Augusta, 'lamenting my presence and her absence'. Annabella tried to hint at this in her letters, but Augusta closed her mind to the dangerous game that her brother was playing:

I wish I deserved half the kindness he feels and expresses towards me. I may think myself most fortunate that he has a Wife who is *not* 'affronted' at such declarations as ye one you tell me of . . .

Annabella was engaged in a complicated exercise, deliberately minimising the horrors that surrounded her at Halnaby because, or so she later made out, she feared Byron's reaction if he discovered that she was sending adverse reports to his sister: 'He had also seemed wretched at the idea of her knowing his state of mind – so much so that he objected when I wished to send her his gloomy compositions.' Augusta was not greatly distressed. Byron had rarely shown her his poetry – 'it has normally been my fate to meet with the lines of his in some *fine lady's* album' – and he evidently did not have very much faith in her powers of judgement. 'My dear you know you don't care about them – you can't understand them, you are a ninny . . .' he would tell her.

After three weeks alone together at Halnaby, the Byrons decided that it was time for them to return to Seaham, or at least Annabella did. All Byron wanted was to be back with his friends in London and he did his utmost to convince his bride that, since he had urgent business in town concerning the sale of Newstead, she should go on to her parents' house alone. Annabella would have none of it, and Augusta, letting the mask slip a little, could only agree: 'I do not wonder at your unwillingness to part with B. I am sure I should feel ye same, were I his wife...' Only to Hodgson did she reveal anything of her doubts about the marriage. With him she never felt the need to conceal or to pretend:

> I will own to you, what I would not scarcely to any other person, that I HAD *many fears* and much anxiety founded upon many causes and circumstances of which I cannot *write*. Thank God! that they do not appear likely to be realised...

At Seaham, Byron acted the part of the happy bridegroom with an almost manic determination. There were revels with the Milbankes, when he dressed up in Judith's long-haired wig, 'snatched from her head for the purpose', while Annabella cut a dash in Byron's travelling cap and cloak, 'with whiskers and mustachios'. He played endless games of cards and draughts with his mother-in-law, ate vast meals, went for long walks and even ran races with his wife.

All this brought back to Augusta memories of Hastings and, as Annabella continued to send her daily bulletins of their 'ramble-scramble-tumble-cum-jumble' fun and games, she began to show signs of fraying at the edges, while doing her best to respond as a good sister-in-law should:

> I am just recovering from one of *B.*'s fits of laughing at the account of 'Duck and Devil' – Oh dear!!! I am so glad of his continuance in 'well-doing' and cannot sufficiently praise you for having brought such improvements. After having been so liberal of my approbation I cannot resist saying that I am also glad poor 'Guss' is not quite forgotten.

Forgotten Augusta was not, and there were times when Annabella must have thought her a Banquo's ghost come to haunt her evenings with Byron. There was a game of bouts-rimés at the end of which he asked her to send the results to Augusta. Annabella suggested that they mark the lines with crosses to identify who had written them. Byron turned pale and said that it would frighten Augusta to death. It was some time later that Annabella discovered that crosses were part of their secret code of love. 'He wore a broach of hair,' she noted, 'on which were three of these crosses, and she had a similar one of his.'

Compared with the high junks at Seaham, with Byron 'jumping and squeaking on the sands', life for Augusta at Six Mile Bottom must have appeared very dreary indeed. When George was at home, she had '5000 things to do for him'. She wrote all his letters and did her best to sort out his affairs, while he occupied himself with his little errands or went off shooting (at least the larder must have been kept well supplied with game). There was the children's schooling to be seen to – 'Here comes Georgiana with her lesson.' George suffered from perpetual coughs and colds – and one or other of the children was invariably ill. Her only diversions were the family gatherings at Gogmagog.

But Byron was growing dangerously bored: the interminable games of draughts were beginning to take their toll. He listened as patiently as he could to Sir Ralph repeating a speech he had made to a Durham tax-meeting, but was chafing to be in London. 'Upon this dreary coast,' he told Moore, 'we have nothing but county meetings and shipwrecks . . .' One night Byron collapsed from the fumes of his dressing-room fire, 'diabolically pregnant with charcoal', and was only brought round by Annabella dowsing him with Eau-de-Cologne. When he was revived he began raving that he was going to hell, swearing that he would defy his Maker to the last. Augusta, who knew her brother's histrionically violent moods all too well, suspected that drink (which was liberally available at Seaham, since Sir Ralph and Lady Milbanke were both great topers) might have had something to do with it:

> Oh! Yes his own account of this exploit would I dare say be comic, but dearest Annabella don't allow him to play the fool any more in this way, and do hide your *Brandy Bottle* – I suspect he had stolen it again.

She added:

> You must not mind all his ideas about his 'predestined' Misfortunes. I must tell you that it is a family failing in ye B.'s to have *uneven* spirits. I have even remarked it in a much stronger degree in some of us than in B. – and when the *glooms* prevail I too well know the effects.

She was, of course, referring to her problems with her own husband.

Before the wedding it had been agreed that Byron and Annabella would visit Six Mile Bottom. 'We shall form a very amicable trio I am certain,' Annabella had told Augusta.

Augusta was understandably reluctant for the three of them to be together, for the first time, under the same roof. There was little doubt in her mind that the moment she and Byron were left alone together, he would do everything in his power to put their relationship back on its old footing, and she was not at all confident that, when it came to it, she would have the strength to resist. She was all too aware of the fragility of human nature in general, and of her own in particular. She set out to find a 'castle' or a 'hole' somewhere in the area, a comfortable carriage drive away. She wrote to Annabella:

> Don't imagine from my discussing this part of the plan first that my 'hospitality' would be easily or soon tired of such guests – but ye truth is that your patience or B.'s would incur some risk of being so from the inconveniences and small dimensions of this building.

Augusta's problem was that she had not the least idea how to set about looking for suitable accommodation. 'You would not fancy the town of Newmarket ... This is a miserable desert country – with no village within 3 miles and shocking roads to them.' Even if there had been a possible 'hole', there was no way she could have taken a look at it. With George away, she was a 'prisoner' in the house, for they had no carriage.

It then occurred to her that it might be better if she could find some reason for deferring the Byrons' visit indefinitely. 'Sometime ago,' she told them, 'my spouse somewhat to my astonishment – proposed to *Aunt Sophy* to come and pay me a little visit during her trip into ye North.' Since George and her aunt had not been on good terms 'ever since our marriage and long before it', on account of the long-standing antipathy between his father and Aunt Sophy, Augusta did not want 'to throw cold water upon the proposal'. She was in a state of 'agitation and vexation' that the two arrivals might clash.

None of this sounds in the least plausible, but it did give her an excuse for delaying any positive decision for three weeks. Unfortunately by the end of that time she had still settled nothing. She had found neither a 'hole' nor a 'castle', had heard nothing from Aunt Sophy (who was in France) and did not even know when George would be returning or whether he proposed to leave again immediately on one of his long trips north – 'in short, I am utterly distracted'.

Byron, meanwhile, had been making his own plans. On 28 February he sent off a letter to Hobhouse, who ever since the wedding had been doing his best to look after Byron's business affairs: 'I shall set off from this place on Monday next furthest and *solus* – any letters after that you had best address to Six Mile Bottom Newmarket.'

He was not to escape so easily. Annabella had no intention of letting her husband go anywhere without her and her parents backed her up. He now realised that there was no way out: he would have to come face to face with Augusta, for the first time since his marriage, in the company of his wife.

Time was running out for Augusta and in the end she simply gave up, resigned herself to the inevitable and, as she always did, consigned the whole matter to the care of providence:

> If Aunt does not come I see no reason (but perhaps I am blind) why you should not both partake of all the inconveniences of this most inconvenient dwelling as long as you could tolerate them and B. could go from hence to town leaving *you* under my protection!!!

Perhaps she hoped that Annabella might take the hint and refuse, but she gratefully accepted. As for Byron going 'from hence to town' alone, Annabella would not hear of it. She was determined not to let her husband out of her sight.

CHAPTER 14

'So You Wouldn't, Guss'

All the time that Byron had been obligingly playing the fool at Seaham he had been trying to close his mind to his money troubles and may well have been privately grateful that he was away from London. He had run up bills lavishly and thoughtlessly and he was heavily in debt to jewellers and gunsmiths, tailors and carriage makers, wine merchants and sword cutlers, telescope makers and livery stables. 'My debts can hardly be less than thirty thousand,' he told Hobhouse while reviewing the follies of his generosity. 'I lent rather more than £1,600 to Hodgson – £1,000 to "bold" Webster – and nearly £3,000 to George L. or rather to Augusta – the *last* sums I never *wish* to see again . . .'

For months he had been counting on the sale of Newstead to free him from his troubles, but by the end of February 1815 negotiations with Claughton had become hopelessly bogged down, while Hanson was still more concerned to establish the sanity of his son-in-law than to do anything that might save Byron's.

To compound his money problems, Lady Melbourne – who had, at Annabella's request, been searching for a London home on their behalf – announced that she had arranged for them to take the lease of 13 Piccadilly Terrace, belonging to the widowed Duchess of Devonshire, the former Lady Elizabeth Foster. The rent was £700 a year, a prodigious sum for a person in Byron's circumstances, and Augusta made no attempt to conceal her disapproval: 'Could not B. – content himself with a *small* house in Town. Oh no – I know his *soaring* spirit – but why not – *till* he *could* have a *great* one?'

On 1 March, Byron, who always hated leaving anywhere once he had established himself for more than a few days, was 'in the agonies of packing and parting' from Seaham, but it was not until 9 March that he and Annabella managed to set out. Byron was deliberately taking his time and their progress south was almost as slow as his reluctant journey north to his wedding had been. It took them three days to reach Wansford and the Haycock Inn, with all its disturbing memories. 'Oh! You lazy travellers!!' wrote Judith Milbanke. 'I should have *dined* at Six Mile Bottom that day.' That night, as Annabella recalled, Byron spoke to her:

> the kindest words I could ever have wished to hear – 'You married me to make me happy, didn't you' – I answered with some expression of attachment. 'Well then, you *do* make me happy!' – with passionate affection, I fancied. I was silent, and he saw not, but felt the tears of joy which rose from my heart. Then again he seemed to pity me for some impending, inevitable misery.

According to Annabella, Byron was in a great state of agitation long before they reached Six Mile Bottom. 'I feel as if I was just going to be married,' he said and despite the fact that her maid was sharing the carriage, he began to caress Annabella and wanted her to kiss him. When the carriage drew up outside the house, Byron went in alone to 'prepare Guss'.

Augusta, in a state of even greater nervous apprehension than her brother, was still upstairs in her room, trying to summon the courage to come down and meet him and his bride. This threw Byron into one of his black rages and he brought Annabella into the house in a state of great 'perturbation', made even worse by discovering a letter awaiting him from Claughton admitting his inability to comply with the terms of the sale of Newstead.

Eventually Augusta came down the stairs in a flurry of embarrassment and shyness, and in her confusion omitted to kiss her sister-in-law, a detail that escaped no one's notice. Annabella recalled: '. . . he afterwards rallied her in my presence maliciously, for not having greeted my arrival more warmly. Her manners were sedate yet timid & guarded.' Augusta had done her best to find room for them in the cramped and inconvenient house. George had gone off to hunt at Raby Castle with the Earl of Darlington, so the principal bedroom could be turned over to Byron and Annabella, while her 'Abigail' was put in George's dressing room. Augusta herself moved into the small spare room. They were all thrown together much too closely for comfort.

On the first night, Byron sent Annabella off to bed early and sat talking downstairs to Augusta. When eventually he did go up he was 'in a state of frenzy' and had been drinking heavily. He was 'black enraged – manifested his loathing for me in every possible way' and (so Annabella recounted) told her, 'Now I have *her* you will find I can do without *you*.' 'He gave me to understand,' she continued, 'that he had been indulging in a criminal passion for her – but never that she had indulged him in it.'

What is clear is that, the moment Byron was left alone with his sister that night, any good intentions he might have had were swept aside. When Augusta resisted him, and continued to resist, he was driven into a frenzy and, fortified by brandy, went off to take his revenge on his unfortunate wife.

'In the morning,' Annabella noted, 'her calm & unconcerned manner of embracing him again lulled my suspicions.' In the course of that day he asked his sister ironically, 'Well, Guss, I'm a reformed character, a'nt I?' She looked disconcerted by the question and said that she '*had* observed some improvements already'.

Every night the same performance would be repeated. Annabella would be abruptly dismissed to go up to bed and, if she attempted to resist, Byron would treat her with such 'aversion and insult' that she was forced to retreat to avoid bursting into tears. In her room she would do all that she could to shut out the sound of their voices drifting up from below. 'I was so miserable at night that I could not go to my restless bed till near the time of his leaving A. and I trembled to hear his terrible step.' He would thrust aside her embraces, screaming, 'Don't touch me!' The humiliation of her rejection would be compounded by Byron doing the unthinkable: getting up early in the morning 'to leave me and go to her'.

Augusta continued in her determination not to give in to his attempts to make love to her, and Byron took his revenge by doing everything possible to draw Annabella's attention to this, once saying mischievously, 'So you wouldn't, Guss'. His insinuations of the passion that he felt for her were continual. On one occasion he lay down on the sofa and commanded them to take turns in kissing him, but Annabella noted that 'I was sensible that he was more warm towards her than me'.

It was his sexual rejection of her that came as the ultimate humiliation for Annabella. He had aroused feelings in her that she had scarcely known existed but, once under his sister's roof, he brutally repudiated her. In one of her notes written in shorthand* she recorded that Byron discontinued 'personal intercourse' with

---

* Annabella made copious notes on, and wrote various accounts of, the sixteen days that the Byrons spent at Six Mile Bottom. Some of her narrative is written in shorthand, when she wished to conceal events that she considered too shocking for the tender sensibilities of her solicitors.

her during their stay and, when it was resumed, it was without 'any appearance of personal affection for me'. It was, he said, only because Augusta was 'in a particular way', and remarked, 'I know what makes you look black around the eyes, since I've been here don't I.' He also made a great point of telling Annabella that he knew that his sister wore drawers.

All this might have been dismissed as the behaviour of an overgrown schoolboy, but Byron was feeling hurt, angry and deeply unhappy and was determined to make someone suffer for it. He wanted to punish Augusta for refusing to let him make love to her, and his wife for daring to marry him. His games began to grow more dangerous. He pointed to Medora, saying, 'You know that is my Child!' but, since she was his godchild, Annabella admitted that this was 'equivocal'. Less equivocal was his calculation of the dates of George Leigh's absence around the time of the child's conception, to prove that she could not have been his daughter.

Augusta's world was tumbling about her ears. She had not wanted her brother and his wife in the house in the first place, but the reality was worse than her wildest imaginings. What made the situation even more impossible for her was that her sister-in-law was constantly turning to her for comfort and advice. Annabella had always leaned heavily for support on her network of devoted female friends and, despite circumstances that seemed more likely to drive them apart than bring them together, she was beginning to realise that Augusta was the only person to whom she could look for help in a marriage that was rapidly becoming like a bad dream.

They walked out together in the bleak, uninviting March weather and Annabella asked Augusta whether she thought that Byron loved her: his behaviour immediately after their marriage, she said, had convinced her that he did not care for her. Augusta was far from reassuring, saying only that she hoped Annabella was now of a contrary opinion, 'or perhaps she said undeceived,' Annabella recalled, 'but the import of the phrase was not such as could justify me in believing *her* of the opinion that he married me for love'.

On 18 March, Augusta wrote to Francis Hodgson, who, having heard nothing from Byron for some months, was worried that he might in some way have offended him. Augusta did what she could to relieve his anxiety by passing on to him Byron's reaction to his letter: 'Oh dear! do tell him I am married and cannot write. I have not answered a single letter since that event.' The rest of her letter was uncharacteristically guarded. She could scarcely describe, even to Hodgson, the melodrama that was being enacted round her and confined herself to saying, with no trace of her usual warmth, that she would regret 'their departure, whenever it takes place, as much as I now delight in their society . . .' Scrupulously, she reserved her enthusiasm for the one topic about which she could be enthusiastic:

> . . . of Lady B. I scarcely know how to write, for I have a sad trick of being struck dumb when I am most happy or pleased. The expectations I had formed could not be *exceeded*, but at least they are *fully* answered. I think I never saw or heard of a more perfect being in mortal mould than she appears to be, and scarcely dared flatter myself such a one would fall to the lot of my dear B.

She then came as close as she could to admitting that all was not well at Six Mile Bottom. 'He seems quite sensible of her value, and as happy as the present alarming state of *public* and the tormenting uncertainties of his own private affairs will admit of . . .'

'Alarming' was no exaggeration. Napoleon had escaped from Elba and after a twenty-day march was back in the Tuileries, Louis XVIII had fled to Belgium bewailing the loss of his bedroom slippers and, in London, the foreign secretary, Lord Castlereagh, had his windows smashed. At Six Mile Bottom, only the children seemed to be deriving any pleasure from Byron's visit, noisily demanding his attention and playing with their new aunt, who was at the same time keeping a sharp eye on her sister-in-law to see if she could detect 'the slightest emotion of too warm a nature towards him. She submitted to his affection, but never appeared gratified by it.'

By 28 March, the Byrons had more than outstayed their welcome. Byron was, as usual, reluctant to move on, but Annabella could see all too well that Augusta 'did not wish to detain us'. Byron waved his handkerchief to her 'in the most passionate manner' as their carriage drove away, and during the days that followed Annabella noticed that he was kinder to her than he had ever been, and hoped that this might somehow be due to her sister-in-law's influence. Perhaps it was because Annabella was showing the first indications of pregnancy.

The whole episode had badly shaken Augusta. Not only had she had to go through the bitter experience of welcoming into her house the woman whom the man she loved had married, but she had found herself having to defend that woman against her brother's sadistic games, while she herself had been tormented and humiliated. Worse, she had been confronted with a side of her brother of which she had been completely unaware, and she could only cling to the hope that her sister-in-law had not been convinced by Byron's determined attempt to frighten her with the spectre of their incest. Something of Augusta's anger and despair showed itself in the letter she wrote to Francis Hodgson three days after the Byrons' departure, although typically she did everything she could to justify her brother's behaviour:

> I am sorry to say his energies and spirits are very far from what I wish them, but don't speak of this to him on any account. I think the uncomfortable state of his affairs is the cause; at least I can discern no other . . .

While the Byrons were still at Six Mile Bottom, Judith Milbanke, who made it her business to know everything that went on in the world, wrote to her daughter: 'Is it true that Mrs Leigh is appointed to the situation Mrs Feilding had – viz. Bedchamber Woman? I heard this from London.' It was certainly true. Augusta had been appointed to Queen Charlotte's household as a Woman of the Bedchamber. The Queen had finally forgiven the sins of her mother and was taking Augusta into her circle – the very world that Amelia had rejected for Jack Byron.

Augusta's good fortune owed as much to the memory of Lady Holdernesse as to any virtues of her own, as Princess Elizabeth, the most devoted of Queen Charlotte's daughters, made clear in a letter to Lady Chichester:

> You cannot think how rejoiced all are at the Queen's nomination of your sister . . . She has written me one of the prettiest letters possible which I shewed the Queen & I can assure you that my Mother has felt . . . no less pleasure in doing what she knew would be so agreeable to you besides feeling that if ever dear Lady Holdernesse could know it would make her happy – for to do my mother justice she never forgets her old friends . . .

Although the stipend of £300 that the post carried was no fortune, any addition to the Leighs' overstretched resources was welcome, provided that George did not spend it in advance. There was the additional benefit of apartments at 'St James's Palace', which could be put at Augusta's disposal whenever her court duties required her to be in town.

Not that the Queen passed much of her time in London any more, preferring to be at Frognal in Windsor Great Park where Augusta's childhood guardian, Christopher Alderson, had helped create her 'little paradise'. She rarely visited the King now, finding it too distressing. He had not appeared in public since 1811 and was virtually a prisoner at Windsor: blind, talking ceaselessly, existing in a twilight world, unable to distinguish between the living and the dead. Indeed, he was not certain whether he himself might not belong to the latter category, for when playing on the harpsichord a composition by Handel, he remarked that it had been a favourite piece of the King when he was alive.

Augusta's duties were not demanding. She was required to attend the Queen when she was in London and on state occasions, royal marriages and funerals, plus the increasingly rare 'Drawing Rooms', or receptions, at 'St James's Palace'. The Queen's court, as opposed to that of her son, was a dowdy, rather old-fashioned affair, a dusty survival from the eighteenth century, as was the Queen: 'I am a piece of Antiquity myself.' In contrast to her sons, she insisted on the highest standards of morality in private life. 'Tho I may be called Hum drum,' she informed Lady Harcourt, 'n'importe. My Conscience is free from accusation.'

The appointment could hardly have come at a better time. Whatever the limitations of Queen Charlotte's court, it was a considerable improvement on a life of drudgery at Six Mile Bottom, where Augusta had little company save that of her children, her chief purpose in life being to prop up an increasingly ineffectual husband.

For years, apart from her rare visits to London, Augusta had been far removed from the fashionable world of her girlhood. It is small wonder that visitors found her dowdy. At Six Mile Bottom she was marooned in a desert where there were no shops, dressmakers or milliners within reach – not even a circulating library. She was not by nature a solitary person; she loved company and gossip and scandal, music and dancing, plays and operas and concerts. Now she had the opportunity to rediscover the life she had once known.

As soon as Augusta's appointment was confirmed, Annabella invited her to stay at Piccadilly Terrace, since the apartment in 'St James's Palace' was not going to be immediately available. After the season in hell they had all three endured at Six Mile Bottom, Annabella must have known that this was an act of utter folly, but it is difficult to see what else she could have done. She could not be entirely certain whether the hints, often considerably more than hints, that Byron had dropped about his sister were not merely another of his malicious games. Not to have invited Augusta would have been discourteous. It would also have suggested that she believed the incest to be a reality.

Augusta was caught in a similar trap. To refuse would have appeared to confirm Annabella's suspicions; to accept was to give them the lie. In her letter to her sister-in-law she did her best to pretend that nothing was, or ever had been, wrong:

> Dearest Sis, I do not require your account of the view from yr Windows as an inducement to pay you a visit. You will perhaps be a better judge by & bye whether I shall not be a plague – & you must tell me *truly* if I am likely to prove so . . . My *youngsters* do not forget 'Aunt Bella' & 'Uncle B.', Georgey looked at the chair B. used to sit in last night & very piteously exclaimed, 'Nobody in that chair NOW!' God bless you dear Annabella – kiss '*Duckey*'! for Sis & if possible give me a favorable report of the 'Wind & the Weather-cock'.

Only Byron appeared to be totally opposed to the idea. In the last days at Six Mile Bottom, when he was unwilling to leave, he had asked his sister to come and stay with them. Once back in London, however, he knew that her being in Piccadilly Terrace would only reignite the situation. 'He told me *I was a fool for letting her come and I should find it so – that it would make a great difference to me in ALL ways*,' Annabella recorded.

Augusta came up to London at the beginning of the second week in April, bringing seven-year-old Georgiana with her. Knowing Byron's fondness for the little girl, she may have hoped that Georgiana's presence in the house might help to diffuse some of the tension. Byron deliberately kept out of the house to avoid the moment of his sister's arrival and, when he returned, it was with the 'lowering looks of disgust and hatred which he had shown on meeting her at Six Mile Bottom'.

For the first few days after her arrival, Augusta was kept busy helping Annabella prepare to be presented in her '*white Satin and Blond*' to Queen Charlotte at the next 'Drawing Room', but on 12 April they received 'alarming' reports that Lord Wentworth,

Annabella's uncle, had only a little while to live. Judith immediately set out from Seaham and Annabella left for Wentworth's house, where she remained for the next few days: 'I felt that death-bed scene a relief from the horrors of an incestuous home – for my suspicions were then at the height . . . I was almost mad.' Annabella was almost certainly reviewing the situation with the benefit of hindsight when she wrote that and was revising it to suit her own ends.

Augusta had been in the house for less than a week, scarcely long enough time for it to qualify as an 'incestuous home'. To judge from a note sent round to Wentworth's house on 15 April, the day of Judith's arrival in London, Byron was full of concern for his wife, who by then would have been sure that she was pregnant:

> Dearest – Now your mother is come I won't have you worried any longer – more particularly in your present situation which is rendered precarious by what you have already gone through. Pray come home.

It is possible that the note was written at the bidding of Augusta, who may have felt embarrassed at her brother paying too little attention to his absent wife and too much to her. The 'black agitation' that Byron had shown on her arrival soon evaporated and, as the days passed, they began to fall back into something of their old ways, sitting up late into the night together, talking, laughing and playing the fool.

By the beginning of May, Piccadilly Terrace was witnessing a rerun of the scenes at Six Mile Bottom, which soon confirmed all Annabella's fears. Byron no longer made love to her; she was sent off early to bed and paced about the room or lay awake half the night, weeping into her pillow and listening to the laughter of her husband and his sister drifting up from below. She admitted that there were times when she was tempted to seize Byron's dagger from the next room and plunge it into Augusta's heart. However, being Annabella, she managed to transfer her feelings to a more exalted and self-righteous plane:

> it was hopeless to keep them apart – it was not hopeless, in my opinion, to keep them innocent. I felt myself the guardian of these two beings *indeed* 'on the brink of a precipice'; – and in this I sought to forget my own miserable and most humiliating condition.

In one respect their situation was an improvement on Six Mile

Bottom, since they were no longer cooped up claustrophobically together. Augusta was settling into her duties at 'St James's Palace' and Byron had plunged back happily into London's literary world. He had also found an occupation of sorts. At the instigation of his friend Douglas Kinnaird,* he had been appointed to the management of Drury Lane Theatre and threw himself into this new role with relish: '... the Scenes I had to go through! The authors – and the authoresses – the Milliners – the Wild Irishmen'. Byron was completely at home among all the backstage intrigue, protecting a pretty dancer 'who had been wronged about a hornpipe', trying to persuade Coleridge to write a play for the theatre, and even appearing on stage in a masquerade.

Annabella was now trapped between two fires: when Byron was at home his attention was invariably given to Augusta; when he was at Drury Lane, 'superintending the candle-snuffers', as his wife bitterly put it, he was making up to the actresses. Yet at least the world of grease-paint and tinsel provided Byron with a temporary diversion from his increasingly obsessional fears of imminent financial ruin. The death of Lord Wentworth had brought nothing in real terms to the Milbankes. They had been required to assume the name of Noel, but they could not touch the Noel money and Sir Ralph was still unable to honour his side of the marriage settlement. Meanwhile news had spread round Byron's creditors that his wife had come into a fortune and they renewed their pressure.

All this sent Byron straight to the brandy bottle and there were violent and frequent tirades against Annabella and her parents. Augusta could hardly remain a passive spectator, and she found herself hotly defending Annabella and the Noels. This served only to increase Byron's fury, and Augusta protested that she would not stay in the house to see Annabella so badly treated, while at the same time reassuring her sister-in-law that she would not leave her until the baby was born.

Byron responded to this with a renewal of his mischief-making, doing his best to shame his sister with a series of pointed innuendoes and thinly veiled allusions, which were not lost on Annabella:

He said to her 'Ly M. does not like you Guss'. She expressed

---

* The Honourable Douglas Kinnaird (1788–1830), 5th son of the 7th Baron Kinnaird and a partner in Ransom's Bank.

something to this effect – that she was ignorant of any offence she had committed against her. He replied very significantly he would tell her why, and went up to whisper something, after which she looked embarrassed. He would sometimes threaten her – half-jesting, half-serious – 'I'll tell, Augusta' – to which she one day replied (desperately I thought) 'I don't care'. He said 'Well if ever I heard anything like the impudence of the woman'.

After more than two months of this, Annabella had had enough of it all. Augusta's term of duty at the palace was coming to an end and Annabella made it very clear to her that it would be best if they were to agree on a day for her and Georgey to return to Six Mile Bottom. She could no longer put up with the continued presence in the house of a rival for her husband's attention. She was now convinced that her only hope of regaining Byron's affection was to make sure that Augusta stayed away from 13 Piccadilly Terrace.

On 18 June, the Earl of Carlisle's third son and George's and Augusta's close friend, their cousin Frederick Howard, was killed at the Battle of Waterloo. A few days later, Augusta and Georgey set off back home.

CHAPTER 15

'A Time of Much Hurry and Confusion'

Rarely can Six Mile Bottom have appeared more familiar and reassuring than it did to Augusta in June 1815 after two months spent in the histrionic and hysterical company of her brother and sister-in-law. But Piccadilly Terrace cast a long shadow. Byron had asked her to write on his behalf to Hobhouse, who had been sending him 'kind and interesting' letters from France to which he could not summon up sufficient energy to reply. Since she did not altogether trust Hobhouse – indeed, there were times when she regarded him as her brother's evil genius – Augusta's letter to him was guarded, painting a not very convincing picture of the life that the married couple were leading in London. Byron was well and eating heartily, seldom dining out and confining himself to half a pint of claret at dinner:

> The only drawbacks to their perfect happiness and comfort are *pecuniary* concerns & I grieve to say the remedy is to be the sale of Rochdale and Newstead, on the 28th of this month. Alas! for the dear old Abbey!

Byron and Annabella were in fact enjoying a brief period of domestic harmony. He had made a new will and Annabella wrote, a little coyly, to tell Augusta about it:

> I must tell you how lovingly B. has been talking of 'dear Goose' till he had half a mind to cry – and so had I. The conversation arose from his telling me the contents of a Will that he had just made . . . and though *you* could never derive any pleasure from the possession of what he might *leave*, you should have satisfaction in knowing that your children will afterwards have a provision besides what may afterwards devolve to them . . .

What little comfort this may have brought Augusta was almost immediately forgotten, for on 7 August Charles Leigh died unexpectedly, having failed to leave a will. Although relations between father and son had been cool, to say the least, since the trouble with the Prince Regent and the inglorious end to George's military career, which had cost his father so much to promote, George had had considerable expectations. The General's intestacy was bad enough, but worse was to come, when a Mrs Longe appeared on the scene and laid claim to his estate. Augusta and George were yet again plunged into crisis and, as always, Augusta turned to her brother for help. Byron did the practical thing and instructed Hanson to look into the situation on George's behalf:

> . . . his father is dead & has left his affairs in confusion – I wish you would see his Attorney – whose report of them *I* don't altogether believe – & enquire into the real nature of the property & the claims upon it . . .

George seemed to have been nonplussed by Mrs Longe and professed ignorance about her claim, which was connected with a plantation on the island of St Kitts that Charles Leigh had inherited in 1791. In serious need of money at the time, to set George up in a fashionable regiment and to consolidate his own military career – he was proposing to raise a regiment – Charles Leigh had decided on selling or mortgaging at least part of the property. To do this, he had first to disentail it, which required his heir, George, to resign his own rights of inheritance and then resettle the estate on his father for life. It was a common enough practice where money was locked up in property, but usually, once its purpose had been achieved, measures were taken to reinstate the heir. Unfortunately for George, this was a step that his father had managed to overlook and, far from inheriting a plantation in the West Indies, his legacy from the General turned out to be a lengthy legal dispute with Mrs Longe.

Exactly who Mrs Longe was remains something of a mystery, but she had either been left money or was owed money by Charles Leigh and she certainly appeared to know more about his affairs than most. Before long her statements and affidavits were arriving on the Leighs' doorstep. Augusta was beside herself with rage and consternation: 'I think Mrs Longe a Devil & *the* Devil! Oh fie, but never mind I can't help it . . .' Mrs Longe's depositions were passed round the family for their consideration. While the Earl of Chichester pondered their legal content, Francis Osborne was all for cruder tactics: '. . . he thinks *fear* would operate as if not *more* favourably than *coaxing*. I'm not sure that I don't agree with him,' Augusta confessed to Annabella. But Mrs Longe was neither to be frightened nor coaxed. Her lawyers were well primed and her claim was plausible.

To complicate matters further, the General's death had lured his estranged wife out into the open. Always one with an eye to the main chance, Frances Leigh now demanded her right, as his widow, to administer her deceased husband's estate. After nearly forty years spent apart from him, not to mention intervening affairs and at least one illegitimate child, Hanson did not rate her chances highly. 'I am sorry for Hanson's opinion of my Mother-in-law's concerns,' wrote Augusta, to whom anyone's intervention would probably have been preferable to that of Mrs Longe, 'she seems well disposed not to resign her *right* of administering . . .' But Frances Leigh's motives were all too blatant and no one could have taken her seriously, as Augusta was forced to admit. 'I can just see ye smirks.'

Frances Leigh's claim failed, as expected, leaving the field clear for Mrs Longe, whose next move was to put herself forward for the task of administration. 'Would she without a security of its proving advantageous to her?' wondered Annabella in a letter to Augusta's close friend, Theresa Villiers, whom she had taken it upon herself to keep informed of the Leighs' tortuous affairs, which had now been overtaken by an unanticipated turn of events.

After the General's death George received messages of sympathy from the Prince Regent. It may have been that the Prince was embarrassed into this by a view, being openly expressed in the newspapers, that his old friend and Groom of the Bedchamber, Charles Leigh,

> . . . should have become almost the oldest General in the army, with no higher remuneration for rank and services than a Lieutenant-Government . . .*

Persuading himself that the Prince's condolences constituted a royal olive branch, George felt sufficiently vindicated to make an approach to his former master and was granted an audience. Cock-a-hoop at the prospect, he was convinced that his return to favour was a foregone conclusion.

After the interview, during which the Prince 'was very gracious, tho' not familiar', George called at Piccadilly Terrace to give Annabella the news that the Regent had promised to 'give him some

---

* In 1811 Charles Leigh had been appointed Colonel of the East Kent Regiment (known as the Buffs) and, in 1813, one of the Lieutenant Governors of the Isle of Wight – a military post which paid £345 per annum.

place or appointment'. Not, it seemed, that anyone had anything specific in mind. Nor did anyone have a ready answer when it came to the question: 'For what is the Petitioner qualified?' Annabella thought it a 'puzzling' one, which 'his R.H. may *fairly* take time to consider – unless any situation can be pointed out by application from Col Leigh's friends, who should now exert themselves in this way before the promise is forgotten . . .' George had no such misgivings. 'He is so elated by the favour of an interview, that he thinks no further exertion necessary,' Annabella reported to Mrs Villiers, but she also went on to note, 'From the same cause he has grown quite indifferent to the chances of his inheritance . . .'

George may have been complacent about his future, but Augusta was not. There was also the matter of George's pension, which had been paid only intermittently and about which (as with everything else) he felt no need to take any action. She asked Annabella whether her parents might know what course she should pursue, and Judith Milbanke obligingly took up the case:

> Mrs Leigh must apply to the *Secretary at War*, when in course it will be granted. I am truly grieved that the Leigh affairs turn out so ill – but everything is unfortunate with *us all* at present – too much to write about – without pain.

Mrs Longe was steadily gaining the upper hand, and Augusta was at her wits' end over letters '. . . full of *Law* and *law terms* I cannot understand . . .' The news that there was to be an audit was about the last straw, knowing, as she did, that among the discrepancies that must inevitably come to light would be Charles Leigh's failure to reverse the disentailing process, which George had been at pains to conceal. 'I tremble about the two auditors who I fear may have a hold upon him in consequence of the paper he signed in concert with his Father . . . It haunts me,' she wrote despairingly to Annabella.*

Byron's own affairs appeared to be growing more unsalvageable by the day and it began to look as if even the sale of Newstead would not put him in the clear. At the end of August, in the lowest of spirits he announced that he was going to spend a few days with

---

* The whole business dragged on for nearly a year and a half and it was not until January 1817 that George was finally granted Limited Administration to enable his father's affairs to be officially wound up. Mrs Longe's claim was upheld and the property, such as it was, in St Kitts was sold in the hope of settling it, but it is unlikely that she profited much. The Leighs profited not at all.

Augusta and set out for Six Mile Bottom 'after', as Annabella recorded, 'having been perfectly ferocious to me for 4 days'. On hearing of the visit, Judith Noel wrote to her daughter fearing that 'Ld B. would find his Sister much distressed God send us all a good deliverance', which provoked a very sharp rebuke from Annabella:

> She is much the best of the bad families with which she is connected
> in spirits, having a sanguine temperament that enables her to hope in
> the face of despair. Do ask her to give you some lessons.'

Six Mile Bottom did nothing to improve Byron's bad humour. He and Augusta quarrelled constantly, about his drinking, his gratuitous rudeness about the Noels and, probably, and this may have been the underlying cause of their rows, about her refusal to allow him to make love to her. In his letters to Annabella, he did his best to make light of it all, telling her that he had nearly lost a toe in a mouse trap that Augusta had left in his room. Augusta too tried to put a brave face on things. Apologising to Hodgson for failing to congratulate him on his marriage on account of 'much hurry and confusion', she wrote to him that she had never seen her brother '*so well* – & he is in the best of spirits . . .'

Byron was certainly not in the best of spirits where his sister was concerned: he was furious with Augusta for defending Annabella's parents. On his return to Piccadilly Terrace, he took his revenge by dropping suggestive comments about her to Annabella:

> Something he told me . . . revived the suspicion that she wished to
> flutter him into a guilty passion for her – I can scarcely repeat it from
> its indelicacy, but it did not afford evidence enough to have any
> lasting effect.

Byron's creditors were steadily closing in on him and he was beginning to fear that the bailiffs would seize the contents of 13 Piccadilly Terrace as soon as he set foot outside it. This provided him with a heaven-sent opportunity to avoid accompanying his wife to Seaham – or to Kirkby Mallory, which Judith Noel was now suggesting – for her confinement. 'He is in great anxiety about me,' Annabella explained to her mother, 'and would have me go by myself – which I *will not*.'

Byron of course wanted to be left alone. Annabella's unrelenting presence was only increasing the agony of his ordeal. The financial mesh in which he was now so hopelessly entangled was beginning to undermine the balance of his mind: '. . . he feels it dreadfully, and distracts himself with the idea of Bailiffs in the House at the same time with the Midwife . . .' Annabella was determined to stand by him. If only she had had the perception to let Byron battle it out by himself, the marriage might not have gone the way that it did. By remaining she was simply adding to his anxieties, making it inevitable that, in his misery, he would turn on her the full force of his bitterness and resentment.

On 8 November 1815, a day when John Murray in all innocence told Sir Walter Scott, 'Lord Byron is perfectly well, and is in better dancing spirits than I ever knew him . . .', a bailiff arrived at Piccadilly Terrace, confirming all Byron's worst superstitions about living in a house numbered thirteen, and sending him into a paroxysm of rage and torment. He turned on Annabella like a madman, attacking her for marrying him 'when he wished it not' and telling her that she must consider herself to be responsible for the 'vicious course' to which his despair would drive him. She sent a distraught account to Six Mile Bottom:

> O Augusta will it ever change for me – I scarcely know what I say. Tho' I have been making the best of things till yesterday, when self-deception became impossible, I have thought that since last Saturday (on which night he sat drinking with Kinnaird's party till ½ past four in the morning) his *head* has never been right – and I fear he will add more and more to the cause . . .

Byron was rapidly cracking up. Beyond all self-control, he roamed around the house breaking ornaments, destroying a watch that he had had since his Harrow days and hurling into the fire a picture of Augusta. 'He loves or hates us together,' Annabella told Augusta.

To add to Annabella's anguish he announced that he had taken a mistress, Susan Boyce, a very minor actress at Drury Lane: 'He studiously and maliciously informed me of the times of his visits to that woman and seemed to have a pleasure in alluding to the subject before me and others . . .' It was all too much for Annabella. She wrote to Augusta beseeching her to return to Piccadilly Terrace immediately: '. . . let me see you the middle of next week – at latest. You will do good I think – if any can be done.'

Annabella had convinced herself that only Augusta could help her, yet there were other friends to whom she could have turned. She had a whole gallery of confidantes, from the celebrated actress

Sarah Siddons to her closest of friends, Selina Doyle. Certain, now, that incest had taken place, she had every reason to be suspicious of Augusta but she believed that Augusta alone could cope with Byron. Pregnant again herself, Augusta had already agreed to join forces with Judith Noel for Annabella's confinement but now she was worried that her presence in Piccadilly might only inflame the situation. In her indecision, she took the fatal step of turning to her old friend Mrs Villiers, who advised her 'unequivocally' that, after the kindness she had received from Annabella, Augusta should not hesitate to go to her sister-in-law's aid.

She arrived on 15 November, accompanied once again by Georgiana and her maid Mrs Anderson. Byron received her with chilly indifference but, according to Annabella, 'soon turned to his former habits of familiar confidence towards her'. Perhaps because of his preoccupation with Susan Boyce he showed none (or at least none that Annabella could detect) of those 'inclinations of special intimacy with Augusta'.

Augusta could hardly fail to notice the change that had overtaken her brother in the few weeks since she had last seen him. She had always been confident of her ability to joke and cajole him out of his black moods, but now her laughter had no effect and she was frightened by his violence, his cruelty towards Annabella and his unremitting savage gloom. Annabella was in an advanced stage of pregnancy, and Augusta even began to fear for her safety and for the safety of her unborn child; she begged her former maid Mrs Clermont,* who had arrived in London from Seaham, to come and sleep in the house at the time of Annabella's confinement. Even the faithful Fletcher, who had witnessed his master in his wildest moods, began to be alarmed at the sight of Byron habitually carrying his pistols about with him: 'I hope my Lord won't do you or my Lady any harm,' he muttered to Augusta.

Augusta took refuge in the conviction that her brother had suffered a mental breakdown brought on by the strain of his rapidly worsening financial situation and by his excessive drinking. Aunt Sophy, who was in London for the rest of that year, agreed with her. She feared that Byron might have inherited the bad blood of his mother's Gordon ancestors and advised an immediate consultation with the fashionable London specialist Dr Baillie.

---

* Mrs Clermont had retired from the Milbankes' service in 1811 but remained a close friend of the family.

Annabella was by now seriously considering leaving the house for the delivery of her baby. The prospect of childbirth was daunting enough without the threat of Byron's increasingly erratic behaviour. With Augusta's 'concurrence' she consulted a family friend, the lawyer Samuel Heywood, but then decided to stay put. In one of her many 'statements', Annabella subsequently recorded that she and Augusta were left alone together for much of the time while Byron went out:

> ... professedly to indulge his most depraved propensities ... One evening, when I said if he had had a friend of firm principle he might perhaps have been saved from such depravity, her remorseful feeling almost overpowered her. She said 'Ah – you don't know *what* a fool I have been about him' – ! – The bitterness of her look as she threw her hair back from her forehead with a trembling hand, wrung my heart. I kissed that forehead where I saw penitential anguish, and left the room. Will you condemn me, reader?*

Augusta, who had left her family to give comfort and companionship to her sister-in-law, now found herself having to defend her against the 'utmost excesses' of her brother's malevolence. There was little sign now of Augusta's reputed reticence and timidity. She had no hesitation in standing up to Byron's threats and rages and did her utmost never to let him be alone with Annabella. '... her accounts of his angry rages towards her', noted Annabella with her customary lack of gratitude, 'prevented my suspicions of worse during the midnight hours she passed with him to prevent in some degree his wilful disturbance of my rest.'

Augusta was certain that they would all sleep more soundly in their beds if there were a few more level-headed people about the house, and she persuaded their cousin George Anson to move in with them, hoping that he might be able to laugh Byron out of his horrors over the bills and bailiffs. This may have brought a little reassurance to the women but there was no noticeable improvement in Byron's behaviour. Judith Noel had arrived in London on 16 November but Annabella was anxious to keep her out of the house as far away from Byron as possible. By the time Annabella went

---

* Although this might suggest that Annabella could have made quite a profitable living by writing novels for the popular circulating libraries, it can hardly be taken as fact, any more than any other of Augusta's supposed 'confessions'. And for what kind of 'reader' did Annabella imagine her various statements and depositions were intended, other than her lawyers?

into labour on 9 December Judith had been taken ill with a high fever and was confined to her bed in Mivart's Hotel.*

The events surrounding the birth of Annabella's child have been embellished with so many horror stories from herself and her supporters that it is difficult to separate fact from fiction. Byron allegedly told his wife before she went into labour that he hoped both she and the child would die, threw soda-water bottles at the ceiling of the room below hers to prevent her sleeping, demanded to know, while she was actually in labour, whether the child were dead and gazed at his new-born daughter and exclaimed, 'Oh! what an implement of torture I have acquired in you!!'

The child who was the subject of so much speculative anecdote was born on 10 December and named Augusta Ada. Augusta herself wrote rather cautiously to Hodgson telling him of the 'fine little girl' and doing her best to paint a cheerful picture:

> B. is in great good looks, and much pleased with his *daughter*, though I believe he would have preferred a son. I am one of those who always endeavour to think 'whatever *is*, is right', and independent of that I see several reasons for being well satisfied with Miss Byron.

Her real feelings were revealed in what followed, telling Hodgson that she would give 'half the world *at least*' for an hour's talk with him and asking whether there was any chance that he might come to London. She needed to find a disinterested friend with whom she could discuss the state of her brother's mind, but she could not mention this in a letter and she was insistent that, even in replying, he must not refer to what she had asked: 'don't repeat it even to the winds'.

The coming of the child had done nothing to soothe Byron's spirits or soften his apparent loathing of Annabella, who later stated that, only hours after the birth, he had sent word to her that her mother was dead. Judith was, in fact, extremely ill. A week later, not much improved, but determined to see her granddaughter, she had herself carried up the stairs at Piccadilly Terrace. Augusta and Annabella made a brave effort to conceal from her the real state of affairs in the house, since they felt that the knowledge might 'seriously damage' her health. Judith immediately took to Augusta

---

* Mivart's Hotel in Brook Street became what is now Claridges. It was the hotel at which Annabella and her parents always stayed.

and was greatly liked by little Georgiana. When she left for Kirkby Mallory on 28 December, she was still happily unaware that anything was wrong. On her arrival she wrote suggesting that Annabella and 'the Dear Babe' should travel up to Kirkby as soon as they could: 'I hope that Lord B. will *also come* and have written a letter to ask it – which *Mrs Leigh* approves.'

Whatever his sister may have approved, Byron had no intention of going anywhere with his wife and daughter. All that Byron wanted was to escape from his marriage, which, he told Hobhouse, had doubled his misfortunes. He talked of going abroad as soon as Annabella and little Augusta Ada had left for Kirkby Mallory, or of continuing to live on in London as a 'single man'.

Annabella was keeping up the pretence that nothing was wrong. On 4 January 1816 she wrote to Lady Melbourne: 'My confinement has been rendered so comfortable by Mrs Leigh's kindness and attention, which I can never forget, that I feel no inclination to break loose.'

Augusta can hardly have shared her sentiments. To add to the tensions and anxieties of protecting Annabella and her child, she now had worries about Georgiana, always a delicate child, whose health was giving her cause to 'fidgit'. She longed to return home, but was too concerned about Byron. Incessant drinking had further damaged his liver, he looked sallow, he suffered constantly from headaches and had taken to mixing laudanum with his brandy.

His behaviour towards his wife was, if anything, growing worse. He informed Annabella that 'a woman had no right to complain if a husband did not beat or confine her and that he had done nothing which would bring him under the law'. On 6 January he abruptly gave Annabella her marching orders:

> When you are disposed to leave London, it would be convenient that a day should be fixed – & (if possible) not a very remote one for that purpose. Of my opinion upon that subject you are sufficiently in possession & of the circumstances which have led to it . . .

What had triggered this sudden acceleration is not clear. Byron could no longer tolerate his wife's presence in the house; he was stretched to breaking point; he needed to be left in peace; he required space in which to try to recover; and Annabella's hovering about him had become an intolerable irritant. If he were to save what was left of his sanity, then she had to go and, since she showed no signs of doing so, he could only issue an ultimatum.

Yet it is difficult to escape the conclusion that some new development had suddenly precipitated his action. The most likely cause is that he had discovered that Annabella had secretly gone through his trunks and letter cases and had found, according to Hobhouse, 'a small bottle of laudanum – and in the same place a few volumes of a work which as a curiosity might be kept, but which was certainly not fit for an open library . . .' The work in question may have been the Marquis de Sade's *Justine or the Misfortunes of Virtue*.

Byron was almost excessively sensitive about his privacy, and the discovery that his wife had been through his private letters, which may well have included those from Augusta, would have been more than enough to make him order her out of the house. This would certainly account for the icy formality of his summary dismissal: 'the sooner you can fix the day the better – though of course your convenience & inclination shall be first consulted'.

Augusta could only conclude that her brother had finally taken leave of his senses. There was a flurry of hasty and secretive consultations with his physicians, Baillie and Le Mann, and a private meeting between Augusta and Hanson, while George Anson kept a careful eye on Byron. Annabella did her best to put a brave face on it all and ostensibly delayed her departure only to be present at the marriage of Fletcher to her maid, Ann Rood, but she was also hoping to see Hanson. She warned her parents that she would be leaving for Kirkby Mallory a little sooner than she had expected, giving no hint of what had happened. Only to Mrs Clermont did she reveal that if Byron were not 'in a state to be put under care', she would 'never return to his roof again'. To everyone else, including Augusta and Hobhouse, she gave the impression that she was expecting Byron to follow her to Kirkby Mallory and she assured Hanson that if she were needed in London she would return at a moment's notice.

She left London on 15 January. According to a statement made the following month, which she was later to recall for the benefit of Harriet Beecher Stowe, the night before Byron had said to her, in Augusta's presence: 'When shall we three meet again?' to which Annabella replied, 'In heaven, I hope,' and left the room in a 'violent agony of tears'. Early the following morning she passed by his door on her way down to the carriage:

> There was a large mat on which his Newfoundland dog used to lie. For a moment I was tempted to throw myself on it, and wait at all hazards, but it was only a moment – and I passed on. That was our parting.

CHAPTER 16

'Too Much Probability of a Separation'

As Annabella's carriage clattered off through the bleak January morning towards the Great North Road, Augusta began to pack her bags for her return to Six Mile Bottom, but almost immediately she began to doubt whether her brother was in any state to be left on his own. His brandy drinking, the state of his liver and his threats of suicide all gave her cause for serious anxiety. That same afternoon the doctor, Le Mann, called on Byron and afterwards advised Augusta to stay on 'for a few days'. Hanson too considered that she should wait until they could be more certain of Byron's state of health.

Augusta was still doing her best to convince herself that her brother's savage treatment of Annabella was the consequence of his illness. Her blind trust in providence led her to believe that the malady would pass and that a reconciliation with Annabella would follow. The possibility that in the event of separation or divorce proceedings, her incest with Byron might be called in as evidence was something that she put firmly to the back of her mind.

Annabella, as she journeyed towards Kirkby Mallory, had no clear idea what she should do next. She told Mrs Clermont that 'if ever I should be fool enough to be persuaded to return I shall never leave his house alive', but she was not prepared to take the 'final step' and demand a separation. She had not ruled out the possibility that Byron might be suffering from mental derangement and she had no wish to be seen as the cause of his self-destruction. There was still the chance that, after a lapse of time, he might follow her up to Kirkby Mallory and come to his senses.

She did not even know what she should say in her letters to Byron. Dr Baillie had advised her to confine herself to 'light and soothing topics for fear of inflaming his mind still further' and the letter that she wrote to her husband after she had reached home on 16 January 1816 gave not the least indication that anything had changed between them. She continued to refer to him as 'Dearest

Duck', told him that she was 'always looking about' for him and concluded:

> Love to the good goose and everybody's love to you both from hence.
>
> > Ever thy most loving
> > Pippin . . . Pip . . . Ip

When she heard from Augusta that she intended to remain for a while at Piccadilly Terrace, a great weight was lifted from Annabella's shoulders, but this did not prevent her from writing to Aunt Sophy to tell her of Byron's 'criminal dispositions' towards his sister, and Mrs Clermont was instructed to keep her eyes open. Annabella was also very concerned to find out from Augusta whether Byron was missing her.

In fact he seemed scarcely aware that she had gone. He was now far more preoccupied by the fact that he was feeling ill – 'very' – and freely admitted it. His face was swollen, he had pains in his 'loins', he was suffering from memory lapses and had convinced himself that he had seen a man trying to break into the house. He had also taken to keeping a loaded pistol on the mantelpiece.

Augusta wrote to her sister-in-law every day, giving her a blow-by-blow account of what was happening at Piccadilly Terrace. For Annabella, the letters were a lifeline; for Augusta, a way of keeping up her spirits. She and George Anson had gone to Drury Lane with Byron, who had burst into floods of tears, which she put down to his excessive drinking. The calomel pills prescribed for his liver by Le Mann had met with a *'miss-for-tin'* (she was mimicking Fletcher's accent) and had been crushed. Byron and Hobhouse had been out to dinner with the editor of the *Morning Chronicle* and had returned home very drunk, the blame for which Augusta had no hesitation in putting on Hobhouse:

> One comfort is *H* looks really dying – God forgive me, I hope he will take him to a better world . . . – but however B. frown'd to such a degree at me to go away that this dear friend (I mean fiend) either was or pretended to be quite shock'd – said he wd go – & when B. pursued me out of the room to apologise for his frowns (when by the bye he tumbled flat on his face up the staircase) H. said to George [Anson] all sorts of tendresses of course to be repeated to me – I was *all the Angels* in ye world & fortunate for him I was married!

> Fletcher has just informed me he left the house door open at 3
> o'clock in ye morn'g & 'lucky we had not all our throats cut!'

The mother of George Anson's fiancée wanted to discuss his
financial prospects with her – 'Heavens & earth! As if I had not
enough to do without such an addition!' – and George Leigh, who
was coming up to London to consult his dentist, wanted to stay at
Piccadilly Terrace. Augusta was all for finding him a 'bed
elsewhere', but Byron would not hear of it:

> So that is settled & my mind & *conscience* more at ease about
> staying till then. He (Sposo) has been seized with such a comical
> fright of B. following me if I go home that he now entreats me to
> stay . . .

Annabella had been careful to conceal from her parents the true
reason for her premature departure from Piccadilly Terrace and had
confined herself to speaking generally of Byron's liver complaint
and his excessive drinking. The Noels were debating whether it
might be more beneficial to Byron's health if he were to come up to
Kirkby Mallory, when, four days after her daughter's return, Judith
happened to read a letter from the closest of Annabella's confidantes, Selina Doyle. Coming upon the phrase 'in spite of all ill
treatment & everything calculated to inspire hatred', she demanded
to know what was meant. Annabella burst into tears and told her
mother all that she had been bottling up inside her since her arrival
– the full facts behind her dismissal from Piccadilly Terrace.

Judith Noel had never much cared for Byron and her daughter's
description of the 'outrages' she had suffered at his hands sent her
into a cold fury. Annabella was settled in a quiet corner to write a
full account of the circumstances that had led to her leaving her
husband's house – the first of the innumerable statements that she
would ultimately make for her lawyers – while Judith hurriedly
made arrangements to travel to London and take legal advice.

Much as she wanted to confide in her 'own dear sis', Annabella
was far from confident that Augusta would keep the news of what
had happened to herself. On the other hand, she could scarcely
conceal from her sister-in-law that her mother was on the war path
and would arrive in London at any moment. Choosing her words
with care, she told Augusta that she had placed herself in her
parents' hands and that they were seeking confidential advice:

'Knowing your anxiety for *me*, I do not withhold the knowledge of this intention.'

Augusta had been sending off regular bulletins on Byron's health, clutching at anything that gave hope for improvement – 'B came home very well last night – no brandy – & he took ye Calomel again & I have ordered a Fowl for his dinner' – but the moment she heard of Judith's arrival in London she began to step up her references to Byron's supposed mental derangement:

> One of the things he did & said last night was desiring George [Anson] to go & live at Seaham exactly as if it were his own! & even before our dinner he said he considered himself *the greatest man existing*. G. said laughing 'Except Buonaparte!' Ye answer was 'God! I don't know that I do except even him!' ... There was *wildness* & *incoherency* to the greatest degree in all he said last night. G.A. was astonished never having seen him so bad.

Judith arrived in London on 21 January and immediately went into action consulting her friend Samuel Heywood, a Serjeant-at-Law, and Selina Doyle's brother, Francis. Annabella had impressed upon her that she must do everything in her power to avoid legal proceedings in open court: 'It would be a death-blow to me to be obliged to come forward publicly.' Doyle advised a legal separation of bed and board, which, if both parties were agreed, could be effected privately. The first step should be for Sir Ralph to write to his son-in-law, 'taking upon himself the authority which both nature and custom allow to a parent, in any case of a Child suffering injury or being distressed'.

The fact that Lady Noel was in London could hardly be kept from Byron, and he was 'excessively horrified' when he got to hear of it. He wanted to know whether she had come to take him back to Kirkby Mallory.

> He seemed harping on Ly N.'s coming all the Evg & came out with it repeatedly said once 'by the bye Augusta she is I suppose (or I fear) in a devil of a pucker with me'. I answered 'Why?' – 'Oh! because I've not written or gone there'. I turned it off *lightly* & pretended to know nothing which must be ye case without ye thunder is to crush him at once.

Judith paid several visits to Piccadilly Terrace to form her own assessment of Byron's sanity and was far from convinced by Augusta's insistence that '*Lunacy* not *depravity*' was at the heart of the trouble. What she did observe was that Byron talked in such an 'obscene stile' before Georgiana that Augusta was obliged to keep her daughter out of the room. Augusta was constantly expressing concern about Georgiana's health but seems never to have admitted to herself that it was the tensions at Piccadilly Terrace that were causing the child's anxiety: 'she is at times so *excessively* irritable as to make me uneasy . . . last night she told me she felt inclined *to laugh or to cry* she *did not know which*'.

Mrs Clermont, whose sharp eyes missed nothing that was going on in the house, considered that Judith had spoken too harshly of Byron to Augusta, 'although she has on the whole behaved very well', and urged Annabella to speak kindly of her sister-in-law in her letters to her mother, 'or rather as she *has deserved* from you & do not suffer any wild fancies to make you unjust . . .'

On 24 January Judith had her first meeting with Dr Stephen Lushington,* a 'civilian' or specialist in civil law: 'He seems the most *gentlemanlike*, clear-headed and clever Man I ever met with.' With Lushington's involvement the proceedings passed the point of no return. There was to be no talk now of reconciliation, only of the necessary legal measures. If Byron chose to oppose a private settlement, Lushington was confident that the 'Spiritual Court' would grant a separation on the grounds of 'cruelty and temper'.

Augusta was by now well aware that Judith was intent on a separation, but she was still clinging to the vain hope that an improvement in her brother's health might yet pave the way towards a reconciliation. On 26 January, the evening before Judith's return to Kirkby Mallory, Augusta was alone in the house with Byron:

> He gave me an opportunity of saying much more of *derangement*, & took it very quietly . . . Told me about Grandfather's end & his Mother always perceiving a resemblance between them – talked quietly & rationally abt it, but seemed rather alarmed at the thought.

'Grandfather' Gordon (Catherine's father) had drowned himself in the Bath Canal and Byron's forebodings only echoed Augusta's, that it would take very little to drive him to take his own life. He talked, she told Annabella, 'as if in expectation of what is going to

---

* Stephen Lushington (1782–1873), M.P. One of the most eminent lawyers of his day and a member of the team who defended Queen Caroline at her trial in 1820. In 1821 he married Annabella's great friend Sarah Carr.

happen', and said, 'I think things can't go on as they are, don't you.'
Augusta, believing that he was in no state to be told what steps the
Noels were planning to take, chose to keep silent.

Throughout the week that her mother was in London, Annabella
was in a permanent state of trepidation. 'Shall I still be your sister?'
she wrote, and in a letter to Judith begged her to be forbearing with
Augusta:

> She had been the truest of friends to me & I hope you regard her &
> *seem* to regard her as such, for I very much fear that She may be
> supposed the cause of separation by many & it would be a cruel
> injustice.

When her mother, accompanied by Mrs Clermont and Selina
Doyle, reached home on the evening of 28 January, Annabella was
so agitated that she nearly fainted. For the first time she fully
realised that there was now no possibility of going back. Judith had
brought with her a letter that Lushington had drafted for Sir Ralph
to send to Byron and he set to work on it immediately: '*Very
recently* circumstances have come to my knowledge, which convince
me, that with your opinions it cannot tend to your happiness to
continue to live with lady Byron . . .' After Annabella's 'dismissal'
and the 'treatment she experienced', Sir Ralph could not permit her
to return and proposed that Byron should instruct a 'profes-
sional friend' to confer with his own legal representative to discuss
the terms of separation.

Warned by Annabella that the letter was on its way, Augusta's
only thought was that somehow her brother must be prevented
from reading it. She was convinced that it would be a 'death blow'.
All that was needed, she told herself, was time – time for Byron to
recover his health and his wits; time for some kind of reconciliation
to be effected. In a moment of wild desperation she intercepted the
letter on its arrival and sent it back, unopened, to Sir Ralph. She
told her sister-in-law:

> For once in my life I have ventured to act according to my own
> judgement – not without 1000 fears I assure you. but I do it *for the
> best* & I do hope at least it will not be productive of evil, as I only
> wish a *few days delay* & that you would hear all that I have to say
> . . . It appears to me of the VERY utmost consideration that you
> should *pause* . . .

Confident that Le Mann at least would be of her own opinion, she begged Annabella to ask her mother what had passed between her, Le Mann and Sir Henry Halford, the medical men with whom she had discussed Byron's condition.

Augusta's rash act managed to be both heroic and pathetic at the same time. It was a gesture born out of panic and confusion and proved to be totally futile. On finding his letter back on his doorstep, Sir Ralph, accompanied by Mrs Clermont, set out for London to deliver it by hand. What Augusta never seems to have anticipated – she was not the kind of person who calculated the effects of her actions – was that, by returning the letter, she would forfeit irrevocably the goodwill of the Noels. Judith was spitting with rage:

> Annabella has just received your letter. I believe that not much longer will any care for her in this world be necessary. She is in a dreadful state and agitated in a degree that it has become *terrifying*. Your *cruel wicked* Brother has broken her heart.

The opinion of the doctors was brushed contemptuously aside:

> The reasons for stopping the letter will be the same next week, next month and next year and so on – Would you wish my poor miserable Daughter to be exposed to the attempts of either a Madman, or a Cruel Savage? for one of the two he is – that she must continue to live terrified at what he may do next? . . .
>
> You have done infinite mischief, which, if you really love and pity Annabella, You will regret and lament – and for what reason do you imagine that a few days will *change his nature*? – or why favour him at her expense?

Fortunately, Annabella managed to prevail on her mother not to send this letter, but it does give a clear indication of what awaited George Anson when he arrived at Kirkby Mallory bearing a letter from Augusta to the Noels. Judith, he told Hobhouse, received him like a 'Fury'. Under the circumstances it is not surprising that he failed to argue Augusta's case. George Anson even dismissed any fear of 'self-violence' on Byron's part and revealed that he had said that the sooner '*we* took measures for a *separation* the better' – a fact that Judith immediately instructed Mrs Clermont to communicate to Lushington. '. . . the business is now very publickly talked of,' she told her, '. . . the Dowr Dss of Leeds said to Mrs Leigh – that she *ought* to *quit* Ld B.'s House – and *so She ought*, but She is a fool – and perhaps her Brothers having left *her* all he has to dispose of may make her shy of offending him'.

By now everyone but Byron seemed to be aware of what was happening. Aunt Sophy, the buttress of the Byrons, was lamenting the sorry course of events that would remove her 'niece' (as she called Annabella) from the family circle. She thanked her for the letter in which she had broken the news to her, 'notwithstanding the many tears it caused to flow, for *your* sake and for the sake of *others* and my *own* more selfish sorrow. My mournful fancy induced me to think it seemed a Farewell as if all intercourse was to cease between us . . .'

It was not long before the rumours reached the ears of Lady Melbourne, and she summoned Byron to account for himself. 'As yet,' Augusta warned Annabella, 'her whole aim has been evidently to be a peace maker . . .'

Judith was outraged. The last thing she was prepared to countenance was Lady Melbourne's intervention and she was determined that Sir Ralph should not fall under his sister's influence while he was in London. Annabella had already provided her with the ammunition with which to demolish Lady Melbourne for good, and this Judith took great satisfaction in passing on to her husband:

> Ld — [Byron] has told his Wife that in 1813 he had *absolute criminal* Connection with an *old Lady*, at the same time as with her Daughters-in-Law – that *She* absolutely *proposed it to him* – and that he said 'She [was] *so old* he hardly knew how to set about it'. Ld B. has also told this to his *Sister – this explains much*, which was before *inexplicable*.

Sir Ralph was instructed to communicate this information to Lushington and, for good measure, to read *Les Liaisons Dangereuses*: 'You will *there* find the *Viscountess* [Lady Melbourne] depicted exactly in La Marquise.'

The whole story was nothing more than a tale concocted by Byron to test his wife's credulity and how far she could be shocked, and she had, of course, believed it. Sir Ralph dismissed it for the nonsense he knew it to be, and so, one hopes, did Lushington.

On 2 February, a special messenger from Mivart's Hotel finally delivered Sir Ralph's letter to Byron. It was a Friday, a detail not lost on his deeply superstitious mind. Augusta was so apprehensive of his reaction that she could not summon up the courage to talk about it. 'My opinion,' she told Annabella, 'is that he might take the letter quietly *at first* but a few hours might produce other effects – & then the advisers & the friends we dread might have more to work on than if the thing came from himself which I can't help feeling it would in a few days . . .'

That evening George Leigh arrived from Six Mile Bottom. He judged, very sensibly, that there was no role for him in the events being acted out in Piccadilly Terrace and decided to have as little as possible to do with it all. He had friends enough in London who were only too glad of his company.

As Augusta had predicted, Byron took it all very quietly at first and began to compose a 'temperate reply', but by the following day it had not been sent and he was having second thoughts. He simply could not believe that Annabella herself wanted a separation; he probably could not bring himself to acknowledge that any woman would ever want to leave him. Accordingly he dictated to Augusta a note to send to Annabella, asking his wife if it was her own wish that they should part: 'if so he will acquiesce, & . . . you need not be under any apprehension of intemperate feelings or conduct towards those belonging to you . . .' Byron then began a letter to Sir Ralph, giving his own version of what had taken place. There had been no 'dismissal'; Annabella had left as a result of medical advice, although he did admit that he had suggested the expedience of 'temporary residence' with her parents. The cause was the embarrassment of his financial situation and his 'inability to maintain our present establishment'.

On Augusta's advice he laid great emphasis on 'distress without & disease within'. His illness, he admitted, may have rendered him 'little less disagreeable to others than I am to myself', but this was as far as he was prepared to go:

> I am however ignorant of any particular ill treatment which your daughter has encountered: – she may have seen me gloomy – & at times violent – but she knows the causes too well to attribute such inequalities of disposition to herself – or even to me – if all things be fairly considered.

He told Sir Ralph that he would not give him a positive answer until he had received Annabella's sanction of the proceedings.

Having got this out of the way, Byron was ready to write to Annabella, asking her, almost apologetically, if she would explain her father's letter and promising 'eventually' to abide by her decision. By 5 February, having still heard nothing from her, he wrote again, addressing his letter to Mrs Fletcher, with instructions to deliver it personally to her mistress, and trusting that a more decidedly passionate approach might carry the day:

> The whole of my errors – or what harsher name you choose to give them – you know – but I loved you – & will not part from you without your *own* most express & *expressed* refusal to return or to receive me. – Only say the word – that you are still mine in your heart – and 'Kate! – I will buckler thee against a million'.

The quotation from *The Taming of the Shrew* was not perhaps the most fortunate he could have chosen.

On the day he wrote this letter the first of the 'advisers & friends' whose intervention Augusta had feared arrived at Piccadilly Terrace. Hobhouse was horrified to find Byron in lower spirits than he had ever seen him and, unable to believe his ears when he was told of Sir Ralph's letter, he thought his friend must be 'the victim of some *hoax* or *plot* to alarm him'. Subtlety was never one of Hobhouse's virtues. He proposed to set off immediately for Kirkby Mallory and wrote to Annabella 'in great agitation':

> I feel sure that five minutes conversation with you would convince you that the extremity mediated is not the treatment that either the former or present feelings of your husband could be said to deserve . . .

It was unreasonable, he told her, to separate after only a year 'merely for a difference of taste & feelings'. Annabella bluntly informed him that he must be ignorant of '*the long series of circumstances*' that had 'necessitated this afflicting step' and flatly declined to see him.

By now Augusta had at last received Annabella's answer to Byron's question about her father's letter. It was uncompromising:

> You are desired by your brother to ask, if my father has my concurrence in proposing a separation. He has . . . I will only recall to Lord Byron's mind his avowed and insurmountable aversion to the married state, and the desire and determination he has expressed ever since its commencement to free himself from that bondage . . .

The letter had been sent to Sir Ralph for his approval, which accounted for the delay. On Judith's advice, it was accompanied by a sharp letter to Augusta:

> I hope, my dear A., that you would on no account withhold from your brother the letter which I sent yesterday, in answer to yours written by his desire: particularly as one which I have received from himself today renders it still more important that he should know the contents of that addressed to you. I am in haste, and not very well.

Byron had promised to abide by Annabella's decision, but he did not do so. Hanson, whom Augusta had been vainly seeking for days, at last surfaced in London and urged him 'not to acquiesce': there was nothing that could not be 'amicably adjusted' by the mediation of 'respectable friends'.

Augusta, too, was still in favour of mediation. She had had no faith in Hobhouse's initiative, but then she had no faith in Hobhouse. She turned to the one person she knew she could trust, and the one person to whom she believed Annabella might listen. For some days, even before the arrival of Sir Ralph's letter, she had been 'having serious thoughts' of approaching Francis Hodgson and on 7 February she wrote to ask him if he could come to town:

> there is too much probability of a *separation* between him and his Wife – no time is to be lost, but even if you are *too late* to prevent that happening *decidedly*, yet it would be the very greatest comfort and relief to me to confide other circumstances to you and consult you; and so, IF POSSIBLE, oblige me, if only for 24 hours.

The reason why she was so anxious for Hodgson to come to London immediately was that George Leigh was urging her to return home. He felt that in her advanced state of pregnancy, the severe strain to which she was subjecting herself could only be harmful, and he could see little point in her damaging herself trying to save a marriage that he had advised against from the start.

Hodgson came up on the first coach from Towcester. Augusta did not want to give her brother the impression that she had been going behind his back in summoning his old friend, so Byron had not been forewarned. When Hodgson arrived at Piccadilly Terrace, Byron was closeted with Hanson and sent a message to say that he was 'so full of domestic difficulties' that he could see no one.

Augusta was not going to be so easily defeated. Convinced that a talk with Hodgson could only do some good, she persuaded him to stay up until the following day for a meeting with herself and George Anson and, she hoped, her brother:

> The fact is, he is now *afraid* of everybody who would tell him the truth. It is the most dreadful situation, dear Mr H.! . . . He can only bear to see those who flatter him and encourage him to all that is wrong.

She had little difficulty in talking Byron into seeing his old friend and he was happy to agree with Hodgson's suggestion that nothing would be lost in making 'an appeal to Lady Byron's feelings', which might carry more weight coming from him because he was a clergyman. Hodgson composed a respectful and diplomatic letter, stressing that although Byron was full of 'regret and sorrow' for so deeply wounding her, he was 'ignorant of the specific things which had given the principal offence' and wished to know them so that he could make atonement.

Annabella was not to be moved. In a polite but unyielding reply she told Hodgson that Byron had married her 'with the deepest determination of Revenge, avowed on the day of my marriage, and executed ever since with a systematic and unceasing cruelty, which no affection could change'.

Hodgson continued his efforts over the next two weeks but his arguments were firmly, albeit courteously, swept aside. The only positive aspect of his involvement was that Augusta now had an ally, someone in whom she could safely confide. Hodgson's kindness and common sense were a great comfort in a situation where there was now little sign of either.

On 7 February, the day on which Augusta had asked Hodgson to come to London, Annabella had written directly to Byron telling him that she had 'finally determined on the measure of a Separation' and had seized the opportunity to deliver a few telling home truths:

> It is unhappily your disposition to consider what you *have* as worthless – what you have *lost* as invaluable. But remember that you declared yourself *most miserable* when I was yours.

As she had anticipated, the 'Dearest Duck' letter had now come home to roost. Byron wrote to Sir Ralph pointing out the 'affectionate liveliness' of the letter she had written immediately after she had left London:

I am therefore reduced to the melancholy alternative of either believing her capable of duplicity – very foreign to my idea of her character – or that she has lately sunk under influence . . .

Bolstered by Hanson, his old angry arrogance returned; he told Sir Ralph that he refused to compromise his rights as a husband and father and invited his wife's return. 'I fear there is nothing but total war to be expected,' Augusta told Hodgson.

Hobhouse, who by now was beginning to have serious fears for Byron – 'I never knock on his door without expecting to hear some fatal intelligence' – was appalled when he called at Piccadilly Terrace on 12 February, to be told by both Augusta and George Anson that most of the offences against Annabella of which Byron was accused were largely true. 'Whilst I heard these things Mrs Leigh went out and brought word that her brother was crying bitterly in his bedroom – poor, poor fellow . . .' Considering that Hobhouse had been allowed to make a fool of himself by writing to Annabella, trusting in the truth of Byron's absolute denial, he showed himself a person of infinite generosity, concerned only for his friend. But he was hurt: 'I find it difficult to account for his wishing to deceive me . . .' From this point, although he would frequently continue to exasperate her, Augusta began to warm a little towards him.

Although she was no longer sending off daily dispatches from the front line to Kirkby Mallory, Augusta had not given up her attempt to make Annabella see reason and to appreciate the consequences of the case coming before a public court:

> He seems DETERMINED *never willingly* to resign you. What is the alternative my dear A.? That as YOUR Friends ARE *determined* upon a separation this sad business must come before the public. *Supposing* even that nothing is LEGALLY PROVED against him which will procure you this separation, what will the *world think*! Won't his character be blasted for ever! He is convinced of this & *I* am convinced not only will his reputation be sacrificed to this exposure but *his* LIFE . . . What would be your feelings SHOULD *this* be the consequence – or even his eternal disgrace in *this* world – he is in *every* way in *any* way a ruined man.

Augusta was scarcely exaggerating. The most horrifying stories were circulating in the streets of Byron's cruelty to his wife, of his drunkenness and his infidelities, and Caroline Lamb was adding fuel to the flames by accusing him to the Melbournes of '— —'.*

Annabella, too, wanted to avoid being dragged through the courts, but with Byron's growing intransigence this was beginning to look less and less likely. There was, however, one resource available to her that up till now she had hesitated to use: the possibility of bringing pressure to bear on her husband by threatening to implicate Augusta.

In the month since she had left Piccadilly Terrace, Annabella's attitude towards her sister-in-law had been steadily hardening. The fact that Augusta had come to London at her entreaty, and had protected her when Byron's manic behaviour had been at its height, was conveniently forgotten. Now all that counted was that Augusta had committed incest with her brother. For all his malicious blabbing, Byron was still under the impression that his relationship with his sister remained a dark secret. He had never for a moment considered that it could be used against him. As a first step she informed Lushington that she would be of more use in London than at Kirkby Mallory: 'I could put into action some resources which would prevent the ultimate necessity of legal proceedings.'

By now George Leigh had had enough of it all. After two weeks at Piccadilly Terrace, where there were endless conferences behind closed doors, furtive whisperings and outbursts of hysterical melodrama, he decided that his time would be better employed at home. With the greatest reluctance he agreed to Augusta staying on for a little longer and, on 19 February, set off thankfully for Six Mile Bottom.

The day after he left, Augusta wrote again to Annabella, but in such an altered tone that she may well have been put up to it by Hanson:

> . . . I never could forgive myself, if I had omitted everything in my power to contribute to the *future* happiness of both. I do think in my heart dearest A. that *your return* might be the *saving & reclaiming* of him. You could but give it a trial, & if he persisted in his ill-conduct you would be fully justified in *then* abandoning him. Your doing it now, I do think, will be his *ruin*.

---

* Homosexuality. Since the offence was too frightful to be named – it was still technically a capital offence – it was referred to throughout the proceedings only by cryptic dashes.

Little more than a week earlier, she had been telling Hodgson that she could not urge her sister-in-law to return '& expose herself to a repetition of all I have witnessed & heard', but now she was doing just that. She must have been aware that if Annabella were to 'give it a trial' and come back to Piccadilly Terrace, this would seriously undermine her legal position:

> You may know more than I do, of the charges you have to bring against him. Most likely you are aware you will have to depose against him *yrself*, & that without witnesses yr depositions will go for nothing – ye same thing in regard to those who have only heard circumstances from you.

The rest of the letter presents something of a mystery. Augusta asked Annabella what had shaken her opinion as to the 'Principle cause of B.'s conduct'. She had left him under the impression that he was 'insane more or less ... You say subsequent *accts* have convinced you he is not – or words to that effect. The report . . .' At this point the rest of the sheet was torn off (by Augusta, as Annabella scrupulously noted). Was Augusta trying to find out whether any of the 'subsequent *accts*' concerned her, and did she then think better of it?

This letter may well have been instrumental in making up Annabella's mind, for on 22 February she joined her father at Mivart's Hotel. She had given her mother strict instructions never to let Augusta Ada out of her sight, since they were all terrified that Byron might arrange to have the child kidnapped. This was no neurotic fantasy on Annabella's part. Augusta had told Hodgson that there was a plan among Byron's friends to 'go to Kirkby to fetch ye child who has been weaned this month & left with Ly N.' Judith suspected that it was part of Byron's plan to hand the child over to Augusta: 'I am convinced that it is plotted for Mrs Leigh to take it with an allowance which will be of assistance to her *poverty* . . .' As an extra precaution, Judith equipped herself with a pair of pistols. As the law stood at that time, a father was legally entitled to the custody of his child if he chose to exercise the right. Annabella and Judith had no intention of allowing this to happen and they were reckoning that the reputed incest could be used to discredit Byron and Augusta. As a temporary measure, Annabella instructed her mother that the surest way of preventing Byron from taking any action was to keep up a constant flow of information about Ada via Augusta, who, she warned, 'should be spoken of by us in a friendly manner'.

Annabella's discussions with Lushington on the subject of Augusta were very far from friendly. She told him everything she suspected about the incestuous liaison. From the very beginning Lushington had ruled out the possibility of a reconciliation, but now he was convinced that it was out of the question. However, he knew that incest could not possibly form part of the charge against Byron: it would be impossible to secure anything that could be advanced as proof. Annabella's information was based solely on the tantalising titbits that Byron had obligingly dangled before her and these could hardly be advanced as evidence.

If Annabella's suspicions were not sufficient for a court of law, they could be put to a far more destructive use. Her wide network of devotedly loyal friends could be relied on to spread the allegations throughout London. Within a week the rumours had reached the ears of Hobhouse: 'Mrs Leigh has been forbid all intercourse with her [Annabella] at her lawyer's request. A story has now got abroad against *her* [Mrs L.] *and Byron!*'

One of the first to hear of the allegations was Theresa Villiers, who prided herself on being one of Augusta's oldest friends. She had an insatiable appetite for scandal and an unequalled talent for interfering in the affairs of others, but she felt bound to come to Augusta's defence. She wrote to Annabella immediately about the 'infamous reports':

> The fact is that amongst the many very vicious and calumnious reports which are now most industriously circulated in London regarding your separation from Lord Byron there is *one* which is in the *highest degree* prejudicial to *Augusta's character*, and on my vehemently and indignantly resenting *such* a calumny, I was assured that the report was confirmed by *your* refusal to assign a reason for the separation . . .

It was essential, she told her, that for Augusta's sake the report should be contradicted and only Annabella could do this 'with effect' by making known to her friends 'those sentiments of confidence, esteem and affection, which I feel sure you feel for her . . .' She would not 'for worlds' inform Augusta about the report:

but should it continue to be circulated her friends *must insist* I fear on her leaving London, tho' it will destroy the *little* comfort she has remaining which is that of believing that she averts greater evil by continuing in Piccadilly.

Annabella replied cautiously, after consultation with Lushington, taking care to say nothing that would put Mrs Villiers' mind at rest and making no attempt to deny the truth of the rumours. She told her that all her friends had heard her express her gratitude for Augusta's 'good offices' while they were living under the same roof, but she could not make public the real grounds of difference between herself and Byron since this would be 'extremely improper' and contrary to the legal advice she had received. 'It is very painful for me to be obliged in consequence to appear less confidential than I wish towards you . . .'

Having inflicted a considerable amount of damage on Augusta by omission and begun the stealthy process of alienating her from one of her closest friends, Annabella now turned her attention to Aunt Sophy. In a letter, she insinuated that Augusta was in the gravest moral danger from Byron and, if her reputation was to be salvaged, she must be made to leave Piccadilly Terrace without delay.

'It is a constant thorn in my side [Sophy replied] and I know not how to relieve it – without *tearing* a veil from her eyes which might almost overset her *reason*, or induce her to disregard what is so contrary to it. I have written and used every argument in my power to *persuade* her to go from London. Le Sposo and her friends have been equally anxious for it . . . if I could by any means have afforded a journey and visit to L.[ondon] just now I would have spoken to Mrs Villiers who has great weight with her . . . I believe she remains NOW on account of the Drawing Room being shortly expected to take place.'

The 'Drawing Room', the first for many months, was in honour of Princess Charlotte, who had recently become engaged to Prince Leopold of Saxe-Coburg-Saalfeld, to the great satisfaction of the Queen. However, Augusta hardly needed a state occasion to make her remain in London. She told Hobhouse that 'her persuasion of B.'s madness was so strong – that if he was mad nothing should prevent her from nursing him'. To Hodgson she wrote: 'Those who consider his welfare ought not to desire my return. You will be of my opinion hereafter – & at present your bitterest reproach would be forgiven. Heaven knows you have considered me more than one in a thousand would have done – more than anything but my affection for One most dear to *you* could deserve . . .'

The person chosen to announce to Augusta that Lushington had forbidden any further communication between Mivart's Hotel and Piccadilly Terrace was the unfortunate Mrs Clermont, who was now cast in the role of Annabella's evil genius, despite the fact that she was the only person in the Noel camp who continued to defend Augusta. A series of stories about her – some of which originated with Mrs Fletcher – sparked off one of Augusta's rare outbursts of thoroughly bad temper. She wrote to Hodgson on 4 March:

> say what you like of the person who made the communication of a prohibition to communicate with Ly B. – I have been quite ill humoured since yesterday afternoon when I heard she had done her best to put Ly B. against me & Capt. B. – Now I have borne patiently & indeed laughed at all I have heard of reports against me – & it has been a good deal for some days past – the world perhaps has a right to talk – but this woman who knows both Capt. B. & I to have devoted ourselves to Ly B. in every possible manner, considered her comfort & happiness & both suffered such great unhappiness on her acct – I do think it is ABOMINABLE! . . .

Annabella had been observing Lushington's advice not to communicate with 'Piccadilly', but on the day after Augusta wrote her angry letter to Hodgson she suddenly sent for both Augusta and for George Anson Byron. She informed them that she was determined never to return to her husband – 'happen what might' – and that:

> if her own friends even knelt to her to do so she felt herself bound by every moral & religious duty to refuse – & she hinted . . . that she had reason which she hoped would die with her – why she *could never* consistently with her duty to God do so . . .

Annabella afterwards told Lushington that Augusta seemed to think her either mistaken or misguided in her view of the situation, but in fact Augusta's main concern was the state of her sister-in-law's health and her frightening appearance. In a letter to Hodgson she told him of the terrible change that she had observed in Annabella:

> I can never describe Ly B.'s appearance to you – but by comparing it to what I should imagine that of a Being of another world. She is

positively reduced to a Skeleton – pale as *ashes* – a deep hollow tone of voice & a *calm* in her manner quite supernatural. She received *me* kindly, but that really appeared the only SURVIVING *feeling* – all else was *death like* calm. *I* never can forget it – never!

CHAPTER 17

'A Reunion Perfectly Out of the Question'

Throughout the long process of legal shadow-boxing that led up to the separation, Annabella's team acted with unanimity and unswerving determination. Stephen Lushington was one of the most brilliant advocates of his day, while Colonel Francis Doyle, a close friend of the Milbankes, was respected by them for his understanding of the law. Annabella and her father were both prepared to abide by their advice and to see the issue through to the end.

Byron's advisers, by contrast – 'the Piccadilly Crew of Blackguards', as Annabella christened them – were ill-assorted and often at odds with one another. Hobhouse regarded himself as the only person who truly understood his old friend: 'I know more about Byron than anyone else – and much more than I should wish anyone else to know.' Scrope Davies, a wit, a dandy and a gambler, was valued more for keeping the company entertained than for any advice he might be able to contribute. Both were in favour of as speedy and private a settlement as possible, with a minimum of confrontation and certainly as little publicity as could be managed. Hanson and Kinnaird, on the other hand, adopted a much more hawkish stance. Hanson, on the occasions when he was able to give his attention to the business, was as a solicitor prepared to haggle every minute detail to the last semicolon. Kinnaird, as a banker and Byron's financial adviser, was determined to fight doggedly to achieve the most advantageous settlement. Byron himself was constantly changing tack: at one moment wanting to be rid of the whole affair as rapidly as possible so that he could put England and his marriage behind him; at another refusing to countenance the notion of a separation; at yet another ready to take the fight into open court.

At the beginning of March 1816, Robert Wilmot, who had proved so ineffectual in trying to bring about a reconciliation with Lord Carlisle, was recruited as another member of the team. Byron was prepared to put up with his cousin's opinionated pomposity in the hope that he might be a useful mediator. In the event he turned out to be a treacherous double-agent.

At first Augusta welcomed Wilmot's involvement. By now she had given up all hope of a reconciliation and all that she wanted was a painless solution that would leave Annabella relatively unscathed, restore her brother to sanity and prevent her own good name from being dragged through the mire. Writing to Wilmot as soon as she heard he was expected in London, she gave him a brief summary of the progress of the negotiations or, rather, the total lack of any:

> I think a *re-union* perfectly out of the question – & as that is ye case all that remains is to arrange a separation as *quietly* as possible . . . I won't dwell longer on the subject – for I must as long as possible bear up under this misery that I may be of what little use I can – I have been going home 1000 times where everything calls me – but I cannot find it in my heart to leave B. – just now . . .

She concluded with a harrowing round-up of family disasters: their mutual cousin, George Anson Byron's sister Julia, was suffering from a complaint 'very like *St Vitus' Dance*', Lady Parker's eldest brother had died of 'a locked jaw' after a shooting accident, and Lord Carlisle 'will not see or speak to any body or get up – & the old pain continues'.

Never a man to lack confidence in his own abilities, Wilmot was certain that once he had taken charge of the negotiations there would be no further difficulties. Rather jumping the gun, he wrote to Annabella on 5 March telling her that he intended to call on her that day.

> *I give you my solemn word of honour* that it is *my opinion* that Lord Byron *may* be & *will be* induced to sign a separation on proper terms, without going into Court; & to assure you that you may command my services to the *utmost extent*, humble & insignificant as they may be.

Augusta was carried along on Wilmot's wave of optimism and wrote two days later to Hodgson:

> I don't know if you are acquainted with Mr Wilmot a first cousin of ours & a very sensible & good young man – He has seen Ly B. and will I hope undertake to be the go-between in arrangements of an amiable quiet *nature* regarding their separation. He has also spoken to B.'s friends who have been urging him to legal measures – as due

to the defence of his character from the reports now afloat & which I
can't think of consequence . . .

It was typical of Augusta that she should shrug off the stories that
were being eagerly circulated about herself and her brother.
Throughout the negotiations she continued to distance herself from
the rumours, as if they had nothing whatsoever to do with her but
concerned some unidentified third person. Hobhouse, however, was
urgently trying to exact from Annabella a 'positive disavowal' of all
the charges made against Byron, particularly those relating to incest
and '— —' (homosexuality). He drew up a document for her
consideration, brushing aside Byron's concern that this might look
like the price of his agreeing to the separation. Annabella informed
Lushington that under no circumstances would she sign Hobhouse's
disavowal.

On the evening of 7 March there was a council of war at Mivart's
Hotel involving Annabella, Sir Ralph, Lushington and Robert
Wilmot. It was here that Wilmot heard about the accusation of
incest and this was one of the factors that led him to favour
Annabella's cause rather than Byron's. A proposal document for the
separation was approved. The financial provisions were far from
unfavourable to Byron. One issue was left unresolved: the Wentworth inheritance, which would eventually come to Annabella
(and, consequently, to Byron) on Judith Noel's death. It was
decided that this should be left 'unarranged' and 'that when the
period arrives of Lady Byron's succeeding to it, he will *then* consent
to an arrangement upon fair terms of arbitration'. If these terms
were accepted, Annabella reluctantly agreed to make a qualified
disavowal stating that she had not spread reports 'injurious to Lord
Byron's character & conduct', nor had any such reports received
her sanction.

Byron insisted that the 'two grosser enormities' (there were
actually three, since in addition to incest and homosexuality it had
been alleged that he had sodomised Annabella) must be specifically
rebutted. Lushington drew up a new declaration stating that the
specific reports 'do not form any part of the charges which in the
event of a separation by agreement not taking place she should have
been compelled to make against Lord Byron'. This, together with
some minor amendments by Wilmot, Annabella accepted.

On 9 March, Byron, Wilmot and Hobhouse met at Piccadilly

Terrace to review the revised proposals. Byron looked through the declaration and, recorded Hobhouse, 'as it appeared to me – assented'. Scrope Davies, who joined them, 'said that he thought the business satisfactory'. Confident that an agreement had now been reached, Wilmot went off in high spirits to carry the good news to Annabella. Meanwhile Scrope Davies, Hobhouse and Byron took themselves off to Drury Lane and on to Watiers – 'good dinner and convers[ation]', for which a bill of £15 remains in the ledgers of Hoare's Bank.

The next day, a Sunday, all hell broke loose. Hobhouse arrived at Piccadilly Terrace to find 'the whole house in rumpus'. Douglas Kinnaird had taken offence at any financial agreement being concluded in his absence and strong exception to the clause relating to the Wentworth inheritance. Byron, he insisted, was sacrificing a valuable financial asset. Scrope Davies, running for cover, had a convenient fit of amnesia and denied that he had ever seen the document. In any case, he insisted, he 'would not presume to give advice on money matters'. Hobhouse continued stubbornly to defend the agreement, arguing that the 'principle as to the Kirkby property' was perfectly fair. As for Byron, he said that he had regarded the paper simply as a memorandum for discussion and felt in no way bound by it. Hanson, who had not been consulted at all, supported Kinnaird. The whole agreement was in ruins and it was left to Augusta to break the news to Wilmot:

> . . . it is clear to me Hanson & others are driving B. on to destruction – he says in answer to my arguments 'am I to give these men an advantage over me as long as I live by saying I've been bullied into terms'.

Augusta herself, now seven and a half months pregnant, was exhausted. With a new crisis threatening, however, there could be no question of her abandoning her brother:

> With regard to myself – I have ordered fires at St James's – but I am advised strongly, not to stir from hence without an *event* to justify it – such as his quitting this house – or a Drawing room – when I should *immediately* go – this is certainly MY OWN FEELING too – for I think a sudden departure wd give reason to think or say I was *afraid* to stay & face ye reports – however if B. is made to act as I *fear* he is now advised I won't stay a moment to witness or sanction such conduct.

Wilmot was beside himself with rage. He had been humiliated before Annabella and her faction and was determined to make someone pay for it. Did not Byron hear the paper read, and did he not 'distinctly assent to it?' In a long letter to Hobhouse, Wilmot insisted that the document had been agreed '*in your presence under your sanction*' and demanded 'an immediate answer in writing'.

'I really lived for twice 24 hours in the greatest dread of a duel between Mr Wilmot & B. or Mr H. or D.,' Augusta told Hodgson. 'To crown *all I* had been the person who persuaded Mr W. to interfere . . .' She was 'nearly dead with worry & finding that I can do no good'. It now seemed inevitable that the separation would have to be fought out publicly in a court of law and Augusta was working herself into a state of frenzy over what might come to light:

> what is most horrible, dear Mr H. is this – that it is intimated from Ly B.'s side – & I & others even think she has confided it to Mr Wilmot – that there will come out what must *destroy him* FOR EVER in this world – even what will deprive him of all right to his Child, & so blast *his* character that neither Sister nor *Wife* who has lived under the same roof with him can ever be considered as they *have* been again! What this mysterious charge can be is beyond ye utmost stretch of my imagination to guess . . .

Since the accusations of incest and sodomy had been so thoroughly wrangled over, it is difficult to imagine what this further enormity could have been. It is possible that, in the increasingly overheated atmosphere, Annabella's suspicion that at some time in his life Byron had committed a murder had been reawakened.

Torn apart by so many anxieties and conflicts, Augusta at last resigned herself to the necessity of leaving Piccadilly Terrace. Mary Chichester, the Dowager Duchess of Leeds, Aunt Sophy and all her friends had been pressuring her to go and she could hold out against them no longer:

> It is my present intention dear Mr H. to leave this house on Saturday to explain *all* my reasons FOR so doing – all my grief *at* so doing wd be difficult at this distance – but I am told it is positively a duty I owe myself – my Husband & Children not to stay to APPEAR to sanction B.'s conduct – that having staid while there was a *possibility* of reconciliation to do all I could towards it, I had better *now* go – you well know what it costs me to leave my dearest Brother – but indeed I CAN'T express one HALF of what I suffer . . .

On 13 March, Hobhouse called at the house and found Augusta in 'great distress'. She told him that she had stayed with Byron long enough 'to *give the lie* to all rumours respecting herself, which Col Leigh has most handsomely discredited in every way . . .' Hobhouse promised to 'hint' at her departure to Byron, but Augusta was seized with sudden apprehension that her brother would conclude that it was her husband who was forcing her to leave the house. She begged Hobhouse to tell Byron that it was his own opinion that Augusta should leave. George's only concern, she insisted, was that she might have injured her health through anxiety and unhappiness:

> He has never pressed my return since he quitted London, and on the subject of reports has only been indignant and vexed, as it is natural he should feel on the subject . . .

Whatever George felt about his wife and his brother-in-law, he kept to himself. He may well have had his suspicions, but Byron had rescued him from a series of financial difficulties and George was in no position to preach morality to anyone. Life at Uppark and his other regular ports of call involved a good deal of indiscriminate wenching to which Augusta was expected to turn a blind eye.

Still the main voice for moderation in the Byron camp, Hobhouse urged Augusta to see Annabella before she left. Lushington had advised against any contact between them, but Annabella had no intention of cutting herself off completely from her sister-in-law – Augusta was far too useful a source of information about Byron – and she was anxious for the meeting to go ahead. To placate Lushington she drew up her 'principles of conduct in regard to Mrs Leigh', in which she detailed the whole course of the growth of her suspicions about the 'heinous crime' and her reasons for wishing to continue her friendship:

> Lady B. cannot divest her mind of the impressions before stated, but anxious to avoid all possibility of doing injury to Mrs L. & not by any conduct of her own to throw any suspicion upon Mrs L. & it being intimated that Mrs L.'s character can never be so effectually preserved as by a renewal of intercourse with Lady B. she does for the motives & reasons before mentioned consent to renew that intercourse.

This statement was witnessed by Lushington and Doyle and, since the transfer of his allegiance to Annabella's camp was now complete, by Wilmot.

The meeting itself turned out to be something of an anticlimax: Annabella did not even trouble to record what took place and Augusta mentioned it only fleetingly to Hodgson: 'I've seen Ly B. at her own desire – but heard nothing new – the *Citation* is to be out to day! What a business.'

On the same day, 15 March, Byron – who was growing weary of the whole wretched struggle and wanted only to see an end of it – changed his mind and, on Hobhouse's advice, agreed to arbitration over the vexed issue of the Noel inheritance. The matter was placed in the hands of the Solicitor General, Sir Samuel Shepherd. 'There can be no doubt,' crowed Annabella, 'that any man of his understanding & feeling will decide in my favour. In short, it is all as well as possible, and effected at last *through Hobhouse*.'

There was one other factor that had contributed to Byron's climbdown: he had realised, far too late, that the person who had most to lose by the case being fought in open court was his sister. Although incest could not have formed part of the main charge, it would certainly have been used to discredit him and Augusta's position in society would have been severely jeopardised; like her mother, she would have been treated as a social outcast.

On 16 March, Augusta moved into her rooms in 'St James's Palace', postponing yet again her return to Six Mile Bottom, 'as *he* seems to derive some comfort in the idea of my remaining one week longer within reach of him'. She was doing everything she could to spin out her time in London, for she had realised that once the separation proceedings had been concluded, Byron would be off on his travels. 'B. seems . . . to think Alas! Of nothing but going abroad *instantly*,' she told Hodgson:

> I dare not hurt myself with my anticipation dear Mr H. 'sufficient unto the day is the evil thereof'. We must put our trust in a wise & Merciful Providence – but I sometimes think my heart must break when I lose sight of my beloved brother . . .

On Sunday 17 March, having signed the agreement that was to be submitted to the Solicitor General, Annabella called on her sister-in-law at 'St James's Palace'. Now that the case appeared to be proceeding in Annabella's favour Augusta was to be allowed back into the fold, but her self-control was beginning to crack. At a dinner party at the Wilmots' at which Annabella was also present, Augusta pointedly refused to shake hands with Selina Doyle, the closest of Annabella's inner circle:

> Lady B. said Miss Doyle had always taken Mrs L.'s part – on which Augusta observed that she had only one thing to request of Miss Doyle – that she would not take her part at ALL – she did think Miss Doyle had been too forward in her interference . . .

That evening Augusta told her brother that Annabella had complained that he and his friends were talking of her in 'injurious terms'. Byron violently overreacted, sending off an angry letter of denial to Annabella, backed up by letters from Lord Holland, Samuel Rogers and Kinnaird. Annabella made the excuse that Augusta must have 'mis-apprehended', but Augusta was in no mood to give way:

> He *may* have *mis-apprehended* & I daresay the little I did say (for it fell very short of my *own apprehension* of yr impressions) has been magnified greatly in his imagination – but it is a natural feeling surely that he should wish to defend himself on such a point – & tho' I must confess I have very little hope from the observations I have *lately* made, that anything he *can* say will alter yr opinions, yet it was but *just* & *fair* in mine to give him at least a chance of undeceiving you.
>
> You well know, I have never *screened* him where I thought him wrong, but you will allow for my anxiety that he should not be accused *unDESERVEDLY*.

Annabella was not accustomed to opposition – particularly from Augusta – and she was never to forget or to forgive her sister-in-law for this moment of defiance.

By the middle of March the news of the separation had reached the owner of 13 Piccadilly Terrace, Elizabeth, Duchess of Devonshire, in Rome. To judge from her reference to Caligula, in a letter to her son, she had heard all about the incest:

> Lady Byron's fate is the most melancholy I ever heard and he must be mad or a Caligula . . . It is too shocking and her life seems to have been endangered whilst with him from his cruelty, and by now her sufferings. I pity her from my heart: she might have been a happy person . . .

Her son was inclined to take a less charitable view of Annabella:

They were certainly two very opposite people to come together, but she *would* marry a poet and *reform* a rake. As to him, he has at length proved himself the true Childe Harold.

One of the most unexpected consequences of the separation drama was that Augusta and Lady Melbourne had found themselves thrown together. Judith's unrelenting animosity had virtually cut her sister-in-law off from any contact with Annabella – although Sir Ralph did manage to brave his wife's wrath and pay her a brief visit – and Lady Melbourne was anxious to find out what was going on. She could hardly avoid meeting Augusta at court and asked her to call at Melbourne House. Much to her surprise, she found that Augusta took Annabella's part, saying that she had 'great cause of complaint' against Byron, and convinced her that an 'amicable Separation' was now the only solution.

On 27 March, Sir Samuel Shepherd delivered his judgement, stating that Byron should bind himself to arbitration when the Wentworth inheritance should fall to Annabella. Augusta wrote to Hodgson the next evening:

> As this is the *best* we *can* unfortunately hope for, I trust no difficulties can now arise – my poor dear B. talks about being off about the 7th. I scarcely can believe it so soon – I dare not trust myself to think of it – *never* can you know dear Mr H. *half* the interest I must take in whatever concerns him – many a melancholy forboding haunts me! & my spirits sink & have sunk so much of late that I had to be a moment left to my own thoughts – this is *so unlike* MYSELF that I am even surprised tho' perhaps it is not unnatural considering all I have suffered . . .

Once again Augusta postponed her return home – 'my Husband being on a hunting excursion & my children well, I am tolerably free from fidgits . . .'

The Noels hailed Sir Samuel's decision as a victory, but Byron took it as a humiliating defeat, particularly because in accepting Shepherd's arbitration he had gone against the advice of both Hanson and Kinnaird. Someone had to suffer the consequences of his anger. He could hardly attack Lushington or Doyle, still less Annabella or the Noels, but there was one person upon whom he could put the blame for his matrimonial disaster and that was the largely undeserving Mrs Clermont. His vengeance was a poem entitled 'A Sketch'. In a series of blistering couplets the unfortunate woman was compared to a viper, 'the Hecate of domestic hells' with 'a vile mask the Gorgon would disown', 'a cheek of parchment and an eye of stone'.

> Mark, how the channels of her yellow blood
> Ooze to her skin, and stagnate there to mud,
> Cased like the centipede in saffron mail,
> Or darker greenness of the scorpion's scale –

Fifty copies were printed and circulated privately by John Murray. One of them came to the attention of Lady Caroline Lamb. She wrote to Murray telling him that it was a 'shame' to show the verses: 'I give you my solemn word that I would rather starve, or see my child die of want, than I should speak or think of Lord Biron but as a poor paltry hypocrite and a man without a heart. That serpent, his sister, too . . .'

Lady Caroline had been eagerly following the separation drama and, since she was in the thick of writing her Byronic romance *Glenarvon*, she was more obsessed with Byron than ever. She now saw a tremendous opportunity for revenge both on Byron and Augusta and did not hesitate. She wrote a long, absurd letter to Annabella, a curious mélange of flattery, improbable religious sentiment and melodramatic rhetoric, but it was calculated to whet Annabella's appetite:

> Do not think me cunning & crafty because I thus write to you but you are so innocent so good you can not be aware of their arts – truth & virtue will find its way in Heaven & God will preserve & protect you – but to spare you a scene of horror to spare you the agony of having yr child taken from you & consigned to such hands – I urge you to follow my counsel it is from the heart I write it – & urge it – there is a secret – he dares not face that . . .

Another letter followed the next day and, for the first time, Augusta's name was mentioned: 'I believe M. Leigh is your sincere friend – but recollect also that she is his sister . . . there is a difficult game to play & they are playing it skilfully . . .' Caroline was not prepared to reveal any more by letter; her dreadful secret could only be divulged tête-à-tête. 'Remember the situation in which I stand; were it but thought that I espous'd your cause would it not hurt it – so she has joined with Lady C.L. against him – the cast-off Mistress & the Wife make common cause . . .'

Eventually it was agreed that they should come together as if by chance, at the house of 'Caro George',* the wife of Caroline's brother-in-law, George Lamb. The meeting was arranged for 27 March and Annabella kept detailed 'minutes' of their conversation. After a certain amount of preliminary manoeuvring, during which Caroline feigned reluctance to reveal what she had sworn to keep secret, this was what she had to tell Annabella:

> That from the time Mrs L. – came to Bennet St in the year 1813 – Lord B. – had given her various intimations of a criminal intercourse between them – but for some time he spoke of it in a manner which did not enable her to fix it on Mrs L. – thus – 'Oh I never knew what it was to love before – there is a woman I love so passionately she is with child by me, and if a daughter it shall be called *Medora*' – that his avowals of this mysterious intercourse became bolder – till at last she said to him one day, 'I could believe it of *you* – but not of *her*' – on this his vanity appeared piqued to rage, and he said 'Would *she* not?' – assured Ly C.L. – that the seduction had not given him much trouble – that it was soon accomplished – and she was very willing – that in their early years they had been separated by Lady Holdernesse on account of some apparent improprieties . . .

One must remember that Caroline was working on a fictionalised account of her affair with Byron at that time and that her creative instinct more often than not got the better of her. (Brother and sister could scarcely have been 'separated' by Lady Holdernesse, since they did not lay eyes on one another until after her death.)

Nevertheless, Annabella lapped it up. Then Caroline advanced what she regarded as her most damning evidence. She claimed that once in her presence Byron had ordered Fletcher to bring him a portfolio containing Augusta's love letters:

> In which were expressions that must refer to such a connection amidst much foolish levity – but occasionally there appeared feelings of remorse, and she particularly remembered this – 'Oh B. – if we loved one another as we did in childhood – then it was innocent' – but these feelings apparently became less frequent – and there were crosses + + in such positions as could not be mistaken . . .

The crosses, which Annabella had rightly guessed to be part of Byron and Augusta's code of love, provided for her the final piece of

---

* Formerly Caroline St Jules, illegitimate daughter of the 5th Duke of Devonshire and Lady Elizabeth Foster. She married the Hon. George Lamb (1784–1834), 4th son of Lady Melbourne; his father was widely believed to be the Prince of Wales.

the jigsaw. Until now, strong though her suspicions had been, Annabella had been entirely dependent on what Byron had conveyed only by hints and insinuations. Now Caroline Lamb had provided her with what she regarded as unquestionable proof.

She believed that this gave her the ammunition she needed to prevent Byron taking control of their daughter. The problem was that she could never tell anyone how she had obtained her 'proof', for Caroline Lamb was known to be out to destroy Byron and no one trusted a word she said. Annabella could only hint obliquely to Lushington what she had discovered and even to her mother she would only say that Caroline had given her 'some information which may be very important'. Caro George, on the other hand, clearly had a very good idea of what had taken place in her drawing room. 'I do not wish to reveal her [Augusta's] faults,' she told Annabella, 'for I could almost pity her, when I think how unhappy she must be, and I look upon her more as his victim than as his accomplice.' Pity or not, Caro George was happy to be the means of judiciously leaking confirmation of Annabella's suspicions, without, of course, mentioning Lady Caroline's involvement.

Now that all shadow of doubt about the incest had been removed from her mind, Annabella was finally in a position to declare her sister-in-law an unsuitable guardian for Ada, in the event of a battle for the child's custody coming to court. Friendship with Augusta was no longer possible. Being Annabella, she was not prepared to make the break herself, but asked Mrs Wilmot to take on the task, giving the recent quarrel with Augusta as a reason for breaking off relations. In a singularly self-righteous letter to Wilmot himself, Annabella told him that her intention was:

> to convey to Augusta, with the least possible pain, the line of conduct that now seems necessary – for whatever a solitary moment of indignation may have prompted me to express, my permanent feeling will always be to soften, as far as my principles will permit, the misery that awaits her . . .

Hobhouse, who had moved into Augusta's rooms at Piccadilly Terrace, noted with satisfaction: 'This has terminated, I believe, all correspondence between *My dearest Augusta* and *My dearest Annabella*!! Such are female friendships!'

Augusta still could not bring herself to leave London. For another week she stayed on with her sister in Stratton Street, giving as her reason the 'Royal Nuptials'. 'I *wish* to stay *as long* as I *can* on my dear B.'s account,' she confessed to Hodgson. On the night of 8 April, Byron and Augusta together attended a reception given by Lady Jersey in honour of Benjamin Constant, a former lover of Mme de Staël and the author of *Adolphe*, the novel that was the talk of London's literati that season. Caro George and her friends made a point of cutting Byron and Augusta. Now at last Byron realised the degree to which his dangerous games of kiss-and-tell had exposed his sister to public scandal.

Annabella wrote exultantly to tell her parents:

> Lady Jersey has since called on me. So have many people – Lady Derby two or three times . . . Indeed I don't know anybody except the Piccadilly crew of blackguards who is *avowedly* against me . . .

The crew of blackguards were consoling themselves in their accustomed way, dining and drinking into the early hours. Hobhouse glumly recorded:

> We sat up till six in the morning and had a scene between B. and myself at home – poor fellow, he came into my room the next morning to ask how I was – he was very sorry and so was I but our regrets originated from different causes . . .

With scandal breaking around her ears and with the time for her confinement approaching, Augusta could not bear to remain in London. 'I really think of going on Saturday,' she told Judith Noel,* 'as I hear [on] fairly good authority that the Royal Wedding will not be *next* week – & the not being *chez moi* makes me very fidgitty in my present predicament, tho' in fact I believe there is no cause to be as I can't expect these 4 weeks.'

On Easter Sunday, 14 April, Hobhouse went home to the country so that 'Byron might have a free leave taking of his sister'. Byron wrote to the poet Samuel Rogers:

> My sister is now with me and leaves town tomorrow; we shall not meet again for some time, at all events – if ever; and, under these circumstances, I trust to stand excused to you and Mr Sheridan for being unable to wait upon him this evening.

'I never can express what I felt when parting with him,' Augusta

_____
* Annabella, although she had yet again broken off correspondence with Augusta, insisted that the channel of communication between Augusta and Judith Noel be kept open, so that Byron could be kept informed about Ada.

told Hodgson, 'he was so dreadfully affected & overcome that in spite of reason & commonsense my heart is full of melancholy foreboding about him.'

He was now very aware of what he was losing in Augusta. All through the dreadful winter she had remained with him, while he shut himself up with his hysterical despair or roamed about the house in drunken rages, sometimes never even bothering to speak to her. Annabella had told him that he prized a thing only when he had lost it and the truth of this was now borne in on him. When the time came for them to part, Byron was 'convulsed, absolutely convulsed with grief'.

Her farewell gift to her brother was a Bible, which he always kept with him. Writing to Murray six years later and asking him to send him a Bible 'in good legible print', Byron continued: 'I *have* one; but as it was the last gift of my Sister (whom I shall probably never see again), I can only use it carefully, and less frequently, because I like to keep it in good order.'

His remorse, his bitter anger and his misery at leaving Augusta were all poured into a letter written to his wife that night:

> 'More last words' – not many – and such as you will attend to – answer I do not expect – nor does it import – but you will hear me – I have just parted from Augusta – almost the last being you had left me to part with – & the only unshattered tie of my existence – wherever I may go – & I am going far – you & I can never meet again in this world – nor in the next – let this content or atone. – If any accident occurs to me – be kind to *her*. – if she is then nothing – to her children: – some time ago – I informed you that with the knowledge that any child of ours was already provided for by other & better means – I had made my will in favour of her & her children – as prior to my marriage: – this was not done in prejudice to you for we had not then differed – & even this is useless during your life by the settlements – I say therefore – be kind to her & hers – for never has she acted or spoken otherwise towards you – she has ever been your friend – this may seem valueless to one who has now so many: – be kind to her – however – & recollect that though it may be advantage to you to have lost your husband – it is sorrow to her to have the waters now – or the earth hereafter – between her & her brother . . .

'This requires no answer,' was Annabella's only comment.

Augusta was back at Six Mile Bottom for Medora's second birthday on 15 April. George, too, had returned home and she was reunited with the children whom she had not seen for nearly five months. Once again she was faced with having to put together the pieces of a life in which Byron would no longer play a part.

A letter arrived from him that same day, enclosing one from newly married George Anson: 'I trust you got home *safe* – & are well – I am sadly without you – but I won't complain – I will write more soon – ever thine – dearest A.' Then he added a postscript:

I can't bear to send you a short letter – & my heart is too full for a long one – don't think me unkind or ungrateful – dearest A. – & all the *tips* on four *legs* or *two* – ever & again – & for ever

thine

P.P. Clerk of this parish*

For another week Byron remained in London while the final details of the separation were hammered out. He signed the deeds on 21 April. After a night of celebration with Rogers, Scrope Davies and Kinnaird, he managed a short note to his 'own sweet Sis':

All I have now to beg or desire on the subject is – that you will never mention or allude to Lady Byron's name again in any shape – or on any occasion – except indispensible business. – Of the child you will inform me & write about poor little *Da* [Ada] – & see it whenever you can – I am all in the *hurries* – we set off tomorrow – but I will write from Dover – My own dearest – kindest – best Sis –.

By nine-thirty the following morning Byron's vast travelling carriage, custom-built for his journey into exile and modelled on that of Napoleon, was making its way out of London. Hobhouse, who had not been able to obtain a passport, was determined to accompany his friend as far as Dover, as was Scrope Davies. No sooner had they left Piccadilly Terrace than the bailiffs seized everything they could lay their hands on, including Byron's birds, his squirrel and all Fletcher's belongings. For fear that the bailiffs might descend on Dover and distrain even the carriage, it was put on board ship as soon as they arrived.

Contrary winds held them in port, and Byron and his friends put up at the hotel. There, Byron ran into an old Harrow school friend,

---

* 'Clerk of this parish' was an allusion to a now forgotten satire by Alexander Pope, which had been one of their private jokes. 'Tip' was the Leighs' dog.

Thomas Wildman, who had been an aide-de-camp at Waterloo and who gave Byron details of the death of his cousin, Carlisle's son, Frederick Howard. His first thought was to let Augusta know:

> He tells me poor Fred. Howard was *not* mangled, nor in the hands of the French; he was shot through the body charging a party of infantry, and died (*not* on the field) half an hour afterwards at some house not far off, and in no great pain.
>
> I thought this might make his friends easier, as they had heard that he was a sufferer by falling into the enemy's hands. Capt. Wildman was near him at the time, and I believe saw him again shortly before his death, and after his wound.

He instructed Augusta to write to him poste restante, Geneva, and asked again to be given news of 'little Da'. What his last words to Augusta were before leaving England we shall never know, since the rest of the letter has not survived.

On the morning of 25 April the wind changed and Hobhouse hustled Byron, complaining of having to rise so early, down to the quay and onto the packet boat. As it glided out of the harbour, Hobhouse ran to the end of the pier and watched until he could see his friend no longer.

On their last evening together in London before Augusta had left for home, Byron had shown her the poem he had written, after they have been publicly snubbed at Lady Jersey's. It was in praise of her constancy and devotion.

When all around grew drear and dark,
   And reason half withheld her ray –
And hope but shed a dying spark
   Which more misled my lonely way;

In that deep midnight of the mind,
   And that internal strife of heart,
When dreading to be deem'd too kind,
   The weak despair – the cold depart;

When fortune changed – and love fled far,
   And hatred's shafts flew thick and fast,
Thou wert the solitary star
   Which rose and set not to the last.

CHAPTER 18

'Intentionally I Have Never Injured You'

'I am particularly anxious about Augusta's approaching confinement,' Aunt Sophy wrote to Annabella in April 1816. 'She has suffered so much in *Mind*, *Body* and *Estate* for these nine months. I cannot help fearing the effect on her health and energy in the days of darkness.'

Poor Augusta, faced with the ordeal of having to endure another difficult labour, was determined not to allow herself to panic. Only to Francis Hodgson did she manage to give a hint of what she was feeling: 'it will be long before all this misery can cease to be felt as it now is – even the *present* can't obliterate the *past* tho' full of worry for home concerns . . .' The past, or at least the Noels, would not let her go. Judith was still committed to passing on news of Augusta Ada, but constantly nagged about letters going unanswered and a report that Byron was complaining that 'he never heard of his child'. Augusta did her best to deal with it all patiently and politely, 'but I am afraid a *Confinement* is not the happiest prescription for my nerves'. She only hoped 'that this sad business will now perhaps rest', but in this she was reckoning without Annabella, who was determined never to let it rest as long as she lived.

> I felt appalled at the desert which seemed spread before me. At first indeed I felt relief from breathing an atmosphere of innocence – but it was not for long. There was a burning world within which made the external one cold – I had given up all that was congenial with youth – The imagination of what *might have been* was all that remained . . .

In marrying one of the most brilliant and attractive men of her time, Annabella had set her sights high, but she had never doubted that she would be able to control and reform him. According to her own lights she had done everything in her power to make Byron happy; and she had failed. She had been accustomed to put a high value on herself and she had been cast aside. She simply could not bring herself to believe that she was responsible for what had happened to her; the real cause must lie elsewhere – someone else must have brought it about. The obvious scapegoat was Augusta. Had she not existed, had she never indulged in a sexual relationship with her brother, then the marriage would have worked out as Annabella had planned it should. Augusta – and Augusta alone – must bear the blame for what had happened. She must be exposed, punished and forced to acknowledge her guilt. Of course this was not the way in which Annabella would have put it to others, or even to herself. What was at stake, she told herself, was the salvation of Augusta's immortal soul.

The immediate difficulty was that, because she had severed relations with her sister-in-law, Annabella could not work on her directly. Her first thought was to win over Aunt Sophy to her cause, but she either could not or would not understand what Annabella was trying to say and was clearly not going to be drawn into her game:

> there are parts of your last letter that make me very melancholy – parts wholly unintelligible to my apprehension . . . I cannot understand how you can have 'escaped destruction hereafter'. How such purity as yours ever could have been in danger . . .

What Annabella needed was a spy in Augusta's camp. The woman selected for this purpose was Theresa Villiers, whom Annabella knew to be both gullible and impressionable. Ever since Mrs Villiers had sprung to Augusta's defence when the first rumours of incest began to circulate, Annabella had decided that she could exploit her friendship with Augusta and had gradually wormed her way into her confidence, winning her over with flattery.

Although she doubtless did not admit it even to herself, part of Annabella's strategy was to alienate Augusta from those who were closest to her. The vain and opinionated Wilmot had been easily won over, but she could not hope to sow discord among Augusta's grander relations, the Chichesters, the Howards and the Osbornes, who were beyond her sphere of influence. The Honourable Mrs George Villiers, however, presented a simple target.

On 24 April, the day before she left for Kirkby Mallory, Annabella paid a 'long kind and spontaneous visit' to Mrs Villiers at South Place, Knightsbridge, though nothing that she ever did could be described as 'spontaneous'. Her first task was to establish

Augusta's guilt, her 'criminality' with Byron, and this she achieved without any apparent difficulty. Her second was to secure Mrs Villiers' co-operation in achieving her main objective, which was to drive a wedge between Augusta and Byron.

Mrs Villiers was instructed to reopen a channel of communication between the sisters-in-law by dispelling any notions that Augusta might have of Annabella's antagonism towards her after all the accusations and counter-accusations that had followed the Wilmots' dinner party. The following day, Mrs Villiers set to work. 'Nothing could be more warm-hearted, kind, considerate & affectionate than everything [Lady Byron] said about you,' she wrote to Augusta, at the same time taking care to warn her that 'the world *must not, can not* with a proper regard for yourself or your children, be set entirely at defiance . . .' Having sent the letter off, doubts began to set in: she wrote to Annabella to ask why, if Annabella had known about the incest between Byron and Augusta, she had begged Augusta to return to Piccadilly Terrace. Annabella promptly burned the letter, and in her reply resorted to her old trick of hiding behind a veil of words:

> I should have great consolation in thinking that A. was more deluded than deluding on the opinions she now declares – for, to me, duplicity is the most unpardonable crime, the only one that could alienate my kindness from her . . .

But duplicity was precisely what she was urging on Mrs Villiers, although she took care to stress the high moral purpose that lay behind it: 'My great object, next to the security of my Child, is, therefore the restoration of her mind to that state which is religiously desirable . . .' Mrs Villiers was not to be put off so easily. It had, after all, been on her advice that Augusta had returned to Piccadilly Terrace, and she now reiterated her question. Annabella gave her the reply she had worked out with Lushington: her 'conviction was progressively formed' but was 'not yet sufficiently corroborated' at the time she had asked Augusta to come back. She then proceeded to divert Mrs Villiers' attention with a little shameless flattery: 'I honour you, and love you for being her determined friend – it is the best privilege of an unblemished reputation to be kind to victims like her . . .'

Meanwhile the woman whose soul they were so earnestly battling to save from perdition had given birth, on 9 May, to her fifth child and second son, Frederick George. He was baptised on 3 June, with Lord and Lady Jersey (perhaps in a gesture of solidarity after the scene at Lady Jersey's reception) and Lord Frederick Bentinck as sponsors. Fred Bentinck was, like George Leigh, a racing man and a gambler. He was, however, under no illusions about George and throughout his life did all that he could to support Augusta with good advice and a liberal supply of franks for her many letters.

On the day that Frederick was born, *Glenarvon* was published. Although there was no name on the title page, it was common knowledge that the novel had been written by Lady Caroline Lamb and that the irresistible but hypocritical Glenarvon – 'Falsehood and craft were stamped on his countenance' – was Byron.* 'I hope I am not mentioned in it', Augusta wrote to Hobhouse, but the 'Lady Augusta' in the story was based on Caroline's friend Lady Cahir. Annabella appeared, fleetingly and harmlessly. It was a 'HORRID book', Augusta informed Hodgson. 'I can't think of her [Caroline Lamb] with *Christian charity*.'

Byron, knowing nothing of the book as yet, had written to Augusta on 1 May from Brussels. His old spirits seem to have returned the moment he reached Ostend (despite a very choppy crossing) and he was rejoicing in his freedom. He had climbed to the top of the cathedral at Ghent and had galloped across the battlefield of Waterloo, roaring out Turkish songs. Byron wrote again later that month from Coblenz. 'He sends me some beautiful lines *and* some Lilies of the Valley written and gathered by the banks of the Rhine,' Augusta told Hodgson. 'You shall have a copy of the former but don't say they are to me or I shall be accused of all sorts of vanity & I don't know what . . .' The 'beautiful lines' commemorated his sight of the castle of Drachenfels perched high above the river and were eventually to be included in the Third Canto of *Childe Harold*:

> I send the lilies given to me;
> Though long before thy hand they touch,
> I know that they must withered be,
> But yet reject them not as such;
> For I have cherish'd them as dear,

---

* Glenarvon was also a murderer. Byron had evidently dropped the same dark hints to Caroline Lamb as he had to Annabella. Both Goethe and Stendhal seem to have believed that Byron had committed a murder.

> Because they yet may meet thine eye,
> And guide thy soul to mine even here,
> When thou behold'st them drooping nigh,
> And know'st them gathered by the Rhine,
> And offered from my heart to thine!

The undermining of Augusta's faith in Byron was not going to be so easily achieved as Annabella anticipated. Mrs Villiers had already done what she could to sow the seeds of doubt in Augusta's mind by suggesting that the real source of the scandalous stories widely circulating about her relationship with her brother was not, as Augusta frequently asserted, Melbourne House and Lady Caroline Lamb, but rather Byron himself: 'Ld B. had by his imprudent way of talking given ample grounds for such reports . . .' Augusta had angrily refused to accept this and insisted that Mrs Villiers had been 'misinformed'. Mrs Villiers, her defection to Annabella's camp now total, felt free to discuss Augusta with her fellow turncoat Robert Wilmot, who explained his singularly unpleasant plan in a letter to Annabella:

> I have seen Mrs Villiers several times & the last time we sat in judgement on a letter of yours to her, & we came to this conclusion – that it would be proper that I should take the first opportunity of speaking to – – [Augusta] after her *complete recovery*, & that I should tell her that I *knew* – –, & that it was all in vain to deny it . . . I should . . . insist *as from myself* that she broke off all connection [and] assure her that it only remained *with herself* to conceal everything . . . I should tell her distinctly that *he had betrayed her*. This is the outline of what I propose to do with *your permission*.

One can quite see why Byron regretted that he had not put a bullet through Wilmot. Mrs Villiers, endorsing his proposal, gave a more urgent reason for telling Augusta of Byron's betrayal:

> Without it I cannot but foresee a probable evil – that from the state of their circumstances he may propose to her to go abroad with him, she may think it a better alternative than starvation (believing the world ignorant & Col L. is *quite* capable of acquiescing in it).

Annabella rejected the conspirators' proposal. She was the heroine of her own private melodrama and she was not going to let herself be upstaged by Wilmot. Nor could she bring herself to admit that her 'conviction' of Augusta's guilt was based on evidence that she could not advance in a court of law and on a clandestine interview that she dared not admit to.

Wilmot's vanity had been injured, and when Annabella showed him the draft of a highly evasive letter she proposed to send to Augusta, he scornfully dismissed it. Partly to appease him and to put heart into her supporters, she announced her intention of taking 'more decisive measures' against her sister-in-law. The prospect sent Mrs Villiers into a paean of self-righteous hypocrisy that is painful to read:

> I think IF it is possible for anything to bring her to her senses, this step will do so, & be the consequences what they may – the bitterest repentance, the greatest degree of misery, even death itself – I should consider it a blessing (loving her as I have done for so many years & still do love her) when compared with the deplorable infatuation under which she is now existing . . .

She concluded on a more down-to-earth note:

> Col L. of *course* left her for Epsom Races, will now I fancy go to Up Park [*sic*] & she seems to think will not return home till the *July Meeting*. She expects an execution in his absence – complains of great weakness & extreme unhappiness . . .

For all her sickening hypocrisy, Theresa Villiers at least gave some thought to the grim realities of Augusta's position: isolated and unwell, the mother of five children,* and the wife of a wastrel who continued to plunge them all still further into debt with his compulsive gambling. They had reached a point where the only solution to their problems would be to sell Six Mile Bottom.

Annabella's letter was far from being the 'decisive' measure she had promised, but it did mark a turning point in her correspondence with her sister-in-law. There was no longer any attempt to hide behind a veil of politeness. It was cold, mean-spirited and, considering all the sacrifices Augusta had made to be with her and to stand by her when Annabella needed her, staggeringly ungrateful:

> Before your confinement I would not risk agitating you, but having the satisfaction of knowing you are recovered, I will no longer conceal from yourself that there are reasons founded on such

---

* Augusta Charlotte, her second child, had always been backward. Now five, she was showing signs of increasing mental abnormality.

circumstances in your conduct as (though thoroughly convinced they have existed) I am most anxious to bury in silence, which indispensably impose on me the duty of *limiting* my intercourse with you.

There was not a word about her suspicions of incest, nor of Byron's treachery. It was the cutting of Selina Doyle that still rankled, and the fact that Augusta had dared publicly to defend her brother:

... you have not disguised your resentment against those who have befriended me, and have countenanced the arts which have been employed to injure me. Can I then longer believe these professions of affection, and even of exclusive zeal for *my* welfare, which I have been most reluctant to mistrust? – And on *this* ground my conduct, if known, would be amply & obviously justified to the world ...

It was the world's opinion that counted above everything else for Annabella, but she was at the same time haunted by her husband's last injunction to her about Augusta – to be 'kind to her & hers' – and it was with this in mind that she tried to conclude on a more conciliatory note:

I shall still not regret having loved & trusted you so entirely – May the blessing of a merciful God be with you & those nearest you – I am truly interested in the welfare of your children, and should your present unhappy disposition be seriously changed, you will not then be deceived in considering me as one who will afford every service and consolation ...

By now Annabella was incapable of writing even a private letter without seeing it as evidence to be used in some possible future litigation, and this was attested to be a 'true copy' and counter-signed by her father. She was greatly pleased with what she had written and told Mrs Villiers that Augusta's 'first feeling will be terror, her second pride & under what influence she will reply I cannot conjecture'.

What she had not anticipated was that Augusta's letter would be firm, dignified and totally unevasive. She was not 'wholly surprised' by the contents of Annabella's letter, she told her:

Your silence towards me during so long an interval, and when all *obvious* necessity for it must have ceased, formed so decided a contrast to your former kindness to me – and to what *my Conscience tells me my conduct towards you deserved from you* – that it could not but require some explanation ... If my feelings have been wounded by your silence, how much more deeply they must now be so by your expressions, I *need* not – *cannot* say. To general accusations I must answer in general terms – and if I were on my death bed I could affirm as I now do that I have uniformly considered you and consulted your happiness before and above anything in this world. No sister ever could have the claims upon me that *you* had – I felt it – & acted up to the feeling to the best of my judgement. We are all perhaps too much inclined to magnify our trials, yet I think I may venture to pronounce my situation to *have been & to be still one* of extraordinary difficulty. I have been assured that the tide of public opinion has been so turned against my Brother that the least appearance of coolness on your part towards me would injure me most seriously – & I am therefore for the sake of my children compelled to accept from your compassion the 'limited intercourse' which is all you can grant to one whom you pronounce no longer worthy of your esteem or affection!

The brush with Selina Doyle, Augusta insisted, had already been sufficiently discussed between them. She too had had great provocation, but her 'irritation' was directed not at those who had befriended Annabella but at those 'whom I often thought con-demned OTHERS too *severely*':

I will not however say more at present than that you need not indeed regret having loved & trusted me so entirely – & the *sincerity of my affection for you & exclusive zeal for your welfare* ALL to whom I ever spoke of you – and who witnessed my conduct – can fully *prove*. I would not dwell a moment on having done what was only my *duty* and *inclination*, but in *self-defence*. My 'present unhappy disposition' – I have indeed in *outward* causes sufficient to make anyone *wretched*, but inward peace which none can take away. It never occurred to me you would act but on the strictest sense of duty – therefore I'm convinced you do so now towards me. God bless you – for every mark of kindness which you have bestowed on me and mine, of which neither time nor circumstances can efface the recollection.

it was, Annabella told Mrs Villiers in an unexpected moment of honesty, perhaps the best letter Augusta could have written.

Augusta had been more shaken by Annabella's silence than she would have cared to admit. However much relations had cooled between them, her correspondence with her sister-in-law had become one of her lifelines. She was beginning to feel neglected and forgotten, and even the faithful Hodgson had failed her. 'I began to marvel at your silence,' she told him when eventually he wrote at the beginning of June. She was 'weak and nervous, and no wonder [it was less than a month since the birth of her son]. None can know *how much* I have suffered from this unhappy business – and indeed I have never known a moment's peace and I begin to despair for the future . . .' Nothing could have been more revealing of how much she had been wounded by Annabella's letter than her request to Hodgson not to destroy any letters she had written to him 'in favour of Lady B. and her family' and to tell her 'if you ever heard me say one word that could detract from *her* merits, or make you partial to *his* side of the question'. Annabella's paranoia was becoming infectious.

On 8 June, Annabella left Kirkby Mallory to spend two months in 'Lowestoffe'. She needed sea air, she told Mrs Villiers, to cure her of 'Sleepless Nights and head-achy days', but she was also going to the rescue of her old friend Mary, Countess of Gosford, who had chaperoned her during her first London season. Lord Gosford had fallen under the influence of his sister, Lady Olivia Sparrow, a fanatical evangelical, and was trying to force his wife into seeing the light and confessing her 'errors'. 'I never knew such a man,' Annabella wrote to her father; 'he is a thousand times worse than *my* Lord, for he professes to be a Christian.'

Pausing only to scoop up Mary Gosford from Worlingham Hall, Annabella arrived at Lowestoft, where the two disaffected wives took neighbouring houses by the sea, which failed to live up to her expectations. There was too little variation between high tide and low, 'it is not the Seaham Sea, though the same German Ocean. There is no reason why its effects should not be equally salutary.'

Although Annabella defiantly informed her mother that she had not felt so well for two years, her need to gorge herself on 'Divine Mutton' and to restrict her diet to 'meat, eggs and biscuits' suggests that food may have become an emotional compensation. At the same time, to judge from her references to 'opening medicines', her frequent use of antimony and her accounts of 'unloading her stomach' by going out to sea in a King's Pilot Boat after eating heavily, it looks very much as if she had an eating disorder. She may have been bulimic.

It might have been hoped that, with someone else's matrimonial problems to occupy her attention, Annabella might have accorded Augusta a little respite, but it was not to be. Mrs Villiers had been instructed to send regular bulletins to Lowestoft, and her news must have given Annabella great satisfaction:

> Her letters of late have been dejected & melancholy to the highest degree & that of today more so than ever – Her letters to Ld F. Bentinck (who is, as you probably know, very much in her confidence & very kind to her) are, he tells me, more melancholy than ever.

The main cause of Augusta's misery was that it was over a month since she had heard a word from Byron, and she was convinced that he had forgotten her. 'I hear . . .' reported the ever vigilant Mrs Villiers, 'that he is living in Geneva in such bad company that no English there visit him & hardly any natives.' Byron had rented the Villa Diodati on a hill overlooking the lake; the 'bad company' included Percy Shelley and Mary Godwin, who were living nearby.

Augusta was rather at a loss as to how to pursue the 'limited friendship' that Annabella had accorded her. She wrote to her, of course, filling her letters with domestic detail. Little Augusta was thin and 'dreadfully nervous'; Georgey was talking of writing to her aunt; 'my confinement has been a drawback to her improvement in penmanship'; and she gave Annabella the benefit of her advice on sea-bathing: 'I suppose you only try the warm Bath – not the open Sea – but the Air will soon be of use. I've always found the good effects of bathing after*wards* – not at the time . . .'

Augusta wanted their friendship to be restored. She did not want to have to pay the price for it by having her past sins constantly raked over; 'all my hope & wish is to see you once more,' she told Annabella.

Annabella's reply made it quite clear that Augusta would be required to travel much further down the stony path of repentance before she could be allowed back into Annabella's fold. 'Personal intercourse' would not be renewed, and Annabella tried to nudge Augusta forward towards a full admission of her guilt:

> Do not pain me by recurring to obligations. If I could think you owed me any, it would only be for the endurance of trials of which I endeavoured to keep you innocent – though *you* were their cause. I was not the least anxious to spare your feelings – to hope and trust for the future even when I could not but have the strongest doubts of the past.

Augusta was not prepared to be blamed for the failure of Annabella's marriage. As she tried to defend herself, her writing degenerated into a hasty scrawl, rendered even more difficult to read by cross-hatching:

> I only wish *ever past & present* thought could be open to you – you would *then* think *less ill* of me than you do now. I declare, after the strictest examination of my own heart, there is *not one act or thought towards yourself* I would not wish you acquainted with . . .
>
> Had I even entertained the slightest suspicions of any 'doubts' of yours – I never could or would have entered your house – perhaps I did wrong as it was to do so, but I was under delusion . . . I *endeavoured* to do right . . . Dearest A. *I have not wronged you, I have not abused your generosity* . . . *intentionally* I have never injured you.

That was as far as Augusta was prepared to go, although there is a wealth of ambiguity in that 'intentionally'. But it was not nearly enough for Annabella's supporters. Wilmot was fairly boiling over with indignation: 'she compromises with herself & flatters herself, that as it did not occur during your couverture, she has some merit!!' As he saw it, fear was the only means by which his cousin might be brought to admit a proper feeling of shame: 'She must have knock for knock till feeling is produced.'

Annabella, meanwhile, was unexpectedly drifting heavenwards on wings of charity and self-denial. She had fallen among saints. These were the Cunninghams and their followers who lived in Pakefield, a village to the south of Lowestoft. At first they afforded her a certain amusement and she told her father that she was talking 'pye-house' and was supposed by Gosford 'on the high-road to Heaven as well as to Pakefield', but within days she had adopted the language of the 'saints' and was preaching Christian forgiveness to Mrs Villiers:

> In your sanction I have a valuable support, but were I to stand alone, *I never would forsake her*. Those who judge by cold & general rules might condemn me, but I am justified by my motives, and trust I shall be so by the result likewise. Your feelings are most friendly towards her, but should her pride or self-delusion at any future moment excite your displeasure, I now ask you to forgive her *for my* sake.

Annabella was brought back to earth on hearing from Mrs Villiers that Augusta was coming up to London in the middle of July for the wedding of the Regent's favourite sister, Princess Mary, to her cousin, the stout and weak-legged Duke of Gloucester. It was the Princess's last chance to escape from the royal 'nunnery', but it was widely rumoured that the Queen was sternly opposed to the match because the bridegroom's mother was illegitimate. The Regent, it was said, had gained her consent only by bribing her with half a pint of snuff.

Mrs Villiers was worried that the wedding might distract Augusta from the path to repentance – 'the *tourbillon* of that & present exertions to sell the Six Mile will give her no time for reflection . . .' – but Annabella had decided that Augusta's presence in London would give them the opportunity to work on her more directly. She would compose a letter for Mrs Villiers to put into Augusta's hand, which would 'press still more on her *delusion*, for else her eyes may close again . . . It is also my intention to turn her feelings *for him* [Byron], *against her sin*, by dwelling on its *fatal* consequences for *him* as strongly as I can. I believe I must not spare strong terms with one whose moral feelings are weak.'

CHAPTER 19

'Something to Atone for'

Mrs Villiers had worked herself up into a state of nervous excitement about the role she was being expected to play in the salvation of the soul of her former friend. She had been rehearsing to herself a little scene in which she handed over Annabella's letter, which would leave Augusta in no doubt of the depth of Byron's betrayal; then she would gather the broken and penitent Augusta into her arms. Unfortunately Annabella's letter was still being vetted by Colonel Doyle when Augusta arrived several days early and called on Mrs Villiers 'looking quite stout and well ... & perfectly cool & easy'. She plunged into a discussion about '*Gauzes & Sattins*' for the dress she was to wear at a fête that the Prince of Wales was giving in honour of his sister Mary. 'This rather provoked me,' Mrs Villiers told Annabella and, when the fateful letter arrived the following day, she was so nervous that she could not bring herself to put it into Augusta's hand but was reduced to leaving it for her to find in her carriage.

The letter was not written in anything like the strong, unambiguous terms that Annabella had promised.

> In the last part of the time we were under the same roof, you will now remember some things by which I intimated that I knew more than you thought, and almost offered myself to your confidence – not to betray it, *as it has been betrayed* – but that I might have more power to befriend you . . . for I knew more of your dangers than you did, and acted as if you had trusted me in counteracting them to the best of my power . . .

'Do not suppose I wish to exact any confession,' she added. 'Let the past be *understood* now, to be buried in the future . . .'

But a confession was what she was more and more fanatically set on forcing from Augusta. She had not the least intention of burying the past; she wanted it exhumed and examined down to the least detail. 'Write to me,' she concluded with a sweetness that she was convinced Augusta would be unable to resist, '& tell me if you can that I am still as dear to you as I shall ever wish to be . . .'

Augusta's reply was not all that Annabella might have wished. She did not admit to incest – she probably never did so directly – but rather chose to take it for granted as something that Annabella knew, and therefore did not need to be discussed. She concentrated instead on Annabella's 'sufferings' and the degree of her own responsibility for them:

> It is still like a *horrid dream* to me my dearest A. that *I caused* yr sufferings whose whole anxiety was at least to mitigate them. I felt it as my only consolation to do *all* I could, & *indeed* to the best of my judgement I *did* it. Many a time I should have felt it one to have confided unreservedly in you. But concealment appeared a duty under such circumstances, & you know I am of a sanguine disposition, & to the very last had hopes of better for you – & for him . . . What *can* I say to you of my present & past feelings, except that I wish my heart were open to you, that you might judge of its weaknesses & point out the remedy . . .

Although Annabella's letters had not spelled out Byron's betrayal in the forthright terms that Wilmot would have favoured, it was enough to alarm Augusta and, when she heard that Hobhouse was about to leave with Scrope Davies to join Byron in Geneva, she asked him to call on her. Annabella was immediately suspicious: 'She disliked and distrusted him, & suddenly after I left Ld B. changed – I have never understood why . . .' Mrs Villiers hoped that Augusta intended to tell Hobhouse that she proposed 'breaking off future correspondence'. In fact all Augusta wanted was for Hobhouse to persuade Byron to write to her. It was weeks since she had heard from him and his silence, apart from making her deeply miserable, was rendering her increasingly vulnerable to Annabella's machinations and, more importantly, to her own suspicions. Hobhouse saw this all too clearly when they met: 'Poor thing, she did not know what to say. Lady B. corresponds with her again, on good terms, but not so affectionately as before.'

In the middle of July 1816 George's ever escalating pecuniary problems took a sudden nosedive. 'Nothing can be worse than their affairs financially,' Mrs Villiers told Annabella, 'nothing can be more tiresome & impracticable than Col L. of which alas! She seems more than ever aware. What they are to do I cannot guess . . .'

The situation was so serious that a meeting had been hastily arranged between Augusta, the Duke of Leeds and Mrs Villiers' husband. What George Leigh needed, they all agreed, was a proper salaried appointment and the Duke of Leeds proposed to put this to the Prime Minister, Lord Liverpool. It looked as if there might be a possibility of finding a position for George in the Stamp Office as Commissioner, but the difficulty would be to persuade the present incumbent, Warwick Lake, to take early retirement and stand down in George's favour. Lake, who for many years had managed the Prince of Wales's racing stables, had known George since his boyhood and was well acquainted with his circle of friends. Lord Frederick Bentinck was confident that he would retire if he knew of George's situation, 'for Lake is a very kind-hearted person'. Clearly a diplomatic approach would be needed and Bentinck was of the opinion that Sir Arthur Paget would be the man for the job, 'for I know you are as well disposed as I am towards Leigh'.

The major stumbling-block was George himself. If he were to be made Commissioner of Stamps, it would mean living 'in or *very near* London' and this, as Augusta put it, was not 'palatable' to George, who swore that 'residing in London would be his death'. His life revolved around his country pursuits, playing host to friends for the shooting or the racing and making his own regular circuit of the houses of his old acquaintances. It was not a way of life that he would readily be prepared to sacrifice. Bentinck was as aware of this as he was of the urgent need to put as much distance as possible between George Leigh and the temptations of Newmarket Heath. His proposed remedy was drastic, but it was realistic: 'George is as obstinate & untoward as ever, but I think if he was once arrested which might be arranged, he wd become reasonable . . .'

Augusta went backwards and forwards between all the parties who were attempting to help her husband extricate himself from his difficulties, but George's attitude was rapidly driving even her to despair.

> Ye worst of it is the *indecision* & the horror I have of all one's friends being tired out with it [she told Annabella]; you know it is not everybody who can make allowance for that sort of thing. I am in constant *hot water* & know not which way to turn.

Bentinck's patience was certainly wearing thin: 'were *he* only concerned I should give myself no further trouble upon his account . . .' In the event, the scheme was thwarted not by George but by Lord Liverpool, who merely promised to 'bear it in mind'.

Annabella, still living in the company of her saintly friends at Pakefield while all this was happening, was not in the least interested in her sister-in-law's difficulties. Her only concern was to keep up the pressure on Augusta. On 17 July, she tried a new approach and took Augusta to task for the 'irreparable injury' she had done Byron:

> by the involuntary sacrifices (for to principles like yours they must have been *entirely sacrifices*) which you made to his immediate indulgences . . . I know there were other causes for his despair but I believe these to have been as harmful as any – as far as any human being is concerned, it is towards *him* that expiation is due.

Augusta did her best to wriggle her way out of this accusation, pleading troubles at home and the need to catch the post. In her next letter, fraught with innumerable hesitations and crossings out, she took great care to miss Annabella's point:

> I never witnessed any thing like what you have alas! & describe to have been *his* Agonies, & whatever I have suffered I have always carefully concealed from him . . . I have said little of *him* my dearest A., fearing you might mistake ye *nature* of my feelings. I am *certain* they are & ever have been such as you could not disapprove . . .

The royal wedding took place on 23 July 1816 and Annabella told her parents (informed, presumably, by Mrs Villiers' report) that Augusta had worn a 'very fine dress'. The occasion seems to have been a typically Hanoverian affair, very crowded and very hot, with the guests talking loudly throughout. The Regent, the bride and all her ladies wept copiously.

By now, Annabella was convinced that her campaign was going to plan. Augusta had put herself completely into her sister-in-law's hands and it was only a matter of time before the break with Byron could be effected:

> Undoubtedly, her moral ideas are to the greatest degree confused and she seems to have had no other *principle* than this, 'There is no harm in anything which does not make any body unhappy'.

Annabella, with precious little to occupy her time or her mind at

Pakefield other than propping up the unfortunate Lady Gosford or accompanying the Cunninghams on their charitable visits to the poor of Lowestoft, was now devoting all her energies to trying to break down Augusta's resistance. On 30 July, she wrote her a letter so lengthy that it reads like a chapter from an epistolary novel. God, Annabella informed Augusta (she had become familiar with God's ways through her friends at Pakefield), would deliver from evil only those hearts that sought 'undividedly to turn away from temptation':

> If I think you have something to atone for to him [Byron], much more do I think he owes you atonement . . . Till you realise that he has in reality been your worst friend – indeed *not* your friend – you cannot altogether think rightly . . . Forgive him, desire his welfare – but resign the pernicious hope of being his friend more nearly – do not think me cruel . . . You will not be offended when I say that I think his mind too *powerful* for you – I could not feel secure that he would not bewilder you on any subject. The nature of his character [which] I *could* make clearer to you than it is gives him great advantage over anyone in this respect. Alas, my dear A. you do not, I believe, know him . . .

Annabella had been having second thoughts about whether she wished the correspondence with Byron to be broken off completely, since it was her only way of keeping track of her husband. Augusta was therefore advised to continue to write to her brother but to avoid 'all phrases or marks [by which she meant the crosses] which may recall wrong ideas to his mind'. She was also warned against 'the levity & nonsense which he likes for the worse reason, because it prevents him from reflecting seriously . . .'

Augusta wrote briefly to acknowledge the arrival of Annabella's blockbuster the following day, but pleaded the post hour and 'all sorts of worry' as her reason for not answering it, limply telling her sister-in-law that it was very kind of her to think about her. She was still at a loss to know what to say when she settled down on 5 August to apologise for not responding. The simple fact was that she did not wish to reply and wanted the whole thing to go away. Almost anything that she wrote would be bound to incriminate her further and she was not going to be bullied into accepting Annabella's instructions. As she elaborated her excuses to Annabella, her handwriting grew less and less legible, but eventually she managed to put together an answer of sorts in which she pleaded rather forlornly to be allowed to handle the business her own way:

> I assure you most solemnly, most truly, I have long felt that he has *not* been my friend, but from my very heart I forgive him, & pray to God to forgive him & change his heart – to restore him to peace – & there is nothing I would not do which could be done consistently with my duty to God & to others to contribute to his good . . .

This was not the response Annabella had anticipated and she decided that it was time to leave the wretched Lady Gosford and come to London to conduct the final stages of her campaign in person. Mrs Villiers excitedly urged her not to delay: 'I think your seeing her NOW would very materially assist you in your endeavour to save her. She has already committed herself beyond all hope of resisting.'

Augusta had no good reason to remain in town. Her tour of duty at 'St James's Palace' had come to an end and George was demanding her immediate return to Six Mile Bottom, since he was incapable of handling the sale of the house without her. Nevertheless, Augusta decided to risk her husband's displeasure and stay on in London until Annabella arrived. Mrs Villiers reported that George was 'very cross', but Augusta justified herself remaining on the grounds that Mr Villiers was seeking another meeting with Lord Liverpool to discuss the Stamp Office proposal. George decided that the best tonic for his flagging spirits would be to spend a few days with Sir Harry Fetherstonhaugh and, after calling in at 'St James's Palace', he took himself off to Uppark, as usual leaving everyone else to fight his battles for him. Frederick Bentinck was furious: 'I never in my life met with a man of so spoiled a temper & such a wrong headed disposition.'

Although Augusta told Annabella that she would be glad to have the opportunity of discussing her 'domestic concerns' with her, she must have known that there could be only one topic of conversation between them. Yet she was, as always, irresistibly drawn towards Annabella. She may have hoped, in her muddled, trusting way, that a meeting between them might somehow restore their friendship to its former footing and she did her best to paint a rosy picture of the welcome awaiting her sister-in-law:

> I declare I am quite 'a *ground*' as the sailors say – Georgey is gone to

dine & spend the day with the Duke of Leeds's boy – but desires her love – *ten* kisses & a great deal more which I don't recollect – you can't think how joyfully she talks about your coming. I don't think there is any body she loves better. I am going to dine with Mrs Villiers who by the bye said she would be most happy to see you.

Mrs Villiers was evidently becoming extremely adept at the art of deception.

On 31 August, Annabella, accompanied by maids and nurses and little 'Da' herself, came to London and took rooms at 1 Seymour Street. Her campaign against Augusta had hitherto been carried out entirely by letter, and each letter had been very carefully considered and some of them even handed over to Colonel Doyle for his advice and approval. Now she was to confront her sister-in-law face to face, with no legal adviser holding her hand, and she was determined to take no chances. She had prepared a secular catechism that she intended to put to Augusta:

> Do you sorrow most for the sin or for the consequences? – for the offence towards God – or the injury towards your fellow creatures? Do you sufficiently feel that every *thought* associated with such sin is sinful, that the heart be criminal though the actions are innocent? Whenever you have any communication with him, question your own heart scrupulously whether these be simply your objects – whether you are not deceived by the wish of still being dear to him, or the dread of those consequences from *his* displeasure, which led you to incur God's *anger*.
>
> Are you sincerely resolved never to indulge him or yourself in that self-deceiving way again? And strictly to confine your manifestations of interest for him to what is required by the following considerations – provided they do not interfere with the determination of *never being again on terms of familiar affection with him*.

Her questions are all too disturbingly reminiscent of a medieval witch-trial.

Augusta was singularly ill-prepared for their meeting. For weeks she had been writing to Byron, begging him to reply to her letters. She was haunted by the fears that Mrs Villiers had planted in her mind that he might have betrayed their relationship to others, particularly to Caroline Lamb, and she wanted some kind of assurance that he had not. His silence had only heightened her suspicions, while stories circulated by her old enemy Caro George, concerning Byron's scandalous life at the Villa Diodati with 'those three women',* only added to her misery and uncertainty.

Nevertheless, on her first encounter with Annabella on 1 September Augusta seems to have had the best of it. Annabella's edgy note to her mother that she had no reason to regret the interview does not suggest that it had gone the way she had intended, and the letter written to her by Augusta the following morning does not read like that of a chastened and repentant sinner:

> I am so sorry for your bad night & for your *idea* of my *uncomfortableness*, which is however a *fancy of your own*. But I daresay I *looked* something or other which made you fancy. Pray have a good night & write me a second post note to say when I am likely to see you again, & tell me you are no longer sorry. I assure you I only feel & felt pleasure & comfort in seeing you &c – ALL at least that I am now . . .

Annabella was later to claim that, during one of their meetings that summer, Augusta made a full confession of 'the previous connection – any subsequent to my marriage being stoutly denied', but the few details that she recorded suggest that the confession was rather less than full:

> She acknowledged that the verses ('I speak not' &c.)† of which I have the original were addressed to her.
>
> She told me that she had never felt any suspicions of my suspicions except at the time in the summer of 1815 when I evidently wished she should leave us, but she had often told him he said such things before me as would have led *any other* woman to suspect. He reassured her when these doubts recurred, & she seems to have acted upon the principle that what could be concealed from me was no injury.
>
> She denied that during the business of the separation he had ever addressed any criminal proposals to her.
>
> Augusta told me that she had never seen remorse for his guilt towards her but once – the night before they last parted, previous to his going abroad.

---

* One of 'three women' (probably glimpsed only through a telescope) was almost certainly a man, Percy Bysshe Shelley, with his slight figure and long hair; the second was his mistress, Mary Godwin; and the third was Mary's stepsister, Claire Clairmont. Claire had presented herself on Byron's doorstep shortly after Augusta had moved out of Piccadilly Terrace but while she was still in London, and was now carrying his child. If Augusta knew of her existence it would hardly have contributed to her peace of mind.
† 'Stanzas for Music'.

Augusta was rewarded for her good conduct with what Annabella termed a 'dinner of duty and expediency' (for which Sir Ralph had sent the first partridges of the season), to which Aunt Sophy and Mrs Villiers had also been invited, but Annabella was not altogether happy with the progress she was making. She needed a less equivocal admission of guilt from Augusta and she wanted to alienate her completely from Byron. This might perhaps be achieved, she decided, if Augusta could be encouraged to make a full confession to Mrs Villiers.

Mrs Villiers was not at all enthusiastic. If she were to tell Augusta that she had discovered that the allegations made against her were true and she knew for certain that they 'originated from Lord B.', the double game she had been playing would be exposed, since she could only have obtained that knowledge from Annabella. Her objections were overruled; Mrs Villiers would simply tell Augusta that her 'detailed information' came from a source she could not doubt. Having resolved this difficulty, Annabella informed Augusta that Mrs Villiers wished to communicate to her the 'horrible report she had heard' and had come to Annabella 'conceiving that I must be your most sincere friend'. She was 'too ill at present to undertake a conversation' but hoped to see Augusta before she left town.

Naïvely trusting Augusta may have been, but she was not a fool and she instantly smelled a rat. She told Annabella that she could not see Mrs Villiers. When Augusta called on her the following day, Annabella wrote a letter to Mrs Villiers on her behalf, telling her that Augusta did not wish to cause her agitation in her 'present state'. The moment Augusta was out of the door Annabella added a triumphant postscript of her own:

> She has shown me of her own accord *his* letters to her, having only suppressed them because of the bitterness towards me. They are *absolute love letters*, and she wants to know how she can stop them.

This marked the turning point in Augusta's relationship both with Byron and with Annabella. It is not certain what brought about Augusta's sudden and abject capitulation. The most likely cause lay in her long-awaited letter from Byron.

> Your confidential letter is safe, and all the others. This one has cut me to the heart because I have made you uneasy. Still I think all these apprehensions very groundless. Who can care for such a wretch as C. [Caroline Lamb] or believe such a seventy times

convicted liar? And in the next place, whatever she may suppose or assert – I never 'committed' anyone to her but *myself*. And as to her fancies – she fancies any thing – and every body – Lady M. &c. &c. Really this is starting at shadows. You distress me with – no – it is not *you* . . . do not be uneasy – and do not 'hate yourself' if you hate either let it be *me* – but do not – it would kill me; we are the last persons in the world – who ought – or could cease to love one another . . .

Despite the tenderness of the last words, it was the sheer inadequacy of Byron's reply that reduced Augusta to despair. He could not have failed to understand the implications of her letters, but he had chosen to protect only himself, and Augusta knew her brother too well to be deceived. It might have been better if he had admitted outright that he had revealed the secret of their relationship both to Caroline Lamb and to Lady Melbourne, since his evasiveness only served to confirm Augusta's suspicions. Far from giving her the reassurance she needed, he had only made her realise how isolated she was. But there is also the possibility that she may have got to hear of the existence of Claire Clairmont,* who had been with Byron at Diodati. During the last weeks before he left England, Claire had deliberately set out to seduce Byron and had then gone out to Geneva to await his arrival. The realisation that Byron had been indulging in a casual affair at a time when Augusta was suffering so much misery on his account and was distraught at the prospect of him going away would have been quite enough to make her hand over the letters. Her discovery of Mrs Villiers' treachery must have been the final blow.

Showing Annabella Byron's letters was an act of betrayal, but it was no greater a betrayal than his showing her letters to Lady Melbourne and Caroline Lamb, or, for that matter, Annabella showing her letters to Mrs Villiers. Another major factor was that Augusta's meetings with Annabella had awakened memories of their friendship when they had stood together against Byron in the dark days at Piccadilly Terrace. Augusta realised that she needed Annabella, not simply as an umbrella to protect her from society's disapproval (which was how Annabella saw it), but as a friend and confidante, a sister to talk or write to, someone with whom she

* Claire Clairmont (1797–1879) was the daughter of the second wife of the novelist William Godwin and had travelled, in May 1816, to Switzerland with Shelley and his mistress, Mary, the daughter of Godwin's first wife, Mary Wollstonecraft.

could share her troubles. Passing on Byron's letters became a way of holding on to her. Undoubtedly, there were times when Augusta was all too well aware of the shameful and spineless nature of what she was doing: some of Byron's endearments she scratched out; occasionally pages were torn off; and sometimes entire letters were not passed on.

She does not seem to have had any idea of the extent to which she was putting herself in Annabella's power, but her belief in 'least done soonest mended' no doubt blinded her to Annabella's more sinister designs. Augusta would have done well to follow the advice given to her by Hobhouse in a letter written from Geneva on 9 September. Speaking of Annabella as her 'Lowestoft correspondent', he said:

> Pardon me dear Mrs Leigh if I were there to advise the strictest confinement to very *common* topics in all you say in that quarter. Repay kindness in any other way but confidence. I say this not in reference to the lady's character but as a maxim to serve in all cases.

Mrs Villiers' conscience was now beginning to trouble her. She had been greatly shaken by Augusta's refusal to see her and was deeply embarrassed that her double-dealing had been exposed. 'I felt I was doing unkindly by her,' she told Annabella, 'and I could not reconcile myself to it.' She therefore sent Augusta a 'very long letter'. She told her, amongst much else, that she considered her to be 'the Victim of the most infernal plot that had ever entered the mind of man to conceive' and advised her to place 'unbounded, unreserved confidence' in Lady Byron; 'that not a letter, a note, a word' should pass between Byron and Augusta without being submitted to her; that Annabella was her 'guardian angel & the only person who could assist her to counteract the execrable villainy of the other'. She informed Annabella:

> I told her that my horror, my detestation, my execration of the person who had beguiled & betrayed her exceeded all my powers of expression and that with the exception of forgiveness no other feelings than those I described *could, should, or ought* to exist in her mind towards him.

Having broken down Augusta's defences, Mrs Villiers called on her and was 'very violent' in her expressions of resentment against Byron.

In her clumsy, forthright way she had succeeded where Annabella had failed, bringing home to Augusta the extent to which Byron had abused her trust in him. What Augusta had at first flatly refused to believe she was now forced to admit to herself. She would forgive Byron, for she could always forgive him anything, but the most disturbing result of her realisation of his betrayal was that she had been driven into the arms of the woman she should have done her utmost to avoid – her 'guardian angel', Annabella – and it would now be very difficult to escape from her embrace.

CHAPTER 20

'He Would Never Forgive Me'

September 1816 found George Leigh in uncharacteristically high spirits, although as Augusta observed, 'without any particular cause for affairs are ye same, so of course durability can't be expected'. He had thoroughly enjoyed himself at Uppark, and was about to set off for a reunion of the old sporting fraternity at the Delmé Radcliffes' house, Hitchin Priory. On the day before he left, he rode out to meet the Earl and Countess of Darlington, who were on their way home to Raby Castle in County Durham. They had recently been in Geneva, where, they told George with a certain relish, they had heard that Augusta was living with Byron, disguised as a page, and 'their informer could not be persuaded that it was not so'.

If the 'page' existed at all, it was probably Shelley, since Mary Godwin was not given to dressing up in men's clothes and Claire Clairmont was four months pregnant. Byron had rather sheepishly acknowledged her existence to Augusta in a letter written from Diodati on 8 September:

> Now – don't scold – but what could I do? – a foolish girl – in spite of all I could say or do – would come after me – or rather went before me – for I found her here – and I have had all the plague possible to persuade her to go back again – but at last she went. – Now – dearest – I do most truly tell thee – that I could not help this – that I did all I could to prevent it – & have at last put an end to it. – I am not in love – nor have love left for any, – but I could not exactly play the Stoic with a woman – who had scrambled eight hundred miles to unphilosophise me . . .

In accordance with their agreement, Augusta passed the letter on to Annabella, enclosing her own running commentary:

> Sposo dining out, children asleep – would that you were here to say to instead of write my observations &c upon the enclosed of ye 14th. I have had 20 different determinations as to sending it to you, but I

wish to do right & I really think you ought to see it, tho it may and will give you pain . . .

This was also the letter in which Byron had revealed to her that Annabella had secretly opened his letter trunks. For all that she was in thrall to Annabella, and despite the fact that she was enjoying the limited friendship that had now been accorded her, Augusta seems to have derived a certain amount of quiet satisfaction from passing on to her sister-in-law those letters in which Byron was harshly critical of his wife, while at the same time throwing up her hands in horror with a flurry of quotation marks. She was also curious to find out what Annabella's reaction would be to Byron's accusation that she had been 'in *correspondence* with that self-avowed libeller & strumpet [scratched out] wife' – in other words, with Lady Caroline Lamb. Augusta was by now quite aware that Annabella had had a secret meeting with Caroline and observed, with an irony that was almost certainly wasted on Annabella: 'I think I told you that I had heard from 2 quarters of it, & replied, *if* it were true I was sure it was from some *good* tho' perhaps hidden motive . . .'

Although Byron expected his sister to take a tolerant view of his indulging in 'a little love . . . by way of a novelty', he was not prepared to take her own friendships so lightly. He had heard from Hobhouse that Lord Bentinck was frequently to be found in her apartments: 'pray why is that fool so often a visitor? Is he in love with you?' Bentinck's inclinations were more towards notorious courtesans such as Harriette Wilson* than towards the wives of his friends. For Augusta he felt only 'compassion' and he was prepared to put himself to endless trouble on her behalf, trying to find ways of keeping her husband out of trouble and doing his best to find a purchaser for Six Mile Bottom.

Byron too had plans for rescuing Augusta from her troubles. Perhaps she might come out for a little 'tour' with him, bringing one or two of her children:

I think I could make it pleasing to you, & it should be no expense to L. or to yourself . . . The great obstacle would be that you are so admirably yoked – and necessary as a housekeeper – and a letter writer – & a place-hunter to that very helpless gentleman your Cousin, that I suppose the usual self-love of an elderly person would

* Harriette Wilson (1787–1846). Celebrated courtesan and author of the notorious 'publish and be damned' Memoirs.

interfere between you & any scheme of recreation or relaxation, for however short a period.

It is curious that Byron could not bring himself to refer to George as Augusta's husband. He went on to write one of the most moving of all his declarations of love:

What a fool I was to marry – and *you* not very wise – my dear – we might have lived so single and so happy – as old maids and bachelors; I shall never find any one like you – nor you (vain as it may seem) like me. We are just formed to pass our lives together, and therefore – we – at least – I – am by a crowd of circumstances removed from the only being who could ever have loved me, or whom I can unmixedly feel attached to. Had you been a Nun – and I a Monk – that we might have talked through a grate instead of across the sea – no matter – my voice and my heart are ever thine –

This, too, was passed on to Annabella and must have made painful reading.

She commented acidly to Mrs Villiers: 'The worst . . . is that it leaves her the means of deluding herself into the belief of his loving her *sometimes* as a sister – and then she is naturally softened . . .' In her letter to Annabella enclosing Byron's note, Augusta prudently concentrated on his invitation to join him abroad, pointing out that he had failed to take into account the fact that she could not leave England even for a short time without the permission of Queen Charlotte, '& after *what has been said* such a *petition* wd not do'.

Although the Queen, on the whole, shut her ears to court gossip, she would certainly have known of the scandal surrounding Byron's separation and would hardly have given Augusta leave to join her brother abroad.

In his letter Byron had also expressed a rather vague hope of being able to return to England in the spring and this had sent Augusta into a flutter of apprehension. If the reports of incest and sodomy (she did not refer to them as directly as that) were circulating as fully as Mrs Villiers had suggested, how could he even contemplate returning? She made a great point of asking Annabella not to mention Byron's return to Mrs Villiers, but this was, of course, ignored. Mrs Villiers was told and shown everything. All three women were now linked in a chain of deception. Mrs Villiers did not wish Augusta to know that she had been shown Byron's letters, nor did Annabella wish it to be known that she was breaking her sister-in-law's trust. Augusta, in turn, did not want her brother to find out that she was showing his letters to Annabella:

> don't for Heaven's sake in *any* way let it travel round to *him* that you have seen his letters. You can't be *too* cautious, for I'm certain he wd never forgive me & is perhaps laying a *trap* for me.

Annabella had reluctantly returned to Kirkby Mallory and, left alone with her daughter and her parents, she was in low spirits. Wandering forlornly round the house, she came across an old notebook that she had not opened since 1810, the year of her first London season. 'What a volume of human nature has been opened to me!' she recorded, and began to set down her thoughts on the woman who had now become an inescapable obsession:

> A. – is formed to feel for all – yet from the nature of her situation must not feel as she could – and otherwise circumstances *ought* – The moment her heart softens, its tenderness returns to one from whom it should be banished for ever –
> 'Had I been happy, I too had been gentle' – she has all the unamiable & unendearing duties of life to perform – She must spare the feelings of others and sacrifice her own.

'Had I been happy, I too had been gentle' was perhaps the saddest admission Annabella ever made.

For once Augusta's spirits were soaring. She believed that she had at last found a purchaser for the house. The 'parish curate' had called round at half-past eight in the morning and had been entertained by Georgey until Augusta could come down. Georgey had told the 'curate' that Six Mile Bottom was on the market and he had put in an offer to Augusta for the asking price of £3,000. 'My only fear, is his turning out a *Mad*man – he looks rather crazy,' wrote Augusta.

Georgey herself had now become the latest victim of Annabella's crusading zeal. Having once promised her uncle that the first letter she ever wrote would be to him, she painstakingly composed a brief note to Byron telling him that she had met Ada. Annabella took strong exception when she heard of this, demanding that all communication between Byron and Georgey should cease.

Mrs Villiers, not to be outdone, suggested that Georgey, who was not yet eight years old, should be fully informed of Byron's cruelty to his wife. Augusta would not hear of it: 'I think Georgey is far too young to understand the thing as I would wish her – & why make her unhappy before it is needful?' The necessity to avoid pointless unhappiness was always at the heart of Augusta's philosophy and, however hard-pressed she was by her enemies, she never allowed herself to be deflected from it.

Byron had conveniently put all his sister's troubles out of his mind, and on 17 September he set off from Diodati on an excursion into the Alps. But if her troubles were forgotten, she herself was not and he was keeping a detailed account for her of his adventures, 'thinking it might amuse you'. There was plenty for Annabella and Mrs Villiers to get their teeth into. He told her that he fell asleep thinking of her and that the peasant girls of Oberhasli 'sing too that *Tyrolese air* & song which you love – Augusta – because I love it – & I love because you love it – they are still singing – Dearest – you do not know how I should have liked this – were you with me . . .' All this was harmless enough, though Annabella did not see it in that light.

Byron had been sending back to England poems that praised Augusta at the expense of Annabella. Moved and flattered though Augusta may have been in private, she was deeply embarrassed as far as Annabella was concerned. When Byron asked her to sanction their publication Augusta was put in an invidious situation, caught between her sister-in-law's disapproval and her brother's anger. She could hardly shelter behind the asterisks of 'Stanzas to *****' when it was all too obvious to whom the verses were addressed:

> Though human, thou didst not deceive me,
> Though woman, thou didst not forsake,
> Though loved, thou forbearest to grieve me,
> Though slandered, thou never couldst shake . . .*

Mrs Villiers had taken great exception to the poem, eagerly pointing out to Annabella double-meanings that Augusta (and possibly even Byron) had failed to notice. 'I heartily wish ye verses in the Red Sea,' Augusta wrote to Annabella, '& I never heard or dreamt of them till Mrs V.'s information.'

Mrs Villiers had also been doing her best to make mischief in another quarter. She had called on the Countess of Chichester, whom she had known since they were girls, and had subtly tried to assess the chances of alienating her from her half-sister. She wrote

---

* This poem, after much indecision, Augusta eventually sanctioned for publication. Another, the 'Epistle to Augusta', was suppressed at her insistence.

an account of her visit for Augusta, in which the more sensitive passages were expressed in French, though whether this was for the benefit of the servants or for George is not evident. She took some satisfaction in pointing out to Augusta how much the security of her position in society depended upon her sister-in-law's good will:

> *Je lui ai dit . . . que je trouvait qu'il n'y avait rien de si important pour vous & pour vos enfants que de faire voir au monde l'affection et la bonne intelligence que subsistait entre votre belle-soeur et vous et qu'il n'y avait rien de si essential à votre caractère & à votre bonheur que de donner un démenti absolu aux bruits infâmes que s'étaient répandus, & dont elle m'avait parlée elle même & que aucun démenti ne pouvait être si fort que la certitude de votre liaison avec votre belle soeur . . .**

She was also at pains to point out to Augusta that she had predicted that Byron would ask her to join him on the Continent, '*parce que c'etait le moyen le plus prompt et le plus sûr pour consommer votre ruine . . .*'

It had originally been Annabella's intention, perhaps to please Byron, that Augusta should be one of Ada's godmothers, but there could no longer be any question of this. Her cousin Lady Tamworth was now appointed in her stead. 'It is not necessary that A. should know the change,' she told Mrs Villiers, who was herself put out, since she had hoped that she would be the chosen replacement. George Anson Byron, living only a little way away from the Noels' house at Kirkby Mallory, was to be the godfather, for Annabella was now doing all that she could to bring him into her camp. The news did not take long to reach Augusta, who wrote to Annabella with just the slightest touch of irony:

> By the bye I did [hear] in round about ways that *the* Captain was to be her Parrain [godfather]. Is not that an alteration from the original plan – & would you wish to make another? Dearest A., do as you think *best* – you well know my wishes, so I will say no more.

Annabella now began to work relentlessly to poison George Anson's mind against Augusta and to coax out of him useful titbits

---

* 'I said to her . . . that I felt that there was nothing so important for you & your children to show the world the affection and good understanding that exists between your sister-in-law and you and there was nothing so essential to your reputation & your happiness than to give an absolute denial to the infamous rumours that have been spread & of which she had spoken to me & that no denial could be stronger than the assurance of your relationship with your sister-in-law.'

about life at Piccadilly Terrace when he was staying in the house with Augusta and Byron: 'He was astonished at the *personal familiarities* she permitted him after I left the house.'

Byron returned from his 'journey of lakes & mountains' at the end of September and concluded his journal: 'To you – dearest Augusta – I send – and *for* you – I have kept this record of what I have seen & felt. – Love me as you are beloved by me. –' The Villa Diodati, where he was constantly being spied upon by English visitors, had become intolerable to him. In the middle of October, accompanied by Hobhouse, he crossed the Simplon Pass, 'escaping all perils of precipices and robbers', with the intention of settling permanently in Italy.

In the Ambrosian Library at Milan he came across a lock of the hair of Lucrezia Borgia and the love letters that had passed between her and Cardinal Bembo. 'And pray what do you think is one of her signatures? – why this + a Cross – which she says "is to stand for her name &c." Is not this amusing?'

Nothing was to shock Annabella more deeply than this. 'She has forwarded me one of the most shameless disgusting letters I have ever read,' she wrote to Mrs Villiers. 'The mask of innocence thrown aside, it is calculated to destroy root and branch of principle to make her a complete Lady O[xford] or Lady M.! indifferent to the distinction of vice and virtue as long as the former can escape positive detection.' Augusta was having great difficulty in knowing how to write to Byron and for the most part evaded the problem by not writing at all. 'I have hitherto written to you very regularly,' he told her, conveniently forgetting his long silence after his arrival at Geneva, 'But I now tell you that I will not write again at all – if I wait so long for my answers . . .'

The problem for Augusta was that she had allowed herself to be so completely intimidated by Annabella, and so tightly controlled by her, that she no longer had any idea what she should say in her letters. She had undertaken to write nothing that touched on or might seem to be designed to reawaken his love. It was easy enough to pass on information about little 'Da' or about strictly neutral topics, but that was not what he wished to hear. Byron wanted her to tell him stories and gossip, to make light of the world, to bring to him 'the laughing part of life' as only she could do – and this Annabella had specifically vetoed. Augusta's letters to him were not as yet inspected; if she wrote anything that went beyond the terms of her undertaking with Annabella this would be reflected in his replies. The only way out that Augusta could devise was to write in her most muddled, confused and evasive manner, while trying to half-hint at what was going on, in the vain hope that he might understand that she was not being permitted to write as she wished. At the same time she did her best to be obedient to Annabella's instructions, telling her brother that if he came to England they might not be able to meet. He wrote to her on 28 October:

> I really do not & cannot understand all the mysteries & alarms in your letters & more particularly in the last. All I know is – that no human power short of destruction – shall prevent me from seeing you when – where – & how – I may please – according to time & circumstance; that you are the only comfort (except the remote possibility of my daughter's being so) left me in prospect in existence, and that I can bear the rest – so that you remain; but anything which is to divide us would drive me quite out of my senses ... You surely do not mean to say that if I come to England in Spring, that you & I shall not meet? If so I will never return to it – though I must for many reasons – business &c &c – But I quit this topic for the present.

The remote prospect of Byron's possible return was the least of Augusta's troubles. All her hopes for a speedy resolution to the sale of Six Mile Bottom had yet again been frustrated. The potential purchaser had turned out to be the Vicar of Bottisham himself, the Reverend William Pugh, but there were difficulties concerning the paddocks in front of the house, which the Leighs rented from a neighbour who refused to sell them on to the prospective buyer. Since the Vicar would purchase the property only if the paddocks were part of the sale and since their owner – Charles Wedge, Vicar of Burrough Green, 'the most obstinate impracticable of Mortals & thorough *Wedge* himself' – refused to negotiate, the sale had reached a stalemate. 'This has my dear really given me a fit of the *Jaundice* almost because it will most probably be an objection to every purchase ...' There were times when even Augusta's elasticity was stretched almost to snapping point. The children were all suffering from one ailment or another and the tensions were beginning to get to them all. Georgey was ill-tempered and sulky, and little Augusta had constant headaches and conjunctivitis. On the one occasion when she was hoping to snatch a brief respite from it all with the Osbornes at Gogmagog, Mrs Villiers arrived in

Cambridge and announced her intention to call. Augusta cancelled her visit and waited for her in vain and this, as she told Annabella, 'contributed more largely to my ill humour'.

George, who was seldom at home when he was needed, was beginning to grow tetchy and suspicious, always wanting to know to whom Augusta was writing and trying to find out what was in the letters she received. The letter from Mrs Villiers describing her visit to the Chichesters had caused a tremendous storm, because he thought it had been written in French on purpose to deceive him.

Augusta became highly alarmed when Frederick Bentinck, staying the night at Six Mile Bottom on his way north, casually asked her, 'before *Mon Mari tout bonnemont*', about the Drachenfels verses in *Childe Harold*: 'I suppose it is to you he alludes as wishing you were with him?' Since George had noticed the arrival of the verses during the summer, she could hardly deny it but said that she wished Byron would not write so much, to which Bentinck replied, 'Why? He does not hurt anybody by writing these sort of things.'

This was hardly the opinion of Annabella and her supporters. John Murray had been circulating copies of the Third Canto of *Childe Harold* and Annabella told Augusta that she had heard 'nothing pleasant' about the fifty-fifth stanza:

> And there was one soft breast, as hath been said,
> Which unto his was bound by stronger ties
> Than the church links withal; and, though unwed,
> *That* love was pure, and, far above disguise,
> Had stood the test of mortal enmities
> Still undivided, and cemented more
> By peril, dreaded most in female eyes;
> But this was firm, and from a foreign shore
> Well to that heart might his these absent greetings pour!

Augusta suspected that her old enemy Selina Doyle had been meddling again and for once made no attempt to conceal her feelings from Annabella:

> Depend on one thing dearest A., there are those who – for what reasons I know not – will make out everything in an ill natured light against me – this has been *but too fully proved* to me – & makes me smile now to think there was a day when I foolishly imagined I had not such a thing as an enemy – as I do *not deserve* it from any human being I am less annoyed than I otherwise might be – but I am

sorry to say I do not bear it with ye feelings I *ought* – & the more I know, the less I love myself.

She confessed to Francis Hodgson that she had come to dread the arrival of a new poem, for fear of 'renewing any unpleasant recollections in the public mind towards her who has already suffered too much'. She meant Annabella, but she could just as well have been speaking of herself. Hodgson had now been appointed to the living of Bakewell in Derbyshire by Augusta's cousin-in-law the Duke of Rutland, and he was pressing her to come and stay, but there was no way in which Augusta could leave Six Mile Bottom: 'with *five* children to nurse and educate you will feel that I cannot make any long or distant absence from home'.

Reverend Pugh's offer for the house had fallen through, but there was now a new purchaser in prospect who hoped to negotiate a twenty-one-year lease of the contentious paddocks. Augusta had little confidence that he would succeed, but was at least grateful for the 'intervals' that the hopes of a sale provided in her husband's increasing depression.

On 18 December, Byron wrote from Venice, where he was to remain for the next three years. He was 'more in love than ever' with 'a very pretty Venetian of two and twenty – with great black eyes'. She was Maria Segati, the wife of a draper. Augusta was to tell Aunt Sophy that he had 'consoled' himself and she was to inform Hodgson, who had always said that Byron would fall in love with an Italian, that his prophecy had been fulfilled. Had she read the 'po's' that he had sent to Murray and had they made her cry; or, as he put it: 'Goosey my love – don't they make you "put finger in eye"?' He continued:

> You can have no idea of my thorough wretchedness from the day of my parting from you . . . though I struggled against it with some strength – at present I am better – thank Heaven above – & woman beneath – and will be a very good boy.

None of this could have brought much comfort to poor Augusta; nor would she have been much gratified by his postscript: 'I forgot to tell you – that the *Demoiselle* – who returned to England from Geneva – went there to produce a new baby B. – who is now about to make his appearance . . .' This letter, like all the others, was passed on to Annabella, who sent a copy to Lushington.

*

At the beginning of 1817, Annabella drew up a list of her 'duties'. She intended to 'decline occasion of hostility' where Byron was concerned, but at the same time to take all power over Ada out of his hands, 'as I should take a knife away from a child'. Needless to say, the two aims turned out to be contradictory, while Annabella's duties to Augusta were outweighed by what she saw as Augusta's duties to her.

As a first step Annabella instructed Lushington to begin proceedings to make Ada a Ward of Chancery so that she could not be 'removed out of the Kingdom without the permission of the Lord Chancellor'.* Annabella also felt it incumbent upon her for her daughter's sake (or so she managed to convince herself) to compose what she called her '*histoire*', an account of her marriage and separation.

It was, in effect, a long indictment of Augusta. Since much of this involved rewriting history,† she asked Augusta to return the letters she had written to her at the time of the Piccadilly Terrace crisis, when she had begged her sister-in-law to come back to support her against Byron. Augusta was heartily sick of the whole business and wrote to her wearily:

> About the letters, do as you please, dearest A. – if it regards yourself by all means let Mrs V. see them. If the view is to justify *me* in *any* way, I had rather you did not. Let people think as they please – it matters little now . . .

But when Annabella then asked to see the letters that Byron had written to Augusta immediately before the marriage, Augusta put her foot down and told her that she had burned many letters, 'which I wish you could have read', and that she could not remember any 'vindictive feelings'.

Augusta was in no mood to waste her time on Annabella's tedious games. By March 1817, somewhat to everyone's astonishment, the sale of Six Mile Bottom seemed to be going ahead and half of the Leighs' possessions had been packed up. Where they were to go had not been decided and George had yet again departed

---

* It had reached Byron's ears that Annabella was proposing to take Ada abroad. He instructed Augusta to inform his wife that, although he had intention of removing Ada from her mother, he strongly protested about her being taken out of the country at such an early age.
† Rather in the Stalinist manner.

for Uppark and the reassuring company of Sir Harry Fetherstonhaugh:

> I never saw him in *better spirits* than when he set out! Fortunately I
> can laugh when others wd cry, & so thoroughly understand his
> ways. I am sure he is perfectly happy in PUTTING OFF the *evil* day of
> removal &c. & will not suffer it to come into his thoughts till
> absolutely driven to it. Happily or perhaps *un*happily our Purchaser
> is enamoured of his Purchase & therefore has more patience than
> might be expected, but I am nervous just now & dread the finale . . .
> I have the strength of a *Lioness* & the spirit of a *Tigress* or must
> have died long ago.

Byron's letters had been bursting with fury about Ada being made a
Ward of Court: 'Give me but a *fair share* of my daughter – the half
– my natural right & authority – & I am content; otherwise I come
to England and "law & claw before they get it".' But it was not
until 27 May that he had the courage to reveal to Augusta that
Claire Clairmont had given birth to a daughter in January. He was
determined that this child, at least, should not slip out of his grasp
and his first thought was that the infant should be handed over to
Augusta (an idea she was hardly likely to welcome). However
Claire had stood out resolutely against this, insisting that 'a child
always wanted a parent's care at least till seven years old'. But
Byron was set on exercising his paternal right and it was finally
agreed that little Allegra should join him in Venice:

> They tell me it is very pretty – with blue eyes & dark hair – &
> although I never was attached or pretended attachment to the
> mother – still in case of the eternal war & alienation which I foresee
> about my legitimate daughter – Ada – it may be well to have
> something to repose a hope upon – I must love something in my old
> age . . . I look to nothing from the Noel quarter – but all that can
> harass & torture . . .

If anyone was being harassed and tortured, it was Augusta. It never
seems to have occurred to Byron that she might be hurt or made
jealous by his affair with Claire Clairmont. Augusta concealed her
feelings from him as she was now concealing all her thoughts and
feelings in the calculated obscurity of her letters. The more
cryptically confused they grew, the more exasperated he became:

> For the life of me I can't make out whether your disorder is a broken
> heart or the ear-ache – or whether it is *you* that have been ill or the

children – or what your melancholy – & mysterious apprehensions
tend to – or refer to . . .

One reference at least he did recognise: 'the man of fashion', her
nickname for Wilmot. 'Another disgrace to me & mine,' he
growled. George Anson, too, had incurred his displeasure for siding
with Annabella. Comparing him to 'your exquisite piece of
helplessness G[eorge]. L[eigh].', he concluded that Augusta's
George was 'the best of the two in a devilish deal – but as for the
other I shan't forget him in a hurry.'

Since he rarely bothered to mention his literary productions to his
sister, he did not tell her that he was in the process of dispatching to
Murray the acts of a dramatic poem that would cause her distress
and public embarrassment. The idea of a drama in the 'Faust'
manner had been in his mind ever since his friend Matthew Gregory
Lewis* had given a viva-voce translation for him of Goethe's
play at Diodati in August 1816. *Prometheus*, *Paradise Lost* and
even *The Castle of Otranto* all went into the boiling pot of Byron's
mind, but it was the alpine excursion with Hobhouse that had
really fired his imagination. As he told Murray, 'It was the
Staubrach and the Jungfrau and something else, much more than
Faustus, that made me write "Manfred".' The 'something else' was
his passion for Augusta and his guilt and remorse for the suffering
he had caused her:

> Her faults were mine – her virtues were her own –
> I loved her, and destroy'd her!

Manfred was the archetypal Byronic hero, a magus alienated from
mankind, desolately wandering through the Alps seeking only
'Forgetfulness . . . of that which is within me'. The reader was left in
no doubt of the guilty passion that had consumed Manfred and his
victim, Astarte. Byron was, literally, making a public spectacle of
his love for his sister:

> I say 'tis blood – my blood! the pure warm stream
> Which ran in the veins of my fathers, and in ours
> When we were in our youth, and had one heart,
> And loved each other as we should not love,
> And this was shed: but still it rises up,
> Colouring the clouds, that shut me out from heaven,

* Matthew Gregory Lewis (1775–1818), writer and poet and author of a number of
Gothic novels, notably The Monk (1794).

Where thou art not – and I shall never be.

The play is too full of spirits and witches and Destinies for its own good, but the scene in which Nemesis raises from the dead the phantom of Astarte, the sister whom he had loved and destroyed, is one of the most moving things that Byron ever wrote:

> Astarte! my beloved! speak to me:
> I have so much endured – so much endure –
> Look on me! The grave hath not changed thee more
> Than I am changed for thee. Thou lovedst me
> Too much, as I loved thee: we were not made
> To torture thus each other, though it were
> The deadliest sin to love as we have loved.
> Say that thou loath'st me not – that I do bear
> This punishment for both – that thou wilt be
> One of the blessed – and that I shall die . . .

At the same time it is all monstrously egotistical. It was not Byron who was bearing the 'punishment for both', but Augusta. When the play went on sale, Annabella's supporters were not slow to see that he had put into their hands the ultimate weapon against her.

Mrs Villiers wrote immediately to Annabella, pulling out all the stops:

> I have read it – and certainly was never so disgusted – so *horrified* in my life – no avowal can be more complete – & nothing but a want of faith in *his* veracity can save A. in the eyes of the whole world . . . it is too barefaced for her friends to deny the allusion.

On 23 June, the *Day and New Times* published a review that left no room for doubt:

> Manfred has exiled himself from society, and what is to be the ground of our compassion for the exile? Simply the commission of one of the most revolting of crimes. He has committed incest! Lord Byron has coloured Manfred into his own personal features.

Lady Chichester, who had assumed the mantle of old Lady Holdernesse's piety, was appalled and took the paper to show to Mrs Villiers.

'What does the Queen think, I wonder,' Annabella asked Mrs Villiers, but to her undoubted disappointment Augusta's standing at court was not affected and the whole affair did not have anything like the impact that Annabella's supporters had hoped for. It is unlikely that the Queen, now old and unwell, would have read *Manfred* – and if the matter had been brought to her notice she would probably have dismissed it, as she had dismissed the rumours about incest and worse among her own children.

Augusta's own feelings about *Manfred* are difficult to assess. Annabella had told her that she should write to Byron 'with the most decided expression of your disapprobation', but Augusta knew that nothing that she could say would be of any use; nor did she believe that anything would be gained by breaking off their correspondence. She told Mrs Villiers that she had been shocked and disgusted, but one suspects that she was only saying what Mrs Villiers expected to hear. Augusta was undoubtedly embarrassed, especially with regard to her sister, Mary Chichester, and those closest to her, but what hurt her most was Byron's cruel thoughtlessness. Later in the year, when he wanted to know whether *Manfred* had not caused a 'pucker', she replied: 'I thought there was unkindness which I did not expect, in doing what was but sure to cause one –' Augusta was still capable of letting her sentences hang in the air with devastating effect.

CHAPTER 21

'A Miracle of Strength'

By July 1817 George Leigh, 'more depressed, more bilious, nervous, helpless than ever before', was sounding out the possibilities of taking flight to the Continent – just as his friend Beau Brummell, 'reduced to most exigent and abject want', had done the previous year and Scrope Davies would be obliged to do in 1820. George had neglected to complete the transfer of the deeds of Six Mile Bottom from the Prince, and he was now having difficulty proving his ownership of the property. The prospective buyer was threatening to withdraw his offer, George, harried by creditors, would be faced with imprisonment for debt and, as Augusta told Annabella, could not 'remain an hour safely in England'. She was showing signs of bending under the strain and was beginning to grow slightly paranoiac. If she accompanied George into exile, returning only for the periods when she was on duty at court, would this give 'OTHERS' a greater opportunity to 'effect their schemes & purposes' against her?

Annabella could not have been less interested in her sister-in-law's alarms and anxieties. She was on a tour of the North of England and was preoccupied with a poem she was writing about her emotions on revisiting Seaham:

> The veil of sorrow hath passed between
> and dimmed the hues of the distant scene . . .

Augusta was at her wits' end. The fact that she was already well into a sixth pregnancy can only have increased her despair. She had attempted to write to Byron of their troubles, but she no longer knew how to be straightforward with him. 'Mrs Leigh has written me an uncomfortable letter,' he wrote to John Murray on 7 August, 'from which I suppose George Leigh's affairs are in disorder – is it so? Or what is the matter? I can make out nothing from her letter – it is very foolish to torment me with ambiguities at this distance.' Byron did not reply. He had given up writing to her, except when he required information about Ada. He told Douglas Kinnaird that November:

> If you see Augusta give her my love and tell her – that I do not write because I really and truly do not understand one single word of her letters – to answer them is out of the question – I don't say it out of ill nature – but whatever the subject – there is so much paraphrase – parenthesis – initials – dashes – hints & what Lord Ogilby calls 'Mr Sterling's damned crinkum crankum'* that – Sunburn me! If I know what the meaning or no meaning is . . .

Fortunately disaster was averted. George managed, after all, to establish his title to Six Mile Bottom. Augusta, who had been in London doing her turn 'in waiting', had stood resolutely by him throughout the negotiations. She returned home 'dreading the confusion of a removal and packing up', to find herself having to contend with another problem. Captain Hunter, the purchaser, wanted to move in before the end of the year and Augusta, with her baby due at the end of November, now had to decide whether to leave before or after her confinement. Terrified that staying on in the house might provide the Captain with another last-minute excuse to pull out of the deal, she decided not to delay. Characteristically, George had washed his hands of the whole business of where they were to go to and how they might get there, and Augusta, in an advanced state of pregnancy, was obliged to move out of the house virtually single-handed. On 15 November, with the five children – in an effort that was little short of heroic – she dragged herself up to Brompton,† where she rented a house for eight weeks. George, who had been staying with the Earl of Darlington, did not join them there: '*Mon mari* is in Town as he has been & *will* be till this tiresome business is settled – *very* low – & I've no prospect of any improvement while the uncertainty lasts . . .' And Augusta added, 'I am as usual a miracle of *strength* for I have had *much* to combat with . . .'

Two weeks earlier Princess Charlotte had died after giving birth to a stillborn child. Augusta, with her own infant expected at any time, was unnerved and deeply shocked. Her baby, a girl, was born on 27 November. 'I am essentially well,' she told Annabella, 'but as usual weak & all over nervous languor which is very uncomfortable

---

* *The Clandestine Marriage*: Garrick and Colman.
† Brompton was still fairly rural in 1817 and well known for its nursery gardens and its excellent air.

without one was a *fine Lady* & had nothing to do but get well –'
'Baby is very small,' she added, 'I think ye smallest I ever had – but
seems strong as if she could fight her way.' The child was to be
named Amelia Marianne, and 'probably she will be called Emily if
you will excuse it which was my Mother's name,' Augusta informed
Annabella, who had consented to be the infant's godmother – she
could hardly have refused after her graceless turn-about over Ada.

'I have a sort of maternal feeling for all your little ones, which
may be some qualification for the office I now thankfully accept,'
but Annabella went on to make it abundantly clear that there had
to be strings attached to her acceptance. Augusta must understand
that she would use every means in her power to preserve all the
children 'from the corrupting and ruinous influence of their Uncle's
society in any future circumstances which might thus endanger their
welfare . . .'

This was not the response Augusta had expected but she
managed to contain her temper, telling her sister-in-law that she
'cannot suppose *I* should desire such' and adding that it was
improbable that her children would ever be faced with that danger:
'I do not believe *that person* feels any interest for them or me either.'

Augusta's recovery from Emily's birth was exceptionally slow.
Two successive pregnancies, both of them occurring at times of
extreme personal stress, together with the physical strain and
anxiety of moving out of Six Mile Bottom, had taken their toll. The
baby was 'nervous – she almost flies at every touch or sound poor
child . . .' To add to Augusta's anxiety, Emily had developed
thrush. 'I am suffering torture from ye effects of her mouth . . .
every time she sucks it is really dreadful & I think will give me a
nervous fever if it goes on . . .' Dr Le Mann, whom she now
regularly consulted, was in favour of bringing in a wet-nurse,
'which wd be a disagreeable & inconvenient addition to my
household'. As a compromise it was decided that little Emily should
have 'a Donkey Nurse [donkey milk] over & above her original
donkey (me)'.

Augusta also found herself faced with a spate of domestic
problems. Her nurse was 'unequal to anything but babies' and
could barely cope with Frederick and Medora, who were still in the
nursery which was in a state of permanent confusion. 'A good sort
of steady person' was 'grievously' needed to take charge of the three
older children. 'Not being very strong, you may conceive of the

miserable feeling of thinking I *could not* give them the time and attention requisite . . .' she confessed to Annabella, as ever asking her advice. On this occasion she also consulted George Anson's sister Julia, who had recently married a clergyman, Robert Heath. Annabella of course knew of a 'person not unlikely to suit', but when it came to it, the young woman proved too expensive and absurdly overqualified. 'It is not for Accomplishments,' Augusta tried to explain to her, 'but I wish good temper & method – & for her to be able to superintend teaching reading & needlework & those sort of useful branches – to help me in short and be with the children when I can't . . .' It cannot have pleased Annabella when Julia Heath found exactly the governess Augusta needed, a woman who was 'peculiarly adapted to such *fiery impatient spirits* as she has to govern'.

With the weather 'so bad for pedestrians', Augusta had not been strong enough to venture outside. Her enforced inactivity gave her the opportunity to read *Northanger Abbey* and *Persuasion*, which John Murray had lent her 'to amuse my convalescent hours'. It also gave her more time to devote to her second daughter, Augusta Charlotte, whose mental abnormality was becoming increasingly hard to ignore:

> . . . she may appear to others a very common place character, but to me she is not like anything I ever met with – the quickest feelings & most affectionate heart – a temper as quick – more irritable than anything you can conceive – but the one moment in an agony of grief – the next laughing & forgetting all but the present moment – a disposition to tell FIBS & steal I declare it makes me often tremble, & the former is a great deal from timidity to hide what she has done wrong . . . I hope a great deal from regular good management but have many an anxious moment . . .

She was also having anxious moments over Six Mile Bottom. The sale was not proceeding as had been anticipated and one snag after another seemed to be preventing completion: 'I fear the produce will scarcely pay the lawyers,' she observed despondently. She did not renew the lease on the house in Brompton but moved into town, renting a much cheaper property in Great Quebec Street off Montagu Square.

She soon found, however, that there were compensations for living in town. The George Anson Byrons lived only a few doors away and Aunt Sophy was staying with them, as she frequently did.

Augusta was able to see her friends and Hobhouse called on her twice before she had been there a fortnight. She even managed to survive her first court duty since her confinement, 'and am alive today which is more than I ought to expect . . .'

By the beginning of April 1818 it had become evident that Lady Melbourne, racked with pain, which she attributed to rheumatism or gout, had not long to live. Augusta had seen very little of her for some time, largely because the old lady did not wish her to come to Melbourne House where they might be observed by Caroline Lamb. On 6 April, Augusta called at the house in Whitehall to ask after Lady Melbourne's health and was told that she had died that morning. She wrote immediately to Hobhouse, telling him of the instructions Byron had left her:

> In case of such an event he desired you would apply to her Son George for his B.'s letters to Ly M. – which contain what he does not wish Ly C.L. 'to lay her paws upon'.

There were, she told Hobhouse, 'many hints' 'of her having been his confidante' & 'acquainted with all his intricacies'. Augusta must have had a very good idea of what those letters contained and feared that they would fall into the hands of the woman she regarded as her most dangerous enemy. At the same time, since she always did her best to find good in everyone, she was able to spare a generous thought for Lady Melbourne. 'She was in *many* instances kind to me & I shall ever bear a grateful recollection of it – what a loss she must be in *that House*! I heard (By the bye Mrs V. told me) Ld M. was *dying* of *grief*!'

Annabella, who tended to see everything in terms of the Day of Judgement, was not prepared to be generous. 'I was not unconcerned at Lady M.'s death and there was something particularly awful in the state of previous imbecility which must have precluded reflection . . .'

Hobhouse unceremoniously wrote off to George Lamb demanding Byron's letters. Caro George wrote indignantly to Annabella to tell her of Hobhouse's 'most disgusting letter . . . really one of the most unfeeling I have ever read . . . I always had the worst possible opinion of that man, but I can believe they are all in a great fright.'

Although the Leighs had theoretically left Six Mile Bottom for good, most of their possessions still remained there; the sale of the house was still not completed and George had returned thankfully to his old haunts. He had found a pony for the Duke of York. 'I like the account of him,' the Duke replied, 'and beg that you will secure him for me . . . I shall be anxious to hear news from Newmarket as I think that Tomorrow and Wednesday's start will open up our eyes very much concerning the Derby.' George was still widely relied upon for his advice about racing form, but his continuing involvement in the racing world did not bode well for the Leighs' finances and Augusta was beginning to wonder how long it would be before they had to find accommodation even cheaper than Great Quebec Street.

On 25 April it seemed as if their problems had been solved at a stroke, through the unexpected intervention of the Prince Regent. It was the kind of experience that confirmed Augusta in her belief in the benign workings of providence: they were given 'very comfortable roomy apartments' in 'St James's Palace':

> I am not much used to the smiles of Fortune tho' I have had blessings I did not deserve – but this supernumerary one really stuns me – I am afraid of not feeling sufficiently grateful for what is so wholly unwarranted & unexpected . . .

Their apartments were in Flag Court in the oldest part of the Tudor palace. Augusta began to move in at the end of May and, like anyone else in similar circumstances, was constantly 'waiting for people who do not come'. Soon all the Leighs' worldly possessions were in wagons on the road from Six Mile Bottom and Augusta was rejoicing in her good fortune: 'I can scarcely believe it sometimes – I try to enjoy the present good without spoiling it by fears for the future.' With almost child-like excitement, Augusta could not wait 'to *scrub* & *scour* & arrange my goods & chattels', but 'Sposo' had returned from Newmarket and was constantly getting in her way.

Her determination to make the most of her 'present good' was coloured by 'very disagreeable' reports of Queen Charlotte's health. The Queen could eat little or nothing, her legs were badly swollen and she was in great pain from what her doctors diagnosed as 'dropsy of the chest'. 'If the Queen dies you are no more a Maid of Honour – is it not so,' wrote Byron on 21 September.

It was only the second letter he had written to her since April and he took the opportunity to give her a round-up of his amours. His daughter Allegra was living with him in his *palazzo* on the Grand Canal and her mother, Claire Clairmont, had come 'prancing . . . over the Appenines' to see her. He had acquired a new mistress, the fiery-tempered Margarita Cogni, who refused to let any woman into the house 'unless she is as old & frightful as possible'. 'You see Goose,' he cheerfully concluded, 'that there is no quiet in this world – so be a good woman – & repent of yr sins.'

Poor Augusta had long ago repented of her sins and she could not have been flattered by her brother's reason for breaking his long silence: he wanted a letter to be 'safely delivered' to Lady Frances Webster – whose virtue Byron had 'spared' five years earlier. Lady Frances, to Augusta's great astonishment, had taken to attending Sunday services at the chapel of 'St James's Palace'. 'I really could not help looking a bit occasionally, as you can understand & felt certain it was *really* her,' Augusta confessed to Annabella. Lady Frances sent a note requesting a meeting.

> I did not see what I *could* do but say I was 'flattered' by her wish etc . . . well, my dear A. she came – I had *armed* myself as much as I could for what might ensue – for I feared she might have some view poor soul! in this odd request – but the visit passed off as many other visits. I was as reserved as I could be on what *regarded* him & I wished her to think I was quite ignorant on what regarded HER . . .

Augusta subsequently returned her visit and was confronted with '*La Mere* & *La Soeur*, I think the most disagreeable looking people I ever saw and ALL BUT pointedly uncivil to me . . .' She concluded her letter with a brief mention of little Augusta Charlotte, who had been 'in sad tribulations after the loss of Aunt Annabella's acorn'.

Now that there were fewer letters from Byron to be passed on, Augusta's correspondence with Annabella had greatly diminished, although Augusta, who still saw their tenuous friendship as something of a lifeline, continued obligingly to tell her sister-in-law whatever news she thought might be of interest: Wilmot had been elected M.P. for Newcastle and was more pleased with himself than ever; she wished that George Anson's wife would 'dress & manage her child better'; Aunt Sophy had come to stay with a friend in adjoining apartments at 'St James's Palace':

> My Sposo & she have not met since our Marriage which makes ye circumstances of being next door PLEASANT . . . She has not been

well, but is, I think ye better for seeing *me* – which wd sound vain to those who did not as you do, know her personality . . .

George had been thrown into a great flurry of excitement by the news that a vacancy had occurred in the Stamp Office and that the Regent himself had put him forward for it. Now that he had a permanent base in London, the prospect of becoming Commissioner seemed more attractive to him than it had done previously and Augusta began to worry that he seemed so sure of being appointed that the disappointment of rejection 'would fall more heavily'. Indeed, George was again passed over but, by way of compensation, Lord Liverpool agreed that the Leighs should be granted a pension of £700 per year for their joint lives:

> It is so infinitely beyond all my hopes & expectations that I have felt stunned . . . I wish you wd not say much about it *just yet* till I know whether it is approved of being mentioned as in these days one feels shy of pensions & I hope (it's not ungrateful) I should have preferred earning it – Beggars must not be chusers you know & besides . . .

On 17 November 1818, Queen Charlotte, sitting in her armchair with the Prince Regent holding her hand and the Duke of York at her side, expired, 'without a pang & a sweet smile on her face'. The Queen's ladies – Augusta among them – were required to attend the lying in state at Kew on 1 December. She found it 'a mournful duty – but as a *spectacle* it was ill-managed – want of space the cause I believe'. The following day, with George's valet in attendance and in a 'borrowed carriage', Augusta was driven back to Kew to take her place in the funeral procession to Windsor. There was such a multitude of carriages, with throngs of mourners on horseback and on foot, that the cortège was eight miles long. As it grew dark, soldiers lined the route, bearing torches to light the procession as it wound slowly between them towards St George's Chapel:

> I must say I never was more overcome. The scene in the Chapel was beautiful & affecting to the greatest degree – extremely *well* arranged – The Music, the Torchlight in the Chapel itself which I had scarcely seen before all combined to make it particularly solemn & had it not been for thinking of my poor baby who was awaiting me at the Castle, I would have liked to remain there, there was something so soothing – it will be long before the scene can be effaced from my thoughts . . .

Since the publication of *Manfred*, Augusta had been living in constant anxiety of what her brother might next take into his head to write about her. Aunt Sophy had heard from John Murray that Byron was working on his life story, and Murray now warned Augusta that there was a new poem, 'Don Giovanni', on its way from Venice. Augusta broke the unwelcome news to Annabella: 'No good can be looked for from *that* subject I fear,' she told her. 'I anticipate only evil.' By Boxing Day, the First Canto of *Don Juan* was in Hobhouse's hands and he was appalled: 'the blasphemy and bawdry and the domestic facts overpower even the great genius it displays'.

Augusta was informed that the poem was 'VERY LICENTIOUS' and 'objectionable'.

> This new poem, if persisted in [she wrote to Hodgson], will be the ruin of him from what I can learn. Indeed if his friends (those whom he terms such) allow it, one may believe it but if you write say nothing, for it would not do good, and I was charged not to write of it, as the more opposition and disapprobation manifested, the more obstinate he will be . . .

Byron's friends believe that his exile had put him out of touch with the changes that were overtaking English morals. The year 1819, which was to see the publication of the first cantos of *Don Juan*, also saw the birth of Princess Victoria, who was to give her name to an age in which the cant and hypocrisy Byron derided would be established as public virtues.

In April 1819, while Augusta was reliving memories of her childhood at Eckington Rectory with Christopher Alderson's daughter, Mary, who had come to stay with her for a month at the palace, Byron met the woman who was to be the last love of his life. At a *conversazione* given by the Contessa Marina Querini Benzoni he had reluctantly allowed himself to be introduced as 'Peer of England and its greatest poet' to the nineteen-year-old Contessa Teresa Guiccioli, the third wife of a wealthy count from the Romagna. Because she came from Ravenna, they were soon talking of Dante and Francesca da Rimini, and it was only a matter of days before they became lovers. 'B. was not a man to confine himself to sentiment,' she confessed.

There was something in Teresa that reminded him of Augusta: her gift for laughter, her talent for mimicry, her impulsiveness. He realised that he was becoming deeply entangled, but before he committed himself irrevocably he made one last attempt to break through the fog of evasions and concealments with which Augusta surrounded herself. On 17 May 1819 he wrote her a long love letter that carried with it inescapable undertones of farewell:

> My dearest Love – I have been negligent in not writing, but what can I say. Three years absence & the total change of scene and habit make such a difference – that we now have nothing in common but our affections & our relationship.
>
> But I have never ceased nor can cease to feel for a moment that perfect & boundless attachment which bound & binds me to you – which renders me utterly incapable of *real* love for any other human being – what could they be after *you*? . . .
>
> We may have been very wrong – but I repent of nothing but that cursed marriage – & your refusing to continue to love me as you had loved me – I can neither forget nor *quite forgive* you for that precious piece of reformation – but I can never be other than I have been – and whenever I love anything it is because it reminds me in some way or other of yourself . . . It is heart-breaking to think of our long Separation – and I am sure more than punishment enough for all our sins – Dante is more humane in his 'Hell' for he places his unfortunate lovers (Francesca of Rimini & Paolo whose case fell a good deal short of *ours* – though sufficiently naughty) in company – and though they suffer – it is at least together . . .

He told Augusta that if he ever returned to England it would be to see her. He had been 'grieved and tortured' by what he called her *'new resolution'* and by Annabella's (that 'infernal fiend') persecution:

> but remember that even then *you* were the sole object that cost me a tear – and *what tears*! do you remember *our* parting? . . . When you write to me speak to me of yourself – & say that you love me – never mind common-place people & topics . . . They say absence destroys weak passions – & confirms strong ones – Alas! *mine* for you is the union of all passions & of all affections – Has strengthened itself but will destroy me – I do not speak of *physical* destruction – for I have endured & can endure much – but of the annihilation of all thoughts feelings or hopes – which have not more or less a reference to you & to *our recollections* . . .

Ironically, the letter was written on Annabella's birthday.

Augusta's reaction was hardly what Byron had anticipated. She was horrified – at least, she told Annabella that she was. Byron's passionate declaration of his love for her was the last thing she needed. At a time when she had hopes of being able to rebuild her life, with a home of her own at 'St James's Palace' and at least a minimal guarantee of income, she had no desire for the love that had destroyed and disgraced her to be reawakened. She had been hammered into submission by Annabella and humiliated by gossip. She had been forced to recognise that Byron had betrayed their secret to others and had suffered a further and more public betrayal in Manfred. Even now her enemies, Caro George in particular, were openly snubbing her.

She had, however, no need to show Byron's letter to Annabella. Communications from him now arrived so rarely that Annabella had ceased to expect them. Augusta delayed for several weeks, continually putting off the decision, but, on 25 June, she enclosed it in a letter to her sister-in-law. She told Annabella that her mind had been 'made & unmade on the subject 20 times . . . Yet I can safely affirm not on *my own* acct have I doubted.' She had tried in vain 'in thought & deed & to reply to the letter –'

> I am *so afraid* of saying what might do harm – or omitting any possible good – burn it – & tell me you have & answer me as soon as you can – I shall be *anxious* – & my unusually long silence may cause agitation – which I always avoid – in short he is surely to be considered a *Maniac*.

Whether or not she believed any of this is difficult to judge. She had become so dependent on Annabella that she was now reluctant to take any step without her approval. There remains, however, the possibility that Augusta may have derived a certain satisfaction from showing this ultimate expression of Byron's love for her to the woman who was so determined to keep them apart for ever. 'Pray pardon me if you think me wrong,' she told Annabella, 'for I do not mean to be so – tho I am convinced there are many wd condemn the act as an *insult* but it is yr advice & superior judgment that is wished for.' There was another, more cogent reason for passing on the letter: it contained Byron's corroboration of the ending of their incestuous relationship – 'your refusing to love me as you had loved me . . .' Annabella wrote to Mrs Villiers: 'it absolutely confirms what I have always believed – viz – her reformation as far as *acts* were concerned after my marriage . . .' She did not, of course, burn the letter, but copied and returned it.

She never destroyed anything of Byron's. She then told Augusta that she must either stop writing at all to Byron or 'take no notice of ever having received it.' She knew very well what course Augusta would follow. Having admitted that '*Decision* was never my *forte*' (which was something of an understatement), Augusta opted for the '*gentler* expedient' and never alluded to the letter in her reply, which was 'ye most insipid that can be imagined'.

Byron was bitterly hurt and it was not until 26 July, when he had followed Teresa and her husband back to Ravenna, that he was able to manage a reply:

> I am at too great a distance to scold you – but I *will* ask you – whether *your* letter of 1st July *is an answer* to the letter I wrote you before I quitted Venice? – What? is it come to *this*? – Have you no memory? or no heart? – You *had* both – and I *have* both – at least for *you*. – I write this presuming that you received *that* letter – is it that you fear? do not be afraid of the post – the World has its own affairs without thinking of *ours* and you may write safely . . .

Yet he was sufficiently concerned about her to be worried about her health because she confessed that she had had a pain in her side for some time and warned her, 'always think of your mother's constitution'. If she wished it, he would come to her; or if a warm climate would do her good, he would pay for her and her entire family to come out to Italy, 'including that precious baggage your Husband':

> you need not fear about *me* – I am much altered – and should be little trouble to you – nor would I give you more of my company than you like. – I confess after three years and a half – and *such years*! and *such* a *year* as preceded those three years! it would be a relief to see you again.

Byron knew very well that there was little hope of Augusta ever accepting his invitation. If she could not bring herself to reply openly to his letter, still less could she brave public opinion and risk coming out to see him, even with 'that precious baggage' as her chaperon.

CHAPTER 22

'You'll Probably Never See Me Again
as Long as You Live'

Annabella confided optimistically to Mrs Villiers on 4 July 1819:

> I am in some anxiety lest our unhappy friend should be implicated in
> the poem which is to appear about the 15th. I feel as if a crisis of
> some sort in this strange history were approaching and my conduct
> shall be regulated according to the best opinions I can form of means
> by which she can be saved . . .

The poem in question was *Don Juan* and Murray had been
dragging his feet over its publication for weeks. He had suggested
cuts, which Byron had rejected, but it had been agreed that the
poem should appear without the author's name on the title page
and without the scurrilous dedicatory verses to Robert Southey, the
Poet Laureate.

When Augusta received her copy she could not find a single
reference to herself, even by implication, but this did not stop her
from being thoroughly scandalised: 'Imagine my horror at this
horrid thing appearing ye day of the Carlton House fête to which I
was in *duty bound* to go.' The fête was one of the most extravagant
events in the Regency calendar, but the Prince's guests were 'too
much preoccupied with their own fancies' to have any time for
Byron's poem. 'I have only had *one question* about it,' Augusta told
Annabella, 'and that was from the Dhs of Rutland.'

It was a summer of discontent, with rumours of secret commit-
tees, conspiracies and imminent revolution. In August a mass
meeting of some 60,000 people assembled in Manchester at St
Peter's Fields to hear the celebrated radical, Henry Hunt. The local
magistrates panicked and ordered Hunt's arrest and the mob did its
best to prevent the local yeomanry reaching him. The 15th Hussars,
who had fought beside George Leigh's regiment in the Corunna
campaign, were called in, and in the ensuing mêlée some twelve or
more people were killed and many others injured. This was the

notorious 'Peterloo' massacre. News of it, and of the measures taken by the government to stifle protest and outlaw seditious literature, reached Byron in Venice, and the champion of the Nottinghamshire weavers began to wonder whether he ought not to be in the thick of it. He wrote to Augusta on 15 October:

> If there is to be a scene in England to which all seems approaching – by the violence of the political parties – you will probably see me in England in the next spring, but I have not yet decided the part I ought to take . . . To me it appears that you are on the eve of a revolution which won't be made with rose water however.

To Augusta, a political ignoramus safely cocooned within the ancient red-brick walls of 'St James's Palace' with sentinels patrolling outside day and night, it seemed as if Byron had taken leave of his senses:

> I really could not help laughing as it read so comically, our 'being on the eve of a Revolution' & sitting here quite insensible of the approach or at least not apprehending it so near. I think he cannot live without some *grand* object of excitement . . .

(On the back of her letter was a note concerned with domestic matters that she did understand: 'Will you tell me dear A. whether it is ye yoke only of the *raw egg*.') She may have taken a less flippant view of the political situation when she learned that Hobhouse had been committed to prison for writing a pamphlet 'containing matter calculated to inflame the people into acts of violence against the legislature . . .'

Augusta was thirty-six and pregnant for a seventh time. Already the Leighs' good fortune was beginning to unravel. Their pension had not been paid and she was 'in a pennyless condition which perplexes me . . .' She was also in her habitual state of 'fidgits' about her children. Little George Henry was very naughty and she was anxious that Georgey might be 'growing awry in the hip'.

On 11 December a letter arrived from Byron that put all other troubles out of her head. He was returning to England. The comic-opera absurdities and indignities of life as Teresa's acknowledged '*amico*' were proving too much for him. He was weary of dragging round Italy in the wake of the Guicciolis and worn out by their hysterical confrontations: '. . . this business has rendered Italy hateful to me – and as I left England on account of my own wife – I leave Italy – because of another's . . .' It was two days before

Augusta dared to break the news to Annabella. There was no one else to whom she could turn. Hobhouse was in Newgate, Scrope Davies was hiding from his creditors and there remained only Douglas Kinnaird, 'that shallow brained & hearted man . . .' 'I now consider my approaching confinement a fortunate circumstance as it will lay me low – in my Bed or my Grave.'

Byron wrote again on 4 December, enclosing a letter for Kinnaird on the subject of his will and telling her, 'in case of my not marrying again & having a son – you & yours must eventually be my heirs . . .' He expected to be in England by the new year and if she wished to write to him she should address a line to Calais. Augusta told Annabella, not very truthfully, that she wished the will in question was 'burnt in – – . . . I do not know how to address a letter to Calais it being out of the question to *give him welcome* to England.' She said that she thought he would be 'greatly quiet on the subject of Ada'. Augusta was showing signs of paranoia:

> do not say a word to ANY of YOUR friends nor indeed to anyone even OUR OWN relations . . . they are too closely acquainted & connected with those whom I believe most inimical to me & it wd be echoed to ye *other* side by some means or other.

It was obvious that she was asking Annabella to keep what she had said from the Doyles, the Wilmots and the George Anson Byrons. However, in one of her most unpleasant lies, Annabella informed Mrs Villiers that Augusta 'was frightened that the letter might fall into George's hands'. She paid no attention to Augusta's plea.

Ruthless even by her own standards, Annabella reminded Augusta that she had frequently pointed out the 'pernicious effects' that would result from Byron's associating with her, unless there was unequivocal proof of his reformation. It was clear that he had not relinquished his 'criminal *desires*, & I think I must add *designs* . . .':

> It can scarcely be doubted, from the whole series of his correspondence, that *you* are his principal object in England. – Consider too, as a Mother, that he would corrupt the *morals* of your Children – and recollect that the public mind is such that the strongest suspicion would attach to your personal intercourse with him . . .

Augusta would have realised that if the 'public mind' did not jump to this conclusion, Annabella and her supporters would make sure that it did. But by the time she reached the end of her letter,

Annabella was beginning to have second thoughts. If Byron were to return to England, she might be held to account for this not very subtle attempt at blackmail. In a P.S. she attempted to distance herself from her threat:

> I think I cannot make it too clear to you that I do not *instigate* the measure which I suggest. If my reasons convince you, they become *yours* – if not I have no wish to enforce them.

The letter was submitted to Doyle for his approval and carried to Mrs Villiers' house in Knightsbridge for her to give to Augusta. But Mrs Villiers did not have time to call at 'St James's Palace' and the family governess delivered the letter instead. By the time it reached Augusta, on 28 December, the whole crisis had blown over. Byron had changed his mind about coming to England.

Teresa, frantic at the prospect of losing her lover, had become so alarmingly ill that her husband was obliged to beg Byron to return to her. On 27 December, Murray received a letter telling him of Byron's change of plan: 'Pray let my Sister be informed that I am not coming as I intended – I have not the courage to tell her so myself . . .'

As soon as she heard the news, Annabella tried to retrieve her own letter, but by then it had been passed to Augusta. 'I do not regret the delivery of my letter,' Annabella complacently informed her friend, 'as it will prevent further discussion.' It did nothing of the kind, for Augusta had already made up her mind not to follow her sister-in-law's instructions, and proceeded to tell her why: There was no need for her to do this. If she had followed her customary philosophy of letting well alone, she could have left Annabella in the comfortable belief that she had obediently told Byron that she would not see him. Instead, in an uncharacteristic moment of defiance, she set out her reasons for not taking her advice. The first were practical. Supposing she were to follow Annabella's wishes, what cause could she give for not seeing Byron to her friends and relatives: '. . . but *most of all* my Husband – I really cannot calculate *all* the consequences of that step as far as he is concerned.' She then proceeded to more positive reasons:

> . . . I will honestly confess to you – I never have – I cannot now believe as you do in the *depth & strength* of what is manifested by fits & starts – when there is nothing else – surely it must be a deadful idea that he must necessarily be wicked in *some* way – then dearest

265

A. – I do not feel I could *without one effort* relinquish – the hope –
the chance of making some impression on his better feelings – you
will perhaps think me foolish – vain – I hope not the latter – but
indeed do you think there is one person in Engd who would – who
could say to him what from circumstances *I* might – it might be *lost
now* but perhaps recur hereafter, & it would be a satisfaction to me
at all events to have said it.

Annabella was not used to defiance, particularly from Augusta.
There was a barely repressed anger in the way in which she
demolished her sister-in-law's fragile arguments. *Don Juan* and
Manfred were sufficient reason for justifying a refusal to meet
Byron, and there was not the least hope of Augusta influencing her
brother 'beneficially'. But it was Augusta's reluctance to admit the
'depth and strength' of Byron's 'wicked dispositions' that excited
her greatest scorn: 'Is *experience* nothing? Did you not before
indulge the delusion that he was not in earnest till it was fatally
proved that he was?' She then attempted to blackmail her sister-in-
law into submission. Now that Augusta had made her 'dissent
intelligible', she must reimpose the restriction on their personal
intercourse and they must 'act independently of each other . . .'
Augusta delayed for two weeks before replying and then informed
Annabella very sweetly what a grief it was to her that she could not
'implicitly' accept her advice.

Eventually a letter arrived from Byron explaining, a little
sheepishly, that he had been obliged to postpone his visit and
enclosing what Augusta described as a 'lump' of his long hair. The
letter was passed on to Annabella; the hair she kept.

On 28 January 1820 the last of Augusta's children, her third son,
Henry Francis, was born. The following day, the old King, whom
she and her sister Mary had received on behalf of their grandmother
at Holdernesse House twenty years earlier, was released from his
long confinement at Windsor and died peacefully with the Duke of
York at his bedside.

The break between Annabella and Augusta was not conclusive.
Augusta had developed an almost masochistic dependency on her
sister-in-law, and Annabella soon found, as she had done before,
that there was no substitute for Augusta as a go-between. This was
a role that Augusta did not relish – 'I do not feel very comfortable
about it if ye communications are disagreeable' – but no one paid

much regard to her feelings. The next crisis to come everyone's way posed a peculiarly tricky dilemma.

The rumour that Aunt Sophy had heard from Murray that Byron was writing his life story had proved all too true. In Venice that October he had handed over the manuscript of his memoirs to Thomas Moore. On the last day of 1819 he wrote to Annabella:

> It will not be published till after my death – and in fact it is a 'Memoir' and not 'confessions'. I have omitted the most important & decisive events and passions of my existence not to compromise others. – But it is not so with the part you occupy – which is long and minute – and I could wish you to see, read and mark any part or parts that do not appear to coincide with the truth.

On the face of it nothing could have been more open-handed, but Annabella suspected that she was being lured into a trap. To do as he requested would be to appear to give the book her sanction, and this she would not do. After a consultation with Doyle and Lushington, she decided that her best course was one of 'intimidation'. If Byron went ahead with publication, she would see to it that there would be a 'full disclosure to the world of all the circumstances' – in other words, his incest with Augusta would be made public.

The difficulty was to find some means of conveying this threat to Byron. The eminent Lushington could hardly be seen to be trying his hand at blackmail. Could Augusta herself somehow be forced to pass on the ultimatum? 'You should not be prevented by any feeling for her *immediate feelings*,' advised the cold-blooded Doyle. But this approach, attractive though it was to Annabella's followers, created more problems than it solved. If Augusta were involved, she would have to tell Byron directly what so far she had only hinted at – that Annabella and her circle had full knowledge of their incest – and this might very well backfire. Annabella wrote to Lushington:

> . . . they would combine together against me – he being actuated by revenge – she by fear – whereas her never having dared inform him that she has admitted his guilt to me with her own, they have hitherto been prevented from acting in concert.

In the end Annabella took the rather Augusta-like course of letting the whole issue drag on unresolved until March 1820, when she sent a terse letter to Byron declining to inspect the manuscript and warning him he might lament some of the 'consequences' of its publication. As Byron laconically pointed out in his reply, the consequences were of no great concern to him, since the Memoir could only be published after his death.

By then he had turned his attention to the vexed question of the marriage settlement. Augusta wearily passed on his letters in a protracted negotiation about the 'funds', professing total ignorance of the whole matter. Annabella pointed out that Byron was still committing her to taking care of Augusta and her children after his death, provoking a highly indignant response in which Augusta professed (not entirely convincingly) her lack of interest in her brother's 'pecuniary liberality'. 'All I wish for my children is ye means to exist & *keep out of debt*, & for myself the same.'

There was little hope of that. Half a year of the Leighs' pension had not been paid because the death of the King made a new warrant for it necessary, over which there were endless delays. To complete her misery, the sale of Six Mile Bottom had encountered a new and very unexpected obstacle:

> The purchaser's lawyers were to search some office to see if any judgements were out agst *Mon Mari* – when lo & behold the first thing was one at the suit of *B*. ye £1000 for which a bond was given . . . it has put me into a perfect terror – in the first place downright ruin must be the consequence of the Sale not being completed . . .

George decided to blame Augusta on the grounds that she had asked Byron for the money in the first place, but she was not going to stand for this: 'I can't feel a particle of remorse relative to the transaction because the request was made through me at his own particular desire – I mean for ye loan . . .' George left her to sort out the mess and to her great relief went off for his summer visit to Uppark. 'I do think his hopeless inactivity wd at this moment be *more* than I can bear.' She sent off a desperate note to Byron, who replied that he had forgotten all about the bond and had never had any intention of acting on it: 'I desire to be considered as *not* one of Col Leigh's creditors . . .' He wrote again on 19 August:

> I always loved you better than any earthly existence and I always shall unless I go mad. – And if I did *not* so love you – still I would not persecute or oppress any one wittingly – especially for debts of which I know the *agony by experience* . . .

With the sale of Six Mile Bottom once more back on track, Augusta, blithely setting aside the restrictions that Annabella had placed on their relationship, was trying to bring about a meeting between Ada and her own children, particularly Georgey, who was always affectionately mentioning Ada in the letters that she wrote to Annabella in her best copperplate:

> I am so sorry that you have been ill, poor dear Cat, I hope you are better now, take care of yourself. Now I will tell you something, my poor little bird is dead, the cage gave way from the nail & down it fell, it was a goldfinch.
>
> I am sure Ada will be sorry for it bye the bye I saw a little girl so like Ada the other day . . . I long to see you & dear Ada & to be at your parties; the kittens send love & kisses. Good bye I love you better & better . . .

Annabella pleaded the Leigh children's whooping cough as a pretext. Augusta replied with a hint of ironic exasperation: 'The Hooping cough can only be caught from the Breath but, if you are afraid of me, let us meet on *Hampstead Heath*.' When they did at last meet, with all Augusta's children, Annabella noted in her journal that she 'felt the most tender affection for ——'. The dash can only have indicated Medora, whom she had by now entirely convinced herself was Byron's daughter.

That summer even Augusta could not fail to notice the politically explosive atmosphere on the streets of London. On the death of his father, George IV had begun to institute the divorce proceedings that he hoped would rid him of his wife. Queen Caroline had been living in colourful exile since 1814 and the undisguised notoriety of her love life had been the talk of Europe; George IV was confident that Parliament would sanction a divorce. The country at large took a different view and was far from sympathetically disposed towards a man whose amours had kept every cartoonist and satirist in the country busily occupied for more than quarter of a century and who was now about to put his wife on trial for adultery. Stephen Lushington was one of the team of lawyers defending the Queen. The trial in the House of Lords dragged on through August and into the autumn while the mob grew ever more violent. 'My Sposo has just been down to ye House of Lords,' recorded Augusta, 'quantities of people but no riot at present . . . streets lined with Police & London surrounded by Troops.'

On 27 October 1820, shortly before the final vote was to be taken in the House, Augusta told Annabella that she was 'dreading next week . . . ye people all appear to me *bit* by some mad animal . . .' Her apartments in Flag Court were uncomfortably close to the front gates of 'St James's Palace' and the sentries no longer seemed to constitute an adequate line of defence. On 6 November the bill was carried by only nine votes, so derisory a majority that Lord Liverpool abandoned it. The mob went wild with joy and the King threatened to leave the country. '. . . It is terribly cold,' wrote Augusta on 17 November, 'tho we have had enough to heat the atmosphere lately I'm sure – thanks to the Queen.'

The trial had not tempted Byron to return, although there was a wild rumour that he had been seen in London. 'I did not think it a very creditable thing to be one of the Judges even upon such matters,' he told Augusta. Teresa had left her husband and was now living with her father, Count Gamba, in Ravenna, where she was visited daily by Byron. The Count, and her impetuous brother, Pietro, were making the most of their opportunity to draw Byron into revolutionary politics against the Austrians.

Byron and Annabella were enjoying a brief cooling-off period. Because she was anxious that the protracted haggling over the 'Funds' might bring her husband back to England, Annabella was doing her best to placate him by carrying out his instructions about Augusta. 'Whatever She is or may have been', he wrote on 28 December:

> *you* have never had reason to complain of her – on the contrary – you are not aware of the obligations under which you have been to her. – Her life and mine – & yours & mine were two things perfectly distinct from each other – when one ceased the other began – and now both are closed. – You must be aware of the reasons of my request in fa[vou]r of Augusta & her Childn – which are the restrictions I am under by the Settlement, which death would make yours, at least the available portion . . .

The winter brought with it a return of the little Leighs' ailments: 'Children all ill as usual.' Georgey, at twelve, looked 'like a tallow candle' and by the time the new year arrived she was afflicted with 'langour and weakness flushings, chilblains & all those sorts of miseries – I attribute it to her growth & age'. Augusta herself had managed to escape all the family maladies. 'She is looking very well and *is* very well,' Hobhouse told Byron. 'Seven children have not spoiled her appearance at all.'

Letters from Byron grew increasingly rare and, when they did arrive, Augusta found that she was being used merely as a post-office for Annabella: 'Forward the enclosed to Ly B. . . . desire Mr D. Kin[nair]d to press upon the trustees the selling out of the funds . . .' When, in June 1821, Augusta taxed her brother with this, his response was hardly sympathic: 'What was I to write about? I live in a different world. – You knew from others that I was in a tolerable plight.'

That month Augusta heard that Aunt Sophy was ill, 'with a bilious attack & cold', and then 'a blood vessel gave way on the lungs'. Wilmot, summoned by the old lady's maid, realised that the end was near. 'Aware of her situation, perfectly resigned', she died at four o'clock in the morning on 25 June. Augusta was 'severely grieved for one who loved me so well . . .' Shrewd, tough-minded and incapable of hypocrisy, Aunt Sophy had not allowed herself to be drawn into Annabella's faction against Augusta. She was a friend whom Augusta could ill afford to lose.

While Augusta was sunk in grief, George was briefly buoyed up by a new round of false hopes. Earlier in the year Warwick Lake had died and one of his many posts, the management of the Duke of York's 'Coach Horses and Hackers', was left vacant. In a last-ditch attempt to rehabilitate his career, George decided to apply for it. The Duke of Rutland spoke, on his behalf, to the Duke of York, and it was a confident George who wrote to Sir Benjamin Bloomfield, the King's private secretary, on 24 July:

> Having received such substantial proofs of His Majesty's most gracious and kind forgiveness and goodwill towards me and my family, do you think I may presume to ask him to condescend so far as to approve my appointment – in which case I have every reason to think it would be conferred . . .

Unfortunately, the King's approval was not enough. There were others who saw George as too great a liability. It is unlikely that Augusta ever knew it, but it was Frederick Bentinck who in the end blocked his appointment. Mortified, but burning with righteous indignation, George protested that it was 'not only a disappointment but a blow to his feelings as his character is implicated . . .' For the man who had once driven down the course at Lewes Races lolling back in the Prince of Wales's carriage, with the Prince himself on the box, it represented total humiliation.

The same month Teresa Guiccioli's brother, Pietro Gamba, was expelled from Ravenna because of his anti-Austrian activities and both Teresa and her father were ordered to follow him into exile in Florence. Byron promised to join them there, but instead he lingered on in Ravenna. In a long, reflective letter to Murray that September, he revealed for the first time that he now knew something of the nature of the ordeal to which Augusta had been subjected:

Lady Byron's people and Ly Caroline Lamb's people – and a parcel of that set – got about her, & frightened her with all sorts of hints & menaces – so that she has never since been able to write to *me* a *Clear common letter* – and is so full of mysteries and miseries – that I can only sympathise – without always understanding her. – All my loves too make a point of calling upon her which puts her in a flutter (no difficult matter) [presumably he was thinking of Lady Frances Webster] . . . It is a very odd fancy that they all take to her – it was only six months ago – that I had some difficulty in preventing the Countess G.[uiccioli] from invading her with an Italian letter. – I should like to have seen Augusta's face with an Etruscan Epistle – & all its Meridional style of 'issimas' and other superlatives – before her . . .

He mentioned Teresa's threatened 'Epistle' in a letter written to Augusta the following month, which, despite all he had said to Murray, was not exactly overflowing with sympathy. He told her that his affair with Teresa was a:

finisher – for you know when a woman is separated from her husband for her Amant – he is bound by honour (and inclination at least I am) to live with her all his days, as long as there is no misconduct. – So you see that I have closed as papa *begun* – and you will probably never see me again as long as you live. – Indeed you don't deserve it – for having behaved so *coldly* – . . .

'Papa' was of course their revered father, 'Mad Jack'. In a postscript, he went on to tell Augusta that she should think highly of the 'future Lady B.' because Teresa had no doubt that he had treated Annabella badly, because she too hated *Don Juan* and because she was a great admirer of Augusta. 'She has a great deal of *us* too – I mean that turn for ridicule like Aunt Sophy and you & I and all the Bs.'

CHAPTER 23

'You Must Go to My Poor Dear Sister'

Towards the end of September 1821, Mary Chichester invited Augusta to bring the older children down to stay at Stanmer. Holidays were a rare event in the life of the Leighs and both Georgiana and little George had been suffering from one ailment after another for months. Once they were in Sussex they rapidly recovered and their spirits soared. Georgey, now approaching thirteen, 'bathed in the tepid sea baths' and 'grew fat and rosy', while nine-year-old George spent the days riding a pony across the South Downs 'and scampering about besides on foot'. Their joy at being free from the constraints of palace life and the murky atmosphere of London was so marked that Augusta managed to spin out their stay for more than three weeks, dreading 'a return to Home grievances which it appears my destiny to mourn over perpetually & of course fruitlessly . . .'

Writing to announce his safe arrival in Pisa, Byron seemed to sense his sister's discontent. The house there, the Casa Lanfranchi, was, he told her, large enough to lodge all her family; 'it would save you expences & you would see your brother . . . you could bring your drone of a husband with you – and probably save the lives of the children if they are delicate'. He would pay for them to come out, and life in Italy was inexpensive. He must have known that Augusta would not accept. The same reasons still prevailed: Augusta was not prepared to risk the scandal, and Annabella would not have hesitated to do her worst. Nor could Augusta have lived at ease with either his *contessa* or the circle that was forming around him at Pisa. 'I hear that Leigh Hunt & that infamous *Shelley* are going out to live with him & publish an Atheistical newspaper,'* she told Annabella.

That December the press were yet again up in arms against

* *The Liberal*, a periodical which lasted for only four numbers. It was not at all 'Atheistical' in tone, although Hunt did occasionally speak derisively of bishops. Augusta had probably heard of Shelley's reputation as an atheist.

273

Byron, this time on the subject of his verse drama *Cain*, which had, Moore noted in his journal, created a 'sensation'. 'Parsons preached against it from Kentish Town to Pisa,' Byron told him, and Mrs Piozzi thought that even the yellow fever was 'not so mischievous'. Augusta, characteristically, was in two minds about it:

> . . . to me it is one of the most disagreeable productions I ever tried to read – I skimmed the greatest part *fearfully* – I really grew so afraid of thinking like Cain. I do dislike the sort of thing to read before all I can express – nevertheless I do not know if I am right in thinking it *wonderful* . . .

What, in her fearful skimming, Augusta seems not to have noticed was that the play contained a strongly argued justification of incest.

On 28 January 1822, Judith Noel died at Kirkby Mallory at the age of seventy. Augusta knew that Judith had disliked and distrusted her, but they had kept up a correspondence of sorts on the subject of Ada and she had been unhappy at the thought that Judith might 'leave the world angry at me'. The fact that she had died without according Augusta forgiveness left her 'almost stunned'.

Now the whole problem of the Wentworth inheritance, which had come close to wrecking the separation agreement, was again opened up. Augusta was so apprehensive of Byron's reaction that she delayed breaking the news of Judith's death to him for as long as she could. He responded with a gently chiding letter, ascribing the delay to 'some good *nursery* reason' and pretending no 'violent grief' for Lady Noel. He was far more concerned and 'a little affronted' that Georgey had not written to him, and rather pointedly reminded Augusta that it was his intention to provide for her children in his will, quoting an old phrase from Lady Holdernesse: 'and should therefore like to *hear* now and then from my "residee legatoos . . ." '

Rather to everyone's surprise, negotiations over the Wentworth inheritance progressed remarkably smoothly, the only hiccup being a letter of Byron's to Annabella, which Lushington thought 'of the kindest nature' but which so offended her that she attempted to rally the Wilmots and the Anson Byrons to her defence. Augusta thought she was making a great fuss about nothing and, for once, did not hesitate to say so:

How it can ever be possible for you to have an opportunity of promoting the views of his [Byron's] Family, I cannot imagine, but if they feel as *I* do, they wd desire above all things that you could forget the whole Race & especially

Yr ever grateful & affec.

A.L.

The arbitrators came to the predictable conclusion that the Wentworth estate should be divided equally between husband and wife, and this was accepted by both parties. What annoyed Augusta, however, was that she was now being used as the channel of communication between Byron and Annabella over every trifling point of detail. When a dispute flared up between Kinnaird and Lushington, her patience was pushed dangerously near breaking point and it was a totally trivial incident that finally brought matters to a head. The arbitrators had decided that Byron had a right to half the game from Kirkby Mallory and a consignment was duly dispatched to Augusta at 'St James's Palace'. Annabella, who had still not forgiven her sister-in-law for her earlier outburst, demanded that Augusta send an official acknowledgement of the delivery to her solicitors and took her to task for her unnatural 'spirit of resentment'. Augusta finally snapped:

> Thank you my dearest A. for all the kindness of your letter & I hope I am not wrong in having the game – I will write & mention it as you suggest – in ye meantime may not the Trustees imagine I am *laying violent Hands upon it*? Your Father too perhaps may not like it – I hope you will not consider *me* – I really wish you could forget that I existed . . .

Ironically, Byron, who had not been in touch directly with her for months, chose this moment to break his silence and, on 12 October, wrote to tell her how 'very acceptable' he found his wife's gesture in sending the game 'the first thing of the kind too for these seven years'. He had left Pisa for good and was now living with Teresa at the Villa Saluzzo outside Genoa,* 'a hundred miles nearer to you than I was'.

A week later he wrote again, making one last effort to persuade Augusta to make the journey, 'by *land* too' out to Italy: 'You must find it sad work living in that expensive England with so large a family.' Why could she not come out, with George and the children,

---

* On 20 April, the five-year-old Allegra had died of fever at the convent in Baqnacavallo in which Byron had placed her the previous year. In July, Shelley was drowned in the Bay of Spezia.

to Nice and stay there 'free of any expence'? He would 'remove from Genoa' to be near her, but would live in a separate house. 'The gain in point of economy – would be something of which you have little idea – *Pensez*.' He knew that there was little likelihood that she would accept and did not bother to post the letter until November, 'thinking it useless', but perhaps she might reconsider it in the spring, 'the time of touring'.

Augusta had refused so often that she had run out of excuses. In some desperation she suggested that they might find one another too greatly changed, and said that she had heard that he had lost his teeth. Byron had not lost a tooth since he was twelve and Hobhouse, who had been out to see him at Pisa earlier in the year, was sent round to 'St James's Palace' to give the 'necessary intelligence'. Trusting that Byron might find her real reason for refusing his 'kind offer' more acceptable if it came from Hobhouse, she explained that she feared that if she were to leave England for any length of time she might forfeit her apartments at the palace; on her return she and her family could find themselves without a roof over their heads. It was more than six months before Byron wrote to her again.

If the spring of 1823 did not take Augusta to Nice, it at least brought the 'most gorgeous' Lady Blessington to Genoa. For the next few weeks she and Byron visited one another frequently – although perhaps not as frequently as she subsequently claimed – riding and dining together, and she accumulated sufficient material for a book of some 200 pages of 'Conversations of Lord Byron'.

It was inevitable that Byron's talk should turn to his sister, although for once he was sensibly guarded about their relationship, knowing Lady Blessington to be a prodigious gossip.

> Augusta has great strength of mind, which is displayed not only in her own conduct, but to support the weak and infirm of purpose. To me she was in the hour of need, as a tower of strength. Her affection was my last rallying point, and is now the only bright spot that the horizon of England offers to my view. Augusta knew all my weaknesses, but she had love enough to bear with them . . . She has given me such good advice, and yet, finding me incapable of following it, loved and pitied me but the more, because I was erring. This is true affection, and above all, true Christian feeling; but how rarely is it to be met with in England.

It was the third week of June before Augusta heard again from Byron, and then only a brief note asking her to pass on to Annabella his approval of the appointment of Thomas Noel (who had conducted the fateful marriage service at Seaham) to the living of Kirkby Mallory. Almost as an afterthought he added: 'I sail for Greece in about a fortnight – address to Genoa – as usual – letters will be forwarded.' In all probability Augusta had already learned from Hobhouse and from the newspapers that Byron had agreed to lend his name and his money to the cause of Greek independence, but she had little or no understanding of why he was going or what he hoped to achieve.

She was sending regular bulletins out to Genoa about seven-year-old Ada, who was suffering from a mysterious 'indisposition', whose main symptom seems to have been a series of agonising migraines, perhaps brought on by the strain of living with Annabella. Writing on 12 October, Byron was reminded of the 'dreadful and almost periodic headaches' he himself had suffered up to the age of fourteen, and asked Augusta to send him some account of Ada's disposition and temper. At the same time he did his best to explain to his sister why he had come up 'amongst the Greeks':

> – it was stated to me that my doing so might tend to their advantage in some measure in their present struggle for independence – both as an individual – and as a member for the Committee now in England. – How far this may be realised I cannot pretend to anticipate – but I am willing to do what I can . . .

That year, 1823, saw the death of Augusta's aunt and mother-in-law, Frances Leigh. She had been living in Kent at Hythe in very reduced circumstances subsidised by an aunt in Nottingham.

In the autumn all Augusta's children fell ill and she herself was struck down by what sounds like a particularly virulent fever, for she later told Byron that she had lost her hair.

> Mrs Leigh has had a good deal of sickness in her family [Hobhouse wrote to Byron on 12 February 1824]; she has now, poor thing, eight children [he had somehow managed to add an extra child] with very slender or rather no means of educating those who are growing up. I do not know what would have happened had she been turned out of the palace. Whenever I see her she is most anxious in her enquiries about you . . .

Now that Byron was at Missolonghi, surrounded by fever-ridden swamps and beset by earthquakes, Augusta for the first time began to grow seriously concerned and scanned the papers anxiously every day for news of him. A report that he had been seriously ill, 'a fit and God's what', sent her into 'a sad fret':

> I have made every inquiry of Mr Kinnaird & Mr Hobhouse who have promised me all the intelligence they may receive – but the only certainty seems to be, as yet, in a letter from Col Stanhope who confirms the reports of your having been ill – pray write, I hope you will when you consider the distance and anxiety such reports & accounts on that subject – Fletcher promised me *faithfully* that he would write to me if ever you were ill – remind him of this dearest B. and let me hear of you and that you are well – I daresay you have been fagging yourself to death as you never could do anything in moderation . . .

She enclosed a bulletin about Ada, whom she had recently seen and was in 'very good looks'. Her letter ended: 'I hope you have received all my letters and that this one will reach you.'

It never did. On 9 April, although far from well, Byron insisted on taking his customary early-morning ride with Teresa's brother, Pietro Gamba. A little way outside the town they were overtaken by a heavy storm of rain and were soon soaked to the skin. Shortly after their return, Byron told Gamba that he had a fever and was suffering from rheumatic pains, but he could not be prevented from going out again the following day and was seized by an even more violent fever. As he lay on the sofa he recalled a prophecy made to him as a boy by a Scottish soothsayer, that he should beware of his thirty-seventh year.

Over the next few days his fever continued to rage but he resisted the demands of his bewildered doctors that he should be bled, the only remedy known to them. They insisted that he was trifling with his life, that the disease might rob him of his reason and eventually, with a sirocco blowing round the house and his medical advisers growing increasingly frantic, he consented: 'Come; you are, I see, a d—d set of butchers . . .'

By 18 April, Easter Sunday in Greece, he knew that he was dying:

> Your efforts to preserve my life will be vain. Die I must: I feel it. Its loss I do not lament; for to terminate my weary existence I came to Greece. My wealth, my abilities I devoted to her cause. – Well: there is my life to her.

Outside in the streets the traditional Easter discharge of musketry was forbidden so that his last hours might not be disturbed. He died at six o'clock the following evening in the midst of a thunderstorm, telling Fletcher, 'I must sleep now.'

The Easter festival in Missolonghi was suspended, the shops were ordered to shut for three days and a period of three weeks' general mourning was decreed. Pietro Gamba wrote immediately to Hobhouse – 'Your friend, my friend and father, the light of this century, the saviour of Greece is dead.' At the same time he sent a letter to Lord Sydney Osborne* in Corfu, breaking the news. A grief-stricken Fletcher had written an account of his master's death in heart-breaking detail for Augusta as well as a letter for John Murray, and these Osborne dispatched to England directed to Douglas Kinnaird. It took nearly a month for the package to reach its destination. Early on the morning of 14 May it was delivered to Hobhouse with a note from Kinnaird. Hobhouse opened the note and in an 'agony of grief' read of his friend's death. At a meeting later that morning it was agreed that Kinnaird should inform George Anson, now the 7th Lord Byron, who would carry the news to Annabella, while Sir Francis Burdett was sent off to 'St James's Palace' to see Augusta.

In her final letter to Byron, Augusta had told him that she was 'really becoming more like myself in point of strength' after her recent debilitating illness, but Burdett's news broke her completely. Hobhouse, when he called on her at her request later in the day, found her in 'an afflicting condition'. He handed over Fletcher's letter, which had been enclosed in the one for Murray. Fletcher had been so agitated about the effect of his letter on Augusta that he had suggested to Murray that he should open it first and 'explain to Mrs Leigh For I Fear the Contents of the Letter will be too much for her'.

Fletcher's letter was rendered all the more unbearable and poignant by its naïve, stumbling simplicity:

On the 15th February my Lord was attacked with a convulsive fit which was after the course of a ¼ of an hour quite gone off – But the remembrance of it, was followed up the most strictest almost &

* The son of Augusta's mother's first husband, the Duke of Leeds, by his second marriage.

moderate way of living, so much that his Lordship wd not even take a dish of Fish which is the only thing we have here . . .

Knowing of Augusta's trust in the workings of providence, Fletcher was at pains to point out that Byron had studied 'most fervently' the duty of a Christian:

> for the Bible was placed on his Ldships Breakfast Table as regularly as his simple cup of Tea which his Ldship always drank without cream or sugar – now Madam I must proceed with my fatal history which to the 10th of April was in every respect well excepting a cold, which I did not wonder at, this being so very low & every sort of the most disagreeable filth in every part of the Town which made the people die by Scores in a Day . . .

His account followed the relentless progress of Byron's illness from day to day, culminating in a harrowing account of Byron's desperate and unavailing attempt to convey his last wishes:

> My Lord on the 18th began to make sure of his speedey Deselution and was beginning to Give me Several orders: first that I should instantly come and see Miss Byron, 'and you must go to my poor dr Sister and tell them all', and then where delerious for a short time and then he came to his Reason for a few minutes and began saying 'I should like to do something for you and Tita and Luca.' I cryed out, 'Pray give your other orders of more consequences than this.' He said, 'I have a great deal to tell you which I hope you will see done for I feel I am going . . .' My Lord now again got me by the hand saying, 'be sure mind all I say,' and at this moment his voice began to falter and I was not able to Distinguish one word from another. My Lord continued talking to me for more than a Quarter of an Houre – I may say nearley half an Houre when My Lord said Quite Plain, 'now I have told you all which I hope you will attend to.' I answered, 'My Lord I am very sorry but I have not understood one word which I hope you will now tell me over again.' My Lord in Great agitation said then, 'if you have not understood me it is now too Late . . .'

Augusta passed the letter to Hobhouse, who 'burst out into uncontrollable lamentations' but regained sufficient control of himself to insist that Augusta should keep to herself the portion of the letter in which Fletcher described how he had put the Bible on his breakfast table. 'Mr Hobhouse,' she told Francis Hodgson, 'desired me *not to show it*, as many people might imagine that *terror* had made him Methodistical.' Augusta herself believed that

Byron had died reconciled to religious faith. 'To this thought I cling,' she wrote to Annabella the following night, 'as it is my only consolation.'

Sydney Osborne wrote to Augusta telling her that, had Byron never written a line in his life, what he had done in Greece would be enough to immortalise his name. From being 'England's best poet and her guiltiest Son', Byron had become a national hero almost on a par with Nelson and Wellington. As Samuel Rogers put it:

> If in thy life Not happy, in thy death thou surely wert,
> Thy wish accomplished; dying in the land,
> Where thy young mind had caught ethereal fire,
> Dying for Greece, and in a cause so glorious.

Augusta transcribed this, as she did all the poems written to her brother's memory. In the weeks that followed – in fact for the rest of her life – she began steadily to assemble a collection of newspaper articles, tributes, reviews and letters concerning her brother. Those who had known him well, and even those who had met him for only a few moments, were encouraged to send her their memories and descriptions of him.

His death, paradoxically, had a liberating effect on her. She became the keeper of the flame, honouring her brother in a way that had been impossible while he still lived. Where Annabella continued to spend the rest of her life, as she had done since the separation, assembling every scrap that might serve to justify her own actions to posterity, Augusta was concerned only to keep Byron's memory alive and untarnished.

CHAPTER 24

'God's Will Be Done! I Hope I Shall Resign to It'

O! well Childe Harold has his fame restored –
And well his wayward pilgrimage has clos'd

wrote 'A Harrow School friend of Lord Byron' in the *Morning Chronicle*, and it was Byron's restored 'fame' that Hobhouse was now intent on preserving – 'all that was left to me of my friend'. The chief threat, as he saw it, was constituted by the infamous Memoirs, which Byron had given to Thomas Moore in a gesture intended to ease his friend's financial difficulties, on the understanding that they would only be published posthumously. Hobhouse had never cared for Moore. He was jealous of the easygoing friendship that had existed between him and Byron, and his feeling of antagonism undoubtedly contributed to the indecent haste with which Hobhouse set about planning the immediate destruction of his friend's 'Life'. He even broached the subject to Augusta, whom he was to use as his stalking horse in the enterprise, at their meeting on 14 May 1824, 'the very day I received the fatal intelligence which I really could not from nervousness comprehend'.

In 1821 Moore had accepted 2,000 guineas from Murray for the manuscript but, even before news reached him of Byron's death, Murray had been beginning to get cold feet, and there had been talk of Moore raising the money to buy the Memoirs back. Murray was now firmly of Hobhouse's opinion that the memoirs should never be published and would be better destroyed. Not that either Hobhouse or Murray had actually read them, but Murray had asked the editor of the *Quarterly Review*, William Gifford, to look through them on his behalf and had been told that they would bring Byron 'everlasting infamy' if they were published.

Augusta had not even seen them, let alone read them. She had barely recovered from her illness and was still in a state of shock after the news of Byron's death. Hobhouse had little difficulty in persuading her that the Memoirs should be consigned to oblivion. She needed to cling to the conviction that her brother had faced up to the 'serious duties of a Christian' during his last weeks at Missolonghi, and to see his precious memory defiled by writings that Gifford had told Murray were 'fit only for a brothel' was unthinkable. She may also have been concerned on her own account. Although she had been assured that there was nothing scandalous concerning her in the Memoirs, she knew that Annabella would be in for a rough ride and that her sister-in-law and her allies would not hesitate to revenge themselves if Augusta's devotion to her brother had been praised at Annabella's expense.

Annabella played a shrewd and very carefully calculated game. Well aware that it was she who had most to lose by publication of the Memoirs, she saw equally well that whoever was responsible for getting rid of the manuscript would be held to account by the world at large and by posterity. It was essential to her purpose that the Memoirs should be destroyed, but it was equally important that Augusta and Hobhouse should appear to shoulder the responsibility. Augusta walked blindly into the trap, behaving with an unhappy combination of irresolution and obstinacy.

She told Annabella that Hobhouse came to her and said he had something to tell her that she would be glad to hear:

> that *it was agreed* (& he produced a *written paper* with ye agreement stated on it) and that Moore, Murray, Hobhouse & Wilmot Horton* sd come *here* – Murray receive 2000 G. from Moore & place the Memoirs in Moore's hand who wd resign them into Mine – '& I advise you Mrs L. to burn them in our presence.'

Augusta was horrified, not at the thought of the imminent incineration of her brother's account of his life, but at the prospect of Moore forfeiting 2,000 guineas. She did not care for Moore (although she had never met him) – in fact none of the parties concerned had the least sympathy for him – but she was understandably worried that he would expect to be compensated for his loss.

Hobhouse, however, was in no mood to countenance any opposition: 'H flew into a fit of *vehemence* & never could I understand anything but that I must be a Great fool for *Not* instantly Seizing his Meaning – so I *pretended* I did . . .'

After Hobhouse had left, Augusta realised for the first time the

---

* Robert Wilmot assumed the name Horton in 1823 on the death of his father-in-law, Eusebius Horton, of Catton Park in Derbyshire.

responsibility that had been thrust upon her. The decision to destroy the Memoirs was to be hers, and hers alone. In a panic, she turned for advice to the new Lord Byron, George Anson:

> ... G.B. comforted me by Saying *'oh never mind you must be only glad they will be burnt'* & so I thought I must perform this painful duty – with ye sort of feeling I should have if I were doomed to appear in a Court of Justice or something absolutely Necessary –.

It was arranged that the following day Moore, Murray, Hobhouse and Colonel Doyle (representing Annabella) should convene at 'St James's Palace' 'for the purpose *above mentioned*', but then Wilmot suggested to Augusta that it might be better if she appointed someone to act for her. Relieved to be let off the hook and to escape 'any share in the business', Augusta gratefully agreed, but was less than enthusiastic when Wilmot proposed that he himself should represent her. She feared this might only stir up the old animosity between Wilmot and Hobhouse '& therefore he said why not leave it to Col Doyle? – I told him I had no objection . . .' Doyle would later claim that he knew nothing whatsoever of the business until approached by Wilmot, but this was almost certainly a convenient lapse of memory to conceal Annabella's covert involvement. Doyle was now in the comfortable position of representing both Annabella and Augusta.

Moore, meanwhile, was trying to persuade all concerned to accept a compromise solution by which the Memoirs might be entrusted to Augusta for safe-keeping rather than being destroyed. Had this been put tactfully to Augusta – she was after all naturally attracted to compromise solutions – she might well have accepted. Unfortunately, in the confusion of contradictory notes and messages between the interested parties, she heard that Murray had understood her to have *'expressed a wish to have these Memoirs in my possession!'* This served only to fortify her determination to see the Memoirs burned – 'and I think the sooner the better'. She wrote to Annabella:

> I don't know whether you agree with me dearest A, but there is something to me of *Vanity* & *Egotism* in writing *one's own life* which I cannot bear – & there is quite sufficient known by those who may wish to do so, & can do it well, to answer their purpose without this unfortunate Memoir having to be read & canvassed,

In 1807 Augusta Byron (*above*)
married her cousin, Lieutenant-Colonel
George Leigh of the 10th Hussars
(*right*).

Byron wrote: 'It is true she married a
fool – but she would have him – they
agreed - and agree very well …'

Six Mile Bottom. The house, six miles outside Newmarket, was given to George Leigh by the Prince of Wales. For Augusta, it was 'the Home I have so long wished for and in which I am completely happy'.

Newmarket. 'In spite of the ruin which the racehorse brings to some of its votaries, it has an irresistible charm. ...' Horses were George Leigh's lifeblood and his downfall.

Two of George Leigh's cronies. The Earl of Darlington (*above*) belonged 'to that select coterie who can boast of a close intimacy with the Prince of Wales'. George regularly stayed with him at Raby Castle, for the excellent hunting.

Sir Harry Fetherstonhaugh (*right*) was also a member of the Prince's circle. His house, Uppark, in Sussex, was one of George's favourite haunts. When life became difficult, George would vanish there for weeks at a time.

Byron. His favourite picture of himself. 'I prefer that likeness to any which has been done of me by any artist whatever.' He commissioned the painting for his friend Scrope Davies who gave it to Augusta after Byron's death. 'Keep it as the apple of your eye,' he told her.

Augusta. The half-sister of whom Byron wrote: '...my feelings towards her – are a mixture of good & diabolical – I hardly know one passion which has not some share in them ...'

Annabella, Byron's wife. Tormented by her jealousy of Augusta, she wrote: '... there were moments when I could have plunged a dagger into her heart...'

Newstead Abbey, the ancestral home of the Byrons. Although she only visited it three times, it had a powerful emotional meaning for Augusta and she thought of it as the place 'where if I could but live and die it would seem to me, I would only be too happy...'

Francis Hodgson (*left*) and John Cam Hobhouse: two of Byron's closest friends. Augusta had great affection for Francis Hodgson and she corresponded with her 'dear Mr H' throughout her life. Hobhouse she had, at first, regarded with deep suspicion but came to value him for his devotion to Byron.

Mrs Villiers. Augusta's close friendship with Theresa Villiers dated back to Holdernesse House days. Annabella, however, easily manipulated her into betraying Augusta.

George Anson Byron. The heir to Byron's title, he, too, was loved and trusted by Augusta and he, too, was turned against her by Annabella.

Two of Augusta's daughters: Georgiana and Elizabeth Medora. Medora (*below*) ran away to France with Henry Trevanion, the husband of Georgey (*right*), leaving her with three young children. Annabella believed that Medora was the daughter, not of George Leigh, but of Byron.

St. James's Palace. Augusta spent the last thirty-three years of her life in a grace and favour apartment situated near the tower (right) in Flag Court.

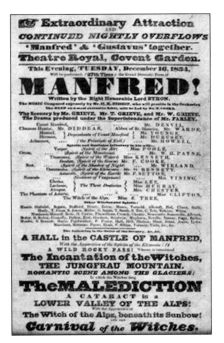

Playbill advertising Alfred Bunn's production *Manfred*. One of the main themes of Byron's verse drama was his love for Augusta. 'It is too barefaced for her friends to deny the allusion.'

Frederick Robertson of Brighton.
A charismatic preacher who became Annabella's close friend and confidant. 'Did *Manfred* shadow a truth?' he asked her.

squabbled over, for what *one* may think desirable *another* not so – so here I am – God knows what will happen tomorrow at 12 . . .

Since Augusta no longer had an active role to play, it was agreed that the parties should meet at John Murray's in Albemarle Street on 17 May. There was a preliminary skirmish in Hobhouse's rooms in Albany, where Henry Luttrell, a lawyer brought in at Moore's request, suggested to Murray and Hobhouse that there 'would be no harm in reading the MSS', but this eminently reasonable notion was summarily dismissed by Hobhouse. The parties then left for Albemarle Street, where Wilmot and Doyle, both claiming to be acting for Augusta, were awaiting them. There followed a lengthy and acrimonious discussion, with Moore arguing strongly against the destruction of the manuscript and Hobhouse and Murray resolutely opposing him. Wilmot Horton suggested that the Memoirs might be deposited 'in the hands of some banker', but although Hobhouse stated that he had no objection to this proposal, this last plea for sanity was overruled, presumably by Murray and Doyle.

It was Francis Doyle (who told Wilmot that he regarded himself 'only as a witness and not a party to the proceedings') who took the decisive action. According to the account set down by Hobhouse:

> Colonel Doyle then said to Mr Moore '*I understand then that you stand to your original proposal to put the MSS at Mrs Leigh's absolute disposal*'. Mr Moore replied '*I do but with the former protestation.*' '*Well then*,' said Colonel Doyle, '*on the part of Mrs Leigh, I put them into the fire*'.

Wilmot and Doyle, on Augusta's behalf, then tore up the pages of Byron's Memoirs and shoved them into the flames.

Doyle was the most ruthlessly partisan of all Annabella's supporters and it is likely that he was carrying out an agenda previously agreed with her. The only account of the marriage and separation that could have contradicted Annabella's version of events had now conveniently been destroyed and the responsibility placed on Hobhouse and Augusta. Annabella had the added satisfaction of being able to tell her sister-in-law: 'had the question been *then* submitted to me, they certainly would not have been consumed by *my* decision. It is therefore perhaps as well it was not.'

The press was predictably outraged by the 'destruction of the

Autobiography of the Greatest Poet of the Age' and the *Morning Chronicle* left no doubt as to who was responsible: 'The MS was placed by Mr Moore and Mr Murray at the disposal of Lord Byron's sister, Mrs Leigh, by whose wish it was immediately & entirely burned.'

The public rehabilitation of Byron brought in its wake a revival of all the old feuds and controversies. One of the first casualties was Mrs Clermont, whom Byron had publicly savaged as 'the Hecate of domestic hells'. At the end of May she wrote to Augusta complaining that she had been 'shamefully traduced in various Newspapers' and demanding, with a degree of thinly veiled blackmail, that Augusta should vindicate her character:

> You are the person most fully acquainted with *all* that caused and *all* that passed at the separation of Lord and Lady Byron – my chief reason for not before taking any public measure for my own justification was a determination not to injure the Interests of another, as I must inevitably have brought you forward.

Augusta's reply fell considerably short of the kind of public declaration that Mrs Clermont had in mind. Augusta sympathised with her annoyance, and had taken every opportunity to deny the calumnies that were being circulated. Mrs Clermont was at liberty to show her letter to her friends and to express Augusta's conviction of her innocence of the charges brought against her, '*except through the channel of a newspaper*'.

Augusta had no intention of giving the press an opportunity to revive old scandals, but the past was now in pursuit of her and nothing would bring this home to her more forcibly than the matter of her brother's will. In the summer of 1815, with the knowledge that Annabella stood to inherit a great deal of money through her parents and, consequently, that any children of their own would be well provided for, Byron had decided to make his will in favour of Augusta and her children. Douglas Kinnaird, his trustee, was of the opinion that he had made a subsequent will in Genoa and a search was duly ordered, but no trace could be found. On 15 June Annabella put Mrs Villiers in the picture:

> I will not leave you ignorant of what appears to be the final disposition of Lord Byron's property as no later Will is to be found than that to which a codicil was added in 1818. The property is bequeathed to the Leighs; Hanson & Hobhouse the Executors. The

amount will be upwards of £100,000 in the end – on this subject I shall inviolably adhere to the determination of making no remarks.

Annabella's letter to Mrs Villiers was deliberately misleading; it contrived to present Augusta in the worst possible light. What she did not reveal was that the major part of the money in question was, in fact, held in trust under the terms of her own marriage settlement to provide her jointure of £2,000 per annum and, over and above that, to provide for Byron's legacy to Ada of £16,000 payable on her coming-of-age or her marriage. Nor did Annabella explain that it was only the residue of Byron's estate that could be of any immediate advantage to Augusta and her children, since the rest of the capital would not become available until after Annabella's death. In short, Augusta was to be placed in the invidious position of being generally regarded as the inheritor of a considerable fortune, while it was not in her power to convert this into ready cash.

It is unlikely that Augusta managed to grasp the full facts of the situation. Her understanding of complex money matters – or even of relatively simple ones – had never been, as she would have put it, her 'forte'. Her first feeling was of guilt towards the new Lord Byron, George Anson, who had been left nothing at all. But she was powerless to do anything. She could not change the will; she could not make him compensation; she could not even, as she pathetically admitted to Annabella, let him continue to have the room he had occupied at 'St James's Palace' while George Leigh was away.

George Anson was now staying with Annabella at her house in Beckenham, and he had no intention of having anything to do with Augusta. Like so many of the Byrons, he was excessively prone to melancholy and his exclusion from Byron's will had driven him into a black depression. Augusta's utter helplessness gave Annabella the perfect opportunity to take the initiative, securing George Anson's lifelong devotion to her and at the same time cutting him off from Augusta for good. Letting it be known that, in her opinion, George had been shabbily treated, she arranged to transfer her jointure to him. This involved no great sacrifice on her part, but was praised in the oiliest terms by the toadying Wilmot:

I consider the proposal as one of the most liberal and magnanimous (if the word were not injured by its frequent misapplication) that *ever was made* by Man or Woman . . .

Either by accident or design, the press got hold of the story, but the report concerning the will in the *Morning Chronicle* – besides describing Augusta's inheritance in terms that must have gladdened the hearts of the Leighs' creditors – took a very curious line on Annabella's benevolence:

> The property which will thus pass to Mrs Leigh and her numerous family, exclusive of the large revenue which must inevitably arise from his great works, will be very considerable . . . Lady Byron, we have authority to state, has most liberally bestowed her jointure of £2000 to Captain George Anson Byron, a proof at least that his Lordship calculated justly on her Lyship's approval of his own dispositions to the female branch of his family [Ada] equally unprovided for . . .

Much as Annabella wished her charity to George Anson not to pass without notice, she had no desire to be perceived to acquiesce in her husband's wholesale bequest to his sister and was not at all pleased. Augusta wrote to her:

> I am very sorry you have been annoyed by it, & you may be sure it does not originate with Mr Hobhouse – My wishes & feelings on this point must be so well known to *you* that it is needless to repeat them – it is a most painful subject to me – but at the same time it is my duty I am sure to be grateful for the very unexpected blessing (& the very unexpected one) of thinking my children will not be Beggars.

Annabella replied to Augusta's letter on 7 July, as always choosing her words with great care:

> It has occurred to me that since the contents of the Will are published, *my* authority for opinions concerning it may be falsely alleged by some . . . I am, however, very far from wishing to deny now what I have more than once said to my husband – that it was his duty to provide for you and yours. How far *exclusively* is a question which I am relieved to be under no necessity of discussing . . .

Augusta seems not to have taken in the implications of this. She had no doubt in her mind that she was perfectly entitled to Byron's legacy but she failed to realise the depth of George Anson's bitterness at being excluded from the will. It was not simply a matter of money, it was George Anson's pride that had been injured. He had become the seventh Lord Byron, with a seat in the

House of Lords, but his ancestral home, Newstead, had been sold and he had inherited not a stick of furniture nor a family portrait.

Nor had Augusta any notion of the degree to which Annabella had poisoned George Anson's mind against her, by revealing to him the incestuous nature of her relationship with Byron. This, he convinced himself, was the reason behind Byron's 'exclusive' bequest: 'Our feelings cannot allow us to receive anything from Augusta,' he told Annabella:

> We are, thank God, independent, and more than that through your generosity . . . but this, my friend, is quite of a different nature. The other will not bear thinking of.

The *Florida*, carrying Byron's remains, was expected any day and, on 25 June, Hobhouse called on Augusta to discuss the funeral. Byron had left no directions, other than a desire to be buried in England.* Augusta wanted Byron to be buried in the family vault in the church at Hucknall, 'near our own dear Abbey', but Kinnaird had far grander ideas. He would be satisfied with nothing less than Westminster Abbey. However, the Dean, Dr Ireland, adamantly refused to admit the author of *Cain*.

Augusta's wishes were therefore observed and it was agreed that Hobhouse should make the necessary arrangements.

Byron's death had made him public property, and London was in the grip of 'Byronmania'. Anything that bore his name or face instantly sold out. Pirated editions of his poems were rushed into print and his fame was commemorated in countless odes and laments. Rossini, one of the few composers for whom Byron had ever shown any enthusiasm, was being fêted everywhere in London that summer, and composed an elegy in Byron's memory. He gave a series of concerts at Almack's and, a detail that Byron would have appreciated, was accosted by a bailiff, 'who had no soul for music', as he was about to sit down to dinner one day.

Byron's body was brought to lie in state at Sir Edward Knatchbull's house, 20 Great George Street. The front parlour had been hastily draped in black to suit the sombre occasion with his coat of arms displayed on a board. The public were admitted by ticket only and crowds 'beyond all precedent' assembled outside. Such were the 'uproar and confusion' that the press reported that

---

* According to Dr Julius Millingen, on his deathbed Byron had asked to be buried at Missolonghi; 'Here let my bones moulder – lay me in the first corner without pomp or nonsense.'

Handley and Veale, 'the two principal officers of the Queens Square establishment', were called out to impose order '. . . and even their presence scarcely tended to abate the violence of the applicants, so eager were they to gain admittance . . .'

On 8 July it was announced that, 'yesterday the Hon. Mrs Lee [sic], sister to his Lordship, was shewn the corpse of her noble brother in the presence of the Executors'. 'I could hardly resist seeing the remains', Augusta wrote to Hodgson, 'he was embalmed so it was still possible'. Byron must have been sadly disfigured by the clumsy post-mortem that had been performed on him in Greece. Hobhouse, when he eventually managed to summon up enough courage to view the body, found that 'it did not bear the slightest resemblance' to his old friend. The mouth was distorted, the teeth discoloured, the skin like parchment. In Missolonghi, Byron had grown a moustache like those of the Suliotes whom he commanded, making his features even less recognisable. Yet Augusta somehow managed to derive a 'melancholy comfort' from the experience:

> . . . for my own part I only envy those who could remain with and watch over him till the last. Such are my feelings, but I know there are many who could not bear it. It was awful to behold what I parted with convulsed, absolutely convulsed with grief, now cold and inanimate, and so altered that I could scarcely persuade myself that it was him – not a vestige of what he was. But God's will be done! I hope I shall resign to it.

Augusta did not attend the funeral, for it was not then customary for women to do so. According to the *Morning Post*, 'Sir Ralph Noel Bart father to Lady Byron, has been written to, to ascertain if it is his intention to follow his lamented son-in-law to the tomb but his answer has not yet been received.' The new Lord Byron, George Anson, did not attend either, pleading ill health, but more probably through pique at having been left out of Byron's will.

The cortège set out from Great George Street at 10 o'clock on Monday morning, 12 July, and slowly made its way through the London streets. Mr Woodeson, the undertaker, rode at the head of the procession, followed by mutes and pages bearing sable plumes, cloakmen on horseback and a black charger carrying Byron's coronet on a velvet cushion. The hearse, attended by eight pages, was drawn by six plumed black horses and was followed by four mourning coaches.

In the first coach came George Leigh, as chief mourner; Captain Richard Byron, Hobhouse and Hanson. In the second and third were Sir Francis Burdett, Kinnaird, Colonel Stanhope and, representing the Caerhays branch of the family, John Trevanion Purnell Bettesworth Trevanion. There followed a literary contingent, Thomas Moore, Thomas Campbell and Samuel Rogers, together with the Greek Deputy in London, Jean Orlando. 'An immense concourse attended,' Hobhouse noted with satisfaction, 'and the windows were full of people in decent mourning.'

Much has been made of the fact that, of the forty-seven carriages that attended the funeral, forty-three were empty; but, far from being a slight, it was considered a mark of respect for the nobility and gentry to send their carriages – among them, those of the Earl of Carlisle, Lord Morpeth, Lord Holland, Lord Melbourne, Earl Grey, the Earl of Jersey and Lord Alvanley.

It was an event that none of those who witnessed it ever forgot. John Clare, already in the grip of the madness that was soon to engulf him, watched the procession slowly making its way along Oxford Street and noticed a beautiful girl in the crowd sighing, 'Poor Lord Byron.' Clare was shortly to believe that he was Byron and set to work to add additional cantos to *Childe Harold* and *Don Juan*. At the corner of Tottenham Court Road there were so many people craning their heads out of the window that the writer George Borrow was reminded of someone being carried to execution.

It was a full hour before the procession reached the end of the paved streets and the carriages turned back. The horses' plumes of feathers were stowed away for the journey north and the hearse set off up the road to Nottingham on a journey that took almost four days. As the cortège travelled slowly northward, Mr Woodeson reported in a letter circulated to the press:

> It is impossible to describe the interest that the funeral excites in every Town the procession passes through, which seems to increase the nearer it approaches Hucknall.

At Kettering it was greeted by 'one of the most tremendous thunderstorms that was ever recorded', inevitably provoking memories of the storm that had broken over Missolonghi at the time of Byron's death.

At Nottingham the body again lay in state, this time at the Blackamoor's Head, where the surrounding streets were jammed with mourners and sightseers. The horses' plumes were unpacked again and the hearse began the final stage of its journey to Hucknall. There Hobhouse, Kinnaird and George Leigh were joined among others by Francis Hodgson and by the new owner and energetic restorer of Newstead, Colonel Wildman, whose name was carved next to Byron's on the panelled wall of a classroom at Harrow School. The church was so crowded that the chief mourners had difficulty in forcing their way after the coffin.

Byron's servants, Lega Zambelli, Benjamin Luigi and Tita Falcieri, who had accompanied his body home from Greece, watched as the coffin, surmounted by the coronet, was lowered into the vault and laid upon that of the Wicked Lord. Fletcher held onto the back of a pew, swaying backwards and forwards 'stunned with grief'. Hodgson wrote an account of the ceremony for Augusta, which has not survived. 'I felt your kindness so deeply in writing me those sad, mournful, yet grateful details,' she wrote. 'I can imagine all you felt that day, and only wish that I had been there too,' and she sent him a mourning ring containing a lock of Byron's hair.

Fletcher brought Augusta the tooled leather pillow on which Byron had lain in his last days at Missolonghi and she seized eagerly on every scrap of information from Fletcher that might confirm her belief that Byron had died reconciled to the Christian faith: 'Towards ye last Fletcher said to him *God's will be done My Lord* – he answered – *"Yes Fletcher & not mine"*.'

A letter from Dr John Kennedy to Fletcher only helped to strengthen her conviction. Kennedy, whom Byron had mentioned to her in one of his few letters from Greece, had debated religion with him for several days in Cephalonia in the August of 1824 and, although he never claimed to have converted Byron, he had at least fully engaged his mind on the subject:

> Though I failed in convincing him of the soundness of those views of Revealed Religion which all Orthodox Members of the Protestant churches all entertain yet he expressed many sentiments which if known will tend to remove part of that obloquy which is attached to his name in the minds of most Christians.

This was all Augusta needed. 'I shall ever bless that man for his endeavours to work upon his mind,' she told Hodgson. 'In some moments one regrets there was not *more time* for them, in others one recollects what threatened if a longer time had been granted, and one ends by a conviction that all must have been for the best.' A very Augustan sentiment.

CHAPTER 25

'The Descent of the Balloon'

George Leigh returned from Byron's funeral satisfied that he had done his duty to the brother-in-law he had so thoroughly 'abominated' and promptly took himself off to the company of Sir Harry Fetherstonhaugh, leaving his wife to cope with a 'very melancholy' situation at 'St James's Palace'. His valet 'who has been very long with us' was dying, 'in the last stages of a liver complaint', the nursery maid was 'threatened with brain fever' and 'the only thing of the servant kind we have left, a Boy, has just run away!!'

It would have been better for Augusta if she had been left to indulge in her grief, slowly to recover herself and come to terms with her brother's death, but she was given no time to achieve this. Rather to her surprise she found that she had become something of a celebrity. The sister whose love and devotion Byron had so publicly, and at times embarrassingly, praised now received the homage of the men who had shared in the uncertain glories of the Missolonghi expedition. The Greek leader, Prince Mavrocordato, wrote assuring her that her own loss was also Europe's loss, but above all an immense and irreparable loss for his own country. Pietro Gamba called on her and, although she was at first alarmed at receiving the brother of Byron's last mistress, she was immediately won over: 'he is pleasing, fine looking & spoke with great feeling'. The same could hardly be said for the blunt rough diamond William Parry, who was given a very frosty welcome – 'a most vulgar rough bearish' person.

Annabella was largely disregarded, but then it was hardly likely that the champions of Greek liberty would pay tribute to the woman who had, as they saw it, deserted their hero. Of Byron's companions at Missolonghi, only Fletcher went to see her, and, as he told his story, she sobbed 'so that her whole frame was shaken'.

But it was Augusta who had, in effect, become Byron's literary widow, the heir not only to his by now mythical fortune, but also to his fame. She was writing busily to his friends and admirers and

294

assembling a collection of his letters for Hobhouse. Scrope Davies, now exiled for his debts in Brussels, sent her the letters that Byron had written to him, with a miniature, and, in gratitude, she gave him some of her brother's rings. In writing to thank her, he warned her to take care of her health: 'for you never go through any worry unless stimulated by a fever – but in the reaction consists the danger – The descent of the balloon is most dreaded by the aeronaut.'

Even before Byron's funeral his would-be biographers were jockeying for position. Pietro Gamba, Parry, Stanhope and Edward Blaquière were all at work on memoirs of the last months of his life and it seemed that anyone who had ever met Byron (and a great many who had not) was rushing into print. Over the full, official biography Augusta and Hobhouse intended to exercise, as far as possible, their control. The first person to put his name forward was the usually reticent Francis Hodgson. Augusta knew that she could trust him to be discreet, but she also knew that the ultimate decision would rest, not with her, but with Hobhouse, Kinnaird and John Murray. 'I cannot help anticipating,' she warned Hodgson, 'that there are still others who will wish me to give my sanction to *them*, and whose feelings I would not wound by *giving* a preference, whatever I may *feel* on the subject . . .'

Scrope Davies had warned her about 'the descent of the balloon' and when Augusta's balloon began to fall, it did so with unnerving rapidity. Even before Byron's remains had arrived back in England, she had heard from George Anson's sister, Julia Heath, that their uncle Robert Dallas was proposing to bring out a collection of letters. This unwelcome news was confirmed on 23 June 1824 by an announcement in the press for the 'PRIVATE PAPERS OF LORD BYRON including his letters to his Mother'. These were to be 'connected by memorandums and Observations forming a Memoir of his life from the year 1808 to 1814 . . . by one of his earliest and most confidential friends'. What made the announcement particularly offensive to Hobhouse and Augusta was that the book was being hailed by the newspapers as 'in a great measure compensation for the loss of Lord Byron's Memoirs'.

Robert Dallas was the brother of George Anson senior's wife, Henrietta Charlotte. Pompous, cantankerous and ingratiating, he had insinuated himself into Byron's life at the time of the publication of *Hours of Idleness*. At first he had proved himself extremely useful; he had found a publisher for *English Bards and*

Scotch Reviewers, had seen the book through the press and had performed a similar service for the first two cantos of *Childe Harold*. He had done very well out of the association, since he had received the copyright of the *Childe Harold* cantos and – although Byron soon wearied of him, calling him 'a *damned nincom*' – also the copyright of the best-selling *Corsair*. Now he was proposing to line his pockets further by selling Byron's private letters to the public.

Hobhouse rushed round to 'St James's Palace' for a conference with a distraught and indignant Augusta, then wrote to Dallas to protest about publishing the letters without consulting either the family or the friends of Lord Byron:

> no man of honour and feeling can for a moment entertain such an idea – and I take the liberty of letting you know, that Mrs Leigh, his Lordship's sister, would consider such a measure quite unpardonable . . .

If Hobhouse had reckoned that this would deter Dallas, he had seriously underestimated his opponent. Dallas did not even condescend to reply, but sent off a highly offensive letter to Augusta, telling her that he did not see 'any obligation to submit his conduct' to any relative of Lord Byron:

> . . . it was my purpose to order a copy of the volume to be sent to you – As I trust you will do me the honour by a few lines to let me know, that it was not your intention to have me insulted, I will hope still to have that pleasure.

He also insinuated that there was material in the letters that might question Byron's friendship for Hobhouse.

Augusta's reply was glacial. She told Dallas she was 'sorry to observe' the spirit of his letter. Hobhouse had written at her request, 'from his being my brother's executor and one of his most intimate and confidential friends'. She concluded:

> I feel equal regret and surprise at your thinking it necessary to call upon me to disclaim an intention of *having you insulted – regret*, that you should so entirely misunderstand my feelings; and *surprise*, because having repeatedly read over Mr Hobhouse's letter, I cannot discover in it one word which could lead to such a conclusion on your part.

Since there were no signs of repentance or retraction from Dallas, and since he could not produce the letter from Byron that he claimed gave him ownership of the letters, Hobhouse secured an injunction to prevent publication on 5 July, four days before the book was due to go on sale. An outraged Dallas returned to his home in France, where he was taken ill, but his son, the Reverend Alexander – a slippery character who combined sanctimoniousness and ruthlessness in equal portions – took up the fight. Knowing that his cousin George Anson Byron would almost certainly side with him against Augusta, he gave the book to him and asked him to read it. On the morning of 26 July, George Anson called on Hobhouse and told him he could see 'nothing offensive to anybody' in the letters. Hobhouse, now preoccupied with Greek affairs, suggested that the book should be submitted to some third party, perhaps Lushington. George Anson was only too happy to go along with this, but the elder Dallas most emphatically was not. There was now no alternative to proceedings in Chancery, and after Dallas, Hobhouse, Augusta and Fletcher had all made sworn depositions, Lord Eldon ruled against publication. But there was no protection for English copyright in France and the Dallases went ahead with the publication in Paris, in a French translation.

In October Augusta, worn out and longing to be away from it all, took refuge with the children in Brighton. 'I hope the sea agrees with you,' Hobhouse told her, 'and that you will come back refreshed enough to bear the fogs and follies of London.'

The sea always agreed with Augusta and she had taken lodgings at 98 King's Road, where she could have an uninterrupted view of it:

> ... it was a comfort to think I need not see anybody but the Fishermen and Bathing women & hear only the waves. I *lived* as close to the water as I could & wind and weather scarcely kept me indoors.

The weather that autumn was dreadful. In freak storms, rain and hail fell in 'drenching quantities' and a 'hurricane', 'one of the most overwhelming for years,' sent the breakers crashing over the bridge of the Chain Pier, flattening the fencing the length of the esplanade. A fire at Blackrock, according to the papers, 'was perceptible throughout Sussex', but none of this deterred Augusta.

Finding comfort in her anonymity, she went out of her way to avoid Brighton's usual complement of fashionable visitors. What was not to be avoided so easily was the fact that all the newspapers were carrying notices of *Medwin's Conversations with Lord Byron*, 'detailing the Principle Occurrences of his private Life, his opinions on Society, Manners, Literature and Literary Men', and by 23 October it was on sale in all the booksellers. 'I am aware that in publishing these reminiscences I shall have to contend with much obloquy from some parts of his family,' Medwin announced in his preface, 'that I shall incur the animosity of many of his friends.' He was right.

Medwin was a cousin of Shelley's, who had been introduced to Byron at Pisa in the winter of 1821–2. They had sat up late into the night with Medwin doing his best, as Scrope Davies put it, 'to become B.'s Boswell'. 'What a worry this *Captain Medwin* is!' Augusta wrote to Annabella before she had even seen the book, 'at least I feel it so – it really keeps me in a fever. I wonder who or what he is, I heard some time ago he is very deficient in *intellect*. He can however *invent*.'

There was nothing in the book to worry Augusta on her own account (she was in fact barely mentioned), but it abounded in misstatements and inaccuracies and, since Hobhouse was throwing all his energies into demolishing 'Captain Medwin's *pretending* conversations', she, as keeper of the flame, could hardly hold back. She was soon dashing letters off to him by every post. She even broke out of her self-imposed seclusion from society to have dinner with Lady Holland at her 'most disagreeable gite, the York Hotel'. Lady Holland observed:

> She is very plain, yet with a strong likeness or caricature of the Howards, Ly Julia* especially. She seems amiable, & desirous that her brother's memory should be spared, alike from friends & foes . . .

Barely had Augusta recovered from the shock of Medwin when she read to her horror in the *Morning Post* on 20 November an announcement that 'The Long-expected Recollections of the Life of Lord Byron by the late R. C. Dallas esq have at length been offered to the public . . .' On 21 October, Dallas had been summoned into the 'presence of his reconciled maker', as his son rather curiously put it, but he had scored a posthumous triumph over his foes.

---

* This was not flattering to Augusta. Lady Julia Howard, Lord Carlisle's sister, was rather eccentric, apparently overdid the rouge and was well into her seventies.

Since Lord Eldon's decision had ruled out publication in England of the letters themselves, Dallas had simply drawn on their content for an account of Byron's life between 1808 and 1814 with liberal quotations from his own letters. The Reverend Alexander had prefaced this with a vitriolic description of the proceedings taken to ban the original, concluding with a savage indictment of Augusta herself:

> it is hardly possible to be believed that all these oaths, as of knowledge upon surmising have for their object to add a few hundreds to the hundred thousand of pounds that Lord Byron has stripped from an ancient and honourable title which they were meant to support – not to give to his daughter, which would have put the silence of feeling upon the reproach of justice, but to enrich his sister *of the half blood* . . .

For good measure he added the accusation that:

> Lord Byron, against all *moral* right, has applied the money procured by the sale of Newstead Abbey, to enrich his half-sister, and left the family title without the family estate which belonged to it . . .

Augusta was hurt and shaken. The public humiliation of the Reverend Dallas's preface was far more punishing than anything she had endured over the *Manfred* crisis, since it was directed so specifically at her. Worse still was the fact that George Anson had played a part in its publication:

> I wish too I had never loved G.B., sufficiently to make me more than angry at his late conduct – I think his sanctioning Mr Dallas's Book is an *outrage* to the living & the dead – such a production *I* never saw – putting aside what is said of myself by his relation Mr Alexander . . .

George Anson had sailed far away beyond the reach of her anger. He was on the long voyage to Hawaii, carrying back home for burial the bodies of the King and Queen of the Sandwich Islands who had died within a few days of one another while on a visit to London, which had been the sensation of the season.

In her misery and rage Augusta turned, as she always did, to her sister-in-law. Annabella was, in fact, far more involved than she dared admit. She had been one of the first to receive a copy of the book, unctuously inscribed by the Reverend Alexander, and she may well have connived at what he had written about Augusta. Yet even Annabella could surely not have sanctioned the accusation that Byron had sold off Newstead to enrich his sister, when she knew very well that the sale was bound up inextricably with her own marriage settlement.

If Augusta had hoped for support or sympathy, she did not receive it; Annabella showed not the least concern for Augusta's predicament, but stood out in George Anson's defence, insisting that he could not possibly have given his approval to the book since at the time of its publication he was on his way to the Sandwich Islands. Augusta knew very well that he had read the book, at least in its original form, since he had told Hobhouse there was no harm in it, and the fact that the Paris edition was now everywhere on sale only added to her sense of outrage:

> G.B. never saw the work entitled 'Recollections &c' – let *that* pass . . . No one I think wd *dare* to affirm that he had given his sanction to the Preface & other parts of the 'Recollections' which are not only offensive, but as I'm told *actionable* – if contempt was not what they best deserve – but to come to the point – What business had Mr Dallas to publish letters of the *late* Lord Byron's? (omitting all that relates to the *Manner* in which he wd have done it) – and what right had the *present* Lord Byron to Sanction such a publication which he did in the original Book I have read, NOW published in French . . .

Annabella, as always caught up in her own web of deception, could not admit that Dallas had sent her a copy of the book, or even that she had read it, and took refuge in suggesting that Augusta was making a great fuss about nothing. Augusta replied, rather sorrowfully:

> I am not given to quarrel *for quarrelling's sake* & had I done so, I think *he* (George) wd have been the LAST *Victim* I shd have chosen! It is impossible you can understand me *quite* if you have never had the Dallas book – & I'm sure I do not wish you to do so – but if you did I think you wd understand why for the sake of *the Dead* I never can again speak to him or be on terms of friendship *unless* he takes the step which wd be right . . .

George Anson had always held a central place in Augusta's affection. Loving and trusting him as she did, she saw his involvement with the Dallases as an act of betrayal far worse than the defection of Wilmot or Mrs Villiers. Worse still, she realised too late that she had failed to appreciate the extent of his resentment towards herself. Now driven to the conclusion that it was George Anson who had prompted Alexander Dallas to denounce the 'sister of the *half*-blood', she was also forced to accept the equally painful truth that he had long ago forsaken her to join Annabella's circle of sycophants and spies. It was her 'peculiar lot', she reflected sadly, 'to mourn over the *living* loss of all I best loved.'

The whole episode, however, had the opposite effect to what her enemies had hoped for. Far from feeling ashamed at being Byron's heir, Augusta now began to take a defiant pride in it. She told Wilmot:

> it was not unnatural that he sd have made some provision for his Sister – even tho of HALF blood, for I am as much a Byron as George so had my Father lived to be Lord B., he wd surely have provided for me – I can regret & I do for my Brother's sake *now* especially that he did not provide for G.B., but I'm growing very sick of the subject, & of hearing his wrongs rung in my ears . . .

To her battles over Medwin and Dallas there was now added the prospect of war on a third front: the threat of a biography from Thomas Moore. Since the burning of the Memoirs Augusta had obstinately refused to let herself off the hook of her obligation to compensate him for the £2,000 he had lost, but since this was inextricably entangled with the tortuous complications of squeezing money out of the Byron trust, she could only worry away at the problem fruitlessly or beg Wilmot to come up with some kind of way out.

Moore was well aware of her embarrassment and took advantage of it to put himself forward as Byron's official biographer. If he could not be compensated for the loss of the Memoirs and his £2,000, then the least that could be done was to allow him to write the Life. Hobhouse refused even to consider the idea and Augusta could only feebly agree not to assist Moore: 'as to giving Mr Moore information I've very little to give, & sd certainly bestow that little on another if I gave it at all . . .' For the moment she did her best to put it all out of her mind and to linger on at Brighton for a few days longer 'to enjoy the dear Sea as long as I can'.

Before she left Brighton she went to Stanmer, to ask the advice of her sister Mary Chichester on the subject of her mentally disturbed daughter, Augusta Charlotte, who was now nearly fourteen. The child's behavioural difficulties and wild moods were becoming impossibly disruptive. Mary knew of a clergyman's widow living on the Stanmer estate in whose family the girl could be safely placed, at least for a time. 'It was not a *school*,' Augusta explained to Annabella, 'but where she is ye only inmate – the Family consists of a Widow Lady & 2 daughters – one of whom is highly recommended for her experience in such cases . . .'

Just before Christmas, Augusta reluctantly made her way back to London. 'I was obliged to take all sorts of nervous medicine before I set out,' she confessed, and the journey 'nearly annihilated' her.

The new year brought no relief. Byron's death, her humiliation at the hands of Dallas and all that she had continued to suffer at the hands of Annabella's faithful furies brought her to the verge of mental breakdown. 'I begin to feel as if my nerves & spirits wd not stand much more,' she admitted, but she drove herself pitilessly on. Always in the past she had been overflowing with sympathy for others. Now she was becoming dangerously self-centred. When Annabella's father died in March 1825, Augusta was so caught up in explaining yet again her grievances over George Anson that she does not seem even to have noticed it.

Annabella was deeply affected by her father's death, far more so than by the loss of her mother, and in the summer she hired a yacht and cruised restlessly along the south coast. Wherever she went, Augusta's letters followed her, endlessly rehearsing her wrongs and her troubles. On 6 June a long epistle reached Annabella at Ramsgate, marked 'To be read at leisure'. Its main theme was that Wilmot, who had been doing what he could to find some way out of the impasse over compensating Moore, had somehow managed to suggest that it was Annabella herself who was actually responsible for the destruction of the Memoirs. Although this was, in fact, not very far from the truth, considering the role played by Colonel Doyle, it was a version of events totally unacceptable to Augusta, who was beginning to take a kind of hysterical pride in the part she had played:

> How can it be possible after all that has passed on the subject between us – when in consequence of his [Wilmot's] coming and proposing the direct reverse of what Mr Hobhouse had the day before – the most extraordinary plans, such as locking up the MS. at HIS [Wilmot's] Bankers!!! publishing the *un*exceptional parts & so on – I declared I would have *nothing* to do with the thing. He said 'you MUST. *Moore will not give them up to anybody else.*' I

answered, 'IF I DO ACCEPT THEM, THEY SHALL BE DESTROYED,' &
that answer closed the whole business!

At the same time it was necessary for her to convince herself that
Byron would have given his blessing to what she had done. She was
as sure as she was of her existence, she insisted, that because of the
'blessed alteration of the last year' her brother would have done his
utmost to prevent publication.

In September, Augusta was invited to a party at Holland House,
'in ye sort of way that it wd have been difficult for me to refuse
going there'. She discovered that one of the guests was Thomas
Moore whom, for nearly a year and a half, she had successfully
managed to avoid. She was convinced that it was a plot. Moore
recalled their meeting:

> Lady Stanhope introduced me to her, found her pleasing, though (as
> I had always heard) nothing above the ordinary run of women. She
> herself began first to talk of [Byron] after some time, by asking
> 'whether I saw any likeness'. I answered I did; and she said it was
> with a string of fears of being answered 'no', that she had asked the
> question. Talked of pictures of him. I found it difficult to keep the
> tears out of my eyes as I spoke with her. She said she would show me
> the miniature she thought the best, if I would call upon her.

When it came to the point, however, Augusta always took great
care to be not at home when 'that detestable LITTLE Moore' called.

CHAPTER 26

'The Hero of My Present Fate'

By the autumn of 1825, Annabella's restless seaside wanderings had taken her to Brighton. Her godchild, Augusta's youngest daughter, Emily, who was nearly eight, was staying there with her governess in the vain hope that the sea air might prove a remedy for her persistent boils. Annabella had promised to go and see her, but was unable to find 10 Western Cottages where she was living. This provided Augusta with the opportunity to send off another of her bulletins of domestic woe:

> I must go and see her [Emily] and Augusta [Charlotte] who becomes more and more a sad and I fear very hopeless anxiety – it is a subject not easily discussed in writing – my Boys are well, but I do not know what plan to hit upon for George who must I think soon be transferred elsewhere [George was thirteen and at school with Frederick in Lewes] – he is not forward in his learning – good abilities but idle – in short what with ye health of some and tempers etc. of others there is no peace.

What Augusta did not mention was that her eldest daughter, Georgey, now almost seventeen, whom Annabella and Mrs Villiers had been so anxious to protect from Byron's evil influence, had acquired a suitor, Henry Trevanion, 'The *Hero* of my Present Fate', as Augusta gushingly described him. Henry was Georgey's second cousin once removed and the second son of the extensively forenamed John Trevanion Purnell Bettesworth Trevanion, who had been a friend of Byron and was the great-nephew of the sister of Augusta's, George's and Byron's grandmother, Sophia Trevanion. Augusta had known the family in the years before her marriage and had been introduced to Henry by his father around the time of Byron's funeral. She broke the news of the couple's engagement to Annabella that December:

> I've seen much of him since from liking him & finding him so far superior to the *common herd* but without the slightest idea till lately

304

that Georgey was likely to attract him or indeed anybody – She is such a *quiet* being – with very sound and excellent sense and good judgement, but not brilliant in any way, and I should have said too *awkwardly shy* to be admired . . .

Henry was twenty-one and very handsome. He was supposed to be reading for the Law, but his studies were constantly interrupted by ill health and by his desire to make a name for himself as a poet. What immediately drew Augusta to him, apart from his good looks, was his total obsession with Byron, to whom he devoted many lines of a long and deeply confused poem, the 'Influence of Apathy'. His verses were a pallid imitation of Byron's, lacking any strength of will and riddled with self-pity. Man's innate moral sense, he believed (as it turned out, with good reason), was insufficient to protect him from the temptations of this world. He brooded incessantly on suicide:

> . . . live I not a curse
> Unto myself – and those – distraction! Worse –
> Those who once loved me? Must I tamely wait
> Till even pity turns to worse than hate?

Like practically everyone else in this story, Henry Trevanion had no money. His father had consumed a fortune tearing down the old family home at Caerhays near Mevagissey in Cornwall, employing John Nash to build a pretty Gothic castle in its place. Henry needed to find an heiress. As one of those in line for Byron's much talked of fortune, Georgey fitted the bill.

'The present state of things,' Augusta told Annabella, 'is that the Father at a distance of 300 miles is approving in ye kindest & most flattering manner but doubting whether there will be *de quoi* to enable to marry at present . . .'

Augusta, on the other hand, was anxious to see them marry as soon as possible. She had, from bitter experience, 'a *horror* of long engagements' and was certain that a delay 'would only render the best years of their lives unhappy'. Unfortunately George Leigh thought otherwise. He did not care at all for Henry Trevanion. His daughter was related to some of the greatest families in the land and would in time benefit substantially from Byron's will. He flatly refused to countenance the idea that Georgey should be thrown away on a sickly, penniless country cousin who wrote bad verses and could hope at best for a minor career in the Law. Augusta brushed aside her husband's objections, and put her faith, as she had always done, in 'the Disposer of all Events, and trust that *He* will order all for her happiness here and hereafter . . .'

The inescapable truth was that Augusta was totally and helplessly infatuated with Henry Trevanion. She may have convinced herself that her feelings were purely maternal – and Henry would certainly have played up to this – but he later claimed that they had been lovers. We shall never know the truth of this, but it is not altogether out of the question. Henry was a considerable charmer, highly plausible in his flattery, and he would not have let the fact that she was twenty years older stand in his way if he thought there was anything to be gained by seducing her. He also made a great show of religiosity, always reading his Bible and taking refuge in prayer, which would certainly have weakened her defences. At the time she grew to know him, she was still deeply shaken by Byron's death and, driven half out of her mind by the repercussions of the Dallas affair and the destruction of the Memoirs, was capable of almost any degree of folly.

On the other hand, it has to be remembered that Trevanion was a compulsive and habitual liar, lacking utterly in principle, and that Augusta was by now over forty and physically worn down by all that she had suffered. In a sense, whether they were actually lovers is irrelevant. Marrying Georgey to Trevanion was a way of holding on to a man in whom Augusta unquestionably saw something of the dangerous and irresistible glamour of her lost brother.

By January 1826 the marriage proceedings were at an impasse. George was as implacably opposed to it as his father had been to his own marriage. As for John Bettesworth Trevanion, he had mortgaged Caerhays to the Bank of England and, to achieve this, had pressured his eldest son into consenting to sign away his rights of inheritance. Fifteen years a widower, the elder Trevanion was now far more concerned to restore his own fortunes by finding a bride for himself – he had set his sights on one of the daughters of Sir Francis Burdett – than in coughing up '*de quoi*' for the marriage of his second son. 'I cannot at this distance describe to you the sort of *unheard misery*', Augusta wrote to Annabella. 'The Lovers are both looking like Ghosts & as for the *Law* there will be no studying* while this state of things lasts as you may easily imagine.'

For a woman habitually given to dithering and procrastination, Augusta began to move with feverish energy and determination. Enthusiastically aided and abetted by Henry Trevanion, she set about raising enough money to enable the marriage to go ahead. The obvious solution, as she saw it, was for Annabella simply to lend her the money. Augusta's inheritance had failed to bring hard cash, but the prospect of the capital sum to come had given her what she perceived to be bargaining power. 'I had rather avoid application to my Leeds and Chichester relations – do you think my dear A. *we* can do this *immediately*?'

The reason for all this frantic haste was that George was away, and Augusta was hoping to have the whole matter arranged before his return, so that she could confront him with a *fait accompli*. Originally it had been intended that Henry should raise half of the money himself, but since the vague expectations on which he proposed to do so proved largely mythical, she was forced to press Annabella for the full amount: 'I expect the return of *my powers* on Saturday.'

Annabella moved swiftly but prudently. She was not prepared to be seen to enter into any direct financial transaction with Augusta, but arranged for a loan to be made in the name of her friend Louisa Chaloner, who was soon to be her travelling companion in Europe. To Augusta's great relief, 'Miss Chaloner' insisted on the transaction being conducted with great secrecy, which meant that she had an excuse for not bringing the loan before the trustees:

> . . . thank heaven Miss C.'s wish of mystery is equal to mine – *for worlds* I would not have to turn to them – they are all kindness but I could not stand the preaching of prudence etc. etc.

Augusta somehow managed to assemble this shaky arrangement before her husband's return. Although he had no grounds now for withholding his consent George refused point-black to have anything to do with the marriage. When, on 4 February 1826, Georgey and Henry Trevanion were married at St James's, Piccadilly, the bride was given away by Colonel Henry Wyndham, '*pour son ami* my sposo!!!!!' Apart from the mother of the bride,

---

* In fact, it took remarkably little to deflect Henry Trevanion from his legal studies.

the only other person present was Georgey's sister, eleven-year-old Elizabeth Medora.

Augusta dashed off a triumphant note to Annabella that evening:

> A line – dearest A. to tell you our Marriage thank God! is happily over and in parting with dearest Georgey I feel I could not to *any*one in the world with such perfect confidence as to Henry Trevanion. I have seen him *daily hourly* for 3 months – in Moments of Sickness, Sorrow, anxiety and suspense – all most trying predicaments to the Lords of Creation – and which Shew the *real* Character – & his has only risen in my estimation! I cannot express all I feel for your kindness on this occasion to which we owe *so much*! But indeed I *am* grateful – so are they –

Georgey and her husband were still on their honeymoon in Brighton when a new cloud began to form on Augusta's horizon. On 8 March she received an anonymous letter offering her 'the refusal of extracts from Lady C. Lamb's journal!!!!' Her correspondent was one J. Wilmington Fleming, an impecunious minor poet who had already made a similar attempt to extract money from Hobhouse with the threat of making the extracts public. Hobhouse had ignored him. Augusta could see nothing likely to endanger her in the passages to which Fleming referred. She passed Fleming's letter on to Annabella:

> Lady Caroline L. has been shewing her *Private Journal* to a man who *took the opportunity* of copying from it!!!! & offers it to me for any small sum *my benevolence* wd bestow!!!! I wish that woman could be sent to the Tread Mill as well as that shame*less* Man her husband!

One of the passages mentioned by Fleming made an oblique reference to Lady Byron's 'last visit to Lady Caroline previous to her separation', and this immediately set alarm bells jangling in Annabella's mind. If the world, not to mention Augusta, got to hear of her secret visit to Caroline Lamb, then the cat really would be out of the bag. However, Annabella was far too clever to suggest any concern on her own account: it must appear that she was acting to protect Augusta. She called off her visit to Europe: 'I cannot go abroad and leave her to such impending danger, if my presence can protect her.' Her chosen audience for this consummate exercise in hypocrisy was the ever gullible Mrs Villiers: 'I have again had occasion to try to be useful to A. – on a very unpleasant business – which I will confide to you . . .'

Annabella was all for paying Fleming off, so long as the money appeared to come from Murray or Augusta; but Augusta herself was not willing to go along with this. Could not Lady Caroline's husband be persuaded to intervene? But William Lamb, for whom his wife's affair with Byron had always been distasteful, refused to be involved.

On 16 March, to her great astonishment, Augusta came face to face with Lady Caroline at a party of Lady Salisbury's:

> We were waiting for the Carriage in the *Cloak Room* – she suddenly jumped before us like *Beelzebub mad* or *drunk*! For the last 10 years or more [ever since the publication of *Glenarvon*] I have never acknowledged an acquaintance with her & all *but* turned my back – Imagine after that, her accosting me & absolutely thrusting her hand into my face! I believe I *just* touched it & made her the most profound Curtsey! Then she made off somewhere – thro' a trap door I believe – for the whole apparition was to me like something from the lower Regions! & I half expected like the man in Der Freischutz to find the Fiend's mark on my hand – not my brow!

Annabella contrived to twist even this hilarious encounter into an example of Augusta's weakness, because she had allowed herself to touch Lady Caroline's hand: 'But half measures will always be her bane.'

The conclusion of the blackmail episode came as an anticlimax. Fleming simply disappeared and nothing was ever heard from him again. But the damage had been done. Annabella had spread the poison. Long after her death, it was still being rumoured that blackmail was the true cause of Augusta's 'abject poverty'.

At the end of March, George Anson, 7th Lord Byron, returned from his long Pacific voyage. His wife had made tentative attempts to make peace with Augusta during his absence, constantly assuring her that he had been in no way involved in the Dallas book (and its preface in particular), but this had done nothing to mollify her:

> '. . . could I never see him again', Augusta wrote to Annabella, '(or go out of Town as he comes into it) it would be a relief to me – such is the state of hurt wounded (I may say) affection – for I loved him most affectionately – & now dear A. – you won't fancy I bear

malice, hatred or any uncharitableness ... I have been most *unfortunate* in all the dearest and nearest ties.'

'Unfortunate!' was the word Annabella seized on. She had, she told Mrs Villiers, who was still basking in her attention, been attempting to reason with Augusta on the subject of George Anson, but had found her implacable: 'All I can do therefore is to persuade Lord B. – not to resent her strangeness – and this will not be difficult with his kind heart and aversion to all quarrels ...'

Annabella had gone back to her old games. It has to be remembered that it was she who had poisoned George Anson's mind against Augusta in the first place, and it was she who had given her blessing to the Dallas biography and had probably been privy to the attack on Augusta in the preface.

Augusta waited until 19 April, the second anniversary of her brother's death, before writing to George Anson. For once there were no exclamation marks and very few underlinings. It was a firmly controlled appeal to him to admit that he was in the wrong. She informed him that it was 'imperative', for the credit and honour of the name he bore and the title he had inherited, 'to remove the stigma which most unquestionably has been cast upon them by Mr A. Dallas's "Recollections of the Life of the Late Lord Byron" ...'

> It is almost unnecessary for me to condescend to add that both Mr A.D. and his work (including his amiable opinion of myself) would have passed unheeded and *unfelt* but for his so cruelly placing on record and endeavouring to incorporate with his own malignant insinuations, the approval and sanction of that person for whom I entertained and have wished to entertain so sincere an affection.

George Anson sent a copy of his reply to Annabella, telling her that Augusta's conduct deserved pity rather than resentment: '*I could have been severe*, but it would have been unmanly and unwise.' It is difficult to imagine how much more severe he could have been. He insisted that he was in no way responsible for the 'misunderstanding' that had arisen between herself and Dallas. Augusta's accusations were 'as unjust as unfounded' and he felt that there was a 'determination' on her part 'to divide the family intercourse which has hitherto subsisted between us'. Far from being an accessory to Dallas's book he had not even read it, since at the time of its publication he had been 'far beyond the reach of any communication with this country'.

All the anger and the sense of humiliation that had been gnawing away at Augusta since she first laid eyes on Dallas's preface exploded in bitter resentment against George Anson. There could have been no 'misunderstanding' with Dallas, she told him, since she had had no contact with him:

> Is it not a fact that you expressed your concurrence and approbation of the original memoirs and letters and even a wish that the publication should proceed – Is it not another fact that the publication was persisted in open defiance of my remonstrances and avowed disapprobation! . . . I do not accuse you of being accessory to Mr Alexander Dallas's publication nor am I either ignorant or forgetful of the circumstances you state relative to it – but I must ask you Was it unnatural that I should feel hurt and indignant at the attempt on his part to interweave (if I may be allowed the expression) *your name, your approval* and *sanction of the original work* (which I so much regretted) with his own disgraceful production . . .

George Anson did not even bother to read the letter. It was returned to Augusta from Bath, unopened. There was to be no further communication between them.

With the Fleming affair securely in limbo, Annabella set off on her tour. It was the first time that she had been abroad and she was determined to make the most of it, travelling through Rotterdam and Heidelberg to Switzerland, which she thought 'like Seaham but much bigger' and then on to Milan and Genoa.

From her writing table in 'St James's Palace' Augusta pursued Annabella across Europe with accounts of her troubles. These were now caused largely by George Leigh, who was straining their marriage to breaking point with his manic displays of intolerance and foul temper. He was taking his revenge for the way she had forced through Georgey's marriage, but he was also venting upon her all his frustrations against the world at large. His failure to get himself back on the royal payroll in 1821 had been the final blow to his self-esteem and it soured him for the rest of his life. His spirits had briefly soared when it appeared that Byron's legacy would provide a passport to the life that he was convinced fate had denied him, but as it became apparent that there was no capital sum on which he could ever get his hands, his savage disappointment vented itself on his wife and his family. Most distressing of all was the way George was unmistakably trying to create, in their eldest son, a carbon copy of himself. Fourteen-year-old George Henry was showing himself to be an apt pupil. When in the autumn of 1826 Augusta discovered that father and son had been, for some months, surreptitiously receiving the racing lists she was horrified:

> What hurt me most in all this was the duplicity and deceit! For had I *known* & it had been done openly – I should have only remonstrated in protest on this ill-judged measure of instilling & encouraging what would with such a desperation become *expensive* – but I really think that I have been only *too passive* from indolence & horror of dissipation . . .

Meanwhile John Bettesworth Trevanion had reduced his son's meagre allowance by half and, unless Henry could find employment, he and Georgey might be forced to live abroad. However, Henry showed very little inclination to help himself, which the ever gullible Augusta put down to his fragile constitution. She prevailed upon her cousin George Howard* to find something for him in one of the government offices under his control, but the post that he did come up with in the Ministry of Woods and Forests carried only £90 a year, and the idle Henry would be expected to put in regular appearances at the office. This was not at all to Henry's liking. Greatly to Augusta's embarrassment, he turned down the job. It was left to her to make his apologies to George Howard.

Augusta refused to allow herself to be crushed and, in a fresh act of defiance, decided to remove George Henry from the 'mischief' of his father's influence and send him to Eton. She set about organising this with the same dogged single-mindedness with which she had raised the money for the Trevanions' marriage. In November 1826, she became a grandmother when Georgey gave birth to a daughter, Betha Rosa. 'My grandchild is flourishing,' she told Annabella, but she was determined that this addition to the family was not going to add to her troubles: 'I try not to attach myself to her: – *à quoi bon* but to increase one's agonies and anxieties . . .'

An inescapable anxiety was Augusta Charlotte, who had proved too much for the family at Stanmer, and was now committed to a 'private establishment' at Kensal Green at a cost of £200 a year. Like George Henry's school fees, it was an additional expense that Augusta could not afford.

---

* The 6th Earl of Carlisle, his father Frederick having died in 1825.

In January 1827, the Duke of York died. It was said that he had never recovered from the death of Augusta's cousin the Duchess of Rutland in 1825. With him went any lingering hopes George may have had of royal patronage as well as a modest source of income: 'It deprives us of the little occupations one had – and of course of future hopes for our children.' The Leighs' financial affairs were yet again at crisis point (although they were rarely at anything else). 'The long standing debts and unlooked for fresh expenses' were driving Augusta to such a pitch of desperation that there were times when she began to fear for her reason:

> The thing I am always afraid of is becoming imbecile; my memory is so dreadful about things which happened a few months or weeks ago – my ideas so confused sometimes even about the particulars of what happened only some days or hours back! . . . I am always dreading being like old Lady Liverpool who they say goes into every room of her house looking for Ld Liverpool her late husband who has been dead between 20 and 30 years to my certain knowledge!!

What was constantly nagging away at her mind was the grotesque contrast between the vast fortune she was popularly supposed to have inherited and the pathetic increase of income that had actually come her way. Hobhouse had warned of this in 1824.

> It will be very difficult if not impossible to make much of the money . . . at present but could we effectuate a change of security your income would be very considerably increased at once . . .

The change of security, which Hobhouse was discussing with Hanson and Kinnaird, was a transfer of the investments from government stocks to a mortgage providing a higher rate of interest. If that could be achieved, less capital would be required to provide for Annabella's jointure and the surplus could then be invested for Augusta, almost doubling her income. The problem was to find a mortgage that was sufficiently cast-iron to satisfy Annabella's trustees and here Kinnaird was making little headway. He was not helped by Wilmot's need continually to interfere in Augusta's affairs.

With the Leighs' backlog of debts reaching catastrophic proportions, Augusta could no longer avoid the need to come to some accommodation with their creditors. On the advice of Annabella and Wilmot, she approached George Stephen, whose company advanced money on reversionary interests. However, Stephen could not proceed without having some knowledge of George Leigh's personal debts, and there was little hope of George agreeing to this. Everyone was by now so greatly in dread of his temper that even George Stephen suggested to Augusta that it might be as well for her to take herself off during 'the explosion'.

In January 1828, Augusta took her courage in both hands and wrote to George, who was conveniently away from home, explaining the mortgage proposal that would ultimately give them a higher income and her interim plans to put their finances straight. Explaining that none of this could be carried through 'without his concurrence and the payment of his private debts', she begged to be allowed to state the amount of these to his solicitor, a Mr Spedding.* George's reply was, to say the least, unworldly:

> My debts are large – you can do nothing by way of assistance – I feel greatly obliged to you for your kind offer – but I own I do not understand it all – hate the subject – I do not fancy Spedding – I do not know why my concurrence is necessary – you can do what you please without me, as you well know.

This, as Augusta pointed out to Annabella, was George in a 'good humour'. In contrary mood, he could be terrifying. 'The Violence I have seen exhibited at times, can only be considered *Insanity* whilst it rages! – sparing nothing in its way!' Augusta then attempted to proceed without his co-operation, reckoning that £2,000 – a previous rough assessment of George's debts – might be an 'accurate calculation':

> . . . I do not know how he *can* owe more – if it were Trades people I *must* know it – and tho he has horses (for Riding purposes) he quarters them with friends & he well knows what he is about with those & with betting – and if he *does* bet which I am confident is not to a large amount . . .

Since she had been so exercised by the discovery that George had been initiating their son into the mysteries of racing form, Augusta was, as always, deliberately deceiving herself.

Augusta's family woes had at least provided a brief diversion from her battles over the official biography of Byron, but in January 1828 the publication of Leigh Hunt's *Lord Byron and Some of His Contemporaries* brought her anxieties back with a vengeance. The

---

* Partner in Bicknell and Spedding, the royal solicitors!

book was a hasty, ill-considered and vindictive account of Byron's life and of the ill-fated collaboration over the *Liberal*, which Hunt had been commissioned to write by Medwin's publisher, Henry Colburn. The effect of his venomous reminiscences of Byron was enough immediately to throw Moore and Murray into one another's arms. They agreed to press ahead as rapidly as possible on a Life that would remove, as Murray put it, 'the odious impression which this villainous work is otherwise calculated to leave'.

Although this would effectively release Augusta from any obligation to pay Moore back his £2,000, she was horrified. What particularly angered her, she told Annabella in a letter that, even by her own standards, was liberal in its exclamation marks, was that Moore was already 'ransacking *all Nottinghamshire*' and that a bewildered Fletcher had been to see her:

> after an interview with the *little* Monster – who said the design of the work had yours and my entire approbation!!! & then complained of *how* he was *Minus* 2000 G.s! For which he was Now paying interest!!! F— *naively* replying he could not understand that, since he had only *repaid* What he had conjointly *received*!!! He (nasty little M.) then desired F. to meet him at Rogers's – F. Said he would *not* till he had seen *me*!

However, yet another crisis at home drove all thoughts of Moore out of her head. In Augusta's eyes, Eton had improved young George Henry 'beyond all I could have hoped for', but now he was begging to go into the Army. George reacted with 'bursts of the most horrid temper' and then washed his hands of the whole business. Once again it was Augusta who had to take charge and who wrote to the King. On 4 December, George Henry entered the 51st Regiment of Light Infantry and twelve days later was gazetted Ensign. It meant kitting him out for his new career, but the Eton fees were as yet unpaid, as were Frederick's school fees – not to mention the governess and little Emily's prescribed stays at the seaside. Augusta, by now so desperate that she was beyond embarrassment, asked Annabella for a loan of £1,000 and was refused. 'I ventured to ask you only as the time was so short before I would have repaid it,' she wrote in a tone reminiscent of Mr Micawber.

The Trevanions now had a second child, Agnes Charlotte Sophia, born in 1828, and Augusta was wearing herself out trying to devise ways in which Georgey and Henry could be supported. One of her schemes was breathtaking in its naïvety. Henry should edit a selection of Byron's letters with a suitable introduction, on which the publisher Colburn (who had already turned down a similar proposition from Caroline Lamb) would advance him £300. That she had previously denounced Dallas, Medwin and Moore for trespassing on Byron's privacy was brushed aside, as was the fact that Colburn had published both the 'Miscreant Medwin's ... falsehoods' and Leigh Hunt's 'infamous biography'. Augusta was prepared to sacrifice all her principles for the sake of Henry Trevanion.

The scheme met with no sympathy at all from Annabella – 'I feel a good deal hurt at the tone of reproach in which you allude to the termination of the Publication business,' Augusta told her – and Hobhouse would not countenance it. For all his jealousy and dislike of Moore, he could not endorse a proposition that would undermine the forthcoming Life and would cause needless antagonism; he 'put at once a stop to it'.

Relations with Annabella now began to follow a relentless downward spiral that was to lead to the complete break-up of their always precarious friendship. In this, two unrelated matters, the trusteeship of Byron's will and Moore's biography, acted upon one another like the constituents in a chemical explosion.

Augusta had recently acquired a new adviser and champion, Colonel George D'Aguilar, an amateur poet and playwright and a fanatical admirer of Byron. His admiration had taken a rather curious course, leading him to produce an emasculated version of *Don Juan*, in which anything likely to give offence had been omitted. It had been much praised by the poetess Felicia Hemans, who told him that she had often pictured to herself 'the pure and delightful satisfaction his [Byron's] sister must derive from your chivalrous affection to his memory'. Gratified Augusta certainly was, and she was soon pouring out her heart to D'Aguilar. He was said to have been so affected by her plight that he was moved to tears.

Augusta's attempt to raise money through George Stephen's Reversionary Society had come to nothing and her only hope of finding a way out of her financial nightmare was by obtaining a considerable increase in her income. Incapable of understanding the difficulties Kinnaird had encountered over the mortgage, Augusta convinced herself that he was incompetent and untrustworthy and she persuaded D'Aguilar to join in the negotiations on her behalf. Kinnaird, by then seriously ill with cancer, was so wounded by this demonstration of Augusta's lack of confidence in him that he resigned his trusteeship of Byron's marriage settlement and of his will.

Augusta had no regrets about Kinnaird's departure, but she naturally assumed that she would be consulted over his replacement and was unpleasantly surprised to be told that Annabella had nominated Stephen Lushington. For Augusta, Lushington – who was a member of Annabella's inner cabinet and had married one of her closest friends – was a proven enemy and totally unacceptable. Annabella's interests were already taken care of by her trustee, John Bland, and Augusta not unreasonably wanted George Leigh's friend Colonel Henry Wyndham to represent her.

Annabella refused. Lushington had told her that it was an act of 'base ingratitude' on Augusta's part, and that a trustee nominated by her 'might injure you and Ada for her advantage'. If Augusta persisted in her opposition, it would be a justifable reason for breaking off from her completely. This may have been exactly what Annabella had in mind from the first. She had long wearied of Augusta's interminable accounts of her misfortunes and her increasingly frequent requests for financial hand-outs. Here was a means of putting an end to it all. Over the next few weeks there was an increasingly acrimonious exchange of letters between them. 'If after full consideration you cannot admit that my assertions are perfectly well founded I must beg you to signify your dissent by silence', wrote Annabella.

Silence was the last thing Augusta had in mind. She refused to be browbeaten, going over the whole issue again point by point. Of all her letters to Annabella, this was the most hard-hitting and concluded on a note of defiance:

> I can forgive and do forgive freely, all and everything that has antagonised and I may say almost destroyed me. I can believe that you have been actuated throughout by a principle which you thought a right one, but my own self-respect will never allow me to acknowledge an obligation where none has been originally con-ferred, or to turn my own self-accuser by admitting imputations which my heart has uniformly disclaimed.

To be given Augusta's forgiveness was more than Annabella could bear. It was an 'insolent' letter, she informed Mrs Villiers. 'I have no resentment on the subject of her present proceedings. She will, I fear, injure herself by them, I have not yet determined what to do in reply to these accusations.'

The means for revenge lay readily to hand. In January 1830, Murray had published the first volume of Moore's Life of Byron. Moore had gone to great lengths not to give offence to Annabella, and Hobhouse, for one, thought that she had been let off far too lightly. Nevertheless, in the chapter dealing with the separation, Annabella took considerable exception to his suggestion that '. . . At the time of their parting, there could not have been any very deep sense of injury on either side.' She was determined to demonstrate that the reasons for the break-up of the marriage had been real and substantial, and she could only do this by implicating Augusta. Had Augusta been more yielding over the question of the trusteeship, Annabella might not have been so bent on vengeance. 'I can never pass over her insolence in offering me her forgiveness,' she told Mrs Lushington. She then proceeded to draw up a statement for publication giving her own version of events, in which she quoted a letter written to her at her request by Stephen Lushington referring to the 'facts utterly unknown communicated to him by Lady Byron which had made any possibility of reconciliation impossible'. He meant, of course, the incest.

Determined to inflict the maximum amount of damage on Augusta, Annabella secured the widest circulation for her pamphlet and even managed to get a copy of it conveyed to the King. If she hoped that Augusta might be deprived of her apartments at the palace as a result, Annabella had greatly deceived herself. The King was too ill to take notice of anything except the racing calendar. To the outside world, Lushington's letter meant nothing. It was not Augusta, but her brother – 'defenceless in the tomb' – who had been needlessly reviled. 'My God, how cruel, how utterly revengeful is the letter of his widow,' exclaimed an angry and outraged Francis Hodgson. Augusta wrote to him:

> I am always afraid of the impetuosity of my feelings on such occasions making me uncharitable. God forgive *her* if she has made me what I never was before, or believed I could be; but I will not dwell on my own feelings; you can guess them.

Nevertheless this marked the final breach with Annabella. Augusta, however, made one further gesture of friendship. On Ada's fifteenth birthday she sent her niece a prayer book. The gift was not even acknowledged.

CHAPTER 27

'I Suppose Mrs Leigh Cannot Be Aware of the Dreadful Tidings'

Although Annabella's 'Remarks' on Moore's Life of Byron had proved less rewarding than she had hoped as a means of punishing Augusta for her 'insolent' conduct over the trustees, she had already begun to take steps that would eventually deliver her enemy into her hands. Just as in the past she had stripped Augusta of those who had been closest to her – Wilmot Horton, Mrs Villiers, George Anson Byron and his wife – so now she began subtly to insinuate herself into the affections of Augusta's children. This process would lead her to the person who was to be the instrument of her vengeance, the girl whom Caroline Lamb had convinced her was Byron's child: Elizabeth Medora Leigh.

Medora had hitherto been the least of Augusta's troubles, the daughter who had caused her the minimum anxiety and the one member of the family on whom she could always rely. 'Elizabeth is wonderful in height and breadth!' she had told Annabella in 1828. 'A great comfort to me – a blessing.' High-spirited and already showing signs of becoming a beauty, Medora had always been George Leigh's favourite.

Back in March 1829 Annabella, out of concern for the young couple's poverty, had lent Georgey and Henry Trevanion a large and rather forbidding house, Bifrons, at Patrixbourne near Canterbury, complete with furniture and servants, so that they might at least have a roof over their heads while awaiting an upturn in their fortunes. The marriage was beginning to show signs of the strain under which they had been living: the couple bickered constantly, and Georgey sulked while Henry wallowed in poetic gloom:

> Bereaved of all that can to life endear
> Hope-seared-heart-broken – ever doomed to bear
> The weight of woes that crush not . . .

He had given up all pretence of looking for employment, pleading his habitual ill health. When Georgey found herself pregnant for the third time in as many years, Augusta decided that it might improve her spirits if Medora were to accompany her to Bifrons. According to Medora's own account: 'the last injunctions and admonitions I received from my Mother on parting were to devote myself in all things to please my brother-in-law and to lay aside the ridicule and dislike I had ever felt and frequently bestowed on him'.

After the child was born – another girl, called Ada after her cousin – Georgey developed severe postnatal depression. She shut herself away in her room, barely speaking to anyone and refusing to allow Henry to come anywhere near her. It was not long before he turned for consolation to the fifteen-year-old Medora, who seems to have needed little persuasion. 'Elizabeth [Medora] writes me she thinks him rather better within the last two days,' Augusta innocently reported, 'but I cannot know to what to attribute the improvement.'

It was only a matter of time before the cause of the improvement discovered that she was pregnant, or, as she put it: 'I was ruined – and likely to become a Mother by one I had ever disliked.' Henry, not conspicuous for his courage, told Medora that she must save him by throwing herself on her sister's mercy. Georgey, who almost certainly had been aware of what was going on, took all the blame upon herself, according to Medora, 'as she had been actuated by jealousy of my superior beauty and talents to expose me to what could not be resisted'.

Unaware of all this, Augusta had seized an opportunity to pay a visit to Newstead with George D'Aguilar and his wife. It was the first time she had been there since the autumn before Byron's marriage: 'I could not divest myself of being still a *child of the Abbey* and I saw his lost image *everywhere*. If I could only live and die there,' she reflected, 'it would seem to me I'd be only too happy.' However, since she was staying as the guest of Colonel Wildman, she confined herself to praising his extensive works of restoration. In the church at Hucknall she saw for the first time the memorial she had had erected to her brother's memory, but the other Byron memorials were so dirty and neglected that she felt bound to stretch her empty purse to have them cleaned. As for the living memorial of Newstead – the Wicked Lord's housekeeper, 'Lady Betty' Hardstaff – Augusta skilfully avoided her: 'it would have been awkward my going to her Sons and my reputed *Cousins*!!!' (the Wicked Lord's bastards). On the morning of her departure Augusta leaned out of her window and picked two ivy leaves, which she pressed in her Bible.

Very soon 'all the farmers' cottages, servants & neighbourhood in general' were talking about the scandalous goings-on at Bifrons. The gossip reached the ears of the vicar of the next village, the Honourable William Eden.* After visiting the Trevanion household, the Reverend Eden was in no doubt that it was his moral duty to communicate what he had discovered to George Anson and his wife.

Since the Anson Byrons were barely on speaking terms with Augusta as a result of the Dallas fracas, Mary Byron decided that she should break the news to Annabella:

> I suppose Mrs Leigh cannot be aware of the dreadful tidings in such active circulation in the neighbourhood of Canterbury, as *she* would be the last person to be informed by the parties concerned.

Annabella at once saw the possibilities. She instructed George Anson to take charge and make arrangements for the Trevanions and Medora to travel to Calais at her expense, so that the baby could be born there in secret (Annabella's name was not to be mentioned), and Augusta was to be told that the Trevanions had gone abroad because of 'pecuniary difficulties' and that Medora's 'spirits' were required to help keep Henry's depression at bay. No mention must be made to Augusta of her daughter's pregnancy.

Medora's baby, a boy, was born prematurely at Calais on 19 February 1830. He was left with the 'Medical Man' who had attended her.† Living in Calais was cheap and the Trevanions spun out their visit until rumours of revolution drove them back to England at the beginning of May. Henry and Georgey went to stay with an aunt of his in Cadogan Square while Medora, now sixteen, returned to her mother at 'St James's Palace'.

Preoccupied as she was with all her other worries, Augusta accepted the situation unquestioningly and seems to have noticed little or no change in her daughter. Her only concern was to prepare Medora for making her début in society – as Medora claimed:

---

* William Eden was a cousin of Annabella's former admirer, George Eden. He was married to the widow of the one-time tenant of Newstead Abbey, Lord Grey de Ruthyn.
† The sad child apparently survived for only three months.

against my wish (and she must have seen this) and in spite of my extreme youth, my mourning for a sister* and my entreaties and prayers to be spared only till I was a little older.

Medora's protestations hardly ring true.

On 26 June, George IV died at Windsor, talking almost to the last about horses and sending out for news of the Derby. Hobhouse noted in his diary that he saw 'nothing like grief or joy, only a bustle in the streets'. The French cooks at Windsor were sent packing, the German band paid off, the royal menagerie exiled to Regent's Park, but the Leighs – also relics of the old King's reign – remained in their grace-and-favour apartments at the palace.

Under the pretext of reading the Bible together, Medora and Henry met every day to pursue their lovemaking. 'During the whole autumn and winter,' wrote Medora, 'I was constantly and daily left in H.'s society and alone and often till a late hour of the night – as much by my Mother as Sister . . .'

Medora was incapable of taking responsibility for her own conduct. This, of course, had to be blamed on her mother. Admittedly Augusta was at times almost wilfully blind to what was going on. A letter from Henry should have set alarm bells ringing:

> MY DEAREST Moé,
>   I owe some explanation for the pain I gave you by my wild note – I took laudanum – I promise you not to do so again – would to God that had been all! Your affectionate kindness distracted me with hopes which are now no more – and Nell [Medora] had half my consent yesterday to have disclosed the fatal cause of my misery – it shall now and ever be a secret. She cannot speak without the consent I have revoked in my note last night, and you are too dear and good to ask of her a confidence the break of which involves – my life. Never again allude to the subject if you have love or pity for your unhappy
>   H.T.

In February 1831, Medora found that she was again pregnant. Henry begged Medora to confide in her mother and he composed a letter for her to copy and sign. Augusta read the letter, threw it on the fire and dashed off an absurdly emotional appeal to Henry.

---

* Augusta Charlotte had died at the private home at Kensal Green in March.

You know I have loved you and regarded you as my own Child – I can never cease to do so! To the last moment of my existence you will find in me the tenderness, the indulgence of a Mother – can I say more? If I could, tell me so! Show me only how I can comfort and support you – confide in me dearest – too much suffering has been caused by a want of confidence. What *might not* have been prevented could I have known, guessed, even *most* REMOTELY suspected! – but – I would not breathe a word if I could help it to give *further* pain! Too well do I feel all that has – that is – and that *must* be suffered! My earnest prayer, God knows! Is to act for the best for ALL and under the trial *He* has inflicted – no doubt for reasons wise and merciful, though unseen by me! Much do I blame myself! But as He who knows our hearts knows my trials, and the circumstances in which I've been placed, and that I have always acted to the *best of my judgement* for the welfare and happiness of others, I trust I shall find pardon!

I am speaking of myself, the *last* person I wish just now to consider! I am convinced, dearest, that as I have opened my heart and feelings to you, you will comfort me! I need not point out the means! Your own heart will dictate them – and as you are dear! MOST dear! *Much*, MUCH is in your power!

This is a prime example of what Annabella termed Augusta's 'moral idiocy'. Henry had judged his victim most perceptively. He knew Augusta's weakness and her gullibility, her determination to believe no wrong of those she loved. He knew also exactly how she could be manipulated. He did not reply with words of comfort or remorse, but wrote what she described as a 'most heart-breaking letter', attacking her for 'acting on a system of distrust'. As he had calculated, Augusta was thrown completely off-balance by this astonishing accusation. There was a hurried consultation with Georgey, whom Augusta begged not to breathe a word to her father. According to Medora, Augusta was in favour of an abortion, but Henry Trevanion would not hear of it. No one saw fit to inform Augusta that Medora had already borne him one child and that George Anson and Annabella had been involved in the conspiracy to conceal the birth from her.

By the following day Augusta had managed to pull herself together sufficiently to write to Henry. In a long, emotionally overweight and at times incomprehensible letter she attempted to defend herself against his accusation of 'distrust':

Dearest, do not mistake me by supposing that I have so little consideration for the weakness of human nature as to think of 'a TOO *precipitate* execution of my purpose' – a purpose on the accomplishment of which depends my only hope of consolation! You say, *you do not respect me* – you would *still less* respect me if I did not entertain such a hope, and do my utmost by the most judicious means I can think of to accomplish that on which the *eternal* welfare of that unhappy Being depends! And the PRESENT welfare – (nay, I may say *existence* and *sanity*) of so many others depends!

If word of what had happened got out, the whole family would be implicated and the scandal might well taint Emily's reputation and jeopardise her chances of ever finding a husband. But the real object of Augusta's concern was not Emily, Georgey or Medora, but Henry himself:

> Now Dearest – let me implore of you to be comforted – to do your utmost to make the best of circumstances – to trust in my affection. That you are tried, SEVERELY tried, I feel – and I pray God to support you and comfort you and guide you! And I feel confident he will never abandon you if you trust in Him!
>
> Do not accuse yourself, dearest, and make yourself out *what you are* NOT!
>
> Remember I do '*depend on your Love*' – and oh! I have loved you! – how I will always love you and God bless you! Dearest.

Her world had been turned upside-down and yet she was deliberately – perversely – blinding herself to reality. She had moved heaven and earth to bring about the marriage, had defied her husband and taken on debts that she had little or no hope of repaying. She simply could not accept that she had been wilfully misguided and had allowed herself to be made Henry Trevanion's compliant dupe.

All Augusta's reproaches were reserved for Medora. It was not the reality of her daughter's predicament that concerned her so much as fear for her immortal soul: 'Reflect that you are – no, not how, – Great God avert it! That (how shall I write it?) you have committed *two* of the most deadly crimes!' The crimes were those that she herself had committed, adultery and incest.* Augusta had, or so she had convinced herself, put her own incest and adultery behind her and now her sins were being reincarnated in her

---

* A sexual relationship between a woman and her brother-in-law was regarded as incest, not only by the Church but also by the Law.

daughter with the full horror of an Old Testament curse. She could hardly tell her daughter that she knew all too well the shame and suffering that were the consequences of her own 'deadly crimes', but she could do her best to point out the perils.

> Recollect who you have injured! – and whom you are injuring – not only your own Soul, but that of another, you think more *dear* than yourself. Think *whom* you have deprived of *his* affection! Think of others upon whom *shame* and *disgrace* must fall, if even now you are not *outwardly circumspect* in your demeanour! Think of his Family – of yours – of your unmarried and innocent sister – of the broken heart of your Father, for that, THAT would be the result, I am *convinced* – you know not his agonies for the loss of that poor Angel* who was from cruel circumstances comparatively an alien to him . . .

George Leigh had always detested Henry Trevanion and, if ever he found out that Henry had debauched his favourite child, there could be no doubt that George would physically assault him and 'no time or place would shield him'. Augusta also knew all too well who would be blamed for it all. As for herself, she told her daughter:

> an obstinate continuance in this DREADFUL affair – or the least deception, will either *upset my reason or break my heart* . . . I have suffered *much* – *long* (neither you or ANY human Being knows *how* much), but – I never knew any sorrow like this! – It was fit perhaps my pride of heart should be humbled – I looked to YOU as the *hope* and *pride* of my life! I felt you might be taken from me by Death! But I was not prepared for this wretchedness – Spare! Oh spare me, Dearest!

Not surprisingly, Medora was totally unmoved by this somewhat operatic appeal; nor would she accept her mother's entreaty that she should be prepared for Confirmation at Easter by a suitably sympathetic clergyman. Augusta's piety was, at times, a positive obstacle to common sense. It was decided that Medora should 'be confined clandestinely' in a 'distant part of the country' and in March she left with the Trevanions for Colerne, a village near Bath, where they borrowed a house belonging to a Trevanion relative. This improbable arrangement seems to have been arrived at largely

---

* This is the only time tht George's grief for Augusta Charlotte is ever mentioned and it casts a revealing light on his unsuspected sensibilities.

at the insistence of Georgey, who refused to be left alone and exposed to Henry's vindictive cruelty, although there was a rumour, spread some years later by none other than Mrs Villiers, that Medora had threatened to take an overdose of laudanum if she were separated from them.

It was also at this time (or so Medora later related) that she was told that she was Byron's daughter. How either Georgey or Henry had come by this information is unclear. Henry always had a sharp ear for information that might be turned to good account with a little subtle blackmail. He could have heard the rumours of the incest and found this confirmed by the Byron letters which Augusta had foolishly allowed him to read when she was planning to publish them. It is also possible that the theory might have been deviously insinuated by Annabella. If Henry really believed that Medora was the child of Byron, it would only have given an added edge to his pursuit of her.

According to Medora, she did not at first believe what she had been told, although the impact of the revelation upon her cannot be exaggerated. Her first reaction seems to have been a strengthening of her devotion to George Leigh:

> I wished to spare him the knowledge of my shame. We were never, any of us, taught to love and honour him. But, strange to say, I was his favourite child and had greater influence over him than any one when he was violent and would have done anything to hide his faults or spare his feelings.

'We were never, any of us, taught to love and honour him' needs to be taken with a pinch of salt, since it is not borne out by anything we know about the Leighs' life.

The immediate consequence of the disclosure was to turn Medora even more emphatically against her mother. The woman who had taxed her with the 'shame and disgrace' she had brought upon herself and her family, and who had warned her of the peril in which she had placed her immortal soul, had herself indulged in the sin of adulterous incest and, as far as her daughter was concerned, her piety was a sham. Augusta had forfeited all right to Medora's respect or obedience.

As the weeks passed the tension between the trio confined together in the house at Colerne steadily increased and Henry's cruelty towards his wife reached a point where she could no longer endure it. Georgey wrote to Augusta telling her that she intended to return with her children to 'St James's Palace'. Augusta, seeing that this would inevitably lead to George Leigh discovering what had happened, panicked. She was still far too terrified of George's reaction to tell him herself, but enlisted Henry Wyndham, who had stood as proxy father to Georgey at the wedding, to break the news.

For once in his life, perhaps for the first time since he had led the 10th Hussars in the cavalry charge at Mayorga, George Leigh took swift and decisive action. In the first week of July he descended upon Colerne in a hired carriage accompanied by 'a woman intended to represent a lady's maid'. When they arrived at the house, an attorney and a man whom Medora described as a 'sheriffs' officer' gained entrance. George informed Medora that he was taking her straight back home. She begged for ten minutes alone with Henry (who was, one imagines, cowering in a corner). Henry made her promise that she would escape at the first opportunity and Medora went upstairs to prepare for the journey.

> I found Georgiana in my room apparently in great distress of mind. She begged forgiveness of me if she had done me any wrong, assured me that she would immediately procure a divorce, and that then I could marry Henry if disposed to do so. Colonel Leigh showed much emotion, as did everyone present; but all his grief seemed dispelled at the first turnpike, in his eagerness *to pass crooked farthings*.

George Leigh had evidently changed little over the years. The Bath road was one of the best in the kingdom and they reached London at around midnight. In the neighbourhood of Oxford Street, George dismissed the carriage and its driver together with the mysterious lady's maid, and took a hackney coach. Only then did Medora realise that she had been deceived and that her father had no intention of taking her back home to 'St James's Palace':

> We were driven I know not whither, until we arrived at a house where I was given into the charge of a lady. The windows of the room into which I was put were securely nailed and fastened down, and there were outside chains and bolts, and other fastenings to the door. There was every show and ostentation of a prison.

After his energetic abduction of his daughter, George seems rather to have run out of steam. He called on Medora three times at her prison in Lisson Grove, but after that she flatly refused to see him.

Augusta visited her once and was given a very hostile reception. Neither of them had the least idea what they were to do next and they laid their troubles before, of all people, Hobhouse:

> The young girl was Lord Byron's favourite niece. I recollect her a little chubby blue eyed creature whom he used to fondle. What a fate. There is retribution in this as . . . . . . knows.

It did not take long for Henry Trevanion to find out where Medora was being held prisoner, and he and Georgey took to driving past the barred windows of her room every day along the carriageway that ran through Regent's Park. After several weeks Medora's gaoler, a Mrs Pollen, told her that if she chose to walk out of the house no one would stop her:

> I did not hesitate . . . but at once put on my bonnet, followed her instructions and found Trevanion waiting to receive me. We left the street with all possible haste and secrecy, which we might have spared ourselves, as nobody attempted to follow us . . .

The likeliest explanation for this rather anticlimactic conclusion is that, typical of George Leigh, Mrs Pollen had not been paid and that Trevanion, with funds squeezed from Augusta, had bribed her to let her captive escape.

Henry and Medora, anxious to put the Channel between themselves and George Leigh, made immediately for France, where they settled on the Cotentin peninsula, living first at Avranches and then at Granville under the name of Monsieur and Madame Aubin. Georgey and her children were left behind.

'I was left in ignorance of Elizabeth's abode – and almost of their existence,' Augusta stated, although she probably made little effort to find out. Both Georgey and Augusta's nephew, the 3rd Earl of Chichester, were in communication with Henry Trevanion, so it would not have been difficult for her to get in touch. After all the lies and betrayals, she simply wanted Henry and Medora out of her life.

Georgey had promised Medora that she would do everything in her power to get a divorce, but Trevanion told her that it 'could not be obtained'. He was lying. He had no wish to be divorced from Georgey, for one of the few assets that lay within his reach was her marriage settlement. It would not have been difficult for Georgey to divorce him, since incest automatically provided sufficient grounds, and there would have been no need for prolonged legal proceedings. Lord Chichester wrote to Henry urging a separation, but Henry was not prepared to go along with that either and took care not to let Medora see the letters that passed between them: 'I was told what they were about, and that he and Lord Chichester could not agree.' In December 1831 Medora put an end to any possibility of marrying Henry by being received into the Catholic Church.

CHAPTER 28

'Misery and Embarrassment in Every Shape'

I must write a line to say how gratified I am that you have seen the nearest and dearest relative of him for whom you sacrificed all, and who would, had Providence spared his life, have consoled you for all. Mrs Leigh is considered to be the most excellent, the most kind, the most faultless woman in England, but were she even less perfect, I well know how your affectionate heart would turn towards her, as the sister of him you so truly loved.

Lady Blessington was writing to Teresa Guiccioli, after the *contessa* had visited Augusta at 'St James's Palace' in the summer of 1832. Byron's last mistress had always been more than a little jealous of Augusta – 'How often I was irritated by Byron's tender affection for his sister Augusta! *C'était un refrain perpetuel*!' – but she was the one person in England that she was determined to meet.

There is no account of what the *contessa*, described by Lady Holland as 'short, fat and carroty', made of the dowdy, forty-nine-year-old Augusta, nor of what they said to one another, except that they were 'always speaking of him'. Teresa told Lady Blessington that 'Mrs Leigh is the most good-natured amiable person in the world', but Augusta merely reported to John Murray that she was 'satisfied' with their meeting. The *contessa* was not inclined to repeat the 'melancholy pleasure' of their encounter when she returned to London from Newstead: 'To say the truth I fear that in the present state of her domestic annoyances to *receive visits* would be to her rather a troublesome than an agreeable thing.'

Life in Augusta's apartments at 'St James's Palace' was far from untroubled. Georgey and her three little girls had now taken up residence and were dependent upon Augusta for everything. Only Emily, who was fifteen that year, brought any calm or comfort to Augusta's life.

George had become rather withdrawn and taciturn, given to walking the streets of St James's at a stately pace in his ankle-length greatcoat, hoping to meet old acquaintances. In the right mood he could still be a good story-teller and, with so many of his contemporaries dead, he could boast that he had fought through the whole Peninsular campaign, and tell of how Colonel Dundas had become so preoccupied with setting the sights of a gun that he failed to notice that a cannon ball had sliced off his arm.

Augusta was not entirely weighed down by her domestic woes. She had engrossed herself in an enthusiastic correspondence with Mary Ann Cursham, daughter of the Vicar of Annesley and a friend of Mary Chaworth Musters, about a book she was writing, *Norman Abbey*. This was set at Newstead and Augusta supposed it to be a historical novel about her ancestors. She wrote breathlessly to Miss Cursham:

> Now listen. You tell me you are anxious to promote the sale of your Book. Do you think it wd have the effect – (*supposing that it is not already dedicated* to *any more likely personage*) to dedicate it to me!! – & not My name – but –
>   'To the Sister Of —!'
> Now pray do not set this down to vanity or conceit – on my own *individual* acct – I know I am *worse* than Nobody – 'I by myself – I' – but – 'The Sister of —' you know alters the case & it has occurred to me whether it might not *attract!* I beseech you *never to breathe* this – but burn it instantly & be honest & candid in your use of it – you know how it is *intended* – & you will forgive the folly if it is one!

When the book eventually appeared, Augusta was so eager to read it that she told Miss Cursham that she had been sending for it 'thrice a day' to 'Cawthorne's where I subscribe'. She sat up reading it until three o'clock in the morning, but her enthusiasm was considerably dampened when she realised that far from being concerned with '*antient* times' it was in fact a fictionalised account of the love of Byron (Lord Evelyn Fontayne) for Mary Chaworth (Bertha). Augusta's more immediate forebears, including the Wicked Lord, her father, Mad Jack, and the Admiral, were superimposed on a background of the Civil War and the Restoration, with Betty Hardstaff putting in an appearance as a garrulous Scottish housekeeper. Since Augusta had 'taken it for granted' that the book would contain 'nothing personal in any way on certain persons and one particular subject', she must have been astonished to find that she herself was portrayed as the 'brunette of the coal-

black eye', Lord Evelyn's hitherto unknown half-sister, the Portu-
guese Donna Isidora:

> 'What a magnificent-looking creature!' exclaimed Evelyn, his eyes
> intently fixed on the young foreigner. 'What a commanding stature!
> what jetty eyes and crescented eyebrows! what a graceful, antelope
> figure!'
>
> 'And how like yourself, my lord, about the nose and chin! Who
> can she be?' asked Sir William.

Miss Cursham had evidently extracted the full story from Mary
Chaworth and had inveigled Augusta into some highly indiscreet
admissions, for the book contained an account of Augusta
dissuading her brother from renewing his friendship with Mary
Chaworth after she had left her husband:

> What balsam will you pour into a heart smarting under the pangs of
> disappointment, which will not secretly and insidiously infuse a
> deadly poison? Be advised, and go not near her.

Augusta's only consolation was that Donna Isidora had been
equipped with a solid and reliable husband – 'The man of her
choice proved one of the best and most amiable of men' – and she
remained on excellent terms with her brother's bride, Lucy Temple:
'the tenderest regard subsisted between the wife and sister of Lord
Fontayne . . .'

Generously, Augusta put her personal feelings aside and wrote to
her bookseller asking him to promote the book.

Far more exciting and rewarding for her were the productions of
Byron's works in the theatre, when she sat in a box at Drury Lane
watching the great tragedian William Macready (who happened to
be a close friend of Colonel D'Aguilar) performing Werner and
Sardanapalus to great acclaim. She sent him a lock of her brother's
hair, fastened by a gold thread to a note which read: 'Werner,
November 1830; Byron, Ravenna, 1821; and Sardanapalus, April
10th.' 'It surprised and delighted me', he recorded in his diary.

However, when in October 1834 Alfred Bunn, a fat, flamboyant
Byron-worshipping showman from Birmingham, announced that
he was putting on Manfred, Augusta was filled with alarm at the
prospect of the drama of her incest being reincarnated on stage. Her
fears proved to be groundless. Bunn was concerned only with the
spectacle, the thunderstorms and cataracts, demons and dancing
witches. Everything in the text likely to give offence had been

expunged. Astarte had become Manfred's cousin and the means of
his redemption. At the conclusion of the play, at the point where
Byron's hero rejects the Abbot's entreaties to prayer, Bunn brought
on the hovering spirit of Astarte in the heavens: 'Manfred! look up
– I do forgive thee!' Manfred rushed towards her and died and, with
thunder, lightning, snow and falling rocks, was received by a troupe
of Good Spirits. It was all that Augusta could have wished for, on a
par with her conviction that Byron had died reconciled to God,
reading her Bible every day at Missolonghi. She wrote to Bunn,
telling him that 'Manfred was splendidly got up and Miss Ellen
Tree's *Witch of the Alps* I shall dream of.' The *Literary Gazette*
thought that it would all have made an excellent Christmas
pantomime.

The public perception of Byron was changing. His admirers who,
in Ruskin's words, had been 'unable to bask themselves in the light
of his glory without fearing to be scorched by his sin' could now
partake of 'one of the noblest feasts that ever fed the human
intellect'. In the prudish new morality that had been ushered in by
Queen Adelaide, the fact that Byron had loved his sister became a
positive virtue, since this was seen as a purified love in which sex
played no part. The poet who had written:

> My sister! my sweet sister! if a name
> Dearer and purer were, it should be thine . . .

was now finding a place on the most respectable domestic
bookshelves.

As a consequence Augusta found herself much sought-after. The
popular novelist Jane Porter was planning to visit Newstead and
asked her to write a few lines pointing out her favourite rooms and
the walks 'where your footsteps and those of your brother (the still
shining light of Revived Greece) so often walked together in sweet
and kindred confidence'. Augusta was only too happy to oblige and
to provide an introduction to the Wildmans. Miss Porter was
delighted at her reception and as a result a succession of pilgrims
from all over Europe was directed to 'St James's Palace'.

But there was one door that remained firmly closed to Augusta
and that was Annabella's. She had frequently seen Ada at social
events in London but, because of Annabella's prohibition on
communication in any shape or form, had refrained from speaking
to her niece. When eventually she summoned up the courage to ask

for Annabella's permission, she met with an unqualified refusal, despite the fact that Ada was now twenty and soon to be married to Lord King. Augusta was longing to bring the unnecessary quarrel to an end, but Annabella would not yield.

For the first two years after their flight to Normandy, Augusta heard nothing of Henry Trevanion or Medora. Their baby was stillborn and Medora suffered a series of miscarriages. In her autobiography she claimed that since she had failed to give Henry a 'living child' they agreed to separate and for her to enter a convent.

At the end of August 1833, they left St Quentin sur-le-Homme outside Avranches, and made their way to the cathedral town of Tréguier in Brittany, where Medora was admitted into the Couvent aux Dames Hospitalières as a boarder. From there she wrote to Augusta, telling her that she was 'very ill & in great distress & penitent' and asking her to send money for the convent fees. Whether she had any genuine intention of retiring from the world is doubtful – it may simply have been a ruse to obtain money from her mother – but within forty-eight hours of her arrival at the convent she realised that, once again, she was pregnant. The Mother Superior, who seems to have had some sympathy for her new boarder, allowed her to move into the convent's Hôtel Dieu.*

To Augusta, with her staunch Protestant upbringing, it was shocking that her daughter had become a Catholic. She delayed and dithered, vainly imploring Medora to come back to England, until she was forced to conclude that the convent was 'the least objectionable' course Medora could take and agreed to provide her with £60 a year. With so many claims on her purse, however, she managed only to send the money in small and irregular sums.

Within a few weeks, Medora and Henry were back together again and in April 1834 they settled in the Manoir de Penhoat, a dilapidated and rat-infested house surrounded by woodland, less than two miles from the little town of Plounéour-Ménez. It was there, on 19 May 1834, that she gave birth to a daughter. Since Henry Trevanion was determined to distance himself from any responsibility, the child was registered as Marie Violette and her parents as 'Henry and Elizabeth Legh'. In the baptismal register he signed 'for the absent father' and, to further add to the confusion, Medora appeared as 'Elizabeth Leigh née Trevanion'.

---

* The hospital attached to the convent.

By that time, Augusta had made the painful discovery that yet again her daughter and Henry had made a fool of her. John Trevanion's brother, Henry Bettesworth, had been scouring Brittany for his errant nephew, aiming, as Augusta put it, 'to induce him to leave that country which was most desirable while Elizabeth remained in it'. He had gone to the convent at Tréguier, where Medora was believed to be leading a life of penitence, and was horrified to learn that she had been there 'only for a short time'. Henry's father sent a furious letter to Augusta, who, shattered by the news, could only beseech him not to withdraw his protection from Georgey and her little girls, 'or embarrass or mix them up with Mr Trevanion's and Elizabeth's conduct'. But she immediately cancelled Medora's allowance.

The discovery effectively put paid to any lingering traces of affection she might have felt for Henry Trevanion. She was determined to force him to contribute towards the maintenance of Georgey and his children, but he refused to acknowledge any responsibility. The Earl of Chichester wrote, rather helplessly: 'There is nothing in the Marriage Settlement to compel Mr Trevanion to do *anything* . . . I wish to God I could see any mode of helping you or poor Georgey.' If Henry Trevanion could not provide money for his wife, he allowed nothing to stand in the way of raising it for himself. He came to England in 1836 and stayed for six weeks. Since there was no hope of extracting anything from his alienated father, who was now married to Sir Francis Burdett's daughter Susannah, he seized upon the only source of cash open to him: Georgey's marriage settlement. With the help of George Stephen's Reversionary Interest Society, he contrived to raise £8,332 against it. The ageing Hanson, his patience exhausted, refused to have any dealings with Henry's solicitors and could only conclude that 'poor Mrs Leigh and all connected with her are mad'.

Although it is difficult to imagine that Augusta's plight could actually get any worse, in 1838, when she was fifty-five, it unquestionably did. She had already forfeited her allowance as a former Woman of the Bedchamber on the accession of Queen Victoria the previous year, and now William Lamb, Lord Melbourne, the young Queen's Prime Minister, chief adviser and father figure, took it upon himself to axe the pension which George IV had awarded the Leighs and on which they were totally dependent. Since there was no need for drastic economies in the royal household, it is difficult to see this as anything other than an act of petty spite against the woman whose brother had so humiliated him more than a quarter of a century earlier. Melbourne's kinswoman Annabella, who looked up to him now as the head of the family, would have noticed the removal of the Leighs' lifeline with satisfaction.

The seriousness of Augusta's situation can be judged by the fact that she could no longer keep up even the pretence of making an allowance to Fletcher. Annabella told Ada that Augusta had 'defrauded' him and that it was 'a breach of promise', but Fletcher took the loss philosophically. Mrs Leigh could not help it, he said, 'as her Sons and Daughters were so expensive to her'.

With the proceeds from his raid on Georgey's marriage settlement, Henry had set himself up in a small farm in the hills above Malguénac, near Pontivy.* According to Medora, she was by now desperate to escape from his clutches, but in the spring of 1838 she fell seriously ill:

> I was considered to be in a consumption & no hopes of my living beyond a few months – the Medical man who attended me was kind and attentive to me. The little experience I had of such during my life made me at his solicitation confide to him my real history & beg him to assist me in freeing myself from the cruelty of one I had never loved & who every day convinced me more & more of his utter worthlessness – & my greatest wish was to die away from him.

The meeting with Victor Carrel, the 'Medical man', was the turning point of Medora's life, for in him she at last had the means of liberating herself from Henry Trevanion. From here on she would always be fortunate in finding admirers and sympathisers who would fight her battles for her. She charmed them, she excited their pity and she relentlessly manipulated them.

It is safe to say that Carrel had never encountered anyone like Medora. Here was a beautiful woman in distress, who was – or so she told him – the daughter of the most renowned poet in Europe, whose mother lived in a royal palace and whose relations belonged to the highest echelons of the British aristocracy. Accordingly, in July 1838 he wrote to Lady Chichester telling her of the dangerous state of her niece's health and of her desire to break free from Henry

---

* The farm was in the hamlet of Botivé and may have been on land that had formerly been part of the estate of the Château de Moustoirlan, since Medora told Annabella that she lived at Moustoirlan before going to Pontivy.

Trevanion, and asking her to intercede with Augusta. He enclosed a letter from Medora which, Augusta stated, gave 'such an account of her health as led me to fear my answer might not reach her alive'. Augusta scraped together what money she could. Lady Chichester sent £5. This was enough to enable Medora to leave Henry and move to Pontivy, where Victor Carrel took her under his wing. Henry was not to be cheated of his prey so easily. He informed everyone that Carrel was trying to get his hands on Medora's money and furthermore asserted that he was Medora's lawful husband. Fortunately Carrel's brother was a lawyer and Augusta sent him a copy of Georgey's marriage certificate to disprove Henry's claim. Augusta even proposed to go over to Pontivy herself, but this would not have suited Medora's game and Carrel wrote to dissuade her. It never occurred to her to question this, and it was possibly with relief that she abandoned any idea of making the journey to Brittany. She did her best to send Medora what she could whenever she could but, as she was the first to admit, the sums were often very small.

Medora appeared to be quite beside herself with gratitude and love and, in a long letter written in December 1838, poured out her devotion in the most hypocritically extravagant fashion:

> Only remember, My OWN DEAREST Mamma, you have never erred but by too great kindness. You did *for* the best, *and* the best, believe me. I have no interest in this world – no good can come to me of deceit – I cannot even hope for the respite of a long life before I answer to God Almighty for all I have done and do. I, who know more in this sad misery than any one, know *only how* innocent you are – how good and kind you have been and are to all concerned therein, and God Almighty will recompense you – we shall be happy hereafter *together*, my *own* dear mamma – pray for me – do – do – pray for me as you alone can do. Keep my letter – and if ever at a future period your kind heart fears having occasioned a pang to your own unfortunate Libby, read this over and believe we *have* been CRUELLY deceived towards each other!!!

One can only hope that Augusta was not taken in by all this, but she probably was. At least she had the good sense to follow her daughter's advice, and kept the letter.

From what Carrel told her, Augusta was convinced that her daughter was at death's door. The best she could do was to try to provide for little Marie by drawing up a settlement that would provide her with £3,000 when the Leighs at last came into the Byron money after Annabella's death. This was not at all what Medora had in mind. She wanted money for herself now, not for her daughter at some unforeseeable point in the future. Carrel was persuaded to write again saying that Medora could not possibly exist on less than £125 a year. This was totally beyond Augusta's means, but Medora had been indulging in a little moral blackmail, telling her that people were saying she had 'no feeling or affection for her daughter'. Foolishly Augusta agreed to do what she could. At the same time she tried to explain that she had only £800 a year *pour tout bien* and this was already committed to 'debts of auld lang syne' and to providing for her own and Georgey's children.

None of this was of any interest to Medora, who had listened to her mother's vapourings over their desperate financial plight ever since her childhood. She needed cash and her only hope of acquiring it lay in the deed that Augusta had executed in favour of Marie. The great obstacle, as she soon discovered, was that no French bank was prepared to advance her money on a mere copy of the document. When she approached her mother for the original deed, Augusta was horrified. It was now plain to her that Medora was trying to deprive her own daughter of her future security. Panic-stricken, she asked Lord Chichester for his advice and he warned her on no account to hand over the deed.

Since there was now no possibility of raising money in France, Medora turned to Sir George Stephen and the Reversionary Society, through which Henry had sold Georgey's marriage settlement. Sir George, who was rather susceptible, fell for her tale of woe, accepted everything she wrote at face value and took it upon himself to write to her mother. Augusta refused to have anything to do with him. Sir George had failed her over her attempt to borrow on her own remote expectations and she no longer trusted him. Seeking some way out of the impasse, Sir George turned for help to Wilmot, whose wife, Anne, was Medora's godmother. Medora's letters, he told him, 'would have moved a heart of stone . . . Mrs Leigh cannot possibly be aware of her daughter's position, or she would not act thus.' Wilmot sent £25 to Medora, but made no mention of this to Augusta who refused to be moved. She was convinced that Medora was being manipulated by someone: Carrel perhaps, or Henry, or even Sir George himself. In an attempt to pacify her daughter, however, she threw herself into the hopeless task of trying to scrape together enough money to pay her debts: 'I was born to be a *"souffre douleurs"* of that I have long been convinced and an illustration of the Fable of the Miller and his Ass!' she wrote, ruefully, to Wilmot.

Like Aesop's ass, Augusta gave way under the strain and became seriously ill, but when Sir George advanced this as a reason for not taking legal proceedings against her to force her to hand over the deed, Medora reponded with another parallel.

> I have been so often deceived & am so accustomed to being told of the state of her nerves that I am now placed in the same position of those in the fable to whom the little Shepherd cried for help . . .

She was now more determined than ever to force her mother's hand and in April fired off an angry letter to Lady Chichester 'begging her influence to obtain the Deed for me'. Lady Chichester knew all too well what Augusta had been going through on her children's behalf and had no sympathy for her niece's loud complaints:

> I cannot help thinking by the tone of your letter you can be aware neither of the extent of your Mother's pecuniary embarrassments, or of the affection she still bears you – her late severe illness was chiefly brought on, and certainly aggravated by distress of mind on your & your sister's accounts . . .

She continued with what might well have served as Augusta's epitaph:

> My dear Libby, she may have been mistaken in her views & unfortunate in her management, but her errors chiefly arose from an excess of indulgence & misguided affection – she could not bear to think ill of those she so dearly loved, forgetting we are *all* by nature prone to evil . . .

Frustrated at every turn, Medora now took the fatal step of asking Sir George to write to 'my Aunt Ly Byron – who were she to know the *truth* of my sad life, would be kind towards me more than any one, for she well appreciates my Mother & knows her more intimately than others . . .'

At this point Henry Trevanion put in an unexpected and unwelcome reappearance. For some months he had been corresponding with Georgey, and now – alone in his farm at Botivé and letting it be known that he feared he had not long to live – he asked her to come out to Brittany with the children and join him.

Augusta, for whom Henry was now little short of the devil incarnate, was appalled and wrote to Medora telling her that it would be 'absolute destruction (body & soul)' for Georgey to do so. Medora's only concern was that if Henry was dying, he must first make a settlement on little Marie. Henry, however, was insisting that the girl was no longer his responsibility, as Medora was married to Carrel. Augusta found herself caught in the crossfire. Both girls, needless to say, blamed Augusta, and Georgey was now furious with her for allowing herself to have been taken in by Medora.

> You & only you could be *so very* (forgive me for saying so) *blind* to the real state of things – . . .
> – After having written you the most affecting letter stating that she was at the point of death, you kindly settle something on her in order that she may provide for the poor child, she gets better & tries to sell the reversion by which means the child would not have a sous, unless H. settled his farm on her which he does not seem likely to do being quite disgusted at L.'s conduct. I cannot think how it is you do not see thro' it . . . [Henry] has acted wickedly & God knows he has also suffered for it – But I do still maintain that he is far the better of the two. I think that situated as he now is, that it is my duty to go to him – and why should I refuse him the comfort & consolation of seeing his children – I really have not the heart to do so – you make him out such a monster that I feel more pity & affection than I might otherwise have felt for him – But supposing him, even all you say, still he is my Husband & but for L. would have been a different Man – I forgive her the past but cannot get over her present conduct . . .

This marked the turning point in Augusta's relationship with Georgey, who never forgave her. As for Medora, she no longer needed her mother. By the end of July she had received 'a most kind and affectionate letter' from her aunt Annabella.

CHAPTER 29

'That Viper Mrs L. . . . She-monster!!'

Annabella was in Paris when Sir George Stephen's letter reached her. It could hardly have come at a better time. She was forty-eight and was casting round for some new object with which to occupy her restless energy. Her former passions were beginning to lose their appeal: the Prison Discipline Society no longer interested her as it had once done; the school that she had founded at Ealing Grove for 'boys of common rank' could run perfectly well without her. Ada, now Countess of Lovelace thanks to the earldom bestowed on her husband by Lord Melbourne, had already given her three grand-children but was now immersed in her mathematical studies. Annabella's life lacked direction and Medora provided her with exactly what she needed.

At first, Annabella was careful to keep her distance. The Bifrons episode had taught her that Medora was a girl to be approached with some caution. She was under the impression that she had been deserted by Trevanion 'and I therefore thought there was little security for her being finally emancipated from his influence'. But the moment she heard that Medora's 'one desire was to be placed anywhere out of Trevanion's reach', she cast all her reservations aside. An English doctor was dispatched to Pontivy. He confirmed Carrel's diagnosis of consumption, and money was sent off to Medora to enable her to travel, together with little Marie and her Breton maid, to meet Annabella at Tours on 21 August 1840.

It had been nearly twenty years since Annabella had last seen Medora, whom she found 'altered beyond the possibility of recognition and in a confused and stupefied state of mind, attended at times with great excitement'. Her original intention had been to place her in the care of a family at Tours, but after their first interview she knew that she must take her under her wing. Within a few days they were on the road to Paris.

As she headed for a life in which all her needs would be catered for and her comforts assured, Medora must have believed that her troubles lay behind her. The only price to be paid was that she would be expected to disparage her mother, but she had no misgivings on that score. She was soon delighting Annabella with tales of her mother's heartless neglect, of the way in which throughout her life she had been deprived both of money and affection.

It was left to Victor Carrel to tell Augusta, but Annabella had no intention of keeping her rescue operation a secret. Ada was immediately informed of it, as were George Anson (now Admiral Lord Byron) and his wife, the Wilmots, Mrs George Lamb (who doubtless made sure the news reached Lord Melbourne), the Misses Doyle, the Lushingtons and, of course, Mrs Villiers.

When they reached Fontainebleu, Annabella was taken ill, and the care and attention that she received from Medora broke down all her emotional defences, the more so, since she believed that Medora had only a short time to live:

> I am particularly happy just now. Feelings that have long lain, like buried forests, beneath the moss of years, are called forth, and seem to give happiness to one for whom I have something like a Mother's affection. This is a little gleam in my life – it will not last, but its memory will be sweet.

Confident that Medora was Byron's child, Annabella encouraged her to call her by his pet name for her, 'Pip'. 'She implored and sought my affection by every means,' Medora recorded, '& almost exacted confidence of the most unlimited kind for all she felt for me.'

It was then that Annabella told her what she had been bursting to say since their first meeting at Tours – '*Her husband had been my father!*' Medora dampened Annabella's satisfaction by telling her that she already knew this from Henry and Georgey, but there can be no doubt that to have her suspicion confirmed in such an unquestionable manner altered her life radically. Any lingering affection she may once have felt for her mother was extinguished and she began to regale Annabella with every vicious slander she could concoct about Augusta. Annabella accepted without question the story of Augusta's adultery with Henry Trevanion and even swallowed Medora's preposterous assertion that her mother had promised Henry the free use of her daughters as they came to

343

maturity. Annabella did not hesitate to inform all her circle of these new instances of her sister-in-law's depravity. She also let it be known that she was encouraging Medora to sue her mother for possession of the deed.

Augusta, meanwhile, had been left in complete ignorance of what was happening to her daughter. Since Carrel's brief communication she had heard nothing. She had written to him enclosing a letter for Medora, 'intreating from *both* an early account of her and her health', but had received no answer. By January 1841, after three months of total silence, she swallowed her pride and wrote to Annabella a downtrodden and pathetically humble letter:

> the suspense & anxiety I must naturally have endured from this most unaccountable silence, is not all that it inflicts on me – I have hitherto complied strictly with Mons. Carrel's request that his letter and information should remain a secret between ourselves, the reasons he assigned appearing to render such secrecy essential, but Elizabeth's long and determined silence, coupled with all that had preceded it, places me in a position the most perplexing, if not bewildering . . .
>
> I have no resource but to turn to you for the information to which I am confident you will consider me entitled . . .

She hoped that the reasons she had advanced for writing would 'prove a sufficient apology for the trouble I have inflicted . . .'

In reply to this grovelling appeal – 'obviously intended for others more than for me' – Annabella sent off what must count as the most shockingly inhuman of all her letters:

> Since last August I am to be considered responsible for the safety and comfort of your daughter Elizabeth Medora . . . If it should become known, I am prepared in justice to Elizabeth and myself, to explain fully the reasons for my thus interesting myself in her welfare . . . Could I have believed that you had a mother's affection for her, you would not have had to ask for information concerning your child. But facts are glaringly opposed to your professions on that point . . . Your affectionate letters to her must appear a cruel mockery to those who know that you left her, for so long a time, only the alternatives of vice or starvation. Her malady, the effect of physical and mental suffering combined can be retarded – only by extreme care and by her avoiding all distressing excitement. The former I can secure but not the latter. I would save you, if it be not too late, from adding the guilt of her death to that of her birth. Leave her in peace! This advice

is given in no hostile spirit, but with the firm determination to protect her to the utmost of my power.

Annabella was tremendously pleased with this letter. 'I may have subjected myself to prosecution for libel,' she proudly informed the Earl of Lovelace, 'but she dares not risk it.'

Stunned and completely unnerved, Augusta began to draw up – on the advice of her nephew Lord Chichester – a statement to refute Annabella's allegations. This recounted, in a plaintive and muddled fashion, the whole course of events since Medora's departure from England. It was true, she admitted, that she had sent her daughter 'but scanty sums', but she *could not* send more'; even to do that had involved her in 'what many would consider painfully humilia-ting' – borrowing from others.

This was not an argument likely to be received with much sympathy by Annabella's supporters, but one person was convinced by it, and that was Mrs Villiers. Up to this point every action of Annabella's had received her unquestioning support, but when she was confronted by Augusta with the manifest injustice of Medora's grievances, she unexpectedly came out forcefully in defence of her former friend:

> Her income is £800 per annum. Out of this she has to board her husband when at home, and her son Henry always, to maintain herself, Emily and her servants entirely. She gives her eldest son George £100 per annum – her son Frederick never costs her less (if so little) as £200 per annum and she has entirely to provide (as far as she can) for the wants and really necessities of Georgiana Trevanion and her three growing-up daughters! As may be supposed, however, the supply has been unequal to the demand and Georgiana is deeply in debt for the bare means of subsistence . . . The parable of the Prodigal Son can only be applicable to cases where there is a fatted calf to kill. In this case there was no Calf at all.

Mrs Villiers did more. As proof of the blatant hypocrisy of Medora's behaviour, she enclosed a copy of the 'OWN DEAREST Mamma' letter:

> Did I not see and know this to be her own handwriting, I could scarcely believe that this is the same daughter who is now engaged in a law-suit against the same mother . . . and all because she *could not* do what she only promised to do IF SHE COULD.

Annabella was not prepared to let the truth stand in the way of a

345

good argument. She did not even bother to respond to Mrs Villiers' defence of Augusta. As for Medora's letter, it was 'very natural from one who believed herself dying, and was worked upon by such a letter as that to which this is obviously a reply'. When she received a copy of Augusta's statement, she sent it back, unopened. By then Ada had joined her mother and Medora at their hotel in the Place Vendôme, and her 'sister' was getting thoroughly into her stride as a story-teller. Ada wrote breathlessly to her husband:

> As for the ruin of Medora, it was effected by the *united efforts* of the *Mother, the Sister Mrs T.* [Georgey]; and Mr T. himself; & by means of *drugging* the victim, who found herself ruined on coming to her senses . . .

Not that Annabella was lagging far behind in her own powers of invention. In an astonishing exercise in revisionism she had convinced herself that Augusta's supposed resistance to Byron was feigned and that she had allowed his advances in private. She had also managed to convince herself that, since Augusta had connived at the ruin of her daughter, she 'must have been capable of injuring a brother in the same way'. From there it was only a short step to the delusion to which she was to cling fanatically for the rest of her life: Augusta had actively stood in the way of any possibility of a reconciliation between herself and Byron after he left England and had done everything she possibly could to prevent it. This was in fact the very opposite of what had happened. Ada wrote to Lovelace on 8 April:

> How comes it that my Mother is not either dead, mad or depraved? . . . A *new language* is requisite to furnish terms strong enough to express my horror & amazement at the appalling facts! – That *viper* Mrs L. crowned all by suppressing letters of my Mother's to my Father when he was abroad after the separation, & *forging others* in their place! *She-monster*!!

The 'She-monster' was still stubbornly refusing to hand over the deed to Medora, and Sir George Stephen was attempting to broker a compromise favoured by the Leighs, by which the document should be placed in the hands of some third party (perhaps the Earl of Chichester) and retained for the benefit of Medora's child so long as Augusta kept up payment of her daughter's allowance of £120 per annum. This was acceptable neither to Medora – who was beginning to grow restive at not being allowed to live life on her own terms, and was impatient for the independence that she believed possession of the deed would afford her – nor to Annabella, who wanted to see Augusta either forced into a humiliating surrender or brought to court.

At the end of May, Annabella and Medora arrived in England to be more closely associated with the case that was making its way through Chancery.* Already Annabella was growing a little unsure of her charge and Medora was showing signs of resentment at not being accorded what she considered to be her proper status. She had, or so she said, been encouraged to believe that she was 'Ada's sister in all things, as I was really'. She had expected to be presented in Parisian society as the daughter of Lord Byron, to be shown off at concerts and theatres, but she had been hidden away even from her aunt's visitors. In England she was instructed to keep a very low profile and was to be known as Madame Aubin, the name she had adopted on first arriving in France with Henry Trevanion.

Proceedings in Chancery were moving at a pace of which even Kenge and Carboy might have approved. Summer changed into autumn and the only moment of excitement came in October when seventy-year-old George Leigh was arrested on the racecourse at Newmarket. Annabella wrote to Lovelace positively effervescing with satisfaction:

> This is under the circumstances the best turn the affair could take. The £1000, and other advantages which Col Leigh received as the wages of his connivance have at last brought a retribution, inadequate indeed, but a beginning . . .

The sum of £1,000 was a considerable underestimate of George's indebtedness to Byron. It has generally been supposed that he was arrested for debt, but it is clear that his offence was towards the Court of Chancery and it seems more likely that he was stubbornly refusing to comply with some legal requirement connected with the case. This would explain why Annabella had high hopes that Augusta might have to share her husband's fate. 'I should regret it but the business must be carried thro, and her own obstinacy has caused this painful result.'

To her great disappointment, not only was her sister-in-law not

---

* Wilmot Horton, who had been involved in the affair from the beginning and could have been relied upon to further complicate an already complex situation, died suddenly on 31 May.

carried off to prison, but George was immediately released. This could not have come soon enough for Medora, who had been so distressed about her father's arrest that she was seized with a 'violent feeling of head & chest' and a burning of her skin. However, in November when the suit was postponed, she became hysterical with fury and lashed out at anyone unlucky enough to be within range.

Annabella had been worried that her niece's uncertain health might not be up to a winter in England, but now she was beginning to realise that Medora's condition was not as serious as she had been led to believe: 'E.'s power of undergoing such immense fatigue discredits the supposition of advanced disease of any kind.' At the same time, Annabella was finding it increasingly difficult to keep up with all Medora's demands. Ada had found her a French lady's maid, Nathalie Beaurepaire, and Annabella had even agreed to pay for her child's schooling in England, as well as that of little Marie. But none of this satisfied Medora: what she wanted was ready cash and her freedom, and these Annabella was not prepared to concede. Medora was deliberately kept short of money and was exiled to Moore Place, Annabella's house at Esher. She was almost twenty-eight, nothing was turning out as she had planned and she was beginning to wonder whether she might not be better off returning to France and looking for a husband instead. However, since she could do nothing until her case came to court, she had no choice but to stay in England.

It was May 1842 before a date was at last set for the hearing, on the thirty-first of the month. On the day before the case was due to come to court, Augusta handed over the deed. She had no intention of allowing herself to be pilloried by her daughter, still less for her family (Emily and Henry in particular) to hear Medora trumpet to the world that she had been conceived in incest and adultery. Medora was beside herself with fury. She had been cheated of seeing her mother exposed and publicly shamed. 'The Chancery suit', she wrote:

> was finished in a way & without consulting me that must shew me that all that had been promised unsolicited & unsought was not sincere – & once more I had been in a manner sacrificed to my Mother's interests.

The full force of her anger was reserved for Annabella. Medora

348

turned on her in hysterical rage and announced her intention of leaving for France as soon as it could be arranged. It was a seriously shaken Annabella who wrote to Selina Doyle:

> I had *never* seen anything like it – She has told me that I was her bitterest enemy and threatened every kind of revenge – I not having from first to last ever uttered an unkind word to her . . .

In a private memorandum she noted: 'There are in my opinion but two holds upon this character – Love of approbation & of money.'

All desire to keep Medora with her was gone. She could not even bear to be in the same house any longer. Her niece had served her purpose in giving Annabella the means of further mortifying her sister-in-law, but now all that she wanted was to see the back of her. The affection that Medora had briefly awakened had been stifled by the realisation that her protégée was an unscrupulous liar, who would stop at nothing to achieve a limited objective: 'In attempting to hurt those who oppose her, she will hurt herself but this will not be from recklessness but miscalculation . . . she expects people to serve her better by bullying . . .'

What had not entered Annabella's own calculations was that Medora would also see through her. Lady Byron, Medora informed Selina Doyle's sister Adelaide, 'does not always act from pure motives – or with truth'. Medora was only too aware that she had been used as a stick to beat her mother and, while she had no great objection to this, she was going to squeeze every last advantage from it. She now agreed to live 'retired and unknown' at Hyères in the South of France, but only on condition that she received an annual allowance of £150. All the expenses of the journey had to be covered by Annabella, as well as those of Medora's maid, and Nathalie Beaurepaire's husband, Victor, was to be engaged as courier for the journey, although he was later to claim that he had been employed as a full-time manservant. As for the deed, which had been the subject of so much bitter contention, it was agreed that it should be deposited with the Earl of Lovelace. A strongbox, containing Medora's letters and papers, was left for safe-keeping at Moore Place.

At the end of the third week of July, Medora went up to London to sit for a daguerreotype as a farewell present for her aunt. While she was returning in her carriage to the Lovelaces' house in St

James's Square she suddenly caught sight of her mother. She sent a lurid description of the encounter to Annabella:

> She could not have seen my face – my veil being down – and I saw her before she saw me – Her sight & perceptions are not quick – & between the door being open & my speaking to William [the footman] she had reached the Duke of Cleveland's before I got out – which I did quickly – she turned round & looked at the carriage – for I observed her from the little back window – probably from curiosity or thinking it might be you – She was followed by a dirty rascally kind of servant out of livery who was playing with his glove & [she] was dressed in a dark brown kind of muslin gown with white pattern & black silk shawl . . . gathered round her as if she was afraid of losing it & a straw leghorn bonnet trimmed with white satin ribbons.
>
> Her large eyes are ever & indeed *unchanged*, her walk is most altered – she shuffles along as if she tried to carry the ground she walks on with her & looks WICKED. Oh were there a thing I had hoped to be spared it was this – . . .
>
> This has shocked me – pained me but it is over – I have drunk quantities of wine since & now there is nothing left for me to suffer that I dread – Oh how dearly fondly I loved her & had she only stifled the existence her sin gave me – but God *is* there – & I will do my best to bear as I have ever done but it is so long & so constant – God forgive her – Oh how horrible she looked – *so* wicked – so hyena like – the sight of her has given me [resolution?] yet more strongly. If for my good or that of Marie intimidate her! – she will grovel on the ground, fawn, lick the dust – all – all that is despicable and bad . . . Now we will try & never mention her name – she will live for *years*. Oh could I only have loved the memory of my mother, but had death passed over me the chill – the horror – could not have been so great. Pity & forgive me if I involuntarily pain, I do not mean – but I *do* suffer . . .*

Annabella later told Ada that this letter had caused her great pain, but the description had been calculated by Medora to please her aunt, painting her mother as she believed Annabella wished to

---

* Whether the encounter ever actually took place anywhere other than in Medora's mind is open to question. The Duke of Cleveland had died the previous January and the one fact that Medora does not mention, which she would have surely noticed, is that her mother's hair had turned white. A description of Augusta at about the same time, by her godson George Holmes, gives a very different picture from Medora's: 'She was tall and elegant of figure and possessed a face which, while not of the type that could be called beautiful, nevertheless bore, as it appeared framed in her silky white hair, the stamp of singular distinction and even of the comeliness of old age.'

imagine her. Medora's terrifying and repulsive vision of Augusta as a shambling, short-sighted hyena was designed to justify both herself and her protectress in the savage course they had adopted against her, in the conspiracy in which they had so effectively joined forces.

Some days later Medora left England. After her departure, Augusta was summarily informed by Lady Wilmot Horton that her daughter's movements would be kept secret from her, lest she should attempt to 'molest' her, but that she would be informed in the event of Medora's death.

Augusta had much the best of the bargain, for within a few weeks Annabella began to regret that she had ever laid eyes on her niece. The money that she had provided for the journey to Hyères was exhausted before the party had got as far as Lyons, and once they were established at Hyères Medora made no attempt to live within the narrow confines of her allowance. Victor Beaurepaire, who clearly saw himself as the Figaro of Medora's little household, claimed that he was 'obliged to exercise his *authority* . . . to prevent her receiving or rather entertaining company', but this cut no ice with Annabella and her first economy was to refuse to continue his wages beyond the end of the year.

The Beaurepaires were outraged and in March 1843 they and Medora took the road to Paris 'to get a more certain and suitable arrangement'. There they installed themselves in the Hôtel du Rhin in the Place Vendôme, one of the most expensive hotels in Paris, and directed their bills to be sent to Annabella. Pierre Antoine Berryer, one of the leading lawyers in France, was engaged to plead their cause.

This was exactly the course that Medora had adopted when she had persuaded Sir George Stephen to take up her case against her mother, and the irony was not lost on Annabella, who told Selina Doyle:

> As long as it was possible I have acted with affection & forbearance
> – I suppose I was a Cat's Paw to pull the Deed out of the fire – when
> I had served that purpose, I was to be turned adrift – yet the policy
> of setting me at defiance is a very mistaken one . . .

Selina Doyle, who was living in Paris, was sent round to the Hôtel du Rhin to attempt to negotiate. 'I felt powerless as to producing any favourable impression –' she reported. 'Pride, Hardness, with a bitter sense of being injured were so predominant that I felt astonished rather than shocked. I looked for symptoms of insanity but only saw the resolution to be independent.'

Medora was drinking heavily, or, as Victor Beaurepaire put it, '*elle boit bien la bouteille*', and was firing off wildly intemperate letters to her benefactress and drunkenly incoherent ones to Ada. Rather as she had once sent Dr Le Mann to assess her husband's sanity, Annabella now dispatched Dr King, proprietor of a lunatic asylum in Sussex, to give an opinion on Medora's state of mind. He satisfied himself that she was sane enough to deal with the second object of his mission, which was to deliver her an ultimatum: if she wished to continue to enjoy the protection and bounty of Lady Byron she must conform to any arrangement made by her concerning her maintenance, 'place of residence, mode of life & other particulars'.

The ultimatum was contemptuously rejected. King, anxious to settle the business, considerably exceeded his brief and offered to double her allowance to £300 a year. This, too, in a splendid fit of *folie de grandeur*, Medora rejected:

> I submitted to all the abuse he was pleased to bestow – though it contributed all the more to make me refuse – when he said, 'Sign, sign, you great fool!' He left Paris next morning.

Berryer then wrote to Annabella's solicitors demanding the surrender of the deed that Medora had deposited with Lord Lovelace. This they refused to do, insisting that to give it up would violate the condition on which 'Lady Noel Byron [Annabella] had agreed to make the annuity'. Annabella now saw clearly how she had been tricked. She had been as gullible as Augusta. She wrote to Olivia Acheson: 'she [Medora] has gone so far that I can never hold intercourse with her again. I think of having a seal with a large *Gull* engraved on it – can you give me a motto?' Annabella now carried the war into the enemy's camp by refusing to pay the fees for Nathalie Beaurepaire's daughter's boarding school. Nathalie came to London to take her child back to Paris and to try and obtain what was owing to Victor for the money he had advanced to Medora. She also carried a letter from Medora to Augusta.

What Medora hoped to get out of her mother can only be imagined. Augusta did not even bother to reply to it, since all her efforts were now concentrated on her son George Henry, whose military career had gone steadily downhill, ending in a predictable muddle of unpaid mess bills and gambling debts.* In 1841 he sold his commission and by June was once more living at 'St James's Palace'.

As her eldest son, George Henry had been assigned a larger share of the Byron money than his brothers and sisters, but this would come to him only after Annabella's death and her own death. In 1843, in a bid to meet his present needs, and possibly her own, she attempted to raise a large sum of money from a certain John and George Foster against George Henry's reversion. Since no financial dealings regarding the Byron trust fund could be concluded without the knowledge of the administrators, Stephen Lushington and Annabella's solicitors Wharton and Ford, this proposed transaction caused them considerable anxiety:

> What sum they [the Leighs] have received for this annuity does not appear. But if Mrs Leigh has got part of the money her appointment to her son for that purpose would be illusory & void – And after her death any of her children then living may file a Bill in Chancery to set aside the appointment.

Hobhouse was appalled. He saw that Augusta was rushing headlong into unsound agreements and feared that by the time the trust fund became payable to Byron's legatees it would in fact be indebted to all those who had advanced the Leighs money on the strength of it. His misgivings and those of Annabella's lawyers were all too justified. When Medora wrote to enquire about charges on her reversion of £3,000, Lushington told her that there were none on her own account but he had received 'many Notices as to the interest of Mrs Leigh in the Funds'. Lovelace commented, rather cold-bloodedly, that 'as for Mrs L. the only thing is suicide or flight'.

It is probable that Augusta's attempt to settle such a large sum on her eldest son led to a permanent rupture with his younger brother Frederick for, from that time, George Henry never spoke to him again. Frederick, whom it was said bore an astonishing resemblance to Byron, had returned from service with the navy in the Chinese

---

* In 1833, he had served for a year with the 51st Regiment of Infantry in the British Protectorate of the Ionian Islands, from where his uncle had crossed ten years earlier to Missolonghi, but this seems to have been one of the few highlights in an otherwise undistinguished record of service.

Opium Wars a violent-tempered drunkard. George Leigh would not allow him in the house, pointedly refusing to acknowledge him if they encountered one another in the street. Frederick's involvement with a notorious gang of upperclass hooligans, whose chief amusement was roaming the streets at night ripping off door knockers and bell-handles, only deepened the rift between them.

In June 1843, Victor Beaurepaire joined his wife in England. His wages had still not been paid, he had left Medora's service and he was set on holding her and Annabella to ransom by seizing the deed for himself. With the help of a middle-aged admirer, Captain Joseph Barrallier, a veteran of Waterloo, Medora followed in hot pursuit. The deed was her lifeline and she was determined that Beaurepaire should not get his hands on it. But she had reckoned without Annabella's lawyers, who, wise to the situation, had resorted to delaying tactics, and she made the fatal mistake of sending an ominously threatening letter to Lord Lovelace:

> You are fully aware My Lord that it is impossible I can comply with such delay & I write to you at the same time as I have written to Messrs Wharton & Ford informing them that unless the Deed is given up to me tomorrow, they will compel me to have recourse to such measures as will place me in possession of it.

As far as Annabella was concerned, this was the end of their relationship. Medora had forfeited any vestige of a claim on her sympathy by breaking their agreement by returning to England and demanding the deed. The annuity was cancelled and all communication between Annabella and her niece ceased.

This jolted Medora back into reality, for at last she realised that she was in danger of losing everything. She had acquired yet another legal adviser, Thomas Smith, a solicitor and one-time army agent, who had briefly known Byron in Ithaca in 1823. Smith urged her to do all she could to 'reconciliate Lady Byron' and she sent off a series of deeply contrite letters, all of which were returned unopened. On Smith's advice, Medora then drew up an autobiographical sketch, setting out all her grievances, putting both her mother and Annabella in the worst possible light:

> Now I cannot though I would say otherwise than that she [Lady Byron] has cruelly deceived me, and is as guilty in thus oppressing and driving me to the utmost extremity as the mother who has only

made me the instrument to serve her avarice and the sacrifice to be made to those she feared.

With a growing sense of panic she proceeded to send off begging letters to anyone she could think of, compromising her appeals for help with tacit threats of exposure. Hobhouse wrote with bewilderment and distaste:

> I have a letter from a person signing herself Elizabeth Medora Leigh stating herself *to be a child of Lord Byron* & asking *for charity* – can it be a daughter of Mrs Leigh's? Can it be *the* daughter who eloped with Trevanion who married her sister. I hear . . . that the woman has threatened her mother with family disclosures, so it is not unlikely she may be my correspondent.

Medora was out to do as much damage as possible. In a letter to her cousin, now the 7th Duke of Leeds, after he had sent her £10, she told how she had been ruined at the age of fifteen 'by the unprincipled man to whom I was exposed by those whose duty it was to watch over and protect me'; how she had been deeply deceived in trusting her aunt, who had left her without the funds necessary for her health or the education of her child, and from whom she had learned that she had been conceived 'in incest and adultery'.

When all her other attempts to raise money failed, she made a last bid to throw herself on her mother's mercy, but whenever she presented herself at the gate of St James's Palace she was told that Augusta was not at home. On 13 August she sent off the last letter she was ever to write to Augusta:

> My Mother,
>   The motive that led me last night to ask what I have long since hoped to be spared, to meet once more, you, I so tenderly loved, was not as you have given me the right yet to do, to accuse and reproach you, nor to seek to awaken your pity for the misery I owe alone to you. Since I was made to understand you could never have loved me, the child of your guilt, to whom you have been but a means to satisfy your ambition, a sacrifice to be made to those you feared, then to throw me on the world, destitute, homeless and friendless. I have expected and sought nothing from you – but now compelled to seek aid and protection from all who will give it. I once more remind you I am your child. The world and strangers will tell you in harsher terms all you owed me – do owe me – could I have felt I was writing to a *Mother*, I would have said much, now I can only beg you, by the

memory of my father, the brother [to] whom you, and the children you love and enrich by my destitution owe all – no longer to forget and neglect what you still owe

> Your child
> Elizabeth Medora Leigh

Augusta had grown immune to Medora's reproaches and accusations. She was more concerned to find out what her daughter was up to and whom she was with. On 2 September she wrote to Wharton and Ford to ask whether or not Annabella had withdrawn her allowance:

> as sad experience prevents all confidence in Elizabeth's statements – & of those with whom she is at present placed or connected I know nothing.

Wharton and Ford passed on a statement from Lady Byron that the 'Dowager Countess of Chichester was put in possession some time ago of the chief facts concerning the allowance which Lady Noel Byron had made for the maintenance of Miss Leigh.' This was neatly side-stepping the issue, since Annabella was no longer providing any sort of maintenance.

The only person who received any satisfaction from the whole affair was the irrepressible Victor Beaurepaire. He threatened to sue Annabella for defamation of character, pointedly addressing a letter to her as 'The Lady Noel Byron, *femme de mauvaise foi*, Esher Surrey', which could not have meant much to the postman. It contained an announcement offering a reward for information about 'the unfortunate Elizabeth Aubin, natural daughter of Lord Byron' and her daughter, who had been cast off by 'the very wicked Lady Noel Byron' and by her half-sister the 'virtuous princess' Lady Lovelace, with the connivance of her 'rascal of a brother-in-law the Seigneur Harpagon de Lovelace'. Anyone prepared to volunteer such information should get in touch with Mrs Leigh at 'St James's Palace', where they would receive the reward – a hundred lashes of the knout.

He threatened to sell the story to the newspapers; to knock down Lord Lovelace in the street, so that when he was brought to court he could reveal the scandal to the world; he even proposed to appeal to Queen Victoria. Annabella was prepared to face him out, but Lushington advised her to pay the rogue off. To complete her humiliation, she was obliged to give the Beaurepaires a character reference.

Medora had succeeded in shutting every door in England against herself and there was nothing left but for her to return to France. She made a new will, leaving everything she possessed to Marie (including her precious strongbox, which remained in England). She then raised £500 on the deed that had at last been surrendered to her and left England for ever in the summer of 1844. In 1845, when she had been reduced to working as a servant at a pension in St-Germain-en-Laye, she met a soldier from a French cavalry regiment, Jean-Louis Taillefer. He was only a batman but, since he was the best that life had to offer, he became her lover and, as had always happened before, she soon found herself pregnant. Fortunately Taillefer was a man of very different metal from Henry Trevanion. He agreed to marry her and to adopt Marie.

Medora and her daughter made the long and arduous journey across France to Jean-Louis's native village of Lapeyre outside Saint-Affrique, in an area chiefly celebrated for the manufacture of Roquefort cheese. Taillefer returned to his regiment and Medora was left to make her own way in the local community as best she could. Once again she adopted the name of Madame Aubin. Her child, a boy, christened Jean-Marie Elie, was born on 27 January 1847. For a year and a half she awaited Jean-Louis's return, and on 23 August 1848 they were at last married. Medora did not have long to enjoy the only experience of stability she had known since childhood. On 28 August 1849, she died of smallpox, aged thirty-five.

In her will, dated five days before her death, 'Elizabeth Medora Leigh' (she never seems to have called herself by her husband's name) bequeathed all her worldly goods 'and all that I possess according to the conventional deed of the late Lord Byron' to Jean-Louis and to her children:

> I declare here that I forgive my mother and all those who have so cruelly persecuted me, as I hope to be forgiven myself. I beg my solicitor Sir John Hughes to send the above mentioned Jean-Louis Taillefer the casket containing my papers which is in his possession.

To the last she insisted that Byron was her father and she would certainly have approved the headstone on her grave, which now records her as:

Elizabeth Medora
Leigh-Byron.

The Taillefers' struggle to obtain the casket which, according to Medora, contained the proof that Byron was her father dragged on until 1863, when, on 19 May, it was at last opened in the office of Sir John Hughes in Bedford Row. By a stroke of irony that Henry James might have envied, the papers alleged to substantiate Byron's paternity were burned as being of no relevance to Medora's estate.

CHAPTER 30

'A Most Happy Release'

By the middle of the 1840s, Byron's reputation was undergoing something of an eclipse. 'That man *never* wrote from the heart,' cried Thackeray. Wordsworth, Keats, even Shelley, were better suited to the Victorian temper. 'Byron's fiercer wine has lost favour,' commented Charles Kingsley. In consequence, Augusta – now in her sixties – found herself no longer much in demand as the sister of the great poet and was beginning to lose much of her purpose in life. 'I do become very superannuated,' she told Hodgson, 'and always think of B.'s horror of "withering at top first", not from the same superabundance of brains but wear and tear of the few that I possess.'

Nor did the family for whom Augusta had sacrificed so much play anything like the same central role in her life. The whole Medora episode had proved deeply divisive, with George Henry siding with Georgey, while Emily refused to take anyone's part. Georgey's relationship with her mother had never recovered as a result of Augusta allowing herself to be taken in, as Georgey saw it, by the sister who had stolen her husband.

The youngest of the Leigh children, Henry Francis, had at least managed to hold down a job at the Board of Control, enabling him to scrape a living for himself. On 18 June 1845 he married Mary Edgar, who gave birth to a daughter, Geraldine Amelia, three and a half months later at their home in Hammersmith. His income was barely enough to maintain a wife and family, but they contrived to keep going until 1851 when ill health forced him to resign from the Board and sell his reversion. Augusta's second son, Frederick, who evidently could turn on the Byron charm if he chose to do so, was lucky enough to acquire a wife from a well-to-do Yorkshire family, Phoebe Althea Rothery, whom he married in Ripon Cathedral on 23 October 1847. A little more than two years later, she bore him a daughter, Ada Mary Augusta, but within three years she had left him, taking the child with her and keeping their whereabouts secret.

'. . . he do not know where she is so I fear she do not wish to see him . . .' George Leigh's valet, John Pollendine, commented sadly. But, like his grandfather Mad Jack Byron, Frederick had always been a wastrel. Mrs Villiers had written of him almost a decade earlier:

> Her [Augusta's] son is a constant drain upon her, and one cannot wonder that she should try and save him from the degradation which has not yet *fallen*, but is constantly impending over him.

Frederick shared the family addiction to the turf, but he was also addicted to alcohol, which was undoubtedly a major factor in the failure of his marriage and the disintegration of his naval career. It was a vicious circle from which he could never extricate himself. 'He will not be long for this world if he do not lead a quieter life,' Pollendine observed. 'I fear he drinks hard . . . I am so sorry for poor Mr Leigh. I wish he were better off. They have been very unlucky with their horses . . .'

John Murray had died in 1843 and the publishing house was now in the hands of his son, John Murray III. Augusta had never felt shy of asking for the odd loan from them, but with ruin omnipresent, she was beginning to use the firm almost as if it were a literary pawnbrokers, sending Emily round there with various scraps of Byroniana and bundles of letters on which to raise often quite considerable sums of money. Even the box of Byron's precious letters to Augusta found its way to 50 Albemarle Street, in spite of the fact that she intended it to go to Emily after her death.

Of all the children, it was Emily who remained loyal and stayed with her parents, a model of devotion and affection. She had a moral integrity conspicuously lacking in the rest of the family and when Augusta's threadbare finances had reached a point of utter catastrophe, Emily unhesitatingly sold her reversion:

> If it had not been for the sad situation she was placed in I should never have raised any money but seeing her, poor thing, in such distress and every chance of my poor father ending his days in prison, I considered it my duty to do all I could to help them – so I raised it for my mother's express use.

But the money was soon gone and by November 1848 there remained only one other possible option open to Augusta and that was to cast herself on Annabella's mercy. The letter she wrote, which must have cost her all the shreds of pride and self-respect still left to her, was returned unopened with a note to the effect that she should communicate its contents through Lushington. Since it was his appointment to the trusteeship that had caused the breach with Annabella in the first place, this was a condition that was little short of inhuman, but Augusta no longer had any alternative. She wrote to him on 9 February 1849:

> a combination of my unfortunate circumstances have placed me in the *most serious* state of pecuniary distress & which if not immediately met, will & must end in the ruin *of us all*. I venture to turn to Lady Byron for assistance but I beg of her to believe that in doing so I *feel* that I have not the slightest claim on her, except what any individual in distress would have upon her Benevolence & her Charity – though there is more for her to forgive in the request from *me* than from any other individual.

To make her self-abasement even more complete she attached an apologetic note to Lushington, telling him that 'no common distress' could have reduced her to 'such a measure'.

Annabella would not condescend to reply directly to Augusta, but sent her answer through Lushington. Lacking any semblance of common compassion, it was distressingly evasive and deliberately obtuse: 'I think Mrs Leigh may be acted upon by those who wish *through her* to act upon *me* –'. She then asked to know why, if Augusta's distress was so urgent, she had not availed herself of the channel of communication via Lushington. This, Augusta patiently pointed out in her reply, was precisely what she had done.

Augusta battled doggedly on, doing everything she could to break the deadlock, but her letters were always returned unopened with the same comment: that there could be no communication with Annabella other than through her lawyer. After months of this humiliating and sterile struggle, Augusta finally lost her temper and made a futile and rather pathetic attempt to reassert her dignity.

> The time may come when Lady Byron will regret her answer – it may easily be believed that no common senses would have induced me to address her after having returned my letter unopened through her solicitor.

There was no alternative but to do the unthinkable – what she had so long resisted – and apply for help from her own relatives. The difficulty was that there was virtually no one left of her own generation, except for her sister Mary, and Augusta was reluctant to ask for money from her nephews. She chose instead to write to the 7th Earl of Carlisle, the grandson of her late cousin, Byron's reluctant guardian. Augusta had been a great favourite with little George William in the days when she had played games with him at Castle Howard and he, not yet able to get his tongue round her name, had known her as 'Miss Bear'. He had grown up to be rather serious and reserved, was fascinated by mesmerism and, like his grandfather, wrote poetry. His only fault, according to Sydney Smith, was that he 'lacked indiscretion'. He could hardly refuse Augusta, and the shakily written letter of thanks that she wrote to him was evidence of her great distress and increasing frailty:

> I hope you will believe that no common cause could induce me to take such a liberty, as that on addressing you on *such* a subject . . . I have no claims but that of former childish recollections and having already received such innumerable proofs of it.

She proposed to repay the loan in quarterly instalments, but before she could even attempt to put this into effect George Leigh died. He was in his eightieth year and had clung to his old way of life to the last: even his arrest in 1841 had taken place at Newmarket. Over the last few years he must have cut a sorry figure trying to sustain the lifestyle of a Regency buck in Victorian England with failing health and no resources. The friends on whom his whole way of life had depended had died off one by one. The last of them, Harry Fetherstonhaugh, had lived on into his nineties, but by the time George died on 3 May 1850 he had been dead for four years.

George had not been easy to live with. In her commonplace book, Augusta had noted down a passage that perhaps encapsulated the perennial problem of trying to help her husband fight off the moods of bleak depression that would descend on him when life, as it so frequently did, went wrong for him:

> None but those who have made the melancholy experiment can tell how cheerless is the labour of supporting the spirit that will make no effort to sustain itself, of soliciting the languid smile, offering the rejected amusement, or striving with vain ingenuity to enliven the oft repulsed conversation . . .

He had been suffering from chronic bronchitis for years and had been shielded and cosseted to the last by Augusta, with Emily and the servants doing everything they could to make his last days as comfortable as possible. For once uncomplaining, he died peacefully at 'St James's Palace' with his devoted valet, John Pollendine, by his side and was buried at Kensal Green. His only bequest to his long-suffering wife was his debts. She told Carlisle:

> I am sure you can understand that my recent loss has, as relates to pecuniary circumstances somewhat changed my position, and I hope that if I repay your kind loan within the given period it may not be inconvenient for you to allow me to send you the instalments somewhat differently to what has been arranged . . .

Carlisle, a friend of that laureate of perennial debtors, Charles Dickens, probably had never expected to see his money back.

George's death was undoubtedly a major factor in the subsequent and rapid decline in Augusta's fragile health. 'I would give my life for him', she had once said. For his sake she had struggled to maintain a pretext of keeping things going and, now this was no longer necessary, she was cast adrift with nothing to focus on. However, the last remnants of respectability had still to be preserved. She managed to keep a few servants about her – it would have been impossible for a woman of her rank to have done otherwise – but their number had been reduced to five: Mary Anne Turner, her maid, of such long standing now that she was virtually one of the family; three younger women; and a twenty-year-old boy called Walter Coe. After George's death, John Pollendine had to go, but continued to keep in close touch with her. For all their improvidence and frequent inability to pay their wages on time – if at all – George, Augusta and their children were able to inspire extraordinary affection and loyalty in their servants.

It was clear to Emily that there was little or nothing that her mother could now do and on 1 February 1851 she made one last attempt to win the sympathy of Lady Byron. Her previous letters, like her mother's, had gone unanswered, but she now had a different pretext for writing to Lushington:

> The death of my Father, although it enables us to retrench in many things that were necessary for his comfort has at the same time deprived us of £300 per annum leaving only 700 to pay debts & to exist upon . . .
> My Mother has been trying for some time to raise a sum of money to enable her to make an arrangement with the creditors. There is no

channel that she has not tried, but Alas! all to no purpose & I now turn to Lady Byron as our last & only hope . . .

Nothing would have induced me to make this application but my unhappiness at seeing My Mother in this wretched state & her health no longer equal to the continual anxiety that she has been existing in for so many years & I may say ruin is now staring us in the face – I should feel so very grateful if you would have the kindness to communicate it to Lady Byron as I fear from her not having answered my letters she was displeased but the recollection of her kindness to me when a child at Brighton induces me to hope she would forgive my appealing to her . . .

The letter could hardly have come at a more opportune time for Annabella. Only a month earlier, on New Year's Day 1851, she had declared: 'I thought Mrs Leigh my friend – I loved her – I love her still! I cannot help it. I shall see her once more before we both die.' The person to whom she spoke these words was the Reverend Frederick Robertson, Minister of Trinity Church, Brighton, and one of the most celebrated and admired preachers of his day. He was in his mid-thirties, intelligent, charismatic, a great lover of poetry and spectacularly handsome. There can be no doubt that Annabella was – spiritually – infatuated with him. After she had been introduced to him by her cousin Robert Noel, she wrote: 'I must thank you for the greatest gift that human being can make to his fellow – the means of intercourse with a great soul.'

Since Byron was one of the poets whom Robertson most admired, his meeting with Annabella was a revelation to him. Soon she was relating to him the whole history of her unhappy marriage. She found in him a steady confidant and a sympathetic friend, and saw him as the person who would justify her to the world after her death.

It was not long before she had decided to reveal to him the whole story of Augusta. She wrote, on 8 January:

A hope has risen in my mind that through your ministry good might be done to that survivor for whom I am so deeply interested . . . You shall know then. If you recollect, in our last conversation I said there was one whom I had not seen for years, but hoped before death to see again. That was the person whose *guilt* made a great part (*not* the whole) of my wretchness . . .

Robertson needed no prompting:

I shrink from suggesting the dreadful fancy that came across me, lest I should have mistaken & should therefore shock you by having conceived it . . . Did 'Manfred' shadow a truth?

Over the years the conviction that Annabella had voiced to Ada when she was with Medora in Paris had become an obsession: Augusta had not merely come between her and Byron as the third person in their marriage and made their separation inevitable; she had also worked to prevent a reconciliation after Byron had gone into exile, concealing, destroying and even forging letters to suit her purpose, so that she could represent Annabella and Byron falsely to one another:

> It is not possible, if I have read human nature rightly, for any one to keep up such bitter resentment without believing in some cause for it . . . Towards the close of his life his feelings towards me were softening – but evil influence had not yet lost its hold entirely. He *must* have come, had he lived, to the belief that *from first to last* I had been his only truly devoted friend – it was not permitted!

All that was needed to set the seal on this astonishing exercise in self-deception was for Augusta to be made to admit the truth of it, and to do so, moreover, in front of Frederick Robertson. To this end, Annabella began to set the machinery in motion. She showed Emily's letter to Robertson (before sending it on to Admiral Lord Byron) and then on 11 February wrote to Augusta giving her address, in a sudden access of paranoia, as the Post Office, Brighton:

> Since the cessation of our personal intercourse you have more than once asked me to see you. If you still feel that wish, I will comply with it. We may not long have it in our power, Augusta, to meet again in this life, and to do so might be the means of leaving to both of us a remembrance of deep though sad thankfulness. But this could not be the effect unless every worldly interest were absolutely excluded from our conversation, and there were the most entire and mutual truthfulness. *No other expectations* must be entertained by you for a moment. On any other terms I cannot see you again, unless summoned to your death-bed. If you decline, these will be the last words of mine ever addressed to you, and as such I wish they could convey to your heart the feelings with which I write them . . .

Augusta can only have felt total despair at this callous stifling of any hope she may have had of receiving assistance from Annabella, but she knew that she had no alternative but to accept. She was all too well aware that she had not very long to live and, financial considerations apart, she wanted to die reconciled to the woman who had been so close to the centre of her existence for more than thirty-six years. Illness held her back from replying until 14 February, when she wrote, on black-bordered paper:

> As you now offer me the opportunity which you know I have so long wished for, and so repeatedly solicited of seeing you once more, I will not delay (tho' almost too unwell to write) telling you that I unhesitatingly and thankfully accept it but at this moment it would be impossible for I am suffering from such a prostration of strength consequent upon an attack of influenza, that I am not equal to much exertion . . .

She trusted that she had turned the corner and would write again 'as soon as I have any strength & I suppose to the same address'. Then, in words that must have fuelled Annabella's hopes, she continued:

> I have no wish to enter upon any subject that should make our interview unpleasant, instead of being, as I trust it may, a consolation to us both – at the same time I shall be prepared if necessary to give & receive any explanation on any subject that concerns myself, where there has been any misapprehension and which it might tend to our mutual comfort to have removed . . .

There was a further brief delay while Augusta's letter was circulated among Annabella's friends and advisers. Mary, the wife of Admiral Lord Byron, confirmed that Augusta was indeed far from well and 'had lately and rather suddenly become a very sunk and aged person'.

While garlanding Annabella with sanctimonious praise for her courage in subjecting herself to such an ordeal, Robertson demonstrated how far he had drifted from either reality or reason under her influence by commenting, 'A *most* unsatisfactory letter. I certainly was not prepared for anything so deep as this . . .' Not to be outdone, Annabella said that it was 'heartless' and 'written for third parties' (one wonders what 'third parties' she could conceivably have had in mind). She was now sufficiently confident to make clear to Augusta the conditions under which the interview must take place. She would not 'venture' into London, but would meet her sister-in-law at the 'nearest convenient hotel' for them both. She would hear whatever Augusta had to say in private:

> . . . but should I after hearing it, want to make any observation you must permit me to do so in the presence of a friend who will accompany me – one who has not been in any way connected with past transactions . . .

Augusta was, at first, not prepared to go along with this. There were things that she might wish to say that '*could* not be communicated before any third person whatever' and she would rather forgo hearing what Annabella might wish to say than have another person present. Would it not be sufficient for Annabella to put in writing what she had to say and for Augusta to countersign it?

Annabella was adamant. These were the only conditions under which their meeting might take place. Byron had once said that she never wrote a letter without a lawyer at her elbow – now she would not meet anyone without a clergyman by her side. She refused to yield an inch. The presence of 'a friend of indispensable honour and character' was essential to attest to what she had to say; nor would she be bound 'by any condition' as to the purport of her remarks. Augusta could take it or leave it and, as Annabella had calculated, she took it, although not without one final protest:

> I can give no better proof of my wishing to see you than by the sacrifice I make of my own feelings in consenting to see any third person during any part of our interview which must be of a painful nature & may be the last we may ever have in this world – however such are your terms, & be it so.

Annabella then revealed the name of her witness, the 'Genius of the Soul's World'. It is doubtful whether the name of Frederick Robertson would have meant much to Augusta, who was too ill to get out of the house, 'except to our Evening Chapel'.

Augusta was still far too unwell to travel and Annabella took advantage of the delay to hold further consultations with her friends and advisers and to draw up a list of points to be put to Augusta: 'Questions – *you* kept up hatred; *you* put things in a false light; *you* supressed what was kindest, most calculated to soften . . .'

As the days passed she began to grow increasingly impatient with the constant postponements of their meeting. 'What is play to you is death to me,' she callously informed the mortally ill Augusta. Eventually a meeting was agreed for 8 April 1851 at Reigate, reckoned by Annabella to be suitably equidistant between herself and Robertson in Brighton and Augusta in London. Augusta wrote to her, rather timorously, on 4 April:

> Will you be so good as to let me know the hour you wish me to be at Reigate on Tuesday & the name of the Hotel at which I am to ask for you & excuse all this trouble in consideration of my inexperience on rail roads, having only taken one journey & back in my life in 1847.

Travelling by the train was not always considered suitable by ladies of Augusta's class or generation, although in this instance any reluctance she may have felt must have been increased by nervousness. Her unease at subjecting herself in her extreme frailty to this alien and terrifying method of transport was not helped by her insistence on travelling alone, with neither Emily nor her maid, Mrs Turner, to accompany her. Annabella had no such qualms. With her endlessly enquiring mind she had taken to the new age and its inventions from their inception, while poor Augusta remained firmly rooted in the previous century. Her journey to Reigate was an extremely apprehensive excursion into the Victorian age. At Reigate station a 'servant in drab livery', who had been instructed to look into all the first-class carriages holding up Annabella's visiting card, escorted Augusta to a waiting carriage to take her to the White Hart Hotel where Annabella had reserved two sitting rooms.

Augusta was sixty-eight, penniless, myopic, suffering from heart disease and greatly unnerved by the train journey. 'I saw Death in her face at once,' Annabella wrote. The Dowager Lady Byron was more than nine years younger, tiny, trim, sharp-faced, tense and expectant. They were face to face for the first time for more than two decades to confront one another over a man whom they had both loved and who had been in his grave for twenty-seven years. After Robertson had been briefly introduced, he retired into the adjoining room to leave them to themselves.

We know nothing of what was actually said, only that Annabella, who had staked so much on the meeting, felt profoundly cheated and dissatisfied by what little Augusta had to say:

> Her communication was very short. I made no comment on it

whatsoever, except, when she ceased to speak: 'Is that all?' Had I spoken, I must have said: 'False – false.' There appeared to be no motive on her part but *self* – no feeling for the nearest kind to her who were gone. The language (now that I reflect upon it) was studiously *equivocal* – no faltering – I think it had been learned by heart.

Since Augusta could have no notion of what Annabella had so eagerly been expecting her to confess, she blundered vaguely on, thanking Annabella for the many past kindnesses she had shown to her family. This only served to exasperate her sister-in-law still further: 'My feelings broke loose from all control, and I said something about its having been all in vain – I felt utterly hopeless, and asked to be left alone to compose myself.'

Augusta went into the next room and did her best to account for her sister-in-law's temporary indisposition to Frederick Robertson. When Annabella eventually joined them she came directly to the point:

> I told her I had become convinced that it was not in human nature for any one to keep up such animosity as Lord Byron had shown towards me, unless it had been *fed* – that for *his* sake, that he might not be blamed more than he deserved, I sought to know the truth about this. I said emphatically that I referred *only* to correspondence subsequent to 1816 when he left England . . . he could not have continued to feel bitterly for so long.

It could only have been a matter of moments before Augusta realised that this handsome clergyman with the piercing dark-blue eyes had been informed of every detail of her story. Nevertheless she tried to defend herself as best she could. Byron's own letters, she asserted, proved that she had never fed his animosity. He had, she admitted, been unjust to Annabella – 'he had said dreadful things' – but she herself had done nothing to bring this about.

Annabella, who had always suspected Augusta's 'smooth way of making mischief', remarked that:

> there was a difference between exasperating and not softening . . . and that as I was confirmed in my own mind that the truth had not been fairly stated . . . but I did not speak as her judge . . .

Annabella seems to have been prepared to let matters rest there, but Augusta was determined to justify herself. Unlike Annabella, she had come to their meeting totally unprepared and was clutching at anything that might bear her out. In an unguarded moment she blurted out that Hobhouse had once said to her that, by taking Annabella's part, 'You not only risked loss of property, but what was much dearer to you, his affection.' Exactly why this should have had the effect it did on Annabella is difficult to grasp (perhaps the very introduction of the name of Hobhouse at this juncture was enough), but it brought Annabella to breaking point:

> At *such* a testimony I started up, and all but uttered an ironical answer – but she *trusted me unconditionally*, and I replied: 'I don't understand it.' From that moment there was a mingling of indignation with the intense pity I had before felt – and I was afraid of myself. I said, I believe, that I should always wish her the blessing I could not give her, or something kind if my tears did not prevent my uttering it – but the strongest desire to be out of her presence took possession of me, lest I should be tempted beyond my strength.

However wilfully misguided and maliciously unjust she may have been, it is difficult not to feel some pity for Annabella. She had so convinced herself during her incessant brooding on the past that Byron and she would have been reconciled, but for Augusta's interference, that she could not let the idea go. All the world had become reconciled to Byron, or so it seemed, except for the Dean of Westminster and herself, the Ice Princess of Parallelograms, who had doomed him to exile. The confession she had sought from Augusta, which would have justified her to posterity, had not been forthcoming. Annabella had been confronted with what was incontestably the truth and she could only exclaim, 'I don't understand it!'

As Augusta travelled back to London alone, she must have known that there was little likelihood she would ever see her 'dearest Sis' again. Any hope of calling on her for help had been completely shattered by a confrontation that left her confused and utterly exhausted. Yet to Annabella's brief notice of her safe return she sent an innocently compassionate reply that was destined to land her in further trouble:

> I am thankful for the few lines I got just as I was going to express my hope that you had not suffered by your exertions on Tuesday – and now grieve to hear that you have inflammation in your eyes . . . I meant to have written to you to enquire yesterday but I was not able. I am better today & cannot resist signing myself
> AFFECTIONATELY YOURS Augusta Leigh.

Harmless enough, but Annabella chose to take offence. 'The tone,' she told Robertson, 'is very unpleasant to me – its *glissant* character, as if everything were smoothed over. To give that impression to others was perhaps her object. I have sought to give a mild rebuke.'

Unlike Annabella, Augusta was not in the habit of circulating her own letters among her friends for their comment and approval. Annabella's 'mild rebuke' was, of course, submitted to Robertson for his prior sanction, and he was required to initial it. She told Augusta that her letter afforded:

> the last proof that during our interview, trying and painful as it was to me, I did not for a moment forget the consideration I was bound to observe by your having trusted me *unconditionally*. As I have received the communication which you have so long and anxiously desired to make – and upon which I offered no comment except 'Is that All?' – I have done all in my power to contribute to your peace of mind. But I remain under the afflicting persuasion that it is not attained by such means as you have taken. Farewell.

In her reply, the last letter she would ever write to Annabella, Augusta insisted that her desire for an interview had been prompted by 'a secret desire to see you once more in this world' and by a need to convince Annabella that the accusations that had been brought against her (presumably over her conduct towards Medora) were unfounded:

> I had not, and never implied that I had, anything to reveal to you with which *you* were not previously acquainted on any other subject. Nor can I at all express to you the regret I have felt since those words escaped you, showing that you imagined I had 'encouraged a bitterness of feeling in Lord Byron towards you'. I can as solemnly declare as if I were on my oath or on my death-bed that I never did so in any one instance, but that I invariably did the contrary. I have letters from him, and of my own to him (and returned to me after his death), which would bear out this assertion, and I am ready at this or any other moment to make the most solemn asseveration of this, in any way you can desire. I would willingly see your friend Mr Robertson and afford him every proof of my veracity in my power.

Augusta had clearly been impressed by Frederick Robertson (most people were) and was distressed that he believed she was keeping something back. It would be a comfort, she said:

> to talk openly with him on such points as might tend to convince you of the truth of what I now say – and without which the remainder of my life will be still more unhappy than the miseries, of various kinds, which surround me must inevitably make me.

Locked as she was within her self-delusion and protected by her self-rectitude, Annabella reverted to her old habits and did not even open the letter, but asked Robertson to return it. Augusta made one last effort. She sent the letter back to Robertson, asking him to read it and requesting an interview:

> You cannot be surprised at my having anxiously wished to remove from her mind impressions so very unfavourable to myself, knowing as I did, and could declare on oath, or on my death bed that they were erroneous, and tho' I never had the pleasure of seeing you before, there was a kindness in your manner which makes me very desirous that you at least should know the truth of which . . . I have in my possession the means of giving . . .

Robertson was now placed in something of a quandary. As a Minister of God, he was uneasy about denying Augusta an opportunity to state her case to him, particularly as he realised that she was seriously ill, but it is clear that Annabella would not countenance this. He replied that, since he was a stranger to Augusta, his 'opinion could be of no importance' and that his investigation of her proofs would be 'inconclusive and useless' without Lady Byron being present and 'she would never consent to another meeting'. For his peroration he fell back on the rhetorical technique that had enthralled so many of those who had attended his sermons:

> If your own conscience is free & clear & Ly Byron is in no way injured by you, the sense of innocence in God's light will make the opinion of any other human being of no consequence. If on the contrary there was anything for the sorrowful acknowledgement of which that meeting was the last opportunity which you can ever have in this world, then of course no opinion of Sir John Hobhouse, nor of Lord Byron himself can reverse that solemn judgement upon the whole matter which must be heard very very soon when you meet God face to face.

Emily later told Annabella that Augusta had been 'very much grieved' by their last meeting. Annabella took refuge, as she always had, in the certainty that what she had done had been right, although she was clearly troubled:

> My calm conclusion is that the state of her mind was absolutely unimpressible by any representation of mine, which is some consolation for my own deficiencies or want of judgement in any respect, overcome as I was by feelings that have not yet been brought under perfect subjection.

There was to be little time for further introspection. On 11 June, knowing that she had not long to live, Augusta made her will, leaving all that she had to leave – her 'furniture plate linen china and all my real and personal estates and effects' – to Emily. It was witnessed by her maid, Mary Anne Turner, and Frances Bennett of Camden Town High Street. By the end of September, it was clear that Robertson's warning that Augusta would be face to face with her Maker 'very very soon' would prove all too true. Annabella was in town, staying in Old Burlington Street, when she heard that Augusta was dying and she wrote immediately to Emily:

> Let me if possible remove any difficulty or afford some comfort. There is no one more anxious to do so. I do not wish your mother to be troubled with my name but if you have need of service trust me.

After the Reigate episode, when her mother had returned deeply hurt and almost hysterically bewildered, Emily was not disposed to accept help from her aunt. 'To this I merely returned a little bulletin,' she remembered. 'I did not know how to acknowledge her sympathy but by signing it *gratefully yours*.'

Annabella left for Esher, instructing her servants to call frequently at 'St James's Palace' for news. It was not long before Emily, with no money at all at her disposal, with doctors' bills to be met and medicines to be paid for, was forced into accepting Annabella's offer, telling her that 'there *was* a pecuniary difficulty' (when had there ever not been?). Annabella gave her the money that was immediately needed, telling her niece that it was 'gratifying to be able to render this poor service'. The feelings that Annabella had struggled to keep in check during their last confrontation in the White Hart were now turned, if not to remorse, than at least to pity. 'I felt so great a desire to send her a message,' she told Robertson, 'that after fully considering what might be the effects I determined to disregard all but those which it might possibly have upon herself . . .' Without Lushington at her elbow or any witness to initial her letter, she wrote to Emily:

> I have a request to make if you can fulfil it without any possible excitement that would be injurious to your Mother to whisper to her *from me* the words 'Dearest Augusta' – I can't think they could hurt her.

Emily did as she was asked and the effect of her words upon Augusta fulfilled all Annabella's hopes. What Augusta most deeply wished was to die reconciled to the woman she had so long regarded as her sister. Emily wrote to Annabella on 5 October:

> She desires me to say that the tears which refused to flow from sorrow were produced by the joy of hearing 'Dearest Augusta' from you – that they were her greatest consolation – her voice has grown weak and thick – that it is with difficulty that I can make out what she says – she said a great deal to me that I could not hear distinctly – I dare say she will mention the subject again . . .

For Annabella this brought back painful memories of Fletcher's account of Byron's death and of the last wishes that his master had been unable to articulate. To the last she hoped that Augusta would confess on her deathbed that she had prevented a reconciliation with Byron, and the only consolation Annabella could contrive for herself was that Augusta had been trying to say this to Emily. 'A second message lost,' she commented bitterly.

In Hyde Park people were crowding into the Crystal Palace in their thousands to catch a last glimpse of the treasures of the Great Exhibition before it closed for ever, and the Duke of Wellington had to be rescued from a mob of overenthusiastic admirers. In 'St James's Palace' Augusta clung to life until 12 October 1851, her mother's birthday, when she was at last released from her debts. Emily, who had never left her bedside, sat down and wrote a brief note to Annabella:

> Poor Mama died this morning a little after three, having suffered most dreadfully since yesterday afternoon – it is indeed a most happy release, but her loss can never be made up to me.

Augusta's body was taken, as George's had been, to the necropolis at Kensal Green, which first opened its gates in 1833. There, in a bay of one of the catacombs – the damp labyrinth of high, colonnaded brick avenues that lie beneath the Anglican chapel – her simple coffin was placed beside his. Now, rows of other coffins are stacked above them and even the corroded metal plates barely distinguish them. Two not very satisfactory lives filed away, half-forgotten footnotes to other, more celebrated lives. Above ground, only a few hundred yards away, stands Annabella's monument – positive and self-assured – justifying her life to the world.

Epilogue

'I wonder if *any*one personally laments Mrs Leigh?' Ada wrote to her mother three days after Augusta's death. 'A sad end to a sad life. I suppose a *bad* life is generally a *sad* one.'

If any of Augusta's children other than Emily saw her during her last illness, they did not stay with her until the end. Mrs Villiers said that Emily had been left 'penniless alone at the Palace with Birds and a Dog'. The financial confusion that had dogged every step of Augusta's life for so many years persisted after her death, for no trace could be found of the will that Mary Anne Turner had witnessed the previous June. Henry Francis, Augusta's youngest son, was granted letters of administration – possibly because his elder brothers, George and Frederick, were out of London; possibly because neither of them could be trusted not to lay their hands on the furniture, the linen, the pictures and the plate that Augusta had intended to bequeath to Emily.

Annabella felt duty bound to make some gesture in the direction of her god-daughter, but, in her customary way, she hedged their meeting round with conditions:

> I should not feel justified in giving you any advice, without referring to some member of your family who must be better acquainted with your circs than I am, therefore I could not accept any confidence which was to be private.

Emily's 'circs' were about as bad as they could be. The apartments at 'St James's Palace' would have to be vacated almost immediately and she had no money whatsoever. Since she had sold her reversion to help her parents through the last years of their lives, she had no expectations at all: 'I have had my portion and I very much lament having raised anything on it but it is done and cannot be undone therefore I must make the best of it.' Mrs Villiers, now old and not in good health, took it upon herself to organise a very modest annuity for Emily. Her difficulty was that most of the likely donors had already been exhausted by Augusta herself:

> . . . the poor girl says her mother has been so helped by Lord C. and the Duke of Sutherland, the Duchess of Norfolk, &c . . . that she can't bear to have her name mentioned to any of them . . .

However, Mrs Villiers did manage to rally enough friends and relatives to provide a sum of £120 a year, to which Annabella contributed a very modest amount, stipulating that she reserved the right to cancel it at any time. She had become incapable of any act of simple generosity; there always had to be strings attached. Lady Wilmot Horton was persuaded to subscribe £4, but with a marked lack of enthusiasm: 'All I protest about is having to do with any other members of her Family. They have long enough been "Beggars" to be quite inured to it, and I fear worse . . .'

The Leighs' creditors were itching to seize anything they could get their hands on and Annabella was most insistent that Emily should not be seen to possess anything of her own. When Emily left the palace in May 1852 to live at 8 Sheffield Terrace, off Kensington Church Street, with her mother's maid, Mary Anne Turner, the lease on the house was taken in Mrs Turner's name: 'therefore I shall be her lodger', Emily explained.

Resolved though Emily may have been to steer well clear of her godmother, it was to her that she turned when forced to dispose of some of the family pictures, naturally assuming that Annabella would want to acquire them. Annabella did not: 'I do not care enough for past generations to wish to purchase them.' But when Emily came back with another offer, perhaps a portrait of Augusta, her aunt changed her tune: 'Yes I should particularly desire to possess what you kindly offer me – but I am sorry to think there are difficulties so pressing as to occasion that necessity . . .'

It might have been hoped that Annabella had sufficiently burned her fingers over Medora ever to involve herself again with another of Augusta's daughters, but once communication with Emily had been renewed, she could not resist an attempt to subvert Emily's devotion to her mother's memory. Once again it was Mrs Villiers who was drafted in to weaken Emily's resistance:

> I am anxious if I can to have you and Ly Byron on a pleasanter footing than you now are . . . I am the last person to wish to destroy the veneration you have for your poor Mother's memory, still I feel

without doing *that* I could explain things to you in a different sort of
way to what you have been accustomed to hear . . .

This was the first premonition that Emily's mother was not going to
be allowed to rest in peace, but that she would be pursued by
Annabella, her supporters and descendants. In her crazed desire for
self-justification, Annabella endeavoured to drive a wedge between
Emily and her faith in her dead mother, just as she had alienated so
many of Augusta's friends and relatives during her lifetime. Truth
had long since ceased to have any meaning for Annabella. Now she
was concerned only to rewrite the past, with herself as Augusta's
rejected guardian angel:

> Before my marriage when your Mother was a stranger to me – I
> resolved to be to her as an own-sister. Mine is not a nature in which
> affection can pass away – nearly 40 years have shown this in regard
> to *her*. She was throughout the object of my unswerving devotedness
> – it was her infatuation (pardon the word) not to recognise in me her
> truest friend – especially as she had in one case been saved by me
> from taking a step that would have ended in irretrievable ruin for
> herself and family. Ask Mrs Villiers if this were not so.

It is difficult to imagine what new fantasy was shaping itself in
Annabella's mind. However, before she could torture poor Emily
any further, it became all too evident that Ada, who had cancer,
had only a short time to live.

Annabella installed herself at her daughter's bedside to watch
over the last months of her life, firmly regulating who was permitted
to see her. Dickens was allowed to read to Ada the Death of Little
Dombey – even Annabella would have been hard put to keep out
Dickens – but all contact with Charles Babbage, Ada's partner in
early computer science, was firmly ruled out. Annabella's spiritual
adviser, Frederick Robertson, was summoned to prepare Ada for
the life to come, and she confessed her sins, her reckless gambling
and her adultery. She died, after weeks of agonising pain, on 27
November 1852, aged thirty-seven. By her express wish she was
buried next to her father in the Byron vault at Hucknall. Less than a
year later Robertson himself was dead, from consumption, and
Annabella began to cast around for someone else to whom she
could entrust her story for posterity.

Over the ensuing years Emily continued to fight a losing battle
against poverty and ill health. From the Isle of Wight in 1857, she

wrote miserably to Annabella: 'You helped my sisters and will you not assist me for the sake of my mother?' Since Annabella had represented herself as nothing short of a saint in her attitude towards Augusta, she could not well refuse and increased her god-daughter's annual allowance by £10. Since Mrs Villiers, one of the main contributors to the annuity, had died, this did nothing to improve Emily's circumstances.

On 16 May 1860, the day before her sixth-eighth birthday, Annabella died at St George's Terrace, Primrose Hill. The surviving members of the Leigh family, not to mention innumerable money lenders and scavengers, might well have been forgiven for hoping that her death might finally have released the Byron money, for despite the fact that all Augusta's children had sold their respective reversions and Augusta herself had borrowed untold sums against her own expectations, the capital that secured Annabella's jointure should have remained intact. This, in the fullness of time, would have benefited Augusta's grandchildren. However, it was not to be. The suit was filed in the dusty corridors of Chancery and by the time that it was concluded most of the claimants were dead.

The last of Augusta's children, Henry Francis, was the first to follow her, dying after a protracted illness on 30 April 1853 at the age of thirty-three, leaving his widow, Mary, and seven-year-old daughter, Geraldine Amelia. By the early 1860s, Augusta's second son, Frederick George, was also dead. His wife, Phoebe Althea, had long since given up the unequal task of trying to live with his temper, his alcoholism and his extravagance and had left him. When Phoebe died in 1863, Emily was made a guardian of their thirteen-year-old daughter, Ada Mary Augusta, although, since the girl lived with her mother's well-to-do relatives in Cheltenham, she probably saw very little of her.

In 1866 Georgey died. She had inherited the proceeds from Henry Trevanion's farm outside Pontivy eleven years earlier, but of her three daughters only the youngest, Ada, survived her. Emily did her best to keep in touch with what remained of the family and in some degree filled the role that Aunt Sophy had played to the previous generation, but as she grew older she became increasingly agoraphobic and was far too nervous to venture from her home in Twickenham, even to attend the wedding in 1868 of Frederick's daughter, Ada Mary Augusta, to John Stephenson. She was certainly in no state to cope with the storm that broke the following year when Harriet Beecher Stowe at last published 'A True Story of Lady Byron's Life', broadcasting her mother's incest to the world.*

Why Mrs Stowe kept the story to herself for so many years is a mystery and her reasons for suddenly breaking her silence were ambiguous, to say the least. The explanation that she gave was that, in his review of Teresa Guiccioli's *Recollections of Lord Byron*, John Paget had denounced Annabella as a 'moral Brinvilliers'† and had added for good measure that 'the most degraded of street-walkers in the Haymarket was a worthier character than Lady Byron'. Mrs Stowe claimed that after this she had no alternative but to speak out, but in fact her article had been written before the offending review was published. She seems to have been activated more by a desire to strike a blow for the feminist cause and to refurbish her own reputation after the indifferent review of her novel *Oldtown Folks*.

Mrs Stowe had predicted that her article would create 'the greatest sensation', but the results were far from what she had hoped. 'A story which would have suited the taste of a Borgia family circle' was the verdict of the writer Justin McCarthy. And the general opinion was that Annabella, in telling her 'hideous story', had been at best a victim of delusion, if not actually insane. Where, the press demanded, was the documentary evidence to substantiate Mrs Stowe's allegations?

The Leighs seem to have received advance warning of the article – probably from John Murray – for even before it appeared in *Macmillan's Magazine*, Emily was frantically looking out letters written by Annabella to her mother, which she was convinced would give the lie to Mrs Stowe's story. The moment her brother George Henry got to hear of the allegations, he sought out his cousin, Augusta's nephew, Lord Chichester, in Whitehall and together they went down to Stanmer to plan a counter-offensive. The correspondence between Augusta and Annabella, augmented with letters from Murray's files, was shown to John Paget, who had written the offending review in *Blackwood's Magazine*, and to

---

* The article appeared in the September number of the *Atlantic Monthly* and was published shortly afterwards in *Macmillan's Magazine*.
† Marie Madeleine, Marquise de Brinvilliers (1630–1676), was executed in Paris for poisoning her father, her brothers and her sister, and for attempting to poison her husband.

Abraham Hayward, Q.C., whose conclusions were far from charitable towards Annabella:

> If we assume the charge to be false, we at all events clear Mrs Leigh. But if the charge was well-founded, or even if Lady Byron believed it to be so well-founded, we do not clear *her*. She still stands self-convicted of a long course of dissimulation and hypocrisy.

Even Annabella's own solicitors, Wharton and Ford, issued a public statement condemning Mrs Stowe's article – '. . . a most gross breach of trust and confidence stated to have been reposed in her' – although they made no attempt to deny the charges made against Augusta.

Those who had known Augusta personally appear to have been totally bemused by the allegations. Lady Frances Shelley dismissed them as the 'height of absurdity': 'She was what I should call a religious woman and her feeling for Byron was that of an elder sister.' Lord Stanhope vouchsafed that he had always thought Augusta 'extremely unprepossessing . . . more like a nun than anything'.

Emily had barely had time to recover from Harriet Beecher Stowe when she was confronted with the spectre of her dead sister's autobiography. Thomas Smith, on whose advice Medora had written her wildly incoherent apologia, had sat on the manuscript for twenty-six years, until the appearance of Mrs Stowe's 'True Story', when he handed it over to the editor of the *Illustrated London News*, Dr Charles Mackay,* who considered it his duty to bring it before the public. Mackay prefaced it with a lengthy introduction and followed it with an even lengthier 'Vindication of Lord Byron'. The allegations of incest and of Medora's parentage he dismissed as a concoction of Georgey's in order to obtain a divorce from Henry Trevanion, but his real purpose was to use Medora as a stick with which to beat Mrs Stowe:

> Lady Byron's story, as told by Mrs Stowe, cannot be true, unless Lady Byron herself were at one and the same time a paragon of superhuman and angelic virtue, and one of the most heartless hypocrites that ever lived.

As a judgement it was, perhaps, not very wide of the mark.

---

* Charles Mackay LLD (1814–1889) was the father of romantic novelist Marie Corelli.

'Poor E.'s biography is as one might have expected,' Lord Chichester wrote to Emily:

a strange and ill-written fragment, evidently written in a hurry & not corrected. It is a shame and disgrace to the English press that it should have been published. Slander cannot happily injure the dead, if it did the Devil would give us more of it.

But Emily had been thoroughly unnerved by the whole episode and when Harriet Beecher Stowe returned to the fray in January 1870 with a book of some three hundred pages,* she declined to release any more of her mother's letters to anyone. Mrs Stowe had prophesied that 'Lady Byron's voice will rise clear as the sun & terrible as any army with banners', which does not say a great deal for her prose style, but since she had no further evidence to put forward she could only repeat at greater length what she had said before. In the end the real victim of her misguided zeal was not Augusta, who emerged relatively unscathed, but Annabella herself. 'Is her memory to be regarded with the deepest horror or the most profound compassion?' asked John Paget.

For weeks the controversy raged on. There were books and pamphlets, indignant vindications of Byron in prose and verse from both sides of the Atlantic. Mrs Stowe was described as a ghoul and a vampire, and as a 'lewd, loquacious literary antic'. A sensational pamphlet, 'Light at Last. The Byron Mystery', was priced at one penny and, desperate for a portrait of Augusta, the publisher resorted to a woodcut that had already done service as a picture of Manon Lescaut, Lola Montez and Madeleine Smith.

By the time Emily died of cancer in January 1876, four weeks after the death of her brother George, the past seemed to have been laid to rest. Geraldine arranged for her to be buried at Kensal Green and John Murray III attended the funeral. Of all the Leighs, now only Ada Trevanion, Geraldine Leigh and Ada Mary Augusta Stephenson were left – and it was Ada Trevanion who, when the Chancery proceedings were finally concluded, directly benefited from what remained of Byron's legacy. The other two girls were reasonably well off. Ada Stephenson came into money from her wealthy mother and made a good marriage, while Geraldine's mother married as her second husband 'a rich Indian'. This was probably as well, since Geraldine appears to have inherited the gene

* *Lady Byron Vindicated – A History of the Byron Controversy.*

that had plagued so many in her family. In October 1872, George Eliot had observed Geraldine at the gaming tables of the Kursaal in Homburg, 'completely in the grasp of this mean, money-raking demon. It made me cry to see her fresh young face among the hags and brutally stupid men around her.' George Henry Lewes noted that she lost £500 and that she looked feverish and excited. The episode provided George Eliot with the opening scene of *Daniel Deronda*, in which Daniel observes Gwendolen Harleth lose her 'last poor heap of Napoleons' at roulette. When Ada Trevanion died, unmarried, in 1882 she left Geraldine a quarter share of her estate. It amounted to £28,000 and, as Ada Mary Augusta commented, was 'rather a godsend'.

The 'Byron Mystery' might have remained a mystery had not Sir Leslie Stephen in his account of Byron's life for the *Dictionary of National Biography*, written ten years after Emily's death, called into question Annabella's motives for confiding in Harriet Beecher Stowe:

> It can only be surmised that Lady Byron had become jealous of Byron's public and pointed expressions of love for his sister, contrasting so forcefully with his utterances about his wife, and brooding upon her wrongs had developed a hateful suspicion communicated to Mrs Stowe, and, it seems, to others.

Up to this point Annabella's grandson, Ralph, now Lord Wentworth, had kept largely silent. Thirteen at the time of Ada's death, he had been brought up under his grandmother's influence, partly as the result of the long-running quarrel between Annabella and his father. Annabella had broken off relations with Lovelace after the revelation of Ada's gambling addiction, for which she chose to regard him as wholly responsible. After Ada's death, Lovelace had made attempts at a reconciliation, but the price that Annabella had placed on this was a signed statement that he had alienated her daughter's affection from her. Annabella had always needed a scapegoat and, since Augusta's death had left that position vacant, Lovelace had now been cast in the role. She had taken charge of his son Ralph, rather as she had attempted to take over Medora, but in this case the boy had proved infinitely more biddable. He was readily susceptible to her stories of the injustice and persecution that she had suffered and she had little difficulty in thoroughly indoctrinating him on the subject of her wicked sister-in-law.

Ralph became his grandmother's champion. He was infuriated by the Leighs' defence of their mother at Annabella's expense during the Beecher Stowe affair, but merely remarked that he could not 'allow that Mrs Stowe's statement is substantially correct'. By the time Sir Leslie Stephen's account appeared, he had thoroughly immersed himself in his grandmother's papers and in 1887 had printed, for circulation only within the family, 'Lady Noel Byron and the Leighs', a short study containing extracts from the correspondence between his grandmother and Augusta and proving, as he saw it, the truth of the story told to Harriet Beecher Stowe. Stephen declared that Lady Byron's allegations had not been dictated 'by resentment or illusion', but it was too late for the account in the *D.N.B* to be changed – nor has it ever been revised.

The study formed the germ of a much more extensive work, *Astarte*, which was begun after Wentworth had succeeded to the title of Earl of Lovelace on his father's death in 1893 and was published in a privately printed edition in 1905. *Astarte* was intended to establish beyond all doubt that the relationship between Byron and Augusta had played a crucial part in the break-up of his grandmother's marriage:

> Augusta Leigh was as fateful an instrument of conflagration . . . as a Greek Love or Nemesis: but she had many loveable and some good qualities, and even the crime of her earlier years was not entirely unwanting in mitigating circumstances.

Although there were those who expressed their regret that the book should ever have been written – 'Lovelace's part in Astarte is wholly lamentable,' complained John Drinkwater – the majority conceded that the issue had been settled. In 1928, when André Maurois was writing his biography of Byron, Lovelace's widow showed him papers of Annabella's that convinced him beyond all doubt. He asked Lord Ernle, who, as Rowland Prothero, had edited Byron's letters and journals, and who had held out strongly against the incest accusation, what he should do. 'If incest took place, say so,' said Ernle, but he added that at the age of eighty he was unlikely to change his own opinion.

Now, one can only wonder why there was so much commotion. That 'incest took place' is beyond doubt. But it was one aspect only of Augusta's abiding and unquestioning love for her brother. Annabella once told Mrs Villiers that Augusta did not consider her 'transgression' to be of consequence, and she probably would never have done so had not those two women worked upon her so relentlessly.

Poor Augusta did not deserve what happened to her. She was not cut out to be a figure of scandal or a *femme fatale*. In comparison with Lady Oxford's or Lady Melbourne's, her life was blameless. She was, as Thomas Moore remarked, 'nothing above the ordinary run of women'. Warm-hearted, easygoing, generous, pious but never prudish, Augusta firmly believed that there was no harm in anything that did not damage others. She seemed destined for an unremarkable life.

But, like her mother, Augusta was very easily swayed by passion, and she had a deeply romantic soul. 'Do not imagine', she once wrote to Wilmot, 'I think of myself as a Heroine de Roman', but that is exactly what she did do all her life, reading late into the night, gazing out of her window at Newstead, dreaming in the Ray Wood at Castle Howard of a dashing hero who would sweep her off her feet and carry her away.

As her mother had done, Augusta turned her back on the safe, law-abiding Holdernesse world in favour of the dangerous, alluring Byrons. She had a marked streak of recklessness, too often acting on the spur of the moment and giving no thought to the consequences. She could also be very stubborn. It was in this defiant spirit that she determined to marry the dashing, devil-may-care George Leigh, the incarnation of her youthful romantic dreams and also a Byron.

Augusta's recklessness was not confined to her choice of a husband. It involved every aspect of her life, her sudden wrong-headed decisions, her impetuous response to people, putting her trust in those who were bound to betray her and mistrusting those who could have helped her. Above all, it showed in her total incapacity to live within her means. Admittedly she lived in a society where few people troubled about paying their bills, but the extent of her debts seems to have been a source of constant wonderment to Augusta and she had the added disadvantage of being married to an addictive gambler. It was the pressure of the Leighs' creditors more than sisterly affection that brought Augusta to Byron in the summer of 1813.

She was not, however, mercenary by nature; nor was she, as Annabella and Mrs Villiers liked to believe, her brother's 'victim'.

Once Augusta and Byron were confronted with each other, she was drawn to him as strongly as he was to her. Each came to see the other as set apart from ordinary mortals – 'Beings who ne'er each other can resign . . .' born under the same star, Aquarius, and bearing, or so they told themselves, a strong resemblance to each other:

> She was like me in lineaments; her eyes,
> Her hair, her features, all, to the very tone
> Even of her voice, they said were like to mine . . .

Augusta understood Byron more completely than any other woman ever could, and, unlike many of the rest, had no desire to change him. She might have preferred to see her brother a better Christian, but, unlike Annabella, she would never have presumed to win glory for herself by saving his soul.

After Byron's death, she was at last able to free herself from the shame and the guilt that had been forced upon her by Annabella and Mrs Villiers. Strengthened by her belief that Byron had died reconciled to God and convinced that she had helped to salvage his reputation by sanctioning the burning of the Memoirs, she no longer felt constrained to conceal her love for him. Even the verses that he had written in her praise and which she had once wished 'in ye Red Sea' were no longer an embarrassment. She could receive them as his tribute to her devotion. In the last decade of her life, when the painter James Holmes suggested that she should write her own recollections of Byron as a means of relieving her 'pecuniary difficulties', she replied:

> All that I know of my dear brother that is not known to everybody is
> of too sacred a nature to be put in a book for all to read.

For all the misery of her abject poverty, Augusta's love for Byron had been preserved intact.

All that remained to Annabella were the boxes in which she had preserved every letter, every statement, every legal document that would justify the rightness of her cause to posterity.

The tragedy of Byron and Augusta was the consequence of the juxtaposition of two ill-starred marriages. Had Augusta not insisted on marrying George Leigh, had Byron accepted Annabella's first rejection, their lives might have been very different. Although monogamy was not in his nature, Byron might have found a wife more capable of handling and understanding him. Annabella, if she had had the good sense to accept her first suitor, George Eden, would, for a time, have found ample scope for her energies as the wife of the Governor General of India. As for Augusta, she would probably have been perfectly happy married to Francis Hodgson, bringing her abounding sense of humour to bear upon the problems of the Rectory at Bakewell and ending her days contentedly as the wife of the Provost of Eton.

NOTES

Abbreviations used in the notes

A.I.B.   Anne Isabella Byron
A.I.M.   Anne Isabella Milbanke
A.L.   Augusta Leigh
B.L.   British Library
D.L.M.   Doris Langley Moore
Hary-O   *Letters of Lady Harriet Cavendish 1796–1809*, ed. Sir George
           Leverson-Gower and Iris Palmer
Judith   Judith Milbanke (later Lady Noel)
L./B.   Lovelace/Byron Papers
L.&J.   *Byron's Letters and Journals*, ed. Leslie Marchand, 13 vols
Mackay   *Medora Leigh. A History and an Autobiography*
MS autobiography *Medora Leigh*. Text from Ada Countess of Lovelace
Mayne   *The Life of Lady Byron*, Ethel Colburn Mayne
Prothero *Letters and Journals of Lord Byron*, ed. Rowland Prothero, 6 vols
W.Y.A.S. West Yorkshire Archive Service

PROLOGUE

Page	Ref.	Source
2	'there was something awful':	Stowe, *Lady Byron Vindicated. A History of the Byron Controversy*

CHAPTER I

Page	Ref.	Source
4	'. . . the calamity of':	Walpole, *Memoirs of the Reign of George III*
	'*Vous savez que*':	B.L. Add. Ms. 33131
	'*Mes enfancts*':	Ibid.
5	'I not only love you':	Ibid.
	'The prettiest man':	*Dictionary of National Biography*
	'Lady A.D.':	Carmarthen to the Duchess of Newcastle B.L. Add. Ms. Leeds Papers

6	'I had heard':	*Letters of Horace Walpole and the Rev. William Mason*, ed. J. Mitford, 2 vols, *1851*
	'Your old friend':	Ibid.
7	*'de mettre comme'*:	Add. Ms. 33131
8	'one of the most striking':	*Morning Chronicle*
	'Camps are the':	*London Chronicle*
	'the plan was':	*Morning Chronicle*
	'He was':	L.&J. 7 (?) July 1823
9	'It is true':	Ibid.
	'her ladyship's chocolate':	W.Y.A.S. Leeds
10	'they laughed a good deal':	Ibid.
	'scarce missed a day':	Ibid.
11	'At the moment':	Private Collection
	'for God's sake':	Ibid.
	'Your Majesty will':	Private Collection
	'marks and stains':	W.Y.A.S
12	'the guilty pair':	Ibid.
	'for God's sake':	Private Collection
	'I cannot think':	Ibid.
	'. . . you are the only':	Ibid.
	'insinuate that':	*St James's Chronicle*, 20 April 1779
13	'She was christened':	St George's, Hanover Square Parish Records. Westminster Archives Centre
	'This was by no means':	William Mason to Horace Walpole. Walpole, op. cit.
	'telling that the':	Ibid.
15	'I am very much surprised':	W.Y.A.S.
	'Augusta Mary Byron':	St George's, Hanover Square, Register of Baptisms. Westminster Archives Centre
	'imprudently insisted':	L.&J. 7 (?) July 1823
	'as usual but':	Admiral Byron to Sophy Byron, 15 June 1783. L./B. Box 161
	'Lady Conyers passera':	Queen Charlotte to General de Budé, *Later Correspondence of George III*
16	'Your present melancholy situation':	B.L. Add. Ms. 33131

CHAPTER 2

Page	Ref.	Source
17	'The Priory of Newstead':	Walker, *The House of Byron*
18	'that whore':	The Diaries of Samuel Pepys, vol. 8. p.182 (Latham and Matthews).
20	'the present lord':	Walker, op. cit.
21	'with a certain sword':	B.L. Add. Ms. 35887
22	'men would willingly':	*Thraliana*
	'A pleasant situation':	*Diary and Letters of Fanny Burney*, ed. Austin Dobson, vol. 1, p. 347

23	'a large quantity':	Admiral Byron to Sophy Byron, 15 June 1783. L. B. Box 161
	'I have on coming home':	The Hon. Sophia Byron to James Sykes. L./B. Box 161
24	'She flatters herself':	B.L. Add. Ms. 31037
	'I have taken':	Walker, op. cit.
26	'I believe':	24 Jan. 1787. L./B. Box 161
	'if you chuse':	4 May 1786. L./B. Box 161
27	'some time after':	Perrigaux to Sykes, 24 July 1786. L./B. Box 161
28	'She is big':	Symon, *Byron in Perspective*, 9
	'Our house is':	George Anson Byron to Frances Leigh, 26 April 1787. L./B. Box 161
	'I still recollect':	Prothero, vol. 1, p. 19
29	'I shall make':	Symon, op. cit.

CHAPTER 3

Page	Ref.	Source
31	'I expect':	Harcourt, *The Harcourt Papers*, vol. VII
32	'Poor Mrs Alderson':	A.L. to A.I.B., 1 April 1817. L./B. Box 81
	'a man of great':	Hedley, *Queen Charlotte*
	'Do you ever hear':	Aeld. Ms. 31037
33	'She is very amicable':	Jack Byron to Frances Leigh, 16 Feb. 1791. L./B. Box 161
	'only persons present':	London Metropolitan Records Office
	'Leeward Islands':	V.L. Oliver, *Caribbeana*, vol. 6, London, 1912–19
34	'as owing to':	Hedley, op. cit.
35	'I declare':	Jack Byron to Frances Leigh, 15 Dec. 1790. L./B. Box 161
	'we had 3 bottles':	Ibid., 24 Nov. 1790. L./B. Box 161
36	'The woman who':	Ibid., 5 Dec. 1790
	'As for La Marigny':	Ibid., 15 Dec. 1790
37	'You do not know':	Ibid., 30 Jan. 1791
	'Your bird':	Ibid., 3 April 1791
	'or go to India':	Ibid., 11 May 1791
	'I would give':	Ibid.
	'I would rather be':	Ibid., 15 May 1791
	'Here is an English':	Ibid., 5 June 1791
38	'You wrong me':	B.L. Add. Ms. 31037
	'I am afraid':	George Anson Byron to Frances Byron. L./B. Box 161
	'The continent':	Ibid.

CHAPTER 4

Page	Ref.	Source
40	'the adoration':	A.L. to A.I.B. 5–6 Oct. 1816. L./B.
	'for there is':	James Sykes. L./B. Box 161
41	'I shall expect':	Sophy Byron to James Sykes, 16 Oct. 1791. L./B. Box 161
42	'she slept in':	A.L. to Miss Cursham. Roe Byron Collection
	'You know Lord Byron':	Boyes, *My Amiable Mamma*. Murray Ms.
	'Miss Byron is':	B.L. Add. Ms 33097
43	'gave and bequeathed':	Derbyshire Records Office, Matlock
44	'This child of mine':	Gunn, *My Dearest Augusta*, pp. 37–8 Murray Mss.
	'which with her long neck':	Ibid.
45	'[Augusta's] taste':	Ibid.
	'I am apprehensive':	Walker, op. cit.
	'On 17 August':	Hanson to Farquhar. Marchand, *Byron: A Biography* vol. 1, p. 49
46	'I hope you will soon':	Add. Ms. 33131, B.L.
47	'The home of thy youth':	Private Collection
	'extreme weakness':	B.L. Pelham Papers
	'for a fair opportunity':	Ibid.
	'I shall be glad':	Add. Ms. 33132
	'. . . tell Miss Byron':	Ibid.
48	'My dearest Lady Mary':	Ibid.
	'new codicil':	Derbyshire Records Office
	'The accounts of':	*The Correspondence of George, Prince of Wales*, ed. Aspinall, vol. 4
	'She flatters herself':	Ibid.
	'game soup':	B.L. Pelham Papers
49	'A point I have':	Ibid.
	'I took the first':	Ibid.
	'Miss Byron has':	Ibid.
	'I do not indulge':	Sophy Byron to James Sykes. L./B. Box 161
50	'It is beyond doubt':	*Dictionary of National Biography*
51	'Lady Charlotte':	Hary-O
	'Miss Byron used':	Ibid.
52	'Somebody who':	Gunn, op. cit.

CHAPTER 5

Page	Ref.	Source
53	'Dear Augusta':	Prothero, vol. 1, p. 18
	'Your Aunt':	Pratt, *Byron at Southwell*, p. 5
54	'I wish':	Boyes, *My Amiable Mamma*. Murray Ms.
	'My sister told me':	L.&J. vol. 9, p. 40

55	'It was by the desire':	Boyes, op. cit. Murray Ms.
56	'Recollect':	Prothero, vol. 1, p. 20
	'Augusta and I':	L.&J., vol. 10, p. 208
57	'When you see':	Prothero, vol. 1, p. 21
	'no society but':	Ibid., p. 24
58	'. . . the truth is':	Ibid., p. 16
	'a circumstance':	Marchand, *Byron. A Portrait*, p. 28
59	'He was once':	Prothero, vol. 1, p. 23
	'I saw poor Joe':	Ibid., p. 21
60	'I don't know':	Boyes, *My Amiable Mamma* p. 103. Murray Ms.
	'Can't you drive':	Prothero, vol. 1, p. 36
	'in a monstrous pet':	Ibid., p. 40
	'Now, Augusta':	Ibid., p. 43
61	'. . . once she let slip':	Ibid.
	'I thought':	Ibid., pp. 45–6
	'. . . she flies into':	Ibid., p. 46
	'You, Augusta':	Ibid., p. 44
	'I am afraid':	Ibid., p. 47
62	'put it in his power':	Ibid., p. 45
	'as she would only':	Ibid.
	'I thank you':	Ibid., p. 49
	'I hear from':	Ibid., p. 39
63	'on further acquaintance':	Ibid., pp. 54–5
	'If your taste':	Ibid.
	'a pleasure':	Ibid., p. 56
	'Within one little hour':	Ibid., p. 62
64	'Believe me':	Ibid., p. 66
	'I *Beg*':	Ibid., p. 68
	'As might be supposed':	Ibid., p. 81
65	'I hope your':	Ibid., p. 91
	'before I disclose':	Ibid., pp. 91–2
66	'All I expect':	Ibid.
	'and to those':	Ibid.
	'I fear the business':	Ibid., p. 94
67	'I am afraid':	Boyes, op. cit. Murray Ms.

CHAPTER 6

Page	Ref.	Source
68	'Your joke about':	Hary-O
	'I cannot forget:	Boyes, op. cit. Murray Ms.
69	'If you are in Town':	Ibid.
	'were married at':	St George's, Hanover Square, Register of Marriages. Westminster Archives Centre
70	'The Prince of Wales':	*Correspondence of the Prince of Wales,* vol. 1

72	'. . . which I hope':	Ibid., vol II
73	'Colonel Leigh':	Ibid., vol IV
	'. . . improper people':	Chifney, *Genius Genuine*
74	'I received':	Ibid.
	'You will not':	*Correspondence of the Prince of Wales*, Aspinall, vol. v., no 1943.

CHAPTER 7

Page	Ref.	Source
76	'In 1750'	Onslow, *Headquarters*
	'the house I have':	A.L. to Lady Morpeth, 5 Sept. 1809. Castle Howard Archives
	'the most beautiful clock':	Aspinall, op. cit. vol VI
77	'enjoyed three days':	Ibid.
78	'Colonel Leigh is said':	Hary-O
	'I shall feel':	Prothero, vol. 1, pp. 187–8
	'I don't know':	Mollo, *The Prince's Dolls*
79	'Mrs Leigh is':	Duchess of Rutland to Gertrude Sloane. Castle Howard Archives
	'my dearest Augusta':	Prothero, vol. 1, p. 203
	'Leigh begs':	Castle Howard Archives
	'almost horseless':	Mollo, op. cit.
81	'Be not disconcerted':	Prothero, vol. 1, p. 138
82	'Though I was happy':	Ibid., p. 283
83/4	'Whatever may':	B.L. Add. Ms. 31037
84	'I hear the cause':	Boyes, op. cit. Murray Ms.
	'for not leaving?:	B. L. Add. Ms. 31037
	'Colonel Leigh will consider':	Ibid.
85	'from fear of':	*Farington Diary*, vol. VI
	'. . . write to the Prince':	L./B. Box 85, ff 94–5
	'Col Leigh arrived':	Castle Howard Archives
	'neglecting to credit':	Doris Langley Moore, *Lord Byron Accounts Rendered*. Murray Ms.
86	'nothing consolatory':	B.L. Add. Ms. 31037

CHAPTER 8

Page	Ref.	Source
88	'Had I been':	L.&J. vol. 1, p. 256
89	'I ought to have answered':	Prothero, vol. 1, p. 332
	'I hear you have':	Ibid.
	'I am determined':	Prothero, vol. 2, pp. 10–11
90	'I don't know':	Ibid., p. 11
	'I have indeed':	Ibid., p. 10
	'clever horse':	Paget Papers. B.L. Add. Ms. 48416

91	'Sir Harry F.':	Ibid.
	'I have so many horses':	Ibid.
	'Col L. said':	Castle Howard Archives
92	'Now, if I could':	Prothero, vol. 2, pp. 16–17
	'My "Satire"':	Ibid., p. 18
	'I feel very uncertain:	Castle Howard Archives
93	'. . . we will travel':	Prothero, vol. 2, p. 18
	'totally enamoured':	L.&J., vol. 2, p. 151
	'How will you carry':	Moore, *Byron's Life and Works*, vol. 1, p. 156
94	'Nobody reads':	Amy Cruse, *An Englishman and His Books*, p. 215
	'The ladies':	Foster, *The Two Duchesses*, p. 364
95	'If she had been':	L.&J., vol. 3, p. 219
	'His mouth continually':	A.I.M., Journal, 23 March 1812. L./B.
96	'He really is':	A.I.M. to Judith, 16 and 25 April 1812. L./B.
	'She certainly is':	Prothero, vol. 2, p. 121
	'. . . shun friendships':	Caroline Lamb to A.I.M., 22 May 1812
	'I admire her':	L.&J., vol. II, p. 199
97	'When indignation':	Mayne, pp. 48–9
	'I thank you':	L.&J., vol. 2, p. 231
	'Tell A.':	Ibid., p. 232

CHAPTER 9

Page	Ref.	Source
98	'. . . at all events':	L.&J., vol. 2, p. 86
	'parish of Bottisham':	Bottisham Parish Records
99	'I did not answer':	Prothero, vol. 2, p. 196
100	'was always buried':	Ibid., p. 199
	'My dearest Augusta':	Ibid., p. 225
101	'If you knew':	Ibid., p. 226
	'There you will see':	Ibid., p. 227
102	'His playful':	A.I.M. Narrative Q. L./B. Box 130
	'I wish she were not':	L.&J., vol. 3, p. 70
103	'He told me':	A.I.M. to Judith, 2 Sept. 1815. L./B.
	'You are quite mistaken':	L.&J., vol. 4, p. 110
105	'. . . we were not made':	*Manfred*, Act 2, Scene 4
	'I don't tell you':	L.&J., vol. 3, p. 83
106	'My sister':	Ibid., p. 85
	'If you have':	Gross, *Byron's 'Corbeau Blanc'*, p. 144
107	'I should have':	L.&J., vol. 3, p. 87
	'I am going':	Ibid., p. 89
	'It would be a terrible':	Castle Howard Archives
108	'She wants to go':	L.&J., vol. 3, p. 93
	'I am in great hopes':	Castle Howard Archives
	'the fact is':	L.&J., vol. 3, p. 96
	'After all':	Ibid., pp. 100–1

109	'Your kind letter':	Ibid., p. 102
	'I am too proud':	Ibid., p. 103
	'I have the right':	Mayne, p. 58
110	'She seems':	L.&J., vol. 3, p. 108
	'I leave town':	Ibid., p. 112
	'You say "write"':	Ibid., p. 113
	'I have not yet determined':	Ibid., pp. 114–15

CHAPTER 10

Page	Ref.	Source
112	'to vanquish':	L.&J., vol. 3, p. 124
	'the same house':	Ibid., p. 122
113	'I have only':	Ibid., p. 138
	'I believe':	Ibid., p. 205
114	'What an odd situation':	Ibid., p. 227
	'Partager tous':	A.L. to Byron. L./B.
115	'The house is':	The Diary of Frances, Lady Shelley
116	'I shall be able':	L.&J., vol. 4, pp. 25–6
	'My dearest Lord':	Boyes, Queen of a Fantastic Realm
	'if you go':	L.&J., vol. 10, p. 209
117	'A very old':	L.&J., vol. 4, p. 35
	'. . . it must be':	Ibid., p. 27
	'The roads are':	Ibid., pp. 36–7
118	'this Lapland':	Ibid., p. 40
	'From this place':	Ibid., p. 44
	'You will very probably':	Ibid., p. 48

CHAPTER 11

Page	Ref.	Source
121	'I wish I could':	Gross, op. cit., p. 171
	'Oh! But it is':	L.&J., vol. 4, p. 121
122	'One of my great':	Ibid., p. 48
123	'You have understood':	Mayne, p. 84
	'As for the report':	Ibid., p. 91
	'A letter from Bella':	L.&J., vol. 3, p. 251
	'. . . there is that shyness':	Ibid., p. 254
124	'Had I no other':	Catton Papers.
	'. . . is not the tempter':	Gross, op. cit., p. 174
125	'she was not':	L.&J., vol. 4, p. 110
	'. . . for Godsake':	Ibid., p. 131
126	'I uttered':	Ibid., p. 127
127	'You talked':	Ibid., p. 132
	'he showed me':	Doris Langley Moore, The Late Lord Byron, p. 241
	'transparencies and':	Cambridge Chronicle, July 1814
	'let my bedroom':	L.&J., vol. 4, p. 137

129 'She wished me':   Ibid., p. 191
    'I very much fear':   Boyes, *Queen of a Fantastic Realm*
    'My doubt then is':   A.I.M. to Byron, 6 Aug. 1814. L./B. Box 38
    'I did – do':   L.&J., vol. 4, p. 155
    'you do not appear':   A.I.M. to Byron, 13 Aug. 1814. L./B. Box
                             38
131 'A few weeks ago':   L.&J., vol. 4, p. 169
132 'It would be absurd':   Mayne, p. 111
    'If it contains':   *Medwin's Conversations of Lord Byron*,
                             p. 35

CHAPTER 12

Page	Ref.	Source
134	'[Augusta] never':	L.&J., vol. 4, p. 191
135	'I am afraid':	A.L. to A.I.M., 1 Oct. 1814. L./B. Box 79
	'she is the least selfish':	L.&J., vol. 4, p. 197
136	'He knows':	Ibid., p. 227
	'He writes me word':	A.L. to A.I.M., 15 Oct. 1814. L./B. Box 79
	'You cannot imagine':	A.L. to A.I.M., 20 Oct. 1814. L./B. Box 79
137	'You would not be':	Ibid.
	'I feel already':	Ibid.
138	'in very good spirits':	L.&J., vol. 4, p. 227
139	'but it is very selfish':	Hodgson, *Memoir* vol. 1, p. 289
	'Do you know':	L.&J., vol. 4, p. 231
140	'The fact is':	A.L. to A.I.M., 30 Nov. 1814. L./B. Box 79
	'I begin to think':	Mayne, p. 138
141	'I am not "wiser"':	A.I.M. to A.L., 9 Dec. 1814. L./B. Box 79
	'Byron, my own':	A.I.M. to Byron, 10 Dec. 1814. L./B. Box 79
	'Hobhouse I believe':	L.&J., vol. 4, p. 246
	'My Dearest B.':	A.L. to Byron, postmarked 15 Dec. 1814. L./B. Box 79
142	'Col L. is opposite':	L.&J., vol. 4, p. 247
	'Never was lover':	Broughton, *Recollections of a Long Life*, vol. 1
143	'somewhat cool':	Ibid.
	'Rather dowdy looking':	Ibid.
	'I am relieved':	A.L. to A.I.M., no date. L./B. Box 79
	'Miss M.':	Broughton, op. cit., vol. 1

CHAPTER 13

Page	Ref.	Source
145	'getting on extremely well':	L.&J., vol. 4, p. 262
	'I have done':	A.I.B. Narrative Q. L./B. Box 130
	'When Byron did not':	*The Literary Life of the Reverend William Harness*

146	'Dearest, first and best':	A.I.B. Narrative Q. L./B. Box 130
	'His terror':	A.I.B. Ibid.
147	'*Would* that I':	A.L. to A.I.B., 8 Jan. 1815. L./B. Box 79
	'It is so like':	A.L. to A.I.B., 9 Jan. 1815. Ibid.
148	'I think and':	A.L. to A.I.B., 18 Jan. 1815. Ibid.
	'I think I see':	Ibid.
	'I wish I':	Ibid.
	'He had also':	Narrative Q. L./B. Box 130
	'it has normally':	A.L. to A.I.M., 30 Jan. 1815. L./B. Box 79
	'My dear you':	Ibid.
149	'I will own':	Hodgson, vol. 2, p. 8.
	'I am just':	A.L. to A.I.B., 28 Jan. 1815. L./B. Box 79
150	'He wore':	A.I.B. Narrative Q. L./B. Box 130
	'Upon this dreary coast':	L.&J., vol. 4, p. 263
	'Oh! Yes his own':	A.L. to A.I.B., 10 Feb. 1815. L./B. Box 79
	'You must not mind':	Ibid.
151	'Don't imagine':	A.L. to A.I.M., 2 Feb. 1815. L./B. Box 79
	'You would not fancy':	Ibid.
152	'I shall set off':	L.&J., vol. 4, p. 276
	'If Aunt':	A.L. to A.I.M., 22 Feb. 1815. L./B. Box 79

CHAPTER 14

Page	Ref.	Source
153	'I lent':	L.&J., vol. 4, p. 259
	'Could not B.':	A.L. to A.I.M., 19 Feb. 1815. L./B. Box 79
154	'Oh! You lazy':	Judith to A.I.B., 14 March 1815. L./B.
	'the kindest words':	A.I.B. Narrative R. L./B. Box 130
	'I feel as if':	Ibid.
	'. . . he afterwards':	Ibid.
155	'Now I have':	Ibid.
	'In the morning':	Ibid.
	'I was so miserable':	Ibid.
	'So you wouldn't':	Ibid.
	'I was sensible':	Ibid.
156	'any appearance':	Ibid.
	'or perhaps she said':	Ibid.
157	'Oh dear!':	Hodgson, op. cit., vol. 2, p. 15
	'their departure':	Ibid., p. 13
	'. . . of Lady B.':	Ibid, p. 13
	'He seems quite sensible':	Ibid., p. 14
	'the slightest emotion':	A.I.B. Narrative R. L./B.
	'did not wish':	Narrative S. L./B.
158	'I am sorry to say':	Hodgson, vol. 2, p. 16
	'Is it true':	Judith to A.I.B. 22 March. L./B.
	'You cannot think':	B.L. Add. Ms. 33131. F101

159	'I am a piece':	Hedley, op. cit.
160	'Dearest Sis':	A.L. to A.I.B. 30 March 1815. L./B.
	'He told me':	Statement E. L./B.
	'white Satin':	Judith to A.I.B., 9 April 1815. L./B.
161	'I felt that':	Statement G. L./B. Box 131
	'Dearest – Now':	L.&J., vol. 4, p. 287
	'it was hopeless':	A.I.B. Narrative S. L./B. Box 130
162	'. . . the Scenes':	L.&J., vol. 9, p. 36
	'superintending':	A.I.B. Statement W. L./B. Box 131
163	'He said to her':	A.I.B. Statement H. L./B. Box 131

CHAPTER 15

Page	Ref.	Source
164	'The only drawbacks':	A.L. to Hobhouse, 5 July 1815. L./B.
	'I must tell you':	Prothero, vol. 7, p. 210. Byron made his will on 29 July
	'Charles Leigh died':	Public Records Office
165	'. . . his father is dead':	L.&J., vol. 4, p. 307
	'I think Mrs Longe':	
	'. . . he thinks *fear*':	A.L. to A.I.B. L./B. transcripts, vol. 361, 1 Sept 1815
166	'I am sorry':	Ibid.
	'. . . should have become':	*Morning Herald*, 9 August 1815
	'was very gracious':	A.I.B. to Mrs Villiers L./B. transcripts, vol. 381
167	'For what is':	Ibid.
	'Mrs Leigh must':	Judith to A.I.B., 1 Sept. 1815. L./B.
	'full of Law':	A.L. to A.I.B. L./B. Box 84 (12 Nov. 1815)
	'I tremble':	Ibid.
168	'She is much':	A.I.B. to Judith, 2 Sept. 1815. L./B.
	'much hurry':	Hodgson, op. cit., vol. 2, p. 19
	'Something he told me':	Statement G. L./B. Box 131
	'He is in great':	A.I.B. to Judith, 8 Sept. 1815. L./B.
169	'. . . he feels it':	A.I.B. to Sir Ralph, 14 Sept. 1815. L./B.
	'Lord Byron is':	Smiles, *A Publisher and His Friends*, vol. 1, p. 286
	'when he wished it':	A.I.B. to A.L., 9 Nov. 1815. L./B.
	'O Augusta':	Ibid.
	'He studiously':	*Statement Given to My Mother*, 18 Jan. 1816. L./B.
	'. . . let me see you':	A.I.B. to A.L., 11 Nov. 1815. L./B. transcripts, vol. 382
170	'unequivocally':	Mrs Villiers to A.I.B., 18 May 1816
	'soon turned':	Statement G. L./B. Box 131
	'inclinations':	Ibid.
171	'. . . professedly':	Statement G. L./B. Box 131
	'. . . her accounts':	Ibid.

172	'Oh! what an implement':	*The Times*, 7 Sept. 1869
	'B. is in great':	Prothero, vol. 3, pp. 291–2
173	'the Dear Babe':	Judith to A.I.B., no date. L./B.
	'My confinement':	Prothero, vol. 3, p. 292
	'a woman had':	*Statement Given to My Mother*, 18 Jan. 1816. L./B.
	'When you are':	L.&J., vol. 5, p. 15
174	'a small bottle':	Broughton, op. cit., vol. 2, p. 250
	'the sooner':	L.&J., vol. 5, p. 15
	'in a state':	Statement by Mrs Clermont. L./B.
	'When shall we':	Stowe, op. cit.
175	'There was':	Mayne, p. 202

CHAPTER 16

Page	Ref.	Source
176	'if ever':	Statement by Mrs Clermont L./B.
	'Dearest Duck':	Mayne, p. 203
177	'criminal dispositions':	Statement G. L./B. Box 131
	'One comfort':	A.L. to A.I.B., 18 Jan. 1816 Box 79
178	'Fletcher has':	A.L. to A.I.B., 18 Jan. 1816. L./B. Box 79
	'So that is settled':	A.L. to A.I.B., 19 Jan. 1816. L./B. Box 79
	'in spite of':	Selina Doyle to A.I.B., 18 Jan. 1816
179	'Knowing your anxiety':	Prothero, vol. 3, p. 297
	'B came home':	A.L. to A.I.B., P.S. to letter of 19 Jan. 1816. L./B. Box 79
	'One of the things':	A.L. to A.I.B., 22 Jan. 1816. L./B. Box 79
	'It would be':	A.I.B. to Judith, 22 Jan. 1816. L./B.
	'He seemed harping':	A.L. to A.I.B., 23 Jan. 1816. L./B. Box 79
180	'obscene stile':	Judith to A.I.B., 23 Jan. 1816. L./B. Box 79
	'she is at times':	A.L. to A.I.B., 25 Jan. 1816. L./B. Box 79
	'although she has':	Mrs Clermont to A.I.B. L./B.
	'He seems the':	Judith to A.I.B. 25 Jan. 1816. L./B.
	'He gave me':	A.L. to A.I.B. 27 Jan. 1816. L./B.
181	'Shall I still':	A.I.B. to A.L., 25 Jan. 1816. Add. Ms. 31037
	'She had been':	A.I.B. to Judith, no date. L./B.
	'*Very recently*':	Sir Ralph Noel to Byron, 2 Feb. 1816. Broughton, vol. II p. 209
	'For once':	A.L. to A.I.B., 29 Jan. 1816. L./B.
182	'Annabella has':	L./B. Box 10, F.125
	'The reasons':	L./B. Box 10, F.103
	'You have done':	L./B. Box 10, F.104
	'. . . the business':	Judith to Mrs Clermont, 31 Jan. 1816. L./B.
183	'notwithstanding':	Sophy Byron to A.I.B. L/B. Box 65, F.14
	'her whole aim':	A.L. to A.I.B., 29 Jan. 1816. L./B.
	'Ld — [Byron]':	Judith Noel to Sir Ralph, 2 Feb. 1816. L./B.

184	'My opinion':	A.L. to A.I.B. 1 Feb. 1816. L./B. Box 80
	'if so he will':	A.L. to A.I.B., 2 Feb. 1816. L./B.
	'inability to':	L.&J., vol. 5, pp. 20–1
	'distress without':	Ibid.
	'I am however':	Ibid.
185	'The whole of':	Ibid., p. 22
	'I feel sure':	Hobhouse to A.I.B. 5 Feb. 1816
	'You are desired':	Prothero, vol. 3, p. 302
186	'I hope':	Ibid., p. 303
	'there is too much':	Ibid.
187	'The fact is':	Prothero, vol. 3, pp. 304–5
	'with the deepest':	Ibid. pp. 312–313
	'It is unhappily':	A.I.B. to Byron, 7 Feb. 1816. Broughton, vol. II, pp. 235–6
188	'I am therefore':	L.&J., vol. 5, pp. 23–4
	'I fear':	A.L. to Hodgson. L./B. Box 84
	'I never knock':	Hobhouse, *Journal*, 12 Feb. 1816.
	'Whilst I heard':	Marchand. vol II, pp. 576–577
	'He seems DETERMINED':	A.L. to A.I.B., 12–13 Feb. 1816. L./B.
189	'I could put':	A.I.B. to Lushington, 15 Feb. 1816. L./B.
	'. . . I never could':	A.L. to A.I.B., 20 Feb. 1816. L./B.
190	'You may know':	A.L. to A.I.B. Ibid.
	'go to Kirkby':	A.L. to Hodgson. 1 March 1816. L./B. Box 84
	'I am convinced':	Judith to Sir Ralph, 6 Feb. 1816. L./B.
191	'should be spoken of':	A.I.B. to Judith, 10 March 1816. L./B.
	'Mrs Leigh has':	Hobhouse, op. cit., 29 Feb. 1816
	'The fact is':	Mrs Villiers to A.I.B., 26 Feb. 1816. L./B.
192	'but should it':	Ibid.
	'It is very painful':	A.I.B. to Mrs Villiers, 26 Feb. 1816. L./B.
	'It is a constant':	Aunt Sophy to A.I.B., 29 Feb. 1816. L./B. Box 65, Ff 21–2
	'her persuasion':	Hobhouse, op. cit.
	'Those who':	A.L. to Hodgson 19 Feb 1816 L./B. 84
193	'say what you like':	A.L. to Hodgson. L./B. Box 84
	'if her own friends':	A.L. to Hodgson. 5 March 1815. L./B. Box 84
	'I can never':	Ibid.

CHAPTER 17

Page	Ref.	Source
195	'I know more':	Thomas Moore, *Journal*, 29 April 1822
196	'I think a':	Catton Papers, no. 1
	'very like *St Vitus*':	Ibid.
	'*I give you*':	Wilmot to A.I.B. L./B.
	'I don't know':	A.L. to Hodgson. 7 March 1816. L./B. Box 84

197	'positive disavowal':	Fox, *The Byron Mystery*, p. 112
	'do not form':	Wilmot to Hobhouse. 8 March 1816
198	'. . . it is clear':	A.L. to Wilmot. L./B. 11 March 1816
	'with regard':	Ibid.
199	'*in your presence*':	Wilmot to Hobhouse. L./B.
	'I really lived':	A.L. to Hodgson, 14 March 1816. L./B. Box 84
	'what is most horrible':	Ibid.
	'It is my present':	Ibid.
200	'On 13 March':	Broughton, op. cit. Hobhouse, op. cit.
	'He has never':	A.L. to Hobhouse. Broughton, op. cit. 2
	'Lady B. cannot':	Memorandum, March 1816. L./B.
201	'I've seen Ly B':	A.L. to Hodgson. L./B. Box 84
	'There can be':	A.I.B. to Judith Noel, 16 March 1816. L./B.
	'as *he* seems':	A.L. to Hodgson, 18 March 1816. L./B. Box 84
	'I dare not':	Ibid.
202	'Lady B. said':	Hobhouse, op. cit.
	'He *may* have':	A.L. to A.I.B., 27 March 1816. L./B. Box 80
	'Lady Byron's fate':	Foster, op. cit., pp. 413–14
203	'They were certainly':	Ibid.
	'As this is':	A.L. to Hodgson. L./B. Box 84
204	'I give you':	Paston and Quennell, *To Lord Byron*, p. 71
	'Do not think':	Doris Langley Moore, *The Late Lord Byron*, p. 234
	'I believe M. Leigh':	Ibid., p. 237
	'Remember the situation':	Ibid.
205	'That from the time':	Ibid. Minutes of meeting with Ly C.L., p. 240
	'In which were':	Ibid. p. 242
206	'to convey to':	A.I.B. to Wilmot. L./B. 29 March 1816
	'This has terminated':	13 April 1816. Add. Ms. 47232
207	'Lady Jersey has':	A.I.B. to Judith Noel, April 1816 L./B.
	'we sat up':	Hobhouse. L Add. Ms. 47232
	'I really think':	A.L. to Judith Noel, 27 March 1816 L./B.
	'My sister':	L.&J., vol. 5, p. 65
	'I never can':	A.L. to Hodgson, 28 April 1816 L./B. 84
208	'in good legible':	L.&J., vol. 8, p. 238
	'More last words':	L.&J., vol. 5, p. 66
209	'I trust you':	Ibid., p. 67
	'All I have':	Ibid., p. 69
210	'He tells me':	Ibid., p. 70

Page	Ref.	Source
211	'I am particularly':	Aunt Sophy to A.I.B., April 1816. L./B. Box 65, F.31
	'it will be long':	A.L. to Hodgson, 28 April 1816. L./B. Box 84
	'but I am afraid':	A.L. to Judith Noel, 9 May 1816 L./B.
	'I felt appalled':	Lovelace, *Astarte*, p. 152
212	'there are parts':	Aunt Sophy to A.I.B., 22 April 1816. L./B. Box 65, F.26
213	'Nothing could be':	Mrs Villiers to A.L., 25 April 1816 L./B.
	'I should have':	A.I.B. to Mrs Villiers, 12 May 1816. L./B. transcripts
	'My great object':	Ibid.
	'I honour you':	Ibid.
214	'He sends me':	A.L. to Hodgson. May 1816. Murray Ms 2
215	'Ld B. had':	Mrs Villiers to A.I.B., 18 May 1816. L./B. transcripts
	'I have seen':	Wilmot to A.I.B., 17 May 1816. L./B.
	'Without it':	Mrs Villiers to A.I.B., 18 May 1816. L./B. transcripts
216	'I think IF':	Mrs Villiers to A.I.B., 3 June 1816. L./B. transcripts
	'Col L. of course':	Ibid.
	'Before your confinement':	A.I.B. to A.L., 3 June 1816. Mayne, p. 235
217	'. . . you have not':	Ibid.
	'I shall still not':	Ibid.
	'first feeling':	A.I.B. to Mrs Villiers, 3 June 1816. L./B. transcripts
	'Your silence':	A.L. to A.I.B. 6 June 1816 Mayne, p. 236
218	'I will not':	Ibid.
	'I began to':	Hodgson, op. cit., vol. 2, p. 34
219	'I never knew':	A.I.B. to Sir Ralph. L./B.
220	'Her letters':	Mrs Villiers to A.I.B., 8 June 1816. L./B. transcripts, vol. 382
	'I hear . . .':	Ibid.
	'I suppose':	A.L. to A.I.B., 22 June 1816. L./B. Box 80
	'all my hope':	Ibid.
	'Do not pain me':	A.I.B. to A.L., 30 June 1816. L./B. Box 80
221	'I only wish':	A.L. to A.I.B., 3–4 July 1816. L./B. Box 80
	'she compromises':	Wilmot to A.I.B., 5 July 1816. L./B. Box 80
	'In your sanction':	A.I.B. to Mrs Villiers, 8 July 1816. L./B. transcripts
222	'the *tourbillon*':	Mrs Villiers to A.I.B. L./B. transcripts
	'press still more':	A.I.B. to Mrs Villiers, 11 July 1816. L./B. transcripts

CHAPTER 19

Page	Ref.	Source
223	'looking quite stout':	Mrs Villiers to A.I.B., 18 July 1816. L./B.
	'In the last part':	A.I.B. to A.L., 11 July 1816. L./B.
224	'It is still like':	A.L. to A.I.B., incorrectly dated 15 July 1816. L./B. Box 80
	'She disliked':	A.I.B. to Mrs Villiers, 11 July 1816. L./B.
	'Poor thing':	Broughton, vol. 1, p. 348
	'Nothing can be':	Mrs Villiers to A.I.B. L./B. transcripts
225	'for Lake is':	Paget Papers. B.L. Add. Mss. 48416
	'George is':	Ibid.
	'Ye worst':	A.L. to A.I.B., 25 July 1816. L./B. Box 80
226	'were *he* only':	F. Bentinck to St Arthur Paget, 13 Aug. 1816. Add. Mss. 48416
	'by the involuntary':	A.I.B. to A.L., 17 July 1816. L./B.
	'"I never witnessed"':	A.L. to A.I.B., 24 July 1816. L./B. Box 80
	'Undoubtedly, her':	A.I.B. to Mrs Villiers. L./B. transcripts
227	'If I think':	A.I.B. to A.L., 30 July 1816. L./B. Box 80
	'all phrases':	Ibid.
228	'I assure you':	A.L. to A.I.B., 5 Aug. 1816. L./B. Box 80
	'I think your':	Mrs Villiers to A.I.B., 5 Aug. 1816. L./B. transcripts 382
	'I never in my life':	Bentinck to Paget. B.L. Add. Mss. 48416
	'I declare':	A.L. to A.I.B., 22 Aug. 1816. L./B. Box 80
229	'Do you sorrow':	Marchand. vol II, pp. 648–9
230	'I am so sorry':	A.L. to A.I.B., 2 Sept. 1816. L./B. Box 80
	'She acknowledged':	Astarte, pp. 162–3
231	'She has shown':	A.I.B. to Mrs Villiers, no date. Ibid., p. 257
	'Your confidential letter':	L.&J., vol. 5, pp. 88–9
233	'Pardon me':	Add. Mss. 39672 (9 Sept. 1816)
	'I felt I was':	Mrs Villiers to A.I.B., 15 Sept. 1816. L./B. transcripts 382
	'the Victim of':	Ibid.

CHAPTER 20

Page	Ref.	Source
235	'without any':	A.L. to A.I.B., 17 Sept. 1816. L./B. Box 80
	'Now – don't scold':	L.&J., vol. 5, pp. 91–2
	'Sposo dining out':	A.L. to A.I.B., 29 Sept. 1816. L./B. Box 80
236	'*in correspondence*':	L.&J., vol. 5, pp. 93–4
	'I think I told':	A.L. to A.I.B., 27 Sept. 1816. L./B. Box 80
	'pray why is':	L.&J., vol. 5, p. 95
	'I think I could':	Ibid.
237	'What a fool':	Ibid.
	'The worst . . .':	A.I.B. to Mrs Villiers, 24 Oct. 1816. L./B. transcripts
	'& after *what*':	A.L. to A.I.B., 29 Sept. 1816. L./B.

238	'don't for Heaven's sake'':	A.L. to A.I.B., 27 Sept. 1816. L./B.
	'What a volume':	L./B. D.D.
	'A. – is formed':	Ibid.
	'My only fear':	A.L. to A.I.B., 21 Sept. 1816. L./B.
	'I think Georgey':	A.L. to A.I.B., 27 Sept. 1816. L./B.
239	'sing too that':	L.&J., vol. 5, p. 102
	'I heartily wish':	A.L. to A.I.B., 6 Nov. 1816. L./B. Box 84
240	'*Je lui ai dit*':	Mrs Villiers to A.L., 20 Oct. 1816. L./B. transcripts, vol. 315
	'parce *que*':	Ibid.
	'By the bye':	A.L. to A.I.B., 2 Nov. 1816. L./B.
241	'He was astonished':	A.I.B. to Mrs Villiers, 2 Nov. 1816. L./B. transcripts
	'To you – dearest':	L.&J., vol. 5, p. 105
	'And pray what':	Ibid., p. 116
	'She has forwarded':	A.I.B. to Mrs Villiers. L./B. transcripts
	'I have hitherto':	L.&J. vol. 5, p. 118
242	'I really do not':	Ibid., p. 119
	'the most obstinate':	A.L. to A.I.B., 13 Oct. 1816. L./B. Box 80
243	'before *Mon Mari*':	A.L. to A.I.B., 20 Nov. 1816. L./B. Box 84
	'Depend on one thing':	A.L. to A.I.B. 22 Dec. 1816. L./B. Box 84
244	'renewing any':	Hodgson, op. cit., 14 Nov. 1816, vol. 2, p. 43
	'with *five* children':	Ibid.
	'more in love':	L.&J., vol. 5, pp. 140–2
	'Goosey my love':	Ibid.
245	'duties':	A.I.B. Memorandum, Jan. 1817. L./B.
	'About the letters':	A.L. to A.I.B., Feb. 1817. L./B. Box 81
	'which I wish':	A.L. to A.I.B., 22 March 1817. L./B. Box 81
246	'I never saw him':	A.L. to A.I.B., 23 March 1817. L./B. Box 81
	'Give me but':	L.&J., vol. 5, p. 223
	'They tell me':	Ibid., p. 228
	'For the life of':	Ibid., pp. 231–2
247	'Another disgrace':	Ibid.
	'It was the Straubach':	L.&J., vol. 7, p. 113
248	'I have read it':	Mrs Villiers to A.I.B., 7 July 1817. L./B. transcripts

CHAPTER 21

Page	Ref.	Source
250	'more depressed':	A.L. to A.I.B., 19 July 1817. L./B. Box 81
	'OTHERS':	Ibid.
	'Mrs Leigh has written':	L.&J., vol. 5, p. 255
251	'If you see Augusta':	Ibid., pp. 273–4
	'*Mon mari* is'':	A.L. to A.I.B., 19 Nov. 1817. L./B. Box 81
	'I am essentially':	A.L. to A.I.B., 17 Dec. 1817. L./B. Box 81

252	'probably she will':	A.L. to A.I.B., no date. L./B. Box 81
	'I have a sort':	A.I.B. to A.L., 22 Dec. 1817. L./B. Box 81
	'cannot suppose':	A.L. to A.I.B., 26 Dec. 1817. L./B. Box 81
	'nervous – she':	A.L. to A.I.B., 23 Jan. 1818. L./B. Box 81
	'which wd be':	A.L. to A.I.B., 30 June 1818. L./B. Box 81
	'unequal to':	A.L. to A.I.B., 17 Dec. 1817. L./B. Box 81
	'A good sort':	Ibid.
253	'person not unlikely':	A.I.B. to A.L., 22 Dec. 1817. L./B. Box 81
	'It is not for':	A.I.B. to A.L., 26 Dec. 1817. L./B. Box 81
	'peculiarly adapted':	A.L. to A.I.B., 11 April 1818. L./B. Box 81
	'. . . she may appear':	A.L. to A.I.B., no date. L./B. Box 81
254	'and am alive':	A.L. to A.I.B., 27 Feb. 1818. L./B. Box 81
	'*In case of*':	Doris Langley Moore, *The Late Lord Byron*, p. 300
	'She was in *many*':	A.L. to A.I.B., 11 April 1818. L./B. Box 81
	'I was not unconcerned':	A.I.B. to A.L., 14 April 1818. L./B.
	'most disgusting letter':	Mayne, p. 276
255	'I like the account':	Duke of York to George Leigh, 21 March 1818. L./B. Box 85
	'I am not much':	A.L. to A.I.B., 25 April 1818. L./B. Box 81
	'I can scarcely':	A.L. to A.I.B., 3 June 1818. L./B. Box 81
	'If the Queen dies'	L.&J., vol. 6, p. 69
256	'I did not see':	A.L. to A.I.B., 21 Aug. 1818. L./B. Box 81
	'*La mère*':	Ibid.
	My Sposo':	Ibid.
257	'It is so infinitely':	A.L. to A.I.B., 25 Oct. 1818
	'without a pang':	Hedley, op. cit.
	'a mournful duty':	A.L. to A.I.B., no date (4 Dec.?). L./B. Box 81
	'I must say':	Ibid.
258	'the blasphemy':	Broughton, op. cit., 26 Dec. 1818 vol. 2, p. 107
	'This new poem':	Hodgson, op. cit., vol. 2, p. 133
	'B. was not a man':	Origo, *The Last Attachment*, p. 40
259	'My dearest love':	L.&J., vol. 6, p. 129
	'but remember':	Ibid.
260	'I am *so afraid*':	A.L. to A.I.B., 25 June 1819. L./B. Box 82
	'Pray pardon me':	Ibid.
	'take no notice':	A.I.B. to A.L., 27 June 1819. L./B. Box 82
261	'*gentler* expedient':	A.L. to A.I.B., 28 June 1819. L./B. Box 82
	'I am at too great':	L.&J., vol. 6, p. 185
	'including that precious':	Ibid.

CHAPTER 22

Page	Ref.	Source
262	'I am in some anxiety':	A.I.B. to Mrs Villiers, 4 July 1819. L./B. transcripts
	'Imagine my horror':	A.L. to A.I.B., 20 July 1819. Box 82
	'too much preoccupied':	Ibid.

263	'If there is':	L.&J., vol. 6, pp. 288–9
	'I really could not':	A.L. to A.I.B., 8 Nov. 1819. L./B. Box 82
	'Will you tell me':	Ibid.
	'in a pennyless condition':	A.L. to A.I.B., 9 Dec. 1819. L./B. Box 82
	'this business':	L.&J., vol. 6, p. 248
264	'that shallow brained':	A.L. to A.I.B., 13 Dec. 1819. L./B. Box 82
	'in case of':	L.&J., vol. 6, p. 251
	'burnt in —':	A.L. to A.I.B., 21 Dec. 1819. L./B. Box 82
	'was frightened':	A.I.B. to Mrs Villiers, 23 Dec. 1819. L./B. transcripts
	'criminal *desires*':	A.I.B. to A.L., 23 Dec. 1819. L./B. Box 82
265	'I think I cannot':	Ibid.
	'Pray let':	L.&J., vol. 6, p. 258 (10 Dec. 1819)
	'I do not regret':	A.I.B. to Mrs Villiers, no date. L./B. transcripts
	'but *most of all*':	A.L. to A.I.B., 28 Dec. 1819. L./B. Box 82
266	'Is *experience* nothing?':	A.I.B. to A.L., 31 Dec. 1819. L./B. Box 82
	'I do not feel':	A.L. to A.I.B., 18 Jan. 1820. L./B. Box 82
267	'It will not':	L.&J., vol. 6, pp. 260–1
	'. . . they would combine':	L./B. Box 68, F54
268	'All I wish':	A.L. to A.I.B., 13 March 1820. L./B. Box 82
	'The purchaser's lawyers':	A.L. to A.I.B., 21 July 1820. L./B. Box 82
	'I desire to be':	L.&J., vol. 7, p. 155
	'I always loved you':	Ibid., p. 159
269	'I am so sorry':	Georgiana Leigh to A.I.B., 20 June 1820. L./B. Box 82
	'My Sposo':	A.L. to A.I.B., 17 Aug. 1820. L./B. Box 82
270	'dreading next week':	A.L to A.I.B., 27 Oct. 1820
	'. . . It is terribly':	A.L. to A.I.B., 17 Nov 1820
	'I did not think':	L.&J., vol. 7, p. 208
	'Whatever She is':	Ibid., p. 256
	'like a tallow candle':	A.L. to A.I.B., Jan. 1821. L./B. Box 82
	'Seven children':	*Byron's Bulldog*, ed. Peter W. Graham, Letter 25, 15 Feb. 1821
271	'Forward the enclosed':	L.&J., vol. 7, p. 257
	'What was I':	L.&J., vol. 8, p. 139
	'severely grieved':	A.L. to A.I.B., 26 June 1821. L./B. Box 82
	'Having received':	Murray Archives
272	'Lady Byron's people':	L.&J., vol. 8, p. 217
	'finisher':	Ibid., pp. 233–5
	'She has a great deal':	Ibid.

CHAPTER 23

Page	Ref.	Source
273	'a return to':	A.L. to A.I.B., 4 Oct. 1821. L./B. Box 82
	'it would save':	L.&J., vol. 9, p. 57
	'I hear that':	A.L. to A.I.B., Dec. 1821. L./B. Box 82
274	'. . . to me':	A.L. to A.I.B., 3 Jan 1822. L./B. Box 83
	'leave the world':	A.L. to A.I.B., 30 Jan. 1822. L./B. Box 83
	'some good *nursery*':	L.&J., vol. 9, p. 120
275	'*How* it can':	A.L. to A.I.B. L./B. Box 83, F.17
	'Thank you':	A.L. to A.I.B., no date. L./B. Box 83
276	'by *land* too':	L.&J., vol. 9, p. 15
	'Augusta has':	Blessington, *Conversations of Lord Byron*
277	'I sail for Greece':	L.&J., vol. 10, p. 204
	'dreadful and':	L.&J., vol. 11, p. 44–5
	'– it was stated':	Ibid.
	'Mrs Leigh has':	*Byron's Bulldog*, Letter 107
278	'I have made':	Murray Archives, 23 April 1824
	'Come; you are':	Julius Millingen, *Memoirs*
279	'Your efforts':	Ibid.
	'agony of grief':	Broughton, op. cit., vol. 3, p. 35
280	'On the 13th February':	Vaughan Library, Harrow
	'for the Bible':	Ibid.
	'My Lord':	Lovell, *His Very Self and Voice*, p. 648
281	'Mr Hobhouse':	Hodgson, op. cit., vol. 2, p.136
	'England's best poet':	Charles Thompson? (Chew, *Byron in England*)
	'If in thy life':	Samuel Rogers, *Italy*

CHAPTER 24

Page	Ref.	Source
282	'O! well':	Chew, op. cit.
	'the very day':	A.L. to A.I.B., 16–17 May 1826. L./B. Box 83
283	'that *it was agreed*':	Ibid.
	'It flew into':	Ibid.
284	'. . . G.B. comforted me':	Ibid.
	'& therefore':	Ibid.
	'*expressed a wish*':	Ibid.
	'I don't know':	Ibid.
285	'Colonel Doyle':	Broughton, op. cit. vol. 3, p. 342
	'had the question':	*Lady Noel Byron and the Leighs*
286	'the MS was':	*Morning Chronicle*, 20 May 1824 (copied from *The Times* of the previous day)
	'shamefully traduced':	Mrs Clermont to A.L. L./B. Box 83
	'*except through*':	A.L. to Mrs Clermont. L./B. Box 83
	'I will not':	A.I.B. to Mrs Villiers, 15 June 1824. L./B. transcripts

287	'I consider':	Wilmot to A.I.B. 1824 L./B.
288	'The property':	*Morning Chronicle*, 3 July 1824
	'I am very sorry':	A.L. to A.I.B., no date. L./B. Box 83, F53
	'It has occurred':	A.I.B. to A.L., 7 July 1824. L./B. Box 83
289	'Our feelings':	George Anson Byron to A.I.B. L./B.
	'who had no soul':	*Morning Post*, 26 July 1824
290	'beyond all precedent':	*Morning Post*, 12 July 1824
	'it did not bear':	Broughton, op. cit., vol. 3, p. 67
	'. . . for my own part':	Hodgson, op. cit., vol. 2, p. 147
291	'An immense concourse':	Broughton, op. cit., vol. 3, p. 68
	'It is impossible':	*Morning Chronicle*, 13 July 1824
	'one of the most':	Ibid.
292	'I felt your kindness':	Hodgson, op. cit., vol. 2, p. 149
	'Though I failed':	Kennedy, *Conversations on Religion with Lord Byron*
	'I shall ever bless':	Hodgson, op. cit., vol. 2, p. 150

CHAPTER 25

Page	Ref.	Source
294	'who has been':	A.L. to A.I.B., 26 July 1824. L./B. Box 83
295	'for you never go':	Scrope Davies to A.L., 22 Sept. 1824. Add. Mss. 31037
	'I cannot help':	Hodgson, op. cit., vol. 2, p. 141
296	'no man of honour':	Hobhouse to Dallas. Add. Mss. 31037, F62 (23 June)
	'. . . it was my purpose':	R.C. Dallas to A.L., 30 June 1824. Add. Mss. 31037, F63
	'I feel equal':	Dallas, *Recollections of Lord Byron*, preface
297	'. . . it was a comfort':	A.L. to A.I.B. no date. L./B. Box 83
	'drenching quantities':	*Morning Post*, 22 Nov. 1824
298	'What a worry':	A.L. to A.I.B. L./B. Box 83
	'She is very plain':	*Elizabeth Holland to Her Son*, pp. 31–2 (18 Nov. 1824)
299	'it is hardly possible':	Dallas, op. cit., preliminary statement, xc
	'Lord Byron':	Ibid., xcii
	'I wish too':	A.L. to A.I.B., 28 Nov. 1824. L./B. Box 83
300	'G.B. never':	A.L. to A.I.B., L./B. Box 83, F170
	'I am not given':	A.L. to A.I.B., 17 March 1825. L./B. Box 83
301	'It was not unnatural':	A.L. to Wilmot. Catton Papers, Letter 695, vol. 16
302	'It was not':	A.L. to A.I.B., 25 Nov. 1824. L./B. Box 83
	'I was obliged':	A.L. to A.I.B., 31 Dec. 1824. L./B. Box 83
	'How can it':	A.L. to A.I.B., 6 June 1824. L./B. Box 83, Ff. 133–42
303	'Lady Stanhope':	Thomas Moore, *Journal*, 4 Sept. 1825

Page	Ref.	Source
304	'I must go':	A.L. to A.I.B., 23 Sept. 1825. L./B. Box 83
	'The *Hero*':	A.L. to A.I.B., 9 Dec. 1825. L./B. Box 83
	'I've seen much':	Ibid.
305	'The present state':	A.L. to A.I.B., 9 Dec. 1825. L./B. Box 83
	'a *horror*':	Ibid.
306	'the Disposer':	Ibid.
	'I cannot':	A.L. to A.I.B., 12 Jan. 1826. L./B. Box 83
307	'I had rather':	Ibid.
	'I expect the return':	Ibid.
	'. . . thank heaven':	A.L. to A.I.B., Feb. 1826. L./B. Box 83
308	'A line':	A.L. to A.I.B., 4 Feb. 1826. L./B. Box 83
	'Lady Caroline L.':	A.L. to A.I.B. L./B. Box 83, F211
	'I cannot go':	A.I.B. to Mrs Villiers, 29 March 1826
309	'We were waiting':	A.L. to A.I.B., 9 March 1826. L./B. Box 83
	'But half measures':	A.I.B. to Mrs Villiers, 16 April 1826. L./B. transcripts
	'. . . I could never':	A.L. to A.I.B., March 1826. L./B. Box 83
310	'All I can do':	A.I.B. to Mrs Villiers, 29 March 1826. L./B. transcripts
	'to remove the':	B.L. Add. Ms. 31037, F115
	'as unjust':	B.L. Add. Ms. 31037, F117 (27 April 1826)
	'far beyond':	Ibid.
311	'Is it not a fact':	B.L. Add. Ms. 31037, F115
312	'What hurt me':	A.L. to A.I.B., 15 Dec. 1826. L./B. Box 83
	'My grandchild':	A.L. to A.I.B., 15 Feb. 1827. L./B. Box 84
313	'It deprives us':	Ibid.
	'The thing I am':	A.L. to A.I.B. L./B. Box 83, F235
	'It will be':	B.L. Add. Ms. 31037 (15 Nov. 1824)
314	'My debts':	A.L. to A.I.B., 19 Jan. 1828. L./B. Box 84
	'The Violence':	Ibid.
	'. . . I do not know':	Ibid.
315	'after an interview':	A.L. to A.I.B., 24 Feb. 1828. L./B. Box 84
	'I ventured':	A.L. to A.I.B., 18 Dec. 1828
316	'I feel':	A.L. to A.I.B., 20 April 1829. L./B. Box 84
	'the pure and':	Mrs Hemans to George D'Aguilar. Add. Ms. 31037
317	'base ingratitude':	*Lady Noel Byron and the Leighs*
	'If after':	Ibid.
	'I can forgive':	Athenaeum, August 1883
318	'I have no':	*Lady Noel Byron and the Leighs*
	'. . . At the time':	Thomas Moore, *Byron's Life and Works* vol. 1, p. 296
	'I can never pass':	A.I.B. to Mrs Lushington, 27 Feb. 1830. L./B.
	'my God':	Hodgson to Henry Drury. Hodgson, op. cit., vol. 2, pp. 203–4
	'I am always':	A.L. to Hodgson. Ibid., p. 202

CHAPTER 27

Page	Ref.	Source
320	'Elizabeth is':	A.L. to A.I.B., 9 Sept. 1828. L./B. Box 84
	'Bereaved of':	Trevanion, *The Influence of Apathy*
321	'the last injunctions':	(Ms autobiography), D.L.M. p. 104
	'Elizabeth [Medora]':	A.L. to A.I.B., July 1829. L./B. Box 84
	'I was ruined':	MS. Autobiography D.L.M., p. 105
	'I could not':	A.L. to Jane Porter. Pforzheimer Collection, New York Public Library. cf. Eisler, p. 415
	'it would have been':	A.L. to Mary Cursham, 5 Oct. 1829. Roe-Byron collection
322	'I suppose':	Mary Byron to A.I.B., 4 Dec. 1829. L./B. Box 65
	'against my wish':	Mackay, p. 125
323	'During the whole autumn':	Mackey, pp. 125–126
	'MY DEAREST Moé':	Mayne, p. 341
	'you know I have':	Ibid., p. 342
324	'Dearest, do not':	Ibid., pp. 343–4
325	'Now Dearest':	Ibid.
	'Reflect that':	Ibid., p. 344
326	'Recollect who':	Ibid., pp. 344–5
	'an obstinate':	Ibid.
327	'I wished to':	Mackay, p. 127
328	'I found Georgiana':	Ibid.
	'We were driven':	Ibid., p. 128
329	'The young girl':	*The Late Lord Byron.* D.L.M. p. 452
	'I did not hesitate':	Mackay, p. 129
330	'I was told':	Ibid., p. 130

CHAPTER 28

Page	Ref.	Source
331	'I must write':	*Literary Life. Correspondence of the Countess of Blessington,* ed. R.R. Madden
	'How often':	Jerningham, *Reminiscences of an Attaché*
	'Mrs Leigh is':	Origo, op. cit.
	'To say the truth':	Ibid.
332	'Now listen':	Roe-Byron Collection
333	'What a magnificent':	Cursham, *Norman Abbey*
	'What balsam':	Ibid.
	'The man of her choice':	Ibid.
	'It surprised':	Macready, *Diaries,* vol. 1, 29 Oct. 1834
334	'Manfred was':	Bunn, *The Stage,* vol. 1, London 1840
	'unable to bask':	Chew, op. cit.
	'where your footsteps':	B.L. Add. Ms.

336	'There is nothing':	B.L. Add. Ms. 31037, F179
337	'I was considered':	Mackay, pp. 132-3
338	'such an account':	A.L., statement no. 2. L./B. Box 84
	'Only remember':	Mayne, pp. 352-3
339	'would have moved':	George Stephen to Robert Wilmot Horton. Derbyshire Records Office
340	'I was born':	A.L. to R. Wilmot. Derbyshire Records Office
	'I have been':	L./B. Box 87, F31-2
	'I cannot help':	L./B. Box 87 (7 May 1840)
	'My dear Libby':	Ibid.
	'my Aunt Ly Byron':	Medora to George Stephen, 2 May 1840. L./B. Box 87
341	'You & only you':	Georgiana to A.L., undated fragment. L./B. Box 85

CHAPTER 29

Page	Ref.	Source
342	'and I therefore':	L./B. Box 87, F141
	'one desire':	Ibid.
343	'I am particularly':	Mayne, p. 353
	'She implored':	Mackay, p. 136
	'*Her husband*':	Mackay, pp. 135-6
344	'the suspense':	A.L. to A.I.B., 16 Jan. 1841. L./B. Box 87
	'Since last August':	A.I.B. to A.L., 20 Jan. 1841. L./B. Box 87
345	'I may have subjected':	A.I.B. to Lord Lovelace, 22 Jan. 1841. L./B. Box 52, F20
	'but scanty sums':	A.L., statement no. 2, 6 Feb. 1841 L./B. Box 87
	'Her income':	Mrs Villiers to A.I.B. L./B. Box 52
	'Did I not see':	Ibid.
346	'very natural':	A.I.B. to Mrs Villiers, L./B. Box 52
	'As for the ruin':	Ada to Lord Lovelace, 8 April 1841. L./B.
	'How comes it':	Ibid.
347	'Ada's sister':	Mackay, p. 137.
	'This is under':	A.I.B. to Lord Lovelace, 7 Oct. 1841. L./B. Box 52, F107
	'I should regret':	A.I.B. to Lord Lovelace, 8 Oct. 1841. L./B. Box 52
348	'E.'s power':	L./B., Box 52, F185
	'was finished':	Mackay, op. cit., pp. 137-8
349	'I had *never*':	A.I.B. to Selina Doyle, 22 March 1843. L./B. Box 68
	'There are':	9 June 1842. L./B. Box 87, F91
	'In attempting':	Ibid.

350	'She could not':	Mayne, pp. 360–1
351	'As long as':	A.I.B. to Selina Doyle, March 1843. L./B. Box 68. F113
	'I felt powerless':	Selina Doyle to A.I.B., 21 March 1843. L./B. Box 68, F115
352	'I submitted':	Mackay, op. cit., p. 150
	'she [Medora]':	Mayne, p. 365
353	'In 1841':	Public Records Office, War Office Papers
	'What sum':	Wharton and Ford to A.I.B., 13 April 1843. L./B. Box 136, F24
	'many Notices':	Lushington to Medora, 5 April 1844. L./B. Box 137, F156
354	'You are fully':	Medora to Lovelace, 12 June 1843. L./B. Box 172, F209
	'Now I cannot':	Mackay, op. cit. p. 154
355	'I have a letter':	Hobhouse, Murray Ms. cf. *The Late Lord Byron* op. cit.
	'by the unprincipled man':	Medora to the Duke of Leeds, 23 Aug. 1843. Mackay, op. cit., pp. 156ff.
	'in incest':	Ibid.
355	'My Mother':	Medora to Augusta. *Medora Leigh. Byron's Daughter*, Turney, p. 245
356	'as sad experience':	A.L. to Wharton and Ford, 2 Sept. 1843. L./B. Box 137, F74
	'The Lady Noel Byron':	L./B. Box 137, F50
	'the unfortunate':	Ibid.
357	'Her child':	Temple, *Le Tombeau de Medora*
	'I declare':	Roger de Vivie de Régie, *Le Secret de Byron*
358	'the headstone':	Temple, op. cit.

CHAPTER 30

Page	Ref.	Source
359	'That man':	Thackeray, *Notes of a Journey from Cornhill to Grand Cairo*
	'Byron's fiercer wine':	Kingsley, *Thoughts on Shelley and Byron*
	'I do become':	Hodgson, op. cit., vol. 2 p. 277
	'On 18 June 1845':	Family Records Centre, London
	'23 October 1847':	Ibid.
360	'. . . he do not know':	John Pollendine to Emily Leigh, 15 May 1853. L./B. Box 85
	'Her [Augusta's son]':	Mrs Villiers to A.I.B. L./B. Box 52
	'He will not':	John Pollendine to Emily Leigh. L./B. Box 85
	'If it had not':	Emily Leigh to A.I.B. L./B. Box 85, F57

361	'a combination':	A.L. to Lushington, 9 Feb. 1849. L./B. Box 90, F80
	'no common distress':	Ibid., F82
	'I think Mrs Leigh':	A.I.B. to Lushington, 20 Feb. 1849. L./B. Box 90, F87
	'The time may come':	A.L. to Lushington, 30 Nov. 1849. L./B. Box 90, F87
362	'I hope you':	Castle Howard Archives
	'None but those':	A.L. Common Place Book. Add. Ms. 58802, F56
363	'I am sure':	Castle Howard Archives
	'reduced to five':	Census Return, Family Records Centre, 30 March 1851
	'The death of':	Emily Leigh to Lushington, 1 Feb. 1851. L./B. Box 90, F88
364	'I thought Mrs Leigh':	A.I.B. to Robertson. L./B.
	'I must thank':	Mayne, p. 399
	'A hope':	A.I.B. to Robertson. L./B.
365	'It is not possible':	Mayne, p. 405
	'Since the cessation':	A.I.B. to A.L., 11 Feb. 1851. L./B. Box 85
366	'As you now':	A.L. to A.I.B., 14 Feb. 1851 Box 85. L./B.
	'as soon as':	Ibid.
	'I have no wish':	Ibid.
	'A *most* unsatisfactory':	Mayne, p. 407
367	'. . . but should I':	Ibid.
	'I can give':	A.L. to A.I.B., 31 March 1851. L./B. Box 85
	'Questions – *you*':	Mayne
368	'Will you':	A.L. to A.I.B., 4 April 1851. L./B. Box 85
	'I saw Death':	A.I.B. to Mrs Villiers, 17 Oct. 1851. L./B. transcripts
	'Her communication':	Mayne, p. 409
369	'My feelings':	Ibid.
	'I told her':	Ibid.
	'there was a difference':	Ibid.
370	'You not only':	Mayne, p. 410.
	'At *such* a testimony':	Ibid.
	'I am thankful':	A.L. to A.I.B., 10 April 1851. L./B. Box 84
371	'is very unpleasant':	Mayne, pp. 411–12
	'the last proof':	Ibid.
	'I had not':	A.L. to A.I.B., 26 April 1851. L./B.
	'to talk openly':	Ibid.
372	'You cannot':	A.L. to Frederick Robertson, 13 May 1851. L./B. Box 84
	'If your own conscience':	Arnold, *Robertson of Brighton*, pp. 184–5
373	'furniture plate':	Augusta's will, Nottingham Central Library
	'Let me if possible':	A.I.B. to Emily Leigh. Add. Ms. 31037, F189
	'To this I':	B.L. Add. Ms. 31037, F183
	'I felt so great':	Mayne, p. 414
	'I have a request':	A.I.B. to Emily Leigh. Add. Ms. 31037

374   'She desires me':   Emily Leigh to A.I.B., 5 Oct. 1851. Ibid.
       'Poor Mama':   Emily Leigh to A.I.B., 12 Oct. 1851. Ibid.

EPILOGUE

Page	Ref.	Source
376	'I wonder':	Ada Lovelace to A.I.B., 15 Oct. 1851. L./B. (Toole, p. 398)
	'I should not feel':	A.I.B. to Emily Leigh. Add. Ms. 31037, F194
	'I have had':	Emily Leigh to A.I.B. L./B. Box 85, F57
377	'. . . the poor girl':	Mrs Villiers to A.I.B. Mayne, p. 417
	'All I protest':	Lady Wilmot Horton to Mrs Villiers. Ibid., p. 416
	'I do not care':	A.I.B. to Emily Leigh, 15 May 1852. Add. Mss. 31037, F195
	'Yes I should':	A.I.B. to Emily Leigh, 20 May 1853. Ibid., F201
	'I am anxious':	Mrs Villiers to Emily Leigh. Add. Ms. 31037, F199
378	'Before my marriage':	A.I.B. to Emily Leigh, 2 July 1852. Add. Ms. 31037
379	'You helped':	Emily Leigh to A.I.B. L./B. Box 85, F62
380	'moral Brinvilliers':	*Blackwood's Magazine*, July 1869
	'A story':	Justin McCarthy, letter to the *Independent*, 26 Aug. 1869
381	'If we assume':	Hayward, *The Quarterly*, Oct. 1869
	'. . . a most gross':	*The Times*, 2 Sept. 1869
	'She was':	Lady Frances Shelley. Mackay, op. cit., p. 181
	'extremely unprepossessing':	Ibid.
	'Lady Byron's story':	Ibid., p. 167
382	'Poor E.'s biography':	3rd Earl of Chichester to Emily Leigh, 30 Dec. 1869. L./B. Box 161
	'Lady Byron's voice':	Harriet Beecher Stowe to Hatty and Eliza Stowe. Hedrick
	'Is her memory':	Paget, *Blackwood's Magazine*, Jan. 1870
	'Light at Last':	Chew, op. cit., p. 281
	'a rich Indian':	Story, *James Holmes and John Varley*
383	'completely in the grasp':	George Eliot, *Letters* 5, p. 314
	'last poor heap':	George Eliot, *Daniel Deronda, Blackwood's Magazine*, 1876, ch. 1
384	'Augusta Leigh was':	*Astarte*, op. cit. (1905)
	'Lovelace's part':	Drinkwater, *The Pilgrim of Eternity*, p. 6
	'If incest took place':	Maurois, *Call No Man Happy*, p. 199

BIBLIOGRAPHY

Manuscript sources

Bodleian Library: Lovelace/Byron Papers, Shelburne Papers

British Library: Add. Mss 19038, 31030–2, 31037, 31038, 39672, 39992, 40517, 58802

—— Broughton Papers (Add. Mss 47230–2)

—— Egerton Papers (2611–13, 3497–500, 3262)

—— Grenville Papers (Add. Mss 41854–6)

—— Leeds Papers (Add. Mss 279914, 28067)

—— Paget Papers (Add. Mss 48416)

—— Pelham Papers (Add. Mss 33082–7, 33097, 33106)

Castle Howard Archives: The papers of Frederick, 5th Earl of Carlisle, and his family

Cornish Records Office, Truro: Trevanion papers

Derbyshire Records Office, Matlock: Catton Papers

Newstead Abbey: Roe-Byron Collection

Nottingham City Archives:

Public Records Office: War Office Papers

West Yorkshire Archive Service: Leeds. Papers of the 5th Duke of Leeds

Published sources and books consulted

Airlie, Mabell, Countess of: *In Whig Society* (Hodder & Stoughton, 1921)

—— *Lady Palmerston and Her Times* (Hodder & Stoughton, 1922)

Arnold, Frederick: *Robertson of Brighton*, (Ward and Downey, 1886)

Aspinall, Arthur, ed.: *The Later Correspondence of George III*, 5 vols (Cambridge University Press, 1962–70)

—— *The Correspondence of George, Prince of Wales 1770–1812*, 8 vols (Cassell, 1963–71)

Ayling, Stanley: *George III* (Collins, 1972)

Barber, Thomas: *Byron and Where He is Buried* (Henry Morley, 1939)

Beresford, Chancellor: *Life in Regency and Early Victorian Times* (Batsford, 1926)

Bessborough, Earl of (in collaboration with A. Aspinall, ed.): *Lady Bessborough and Her Family Circle* (John Murray, 1940)

Bickley, Francis, ed.: *Diaries of Sylvester Douglas, Lord Glenbervie*, 2 vols (Constable, 1928)

Blessington, Marguerite, Countess of: *Conversations of Lord Byron* (London, 1834)

Bloom, Edward and Lillian: *The Piozzi Letters*, 2 vols. (University of Delaware Press, 1989)

Blyth, Henry: *Old Q. The Rake of Piccadilly* (Weidenfeld & Nicolson, 1967)

—— *Caro, The Fatal Passion* (Granada, 1972)

Bolderstone, Katherine, ed.: *Thraliana* (Oxford University Press, 1951)

Bond, Peter, ed.: *A History of St Peter and St Paul* (Eckington)

Boyes, Megan: *Norman Abbey and Its Author*

—— *Queen of a Fantastic Realm* (1986)

—— *Love Without Wings* (1988)

—— *My Amiable Mamma* (1991)

—— *Newstead Abbey Byron Society* (1996)

Broughton, Lord: *Recollections of a Long Life* (John Murray, 1910)

Bunbury, Sir H.: *Narrative of the Campaign in Northern Holland (London, 1853)*

Bunn, Alfred: *The Stage. Both before and Behind the Curtain*, 3 vols (London, 1840)

Burke's Peerage, 7th edition (1915)

Burne, Alfred H.: *The Noble Duke of York* (Staples Press, 1949)

Burnett, T.A.J.: *The Rise and Fall of a Regency Dandy* (John Murray, 1981)

Chapman, John S.: *Byron and the Honourable Augusta Leigh* (Yale University Press, 1975)

Chew, Samuel C.: *Byron in England* (Russell and Russell, New York, 1965)

Chifney, Samuel: *Genius Genuine* (London, 1804)

Chisholm, Kate: *Fanny Burney* (Chatto & Windus, 1998)

Chouteau, Nicole: *Les Rues de Tréguier du XVIII Siècle à nos jours* (Éditions Art, Culture et Patrimonie, Tréguier)

Colchester, Lord: *Diary and Correspondence of Charles Abbot, Lord Colchester* (John Murray, 1861)

Cole, Hubert: *Beau Brummell* (Granada, 1977)

Cruse, Amy: *The Englishman and His Books* (Harrap, 1930)

Cursham, Mary Anne: *Norman Abbey* (James Cochrane, 1832)

Dallas, R.C.: *Recollections of Lord Byron* (Charles Knight, 1824)

David, Saul: *Prince of Pleasure* (Little, Brown, 1998)

Dobson, Austin, ed.: *Diary and Letters of Fanny Burney*, 6 vols (Macmillan, 1904)

Drinkwater, John: *The Pilgrim of Eternity* (Hodder & Stoughton, 1925)

Edgecumbe, Richard, ed.: *The Diary of Frances, Lady Shelley*, 2 vols (1912/13)

Eisler, Benita, *Byron* (Hamish Hamilton, 1999)

Elwin, Malcolm: *Lord Byron's Wife* (Macdonald, 1962)

—— *The Noels and the Milbankes* (Macdonald, 1967)

—— *Lord Byron's Family* (John Murray, 1975)

Farington, Joseph: *The Farington Diary*, ed. James Greig, 8 vols (Hutchinson, 1922–8)

Fleming, Anne: *In Search of Byron in England and Scotland* (Old Forge Press, Ditchling Press, 1988)

Fletcher, Ronald: *The Parkers At Saltram* (BBC Publications, 1970)

Foreman, Amanda: *Georgiana, Duchess of Devonshire* (HarperCollins, 1998)

Foster, Vere: *The Two Duchesses* (Blackie, 1898)

Fox, Sir John: *The Byron Mystery* (Grant Richards, 1924)

Fraser, Flora: *The Unruly Queen* (Macmillan, 1996)

Gittings, Robert and Manton, Jo: *Claire Clairmont and the Shelleys* (Oxford University Press, 1992)

Gore, John, ed.: *Creevey* (John Murray, 1948)

Graham, Peter W., ed.: *Byron's Bulldog* (Ohio State University Press, 1984)

Gross, Jonathan, ed.: *Byron's 'Corbeau Blanc'. The Life and Letters of Lady Melbourne* (Rice University Press, 1997)

Grylls, R. Glynn: *Claire Clairmont* (John Murray, 1939)

Guiccioli, Teresa: *My Recollections of Lord Byron* (Richard Bentley, 1869)

Gunn, Peter: *My Dearest Augusta* (The Bodley Head, 1968)

Hallows, Ian S.: *Regiments and Corps of the British Army* (Arms and Armour Press, 1991)

Harcourt, William: *The Harcourt Papers*, 14 vols (London)

Hartmann, Cyril Hughes: *Enchanting Bellamy* (Heinemann, 1956)

Hedley, Olwen: *Queen Charlotte* (John Murray, 1975)

Hedrick, Joan D.: *Harriet Beecher Stowe* (Oxford University Press, 1994)

Henley, William Ernest: *Byron's World, Essays* (Macmillan, 1878)

Herbert, David: *Lady Byron and Earl Shilton* (Hinckley and District Museum, 1997)

Herold, J. Christopher: *Mistress to an Age. The Life of Madame de Staël* (Hamish Hamilton, 1959)

Hibbert, Christopher: *Corunna* (Batsford, 1961)

—— *George IV, Prince of Wales* (Longman, 1972)

—— *George IV, Regent and King* (Allen Lane, 1975)

—— *George III* (Viking, 1998)

Hibbert, Christopher, *Greville's England* (Folio Society, 1981)

—— *Louis Simmond. An American in Regency England* (Robert Maxwell, 1968)

—— *Captain Gronow* (Kyle Cathie, 1991)

Hodgson, James: *Memoir of the Rev. Francis Hodgson*, 2 vols (Macmillan, 1878)

Howell, Margaret J.: *Byron Tonight* (Springwood Books, 1982)

Huish, Robert: *Memoirs of Her Late Royal Highness, Charlotte Augusta* (Thomas Kelly, 1819)

Illchester, Lord, ed.: *Elizabeth, Lady Holland, to Her Son. 1821–1845* (John Murray, 1946)

Israel, Jonathan D.: *The Dutch Republic* (Oxford University Press, 1995)

Jeaffreson, John Cordy: *The Real Lord Byron* (Hurst and Blackett, 1883)

Jenkins, Elizabeth: *Lady Caroline Lamb* (Victor Gollancz, 1932)

Joyce, Michael: *My Friend H.* (John Murray, 1948)

Kennedy, James: *Conversations on Religion with Lord Byron* (London, 1830)

Keppel, Sonia: *The Sovereign Lady. Elizabeth, Third Lady Holland* (Hamish Hamilton, 1974)

Knight, George Wilson: *Lord Byron's Marriage* (Routledge & Kegan Paul, 1957)

Kroll, Maria: *Sophia, Electress of Hanover* (Victor Gollancz, 1973)

Lees-Milne, James: *The Bachelor Duke* (John Murray, 1991)

Le Guennec, Louis: *Morlaix et Sa Région* (Le Bouquinniste, Morlaix, 1991)

Leslie, Shane: *George IV* (Benn, 1926)

L'Estrange, A.G., ed.: *The Literary Life of the Rev. William Harness* (London, 1871)

Leveson-Gowery, Sir George and Palmer, Iris, eds: *Hary-O. The Letters of Lady Harriet Cavendish 1796–1809* (John Murray, 1940)

Linney, John: *Newstead Abbey and the Relics of Byron* (*Mansfield Advertiser*, 1865)

Longford, Elizabeth: *Byron* (Hutchinson/Weidenfeld & Nicolson, 1976)

Lovelace, Ralph Milbanke, Earl of: *Astarte* (The Chiswick Press, 1905)

Lovell, Ernest J., Jr: *Captain Medwin* (Macdonald, 1962)

Lovell, Ernest J., Jr, ed.: *His Very Self and Voice* (Macmillan, New York, 1954)

—— *Medwin's Conversations with Lord Byron* (Princeton University Press, 1962)

Mackay, Charles, ed.: *Medora Leigh. A History and an Autobiography* (Richard Bentley, 1869)

Macready, William, *Diaries* ed. Toynbee (1912)

Madden, R.R.: *Literary Life. Correspondence of the Countess of Blessington* (London, 1855)

Marchand, Leslie: *Byron: A Biography*, 3 vols (John Murray, 1957)

—— *Byron: A Portrait* (John Murray, 1971)

Marchand, Leslie, ed.: *Byron's Letters and Journals*, 13 vols (John Murray, 1973–94)

Mason, William: *Works*, 4 vols (London, 1811)

Masson, Madeleine: *Lady Anne Barnard* (Allen & Unwin, 1948)

Maurois, André: *Byron* (Jonathan Cape, 1930)

—— *Call No Man Happy* (Jonathan Cape, 1944)

Mayne, Ethel Colburn: *Byron*, 2 vols (Methuen, 1912)

—— *The Life of Lady Byron* (Constable, 1929)

—— *A Regency Chapter* (Macmillan, 1939)

Mitchell, L.G.: *Lord Melbourne* (Oxford University Press, 1997)

Mollo, John: *The Prince's Dolls* (Leo Cooper, 1997)

Moore, Doris Langley: *The Late Lord Byron* (John Murray, 1961)

—— *Lord Byron. Accounts Rendered* (John Murray, 1974)

—— *Ada Countess of Lovelace* (John Murray, 1977)

Moore, Thomas: *Journal* (London, 1853)

—— *Byron's Life and Works*, 2 vols (John Murray, 1873)

Murray, Venetia: *Castle Howard* (Penguin, 1994)

—— *High Society. A Social History of the Regency Period, 1788–1830* (Viking, 1998)

Nightingale, John: *Memoirs of the Public and Private Life of Queen Caroline* (Folio Society, 1978)

Oman, Carola: *Britain Against Napoleon* (Faber & Faber, 1942)

Onslow, Richard: *Headquarters* (Great Ouse Press, Newmarket, 1983)

Origo, Iris: *The Last Attachment* (Jonathan Cape and John Murray, 1949)

Page, Norman, ed.: *Byron, Interviews and Recollections* (Macmillan, 1983)

Paston, George, and Quennell, Peter: *To Lord Byron: Feminine Profiles* (John Murray, 1939)

Pratt, Willis W.: *Byron at Southwell* (Austin, Texas, 1948)

Prothero, Rowland, ed.: *Byron's Works. Letters and Journals of Lord Byron*, 6 vols (John Murray, 1898–1904)

Quennell, Peter: *Byron, the Years of Fame* (Collins, 1935)

—— *Byron in Italy* (Collins, 1941)

Richardson, Joanna: *Lord Byron* (Folio Society, 1988)

Robinson, Henry Crabb: *Diary, Reminiscences and Correspondence* (Macmillan, 1869)

Rowse, A.L.: *The Byrons and Trevanions* (Weidenfeld & Nicolson, 1978)

Rush, Richard: *A Residence at the Court of London* (Century Hutchinson, 1987)

Sadleir, Michael: *Blessington D'Orsay. A Masquerade* (Constable, 1933)

Siltzer, Frank: *Newmarket* (Cassell, 1923)

Smiles, Samuel: *A Publisher and His Friends* (John Murray, 1911)

Smith, E.A.: *George IV* (Yale University Press, 1999)

Stone, Lawrence: *The Family, Sex and Marriage in England* (Weidenfeld & Nicolson, 1977)

—— *Uncertain Unions and Broken Lives* (Oxford University Press, 1990)

—— *Road to Divorce* (Oxford University Press, 1992)

Story, Alfred T.: *James Holmes and John Varley* (Richard Bentley, 1894)

Stowe, Harriet Beecher: *Lady Byron Vindicated. A History of the Byron Controversy* (Sampson Low, 1870)

Strickland, Margot: *The Byron Women* (St Martin's Press, New York, 1974)

Symon, J.D.: *Byron in Perspective* (Frederick A. Stokes, New York, 1925)

Temple, Frédéric-Jacques: *Le Tombeau de Medora* (La Manufacture, 1988)

Templewood, Viscount: *The Unbroken Thread* (Collins, 1949)

Thorne, James: *Handbook to the Environs of London. 1876* (Godfrey Cave Associates, 1983)

Thorold, Peter: *The London Rich* (Viking, 1999)

Tollemache, E.D.H.: *The Tollemaches of Helmingham and Ham*

Toole, Betty: *Ada, the Enchantress of Numbers* (Strawberry Press, 1992)

Trevanion, Henry: *The Influence of Apathy* (Longman, 1827)

Turner, E.S.: *The Court of St James's* (Michael Joseph, 1959)

Turney, Catherine: *Byron's Daughter* (Peter Davies, 1975)

Vickery, Amanda: *The Gentleman's Daughter* (Yale University Press, 1988)

Vivie de Régie, Roger de: *Le Secret de Byron* (Éditions Émile-Paul Frères, 1927)

Walford, Edward, *London Recollected*

Walker, Violet: *The House of Byron* (Quiller Press, 1988)

Walpole, Horace: *Memoirs of the Reign of George III* (London, 1894)

Watson, J. Steven: *The Reign of George III* (Oxford University Press, 1960)

Weinreb, Ben, and Hibbert, Christopher, eds: *The London Encyclopaedia* (Macmillan, 1983)

Williams, Basil: *The Whig Supremacy* (Oxford University Press, 1960)

Wilson, Frances, ed.: *Byronmania* (Macmillan, 1999)

Woolley, Benjamin: *The Bride of Science* (Macmillan, 1999)

Journals

The Annual Register
Blackwood's Magazine
The Gentleman's Magazine

INDEX

ACKNOWLEDGEMENTS

Anyone writing on matters concerning Byron must pay tribute to the work of three great scholars: to Leslie Marchand for his still unsurpassed biographies and for his indispensable edition of Byron's *Letters and Journals*; to Malcolm Elwin for his intrepid investigation of the Lovelace Papers and to Doris Langley Moore whose valuable studies shed so much new light on so many aspects of Byron, his family and his friends.

More particularly, we must thank the Earl of Lytton for permission to quote from the Lovelace Papers and John Murray (Publishers) Ltd for allowing us to quote freely from Byron's *Letters and Journals* edited by Leslie Marchand, from two letters from Lady Melbourne to Byron and for extracts from John Cam Hobhouse's letters, to quote from *Hary-O* edited by Sir George Leveson Gower and Iris Palmer, *Elizabeth Lady Holland to Her Son* edited by the Earl of Ilchester, and *To Lord Byron* edited by George Paston and Peter Quennell. We are very grateful to the Hon. Simon Howard by whose kind permission we have been able to quote from the papers of Frederick Howard, 5th Earl of Carlisle and his family; to Nottingham Museums and Galleries (Newstead Abbey) for permission to quote from the Roe-Byron Collection and most especially to Haidee Jackson, Keeper of Collections at Newstead Abbey who has helped us in such a multitude of ways. For permission to quote from those letters and papers of the Duke of Leeds held in Clarendon Road, Leeds, we must thank the Yorkshire Archive Service; Derbyshire County Council for material relating to Sir Robert Wilmot Horton in the Derbyshire Records Office, Matlock; the Trustees and Governors of Harrow School for giving access to and permission to quote from archive material. The Department of Manuscripts in the British Museum proved to be a treasure trove of information and, there, as at Colindale, the staff were always helpful and accomodating.

Our thanks are due to the Carl H. Pforzheimer Collection of Shelley and his Circle at the New York Public Library, Astor, Lenox and Tilden Foundations, for permission to quote from a letter from Augusta Leigh to Jane Porter and to the J. Pierpont Morgan Library to quote from the Ms Autobiography of Medora Leigh. We are grateful too to the Berg Collection of the New York Public Library for permission to quote an extract from a diary entry by John Cam Hobhouse. We must also thank the Oxford University Press for permission to quote a short extract from *Harriet Beecher Stowe* by Joan Hedrick and Jonathan Cape for an extract from *Call No Man Happy* by André Maurois. For their help and advice in our picture research, we would like to thank Susan Morris and the Richard Green Gallery, Sue Daley of Sotheby's Picture Library, Emma Strouts of Christie's Images, Antonia Leake of the Heinz Archive, Adam Grummitt of the National

ACKNOWLEDGEMENTS

Portrait Gallery Picture Library, the Picture Library at the National Army Museum and Christina La Torre of its Photographic Department.

Others whose assistance has been invaluable in the course of this project include Colin Harris and Nicola Kennan of the Department of Western Manuscripts at the Bodleian Library, Alain Croix of the University of Rennes, the Lord Tollemache and his family archivist, William Sergeant, Dr Christopher Ridgway, the archivist at Castle Howard, Robert Frost and Dr Betteridge of the Yorkshire Archaeological Society, Dr Peter Cochran, Mrs Rita Gibbs, the Harrow School archivist, the Staff at the National Register of Archives (Historical Manuscripts Commission), Sharon Harper of the Jockey Club and The Curator of the National Horse Racing Museum, Graham Snelling who alerted us to the existence of Richard Onslow's excellent history of racing at Newmarket, *Headquarters*, the staff of Nottingham Central Library, Rosalys Coope, Robert Innes Smith, Vivienne Irish of *Derbyshire Life* magazine and the Rector and the Verger of the Church of SS Peter and Paul at Eckington. We are grateful to all of them.

On a personal note we would like to thank Virginia Murray for the interest she has shown in our book, Alex Alec-Smith who never failed to track down the most elusive volumes for us. Anne Fleming, Harry Guest, Brian Butler, Caroline Humphries and Carole Allington. Very special thanks must go to Ralph Lloyd-Jones for arranging a visit to Kensal Green, a memorable experience and one made more so by the eccentric Martin, our guide to the catacombs.

To Barbara Jackson who allowed us to see and quote from valuable manuscript material in her own collection, we owe a huge debt of gratitude. We are no less indebted to John Patrick who gave so generously of his time, energy and expertise and in particular for his work on the family trees. Megan Boyes' contribution has been equally generous and it is impossible to thank her sufficiently for keeping us supplied with so much vital information.

Finally, we must thank our editor Penelope Hoare for her guidance and infinite patience, Stuart Williams who communicated the urgency of deadlines with such good humour that we were never reduced to complete panic, and our agent Deborah Rogers.

Every effort has been made to contact all copyright holders of material quoted in this book. We shall be pleased to hear from anyone not here acknowledged.